# WISH TO LIVE MY LIFE DELIBERATELY

## PATRIC LEEDOM

INKS & BINDINGS

Inks and Bindings
888-290-5218
www.inksandbindings.com
orders@inksandbindings.com

# CONTENTS

## Part One: Dr. Patric Leedom's Autobiography
## NOVEMBER 17—JULY 25, 2022

# PART ONE

## Dr. Patric Leedom's Autobiography

### NOVEMBER 17—JULY 25, 2022

SCORE ONE OF YEARS: Age 1 TO 20 Years

If you were to ask me to define my over-arching life's philosophy on one page, here it is:

To Live Deliberately

Why should we live in such a hurry
And waste of life?

> *We are determined to be starved*
> *Before we are hungry.*

I wish to live deliberately, to front
Only the essential facts of life.

> *I wish to learn what life has to*
> *Teach, and not when I come to*
> *Die, discover that I have not lived.*

I do not wish to live what is not life,
Living is do dear,

*Nor do I wish to practice resignation,*
*Unless it is quite necessary.*

I wish to live deep and suck out all
The marrow of life,

*I want to cut a broad swath to*
*Drive life into a corner, and reduce*
*It to its lowest terms.*

If it proves to be mean, then to get
The whole and genuine meanness of
It, and publish its meanness to the
World;

*Or if it is sublime, to know it by*
*Experience, and to be able to give a true account of it.*

**Henry David Thoreau**

A Note of Emphasis: I first learned of this essay when I was 14 or 15 years old. I took it immediately to heart as a guiding philosophy, and I have followed it every day of my life.

For accomplishing this Abridged Autobiography, I chose to divide my life into Scores of Twenty Years. Score One is the only score not divided into decades.

I have titled this work as ABRIDGED as using the frame work I Believe I Can…I Did It…I Believed I could! I have generally only included events where I was growing and maturing and developing my skills to take on Challenges—even though sometimes I had never done anything like it.

## MY BEGINNINGS

• • • • • • • • • • • • • • • • • • • • •

Life out in the big world started for me in the small town—30,000 population—of Albuquerque, New Mexico on May 13, 1940. My parents, Robert and Georgiana (Joy) had journeyed out from Ohio to launch a new alternative newspaper—The Duke City Times. It lasted about one year and folded. Then Dad was hired by the Albuquerque Tribune—a Scripps-Howard paper. I mention that because a little while later, the famous War Correspondent Ernie Pyle and his wife Gerry moved into town. Ernie worked for the Scripps-Howard syndicate. Both men came from small mid-western towns. Ernie from Dana, Indiana, and Dad from Manchester, Ohio. Both men had similar notions of what was important and life, so the two families became close friends. Ernie was 14 years older, and I am sorry I didn't know to ask Dad what influences did Ernie have on your newspaper reporting and writing; there definitely are similarities.

For a woman in the 1930's my mother was unusual. She had gone straight from high school in Hamilton, to Miami University where she graduated in 1938 with a bachelor's degree in Government and Economics—having been dissuaded from pursuing Accounting by a white male professor in her junior year. Mom and Dad, Georgiana and Bob, had gotten married in Kentucky before Dad had left. With her college degree, no one was hiring that degree, so Mother stayed behind in Ohio for a few months, enrolled in a Business School, and took steno typing (with a machine) and other secretarial skills. When she arrived in Albuquerque, she took a job with the Health and Welfare Department, as she had earlier for the City of Hamilton, Ohio.

Mother, Georgiana, was intellectually bright and a linguist. She took four years of high school Latin and Spanish, and four years of college Latin and Spanish. Consequently, when I was born in Albuquerque, mother hired a Mexican care giver, Mary Lopez, and instructed her to speak only Spanish to me. While I did learn "Toddler Spanish" when the family moved back to Ohio, I lost it all.

My parents married relatively young: Robert 24, and Georgiana (Joy) 22, and they were full of "Piss and Vinegar," and "Wild Oats!" Years later my mother confided in me that I came by my Corny Humor naturally: I was conceived in a corn field! Mother was sure because Dad left town the next day to travel to Albuquerque.

Apparently during those immature years, there was a lot of miscommunications, and misunderstandings: their marriage started to unravel. [And I can't help but wonder if Dad felt insecure and uncomfortable with mother because she had a college degree—and she hung out with American Association of University Women; Dad never had the opportunity to attend college.] However, Dad was extremely bright, and very well educated from the thousands of books he read while "living in the Cincinnati Public Library" instead of going to high school where he was bored. All his life he read hundreds of books—which is a very good idea if, as a newspaper writer and editor who needs to fully comprehend many levels of English, but, in interfacing with the public, must write in simpler terms. Even when Dad died, one of my tasks was to return 13 books to the local library.

Over many years increasingly Dad was widely known in California newspaper circles—having worked for 20+ different ones (Dad often had arguments with the Publishers because of their need to politically slant the news; however, they readily hired him back if he asked, because he was a very effective newspaper man, especially at building circulation.) In the late 1960's, the New York Times first commissioned my father to do a market survey to determine if the New York Times should publish a West Coast Edition. When he reported back that it was a sound idea, the New York Times asked Dad if he would like to be the Editor! He felt honored but deferred because he would really like to be out in the communities where the important events were taking place.

So, when my parents relocated to Cincinnati, Mother obtained an immediate job working for the War Industry—Wright Aeronautical. She was in the accounting department, and who should be her boss? But the nice young man who sat behind her in Miami University's accounting classes, and she helped him with his homework! He took good care of Mom: she had a "Q Clearance" allowing her to travel anywhere in the plant to collect financial data, and on one occasion she almost knocked Senator Harry Truman over as she was about to push her way through some double doors. (Luckily, someone pulled her out of the way just in time.)

Upon their return to Ohio in 1943 Dad was not so fortunate; he wound up moving 50 miles away north to Dayton, to work for the Dayton Daily News. He would travel back for weekends, but I never saw him because my mother's parents, George and Daisy Shelhouse, would drive down from Hamilton on Friday afternoon and pick me up to go home with them for the weekend, returning me on Sunday afternoons, usually after Dad had returned to Dayton.

Dad, in his mind, believed that he had been abandoned when he was 6 years old, by his mother. So, Dad kept looking for someone to fill that void—marrying one woman after another. [In his four marriages, there was hardly a year in between.] So as soon as his divorce was final from Georgiana, he married Mary Ellen Munger, and shortly they relocated to Los Angeles, California.

I saw him when I was 6 years old, for about 8 minutes. Grandma Daisy, Mom and I were on a trip back to Albuquerque and went up through Colorado Springs on the way home. Daisy spotted Bob walking across the street. Mother figured out exactly whom he was visiting, and she telephoned. Yes, he was there, so we all drove over. But I was sent upstairs to play with the other children.

I did not see him again until I was 13; that was when Dad sent me a cross country train ticket. (It was one of those "Marx Brothers" [Movie Comedians Groucho, Harpo, and Chico] who kept tearing off parts of a long paper contract when anyone objected to a paragraph] train tickets a yard long and the conductor had to tear off apiece every time we crossed over some train company's trackage.)

Dad did write to me once or twice a year, sometimes including photographs, and he always telephoned me on Christmas. Still, I was very aware of coming from a divorced family when (outside of our apartment building) every other child seemed to have had a mom and dad, lived in a house rather than an apartment, had automobiles instead of taking the street car, and several families on our block had maids.

## CONTEXTS IN WHICH I GREW UP : A FAMILY SOCIAL ROOTS

• • • • • • • • • • • • • • • • • • • • • •

My family tree on both mother's and father's side fit within the description of "Middle Class." While I recognize that the "Middle Class" category can be measured differently depending upon the specific criteria chosen, e.g., wealth, or education, or social background--can be so wide and broad as to become weakly useful.

On my mother's mother's side, the Hancocks, at the time of Daisy's parents--Lorenzo Dow Hancock (18) was wed to Elizabeth Curry (16), both families were considered to be in the upper middle class possessing a comfortable amount of land and money. Good breeding: Random House Webster's Unabridged Dictionary Page 259. "The result of upbringing or training as shown in behavior and manners; especially good manners."

On mother's father's side, the Shelhouses--they were hard working industrious German Middle Class. My Grandfather, George Robert, worked his way up to be the Foreman of the MAUG GEAR Department, where they made 20-foot-tall gears that could integrate the teeth with another 20-foot gear at right angles. George's formal schooling never went beyond 4$^{th}$ grade in elementary school (which was common in those days—1880's) but he had an excellent mind, and he figured out the mathematical-algebraic formula for cutting all the gear teeth such that fit within required millimeter specifications. George's older brother Maurice was the Superintendent of the Niles Tools Works Plant. And his older brother John also was a "mechanic" there. All three brothers worked steadily throughout the 1930's and the Depression. George always made sure his "little Jossy" (Joy) was dressed in the finest clothes to attend school and college. [When I was born, she continued the practice, so I always had very presentable clothes.] Oh yes, Grandpa George opened a college account for me at the Seven Mile Bank! While the account never had a lot of money in it, the "seed was planted" deep into my mind little Patric is going to go college some day!

On my father's side, his third great grandfather, was William Leedom, who was a Captain in the War of 1812, and a successful businessman and farmer. In the 1790's William joined a group of pioneers who floated down the river to what is now Manchester (Originally Massie's Station—named in honor of Colonel Massie who led the pioneers.)

Manchester was within the "Virginia Military Land Grant" territory (South Central Ohio on the Ohio River). The William Leedoms and two other families, The George Edgington's and the Donalsons joined Colonel Massie in founding the settlement of Manchester, during the 1788-90's. William married George's daughter Tacy (Elizabeth) Edgington. [In recent research, I discovered that George Edgington's daughter was also WILLIAM'S OLDER SISTER ALMIRA'S DAUGHTER, SO WILLIAM MARRIED HIS OWN NEICE!!

William had eleven children by his first wife Tacy—Elijah and Joseph. We are related to Elijah through our grandmother Bessie's lineage, and we are related to Joseph thru our grandfather Chilton A.'s lineage—you might say I received a "Double Dose of Leedom-ness and William fathered nine more children by Tacy. She died in 1824. Later William married Mary Rogers' they had one daughter Talitha They were prolific and courageous: The history book reports that William, along with several other farmers, built the "Flatboats = 200 feet long, 30 feet wide, with a steering oar in back" loaded them with animal furs, and farm produce and whatever else might be sold for money, and floated down the Ohio and Mississippi Rivers and selling everything including the flatboat made from great Hardwoods suitable for building homes in New Orleans. After selling everything, the farmers banded together, and their only way to get back up the rivers to home, was to walk back, e.g., along Natchez's Trace [ A path or trail through a wilderness that has been beaten out by the passage of animals or people.]. These trips by boat down the river and walking back took several weeks. William and fellow farmers made the trip 15 times over 23 years!

[Time Digression] As a teenager going back and forth from Ohio (my mother) to California (my father) that gave me a comparison between my two parents. Observation: I am bi-cultural: my mother was a "conservative Eisenhower-Taft Country Club Republican." Which implied she held to a certain set of political, economic, social beliefs.

My father was a "liberal social Democrat and defender of the common person" which again implied that he held to a certain set of political, economic, and social beliefs." And I had the philosophical advantage of learning from both of them.

## MOVING IN WITH GEORGE AND DAISY SHELHOUSE
• • • • • • • • • • • • • • • • • • • • • •

When the divorce took place, mother and I, age 3, moved from Cincinnati in with her parents in Hamilton, Ohio (where mom had grown up.) Most things have a + and a -. The negative was that I have almost no awareness of having a mother. Years later she explained that she got up earlier than I, to go to work at the Defense Plant. And she returned home after I went to bed with grandma. We went to bed early probably shortly after the sun went down. I don't doubt any of Mother's explanations because mother was always popular in social gatherings, and she did like to have a drink after work, usually a beer with fellow coworkers. I do remember her on some weekends.

Grandma and Grandpa slept in the same bedroom but not in the same bed. [Maybe that wasn't and isn't so unusual.] I slept with Grandma (after we knelt and said our prayers). Grandma always told me a true family story every night—like the time Rebel General John Hunt Morgan [American Commander of Confederate Raiders] came to the Hancock family farm with his men and demanded to be fed. [The farm was on the western side of Colerain Pike, 3 miles south of Oxford. It was still there in the early 1960's when Mother and I drove up to see it. It was vacant so we could see most of the things Grandma told us about.] Grandma's mother, Elizabeth Curry Hancock obliged—even when the flour was filled with ants—or were they weevils? General Morgan was very polite, traded horses as usual. Years after the war, Grandma's uncle, Marion Curry, made a lot of winnings on the Kentucky Racehorse that

Morgan's men left behind. He named the horse "Kit Curry."

I loved my grandpa George very much. [I was told he was a very **kind** person, and that he was never known to say anything unkind about anyone. And I was instructed to take after him in his being **kind.**] And I have. He spent a lot of time with me—taking walks, maybe for us to see a steam locomotive puff its way into the tunnel at the end of our street and emerge out the other side—with smoke and steam enveloping the two of us. Sometimes he and I climbed into his 1934 Studebaker sedan, and we drove into town to Mr. Lee's Cigar Store, where grandpa purchased cigars and I often got a pack of Juicy Fruit gum—and occasionally a rubber ball to play with. Now grandpa was forbidden to smoke cigars in the house, so he smoked on the back porch or in the car. I can still remember distinctly the cigar-smoking aroma of that car. Grandpa was medically retired because of cancer and he did spend on and off time in the hospital. Mother related to me years later that even though Grandpa knew he was dying, he still walked up and down the hospital halls singing **Old Man River** to other patients in his deep baritone voice.

Grandpa and I sat together in the evening to listen to the old-time radio shows when you had to use your imagination; such programs as Lum and Abner, Fibber Magee and Molly, Amos and Andy, and Baby Snooks. On Sundays, he would put me on his lap and read the comic or Funny Pages section to me. I still have many photographs of me and grandpa together (and some letters he wrote to me before I could even read.)

Unfortunately, Grandpa's contracted Cancer of the Colon (which was prevalent in the Shelhouse side.) progressed to the advanced stage; at the time doctors did not know much to do, besides cut out sections of the colon. He died in the hospital when I was four turning five; I was allowed once or twice to go to his room and visit with him. (Not really being aware he was dying.) I was not allowed to attend the funeral, but I remember riding in the car going home, Mother tried to break the news gently to me, but I was sad just the same at losing him.

Grandma Daisy—she was a huge gift to me. She had been an elementary school teacher since September 1896. She graduated high school in June 1896; she followed her next oldest sister, Elizabeth, into teaching. Daisy went to the Board of Education, took the test to be a teacher, passed, and in September 1896 she had her own room schoolhouse—1st through 8th grade (very similar to the one she had gone to school in) in the rural settlement of Urmsten. (I still have a photograph of Daisy and her class from that year.)

Daisy, who had taught elementary grades and "Adjustment Classes" (Now called Special Education) for over 50 years, was an astute observer of children and labeled me as "bright"—for example that I picked up on things quickly and remembered them well. So, she began teaching me or rather "schooling" me every day. Because we went to bed so early, we would be up each morning between 5:30 and 6:00 A.M. After breakfast, sometimes we would go outside in the yard where she instructed me on the names of all the birds (which we fed daily), all of the names of flowers, and yes, they did have a World War II "Victory Garden" where you grew your own vegetables rather than buy them in the market. So, then I had to learn the names of all the vegetables. (And occasionally I had helped Grandpa spread sulfur and cigar ashes around the plants to keep the rabbits away.)

This was during 1943 and 1944 and World War II was still being fought. I remember each of us had a RATION BOOK used to control certain war-critical commodities such as meat, sugar, butter, shoes, gasoline, and tires. Automobile drivers were issued an alphabetic sticker to place on the windshield indicating how many gallons this person was allowed to buy. For example, doctors were issued an "A" sticker because they needed to be able to drive a lot and were allowed to fill up. Ordinary workers received a "B", and non-essential persons received something like a "C" or "D", and they were only allowed two to three gallons.

I remember a few times when Civil Defense would declare a "Black Out Drill" and everyone was required to extinguish all sources of light in the house. Civil Defense wardens patrolled the streets to enforce it. [The fear was, that since so many war defense plants were located in the general area—such as Wright Aeronautical, that enemy bombers would see and use the lights of the town to guide them to the factories.]

Back inside the house, Grandma (who I am sure never heard of the Montessori philosophy of teaching) did Montessori-like activities with me. She "made me her assistant" as we cleaned the house, made the beds. She sometimes taught me to cook, especially cookies and cakes. She let me help wash the clothes on "Wash Day Monday" using the old rippled wash board and Fels-Naphtha brown soap. She even helped me to learn to sew. She would hand me a piece of "Sampler" cloth with a design on it. I would then embroider the designs with colored thread. Later Grandma would fill in the designs with cloth. To this day, hanging in my living room, is a sampler of a fruit bowl in the middle—A banana, apple grapes etc. with different colored flowers (perhaps tulips) on all four sides. I recently had it framed! On occasion, Grandma was called to substitute teach, and when she was, she took me to school and placed me in her friend, Mrs. Slifer's Kindergarten Class, where I spent the day.

Every afternoon when Grandma and I were back home, it was my nap time...on the Davenport (old form of couch or sofa.) Grandma always had an excellent selection of Children's Literature to read to me: A Child's Story of the Bible, Aesop's Fables, Adventures of Anthony Ant; Uncle Lucky Left Hind Foot were some of them. It seemed to me that she would read a full chapter before I drifted off to sleep, but probably there were times when I drifted off earlier. Grandma would note the page where we stopped for the day, and where to re-commence the next day. So, the year and a half that I lived at 317 Milliken Street, Hamilton, Ohio, my life was well nurtured.

As I reflect upon my interactions as a small child with my grandmother, there were lots of "messages" from her, that she loved me, she cared about me not only at the time, but for my future development. They were very positive "messages."

Perhaps now is a good time to mention parenting skills. The average person would say, "Oh, all mothers love and care for their children." I will shift momentarily to the male of the species; it is much more understandable that most men's parenting skills are modeled after what they experienced from their fathers. Agreed? Now switch back to the female of the species. In similar fashion, most women accumulate their mothering skills from their mothers, or perhaps by observing neighborhood mothers; and by baby-sitting and caring for younger children.

My mother, nick-named "Joy," grew up differently. George and Daisy had given birth to a son first, but the doctor used forceps to remove the child, damaging the skull, so Samuel Hiram only lived 20 days!

When Georgiana (named after her father, who perhaps was hoping for a son) was born, they treated her like a queen. Georgiana was immediately a favorite with her father. They spent lots of time together—in teen years even repairing cars together. [Note: during mother's second marriage, it was she who bought and sold their cars, and maintained proper servicing.] I do not really know what happened to the relationship between my Mom and her Mom, Daisy, [Who was 38 years old when mother was born and already an austere teacher, so maybe they had difficulty emotionally bonding.] but it seems to have generated friction from early on. I do have some sense that Daisy was not the huggy, cuddly type. I do know that when Daisy was upset, she became the "Silent Type" not speaking a word to anyone—even to explain why she was upset. I do remember mother telling me that there were times when she said to her father, "Let's divorce Daisy, and you and I can live together!" Added to this, growing up, Georgiana did not babysit nor care for young children. So, she really didn't have much of a reference for caring for me.

At the age of 12, her father George taught Georgiana to drive the car. Note: there were no Driver's Licenses in those years, and Daisy refused to learn, and George thought at least one other person needed to be able to drive.

Georgiana was growing fast into adult hood-like maturity. At age 13, she began taking violin lessons from Giovani Bruno—who was affiliated with the Cincinnati Symphony Orchestra. By age 16, three things happened:

1) She had her own String Quartet that performed publicly e.g., D.A.R. and the YWCA, as well as high school events.

2) By age 16, Giovani Bruno was taking Georgiana to downtown Cincinnati from Hamilton to have an upscale dinner and enjoy the Cincinnati Symphony Orchestra performance; sometimes Giovani and Georgiana went backstage after the performance to socialize with some of the musicians.

3) Also, by age 16, Georgiana was driving herself 70 miles up to Greensburg, Indiana, where her cousin Edward J. Hancock lived. He was in his 60's, his first wife had died, and his eyes were going bad. He was very active in Republican politics and was overseeing a candidate

who was running for the office of Governor. So, mother stepped in as E.J.'s co-host for parties, and drove him to meetings, or important social affairs, such as a Governor's Ball. From these experiences, Georgiana (Joy) developed Savoir Faire—the best of good manners, and the art of engaging others in stimulating conversation.

## *MOTHER AND I MOVE TO CINCINNATI*

• • • • • • • • • • • • • • • • • • • • • •

Right after Mom and I moved to Marion Avenue, North Avondale, Cincinnati, Mom was still working in the Defense Plant in Lockland (Evendale), so she enrolled me into a "War Nursery" (designed for child care for all the women, working three different shifts in defense plants) in Lockland. I am remembering that often it was a male colleague of mother's—I think his name was Jack—would pick us up to drive to the plant. I remember stopping at a delicious bakery every morning and buying rolls, and I always was given one. That was a nice way to start the day.

Mother still had Grandpa's Studebaker car in those days. So sometimes she drove us to Lockland. Either way, Mother dropped me off on the way to work and picked me up right after work. [In 1948, Mother finally had to give up the car because as a 1934 vintage car, the car companies no longer made parts for them such as the mechanical brakes the Studebaker possessed.]

After the war was over, and the defense plants closed, Mom got a job in downtown Cincinnati, so now she moved me to "The Little Flower Hotel"--Miss Campbell's War Nursery in an old mansion across from the Cincinnati Zoo on Eden Ave. Most of the time things were fine. I was excused from Nap Time because I was too full of energy—played outside by myself. But there were three times when life was not fine.

These were painful, traumatic times when the day was ending, and mom usually came to pick me up. But on this particular day, it was a Friday, the adults allowed me to sit in the large living room window watching and waiting for my mother—to pick me up and take me home. They allowed me to sit and observe every car that came by. Sometimes a car did pull into our driveway…BUT IT WAS NOT FOR ME! More watching and waiting and hoping. "Where is she? When is she coming?" I was growing anxious and a bit fearful. I know I sat there over two hours—I watched the sun go down and the sky turn dark. "Where is she? And When is she coming?" Finally, one of the adults, perhaps Miss Campbell, took me upstairs and put me to bed in a bedroom where her visiting niece, Bunny, was staying. Bunny was about my age and fun to be with. Even sneaky. The large iron fire-escape led from our second-floor room down to the side yard. So naturally we had to "check it out" quietly! No adult ever knew.

[Time Digression] That scene played out two more times!! Years later when I was sharing my feelings with my mother, she was shocked! On those three mornings-- Friday mornings, when she dropped me off, she carried in a small suitcase in to Mrs. Campbell and told her she would not be back until the next morning. Apparently, Mom assumed Mrs. Campbell would explain that to me. But Mrs. Campbell didn't, nor did mother when she dropped me off. I would have remembered. The psychological emotional wound was very deep and long-lasting.

A similar situation developed when I was 16-17 living in Laguna Beach and hanging out with "the Brothers" Duane, Bruce, Donnie, and Lorenzo from South Central Los Angeles. They would telephone me the day before and tell me they would stop by and pick me up on their way to party in San Diego. Sometimes I would wait anxiously for two hours and finally telephone them to find: they had changed their minds; they just forgot to tell me!

As an adult, I do have anxiety disorder—largely from some very insecure times when I was trying to succeed in college, but often didn't have much money; I sometimes worried where I was going to live or to sleep, and where the next meal was coming from. I did starve twice while going to school-COLLEGE--losing 28 pounds each time. But the early War Nursery experiences launched it. [End Digression]

I certainly did absorb a message from my Mother:—"The more independent you can become, the happier I will be" which helps to explain why I was going downtown alone at the age of 8 to attend double-feature movies in the evening, sometimes arriving back home around 11:15, 11:30 P.M. or so. [As I reflect all these many years later, I can begin to piece together an "education" of my mind, and spirit. I remember walking the twelve or fourteen blocks to school when I was six and seven years old. I had to be very observant and learn all the streets. I had to have had courage, and a form of security that I probably would be safe as I wandered the neighborhoods….This included walking more than a mile to the movie theatres in Norwood. I do not remember ever being scared. As I write this, I am remembering that I got my hair cut at the Alms Hotel Barber Shop in Walnut Hills. Sometimes mother was with me, but often I took the two buses to get my hair cut, which also gave me the access to Williams YMCA two blocks further, where we went swimming.

Another situation developed shortly after Mother and I moved into the apartment on Marion Avenue, in North Avondale, Cincinnati. In those days, North Avondale was a very desirable neighborhood with an excellent school. The neighborhood was heavily Jewish, so when I finally could start school in the First Grade at the old Avondale School (Rockdale and Reading roads) many of my classmates were sons and daughters of Jewish Doctors, or successful businessmen. The academic standards in the school were high—even for the toe-headed kid who wasn't sure how to make sense of it all. I do remember learning to read in the first grade with Miss Frank. We certainly did use "Dick, Jane, Sally, Spot the dog and Puff the cat" readers. All white middle-class examples. One of my biggest or longest lasting memory is that Miss Frank taught all of us to "Spool Knit." This is where you actually had a thread spool with four nails hammered into the top in 4-square fashion. Then, with knitting yarn, and a knitting needle, we learned to wrap new yarn around the existing yarn, and to lift the existing yarn on each nail up and over the new yarn thus locking it into place. This produced a knitted "tube-like" coming out the lower end of the spool. One could then sew the tubes into objects such as hats. What I remember is that when we added a different color strand of yarn, it took a while to integrate the new color until it appeared coming out the bottom. This slow changing of the colors has stuck with me all my life as a metaphor for how our life's events also take a course of slow integration into our lives—perhaps as the birth of a new baby in the family, or maybe moving into a new neighborhood, or entering the Armed Forces; some kind of a life change that is as gradual as the yarn. Yes, I would like to purchase a kit and once again spool knit as a philosophical exercise. [OK, Since I wrote that, I went out and bought one, and now my knitted variegated "tube" is six feet long!]

## SEEDS OF "I BELIEVE I CAN."

• • • • • • • • • • • • • • • • • • • • • •

Let us start with "Boyhood."

As a three to six-year-old, I remember myself as being "normal sized; normal attractive—nothing about me was unusual or overtly noticeable. Normal haircut. Physically I was quite capable; I could walk long distances; I could run for moderate distances. My eyesight was very good. My teeth appeared in the normal range. My ability to speak, hear, comprehend the English language was ordinary. My health was very good to excellent.

Mentally, I was above average: a) I was able to perceive situations; I was able to formulate a plan of action such as to take myself a mile or two to a movie theatre in Norwood. I believe my "problem solving ability", was above average. For example: I was able to look at a couple of tall pine trees and conceive of constructing a "cable car/tram way." I took the fuselage of a toy airplane to create the cable car. I was able to construct pulley type anchors such that I could thread a string from the ground (where there was a drum reel for "paying out and retrieving the "Running Cable" up the tree to a height of 6 or 7 feet, where I had affixed a pulley-anchor ring then straight across to a neighboring tree and its pulley-anchor ring and down the trunk to the ground to the companion cranked drum reel. I ran pieces of twine through the open windows of the fuselage looping up and over the "Standing Rigging Support Cable" and back to the plane—one forward and one aft, such that the cable car was horizontal. I attached a "Running Cable" to the "bow" or front of the "Cable Car" which was the cable that ran through the pulley and down to the drum reel on the right tree; I attached another running cable to the "stern" or back of the cable car, and similarly to the opposite tree pulley attachment and down the tree trunk to the cranking drum wheel.

Now, I could sit on the ground and crank one drum moving the cable car over to the left tree; then I moved taking the opposite drum crank and move the cable car back across the "High Wire or "Standing Cable." As I recall, the distance between trees was in the neighborhood of around ten feet.

The point I am illustrating is that I could conceive of a project, then locate the apparatus, and create and execute the project. I saw them as challenges.

## *A SENTIMENTAL TRIP BACK TO ALBUQUERQUE*

• • • • • • • • • • • • • • • • • • • • • •

I am reminded that in 1946, Mother, Grandma Daisy, and I took a car trip--in the old 1934 Studebaker sedan—across country, and back to Albuquerque, so we could visit old friends including my care taker Mary Lopez. [1946 was only one year after World War II. New tires were not available. So, we suffered two flat tires-one right next to a flying ant hill. Also, car radiators were "primitive so a thoughtful person carried "Water Bags draped over the Hood Ornament [which sits on top of the radiator cap.] We made a special trip up to Santa Fe to obtain a copy of my Birth Certificate.

Mother had always loved living in Albuquerque, so she went back to the Health and Welfare Office, where she had worked in 1942 and 1943. They offered her her old job back. And mother deeply wanted to move back to Albuquerque. And she told her mother Daisy about it. Daisy apparently responded, "Well if you want to stay out here in this god-forsaken desert you can; BUT I AM GOING BACK HOME!" So, mother declined to take the job. [Years later, Mother was feeling some regret and reported to me, "I should have called her bluff, and kept the job in Albuquerque. She would not have stayed very long back in Hamilton when her only family—you and I were out here."

Would you believe for the first time ever July 2020—I found in an old cardboard box, Grandma Daisy's letters to her niece Jean Woolford, complaining bitterly about our 1946?? Here are some selected excerpts:

Albuquerque, New Mexico July 5th, 1946

*Dear Jean (Woolford)..."It is like being in a foreign country to be in Albuquerque [Population 30-40,000 people] Mexicans chattering Spanish, Indians stolidly walking along, husband leading wife...One* *morning Joy parked the car in the shade...As I sat there I saw Bob Leedom [my father] cross the street in front of me....And I paid $2.17 for our lunch, which wasn't fit to eat....Pat is blowing a whistle and I can't think!... This motel is $6.00 a day, it would be $7.50 if we used the kitchen, so we didn't use the kitchen. The next day it was 105 degrees...one person said it was the hottest day in 96 years....But I think it is always unbearable!*

Albuquerque New Mexico July 8th, 1946

*My very dear (Jean), I'm so glad we are to leave here in the morning. When I was **here three days, I was ready to go home**. How Joy would want to live here I cannot understand. And to think she thought that she could coax me to live here is not understandable.*

*It is perpetually hot and dry. Who would want that? Joy has left Pat with his old nurse, Mary Lopez. He will play with little Ramoncito who is 8 years old and only comes to Pat's shoulder.*

*Pat is tired of being left each evening with me. And I am tired of it too."*

Well, now you have a flavor of Granma Daisy's personality. I do not believe Mother ever read these letters. For years Mother kept saying that in 1946, Mother should have called "Daisy's Bluff" and stayed living and working in Albuquerque. But after I have read the letters—there is no way Daisy would have lived in Albuquerque. She and Georgiana—my mother-- did not have a comfortable relationship.

When her father George died, and a few years later, Mother tried bringing Daisy to live with us. However, Daisy could not keep her mouth shut and was very critical of mother's dating lifestyle, so Daisy had to move out…

I think I might have been Daisy's salvation, because she doted on me, and we always got along. [By the way, I do have several memories of that trip.]

## I TAKE MYSELF TO SCHOOL

• • • • • • • • • • • • • • • • • • • • • • •

I am remembering my experience of enrolling in the first grade at Avondale School. My mother took me on the Municipal Street Car which ran South and North on Reading Road. Our apartment was just a block east of Reading Road and the Avondale School was on Reading Road about 12-14 blocks south. Mother showed me the way to ride the street car to school one (1) time. I was expected to learn it quickly and remember it, because from the second day on, it was up to me to get myself to school and on time! AND, if I missed the street car/bus or if I lost my fare—which was 5 cents, then it was up to me to walk the 12-14 blocks either to school or from school to home! No problem. I clearly remembered the way. [It is worth noting that in the 1940's streets were safe for children—no adult tried to harm them.] It might be important to note that Reading Road was a major route in and out of the city, so it was a busy thoroughfare. Mother taught me how to obey the traffic lights, and cross safely—which I had to do going and coming to school. No problem.

By the way, there were no "school buses" in those days. I am wondering if I didn't have a touch of existential anxiety in my young days: I watched adults board the street car and deposit their dime—10 whole cents—into the Fare Box. And I remember worrying if I could ever afford that much money!

+ + + + + + +

## *AT AGE SEVEN, BABY SITTERS WERE CANCELLED*

• • • • • • • • • • • • • • • • • • • • • •

Well into my seventh year, I had one of those moments: "Mother please, I would rather do it myself!" Was it a strong will that was developing? The need for babysitters WAS CANCELLED. At eight years old, Mother would give me a few dollars, I climbed on the streetcar and went downtown in the evening to see a double-feature movie complete with Newsreel and Cartoon. I would leave the theater around 10:30 pm, do a little shopping, perhaps at Mr. Planter Peanut's shop on Fountain Square, and be back on the streetcar or bus, and ride home. No one ever bothered me, and I didn't bother anyone, and I went straight home at a good pace.

Yes, I was responsible for getting myself back and forth to school at age six. But by age seven I was roaming and learning the streets in the eastern half of the North Avondale neighborhood, and as I approached 8, I was able to walk a mile or so over into Norwood because there were two movie theatres up on Montgomery Road. For a quarter, I could buy a ticket for 15 cents, and a bag of popcorn for 10 cents. And of course, by turning age eight, I was taking a city bus downtown to attend double features in the evening.

[Time Digression] This is a good time to REFLECT on my mother. Up until now my words have painted a picture of "an absentee—hands-off parent." I was given my "independence" at an early age—I was transporting myself back and forth to school at age 6; at age eight I was going downtown Cincinnati to an evening double feature movie. At age nine I went to work at the Xavier football stadium to work with concessions and help manage the money.

I don't remember anything particularly distinguishing about the second grade with Mrs. Gonnard. I think it went smoothly. I do remember several times when they took classes into the big auditorium and showed us movies. And I thought it was some kind of magic when the blank plaster wall in front of us started displaying moving pictures. [How was I to know that there was this machine far behind us that was "projecting" these pictures? I was too small to even be able to look back over the audience's heads to see the machine.]

Now third grade was a very different experience: the teacher, Miss Taylor—who got married during the year and became Mrs. O'Connell and I just did not get along well. I guess my attention in class was wandering a lot and not on the lesson she was teaching. And maybe I was disturbing the classmates around me. Anyway, early in the year, Miss Taylor placed my desk beside hers and that is where I stayed all year long—not able to be with my classmates.

Quoting from a Memoir I wrote September 2, 1964: "For the fourth grade, those of us who lived north of certain streets were transferred to the new North Avondale School. I remember walking up the big hill (Clinton Springs Avenue) and registering myself (For the fourth Grade.) After the first grade, Mother never went with me. There really wasn't much reason to. I was always with the same group of kids from year to year and the school knew all about me and where I belonged. Mrs. Olmstead was our teacher. She was reasonably young and of the "new school of thought" where the teacher paid more attention to individual problems. End of quote. Mrs. Olmstead was the first teacher I thought liked me, and I received my first teacher-hugs from her.

Going to North Avondale school, my clothes and shoes were "normal" for the times. One does not wear blue-jeans to school: those are "play clothes." One does wear corduroy pants. One does not wear tennis shoes to school. One takes tennis shoes in a bag to be put on for gym class. One wears fully leather shoes to school. And I recall all the other boys following that custom. I would further comment that I was not particularly conscious of clothing styles, brands, etc. Only that my appearance was similar to all the other boys. So, I did not "stand out."

Thank God for moving to the new North Avondale School on Clinton Springs Ave. It was much closer to my home—maybe three long blocks—and where the teachers and principal were all warm and positive. With my fourth grade home-room teacher, Mrs. Olmstead, I blossomed. Then, there was the Art teacher, Miss Keller. We did many interesting projects; she knew her stuff. But when the project involved cutting and pasting, I did poorly. I could NEVER cut the paper pieces neatly and cleanly as the model Miss Keller showed us! I got a complex that I was not good at art. However, Joyce, who sat across from me, always seemed to do everything right! Well, she was a girl. Girls are neat. I was a boy. With two thumbs. What do you expect of me?

[Time Digression] This is a good place to relate that when I became a teacher 25 years later at Children's House West Public Montessori School, and insisted on having an art easel available to my students as a choice of activity, I remembered my feelings from Miss Keller's class, and so when I demonstrated how to use the paint brushes to create a painting, I purposely painted abstract designs, and "thought out loud" for the benefit of the students. "I think I feel like using some red, and putting a splotch here, and maybe over there; okay, now I feel like some blue...some yellow..." Then I asked my table full of six students, "When it is your turn to paint, do you have to make exactly what I did?" In my mind their response would be "NO!" But it was notable that some children wanted to know from me what was "the right answer to my question even at the age of five; some are already socialized into thinking the teacher determines "the right answer." Sad.

Back to when Mom and I moved into North Avondale. In order to live comfortably in our beautiful and friendly neighborhood, Mother needed more income in addition to her five days a week job (as the

Secretary and later also the treasurer) of a small mineral brokerage firm for Fluorspar—a "Fluxing Agent" in the process of making steel (in those olden days.) So, when our neighbor up the street on Reading Road, Sammy Rosenbaum, the Dry Cleaner asked Mother to keep his Books one night a week, she accepted. A few weeks later Sammy said his friend Harry Glueck, the Druggist, needed someone one night a week, was mother interested. Yes. A few weeks later Harry said his friend Louis Lesher, the Florist, needed someone one night a week, was she interested? Yes.

In my review of pieces of an old autobiography I must have written about the age of 11, I was reminded when I was seven years old, I had contracted Chicken Pox. That was bad enough; but then the doctor who was doing a house call, had just come away from a patient who had Scarlet Fever (a serious disease.) I *had contracted "surgical* Scarlet Fever—from the doctor's contact with my skin—not as serious. Well, I must have scratched one or two of the pox, because within days, I developed Scarlet Fever," and a very large bag of pus formed on my chest. I was taken immediately to the hospital—I remember being carried out of the apartment to a waiting ambulance by the driver, dressed in ordinary clothes and one of those flat hats popular at the time.

I cannot tell you the exact number of weeks I was quarantined in the hospital, but I believe at least three. The doctors did do surgery on me and drained the large puss bag; I still have the scars. Whenever Mother came to visit, she had to wear a special gown, and she was not allowed to get too close to or touch me. And all the books and toys I had enjoyed in the hospital, had to be burned!

Sometime during all of this, Mother connected with a Catholic Brother, Jerry Sullivan, at the University of Dayton, who had just written his Doctoral Dissertation all in Latin. Mother, with her four years of high school Latin, and four years of College Latin, edited, corrected, and typed his dissertation for extra pay!

And within a year or two after that, Mother was hired into a mineral brokerage firm that regularly communicated with Mexican Mine owners. Mother did all the letter writing and translation in Spanish and handled all phone calls.

I think I can: What I did do, was to set myself to work to learn all the downtown major streets. I would go to a street corner that I knew. I would look down a street I didn't know. I would start carefully walking and observing. I would stop halfway, turn around and check my familiar corner; then I would proceed to the end of that street, and so on. There was motivation: Cincinnati had at least seven movie theaters spread out on different streets. I located them all. I did it! I thought I could.

+ + + + + + + + +

And when I was 7, Mom met and became involved with Matthew G. Long—grandson of the man who put Henry Ford in business by making the steel for the first cars. So, there were nights when they would join the social crowds at upscale cocktail lounges, and I was left home alone.

While they never married, gradually Matt filled in as my stepfather. He loved me, reached out to me, and frequently included me in activities such as swimming at the Country Club. As I became a teenager with a driver's license, he always let me drive his cars. As I started dressing up, he taught me all about quality clothing and shoes and how to take care of them to make them last. Matt did have financial resources, so all of his suits were hand-made. The buttons on the sleeves "un-buttoned!" as they did for the fancy lace-cuff blouses (shirt) in the 1700's.

Matt liked to drink—all through prohibition. He became popular with the hidden "Speakeasys" because he became the "Mobs' " clothing consultant. (I do not know if they really were part of a Mob.) He told me there were times when he was sitting having a drink, and the boss would come over and tell him he had to leave NOW by the back door "because they were going to be RAIDED in ten minutes!" [I wasn't there to observe how true it was, but it sure made a good story!]

+ + + + + + +

## A BUS TRIP AROUND THE CITY

• • • • • • • • • • • • • • • • • • • • • •

*I believe I can. I believe I Can.* One time around age 9 or 10, I boarded a Cincinnati Railway bus, asking myself, "I wonder to where all this bus goes?" So, I rode the entire route observing all the neighborhoods until I was back to where I had boarded. While I did sit near the front of the bus--observing out the window, the bus driver never said a word.

My mother was "absent" a lot in the home: she was busy working evenings for several local merchants; and being divorced, and being highly adept at social engagement, she did have an active social life. I was home alone a lot, or more often, I was "running the streets." There was a time when I went to work for the local drugstore—it was my responsibility to maintain the Comic Book and Magazine Rack. I weekly replaced the old issues with the new. (I also accumulated a collection of 500 Comic Books—which my mother disposed of when I was in California.)

Consequently, that full-route ride in the Western part of Cincinnati turned out to help me a year or so later when my mother had me join "Big Brothers" for young boys who needed a male role model. My

Big Brother lived over on the West side of Cincinnati, and after I was shown the route once, I was expected to take the two buses to get to his house [As an indication of maturing, I had acquired a certain level of confidence and comfort levels when traveling to new destinations, and in this particular case, being comfortable staying overnight in a different bed....] I would take the bus—but I think it was two, and maybe I had to go downtown by myself and transfer to the other bus (but I was confident)—and go over on Friday afternoons for the weekend. He was into cars and owned some midget racers. So, most Friday nights we drove to the Sharonville Racetrack, to watch the midget races. He (I do not remember his name) would allow me to sit atop a brick pillar, right down by the racetrack. One time I fell off and cut my wrist on a broken bottle (I still have the scar). Another time, when we did not go, so I was told, two boys sat up on the pillar. One of the midget racers crashed sending a wheel through the air which killed the two boys.

## AT AGE 9, I GOT TO WORK FOR THE XAVIER FOOTBALL STADIUM CONCESSION STANDS

• • • • • • • • • • • • • • • • • • • • • • • •

When I was 9 years old, I was "hanging out" at the Xavier Football Stadium. This large overweight man came to me. "Hey kid." "Yeah?" "Want a job?" "Doing what?" "Making popcorn, setting up for concessions." [**I believe I can**.] "Yeah, sure, but I need to run home and let my mother know." I worked every football game that fall season of 1949. I would go early to make popcorn and stock up the two concession stands—Bill Decker on the north side, and his brother, John Decker, on the south side. Sometimes before the games I would retrieve footballs for the players who were practicing. During the game I was a "money runner": if John had too many large bills, I would take small bills and exchange them." Very occasionally I sold in the stands, but I was not fond of it. After the game, Bill sat me in a corner with a cardboard box full of loose coin and a fist full of wrappers. I wrapped every single coin, and I never took (stole) a single cent; it didn't even enter my mind to do such a thing. It was time consuming, so often I arrived home between 11:30 P.M. and midnight. **I Did It! I believed I could!**

A related event, a few years later when I was transferring busses to return to the Ohio Military Institute, John Decker was working at a market at one of the transfer points. He would always give me a friendly greeting and a piece of fruit.

At the age of 10, I talked my playmate, Laura Mac St., (my partner in crime) into walking the railroad tracks with me. The tracks headed north so I thought we might make it to my grandmother's home in Hamilton Ohio. So, we started in mid-morning with 17 cents in my pocket. Around noon the tracks crossed a street and there was a candy store there. We bought three flavored ice cones for 5 cents apiece, and two lollypops at 1 cent a piece. [Looking back now, that was a rather mis-guided idea, even though it demonstrated bold adventurous desires.]

After a while, especially walking across train trestle tracks, we discovered that sometimes *YOU CAN'T HEAR A SPEEDING TRAIN BEHIND YOU!* One anxious moment was when Laura got her cowboy boot caught between the ties. But like in the melodramas, she got it free just in time. Yes, a train was heading toward us!

What we did not notice was the track was no longer heading north; instead, it had arched over to the west and then south. Arriving at the train yard down near Union Terminal, we asked the first adult we saw if we were nearing Hamilton? How were we to know he was a Railroad Policeman! [Well, I had thought we could walk to Hamilton. OOOps, wrong!] So, he arrested us, but we would not talk and give him any information. So, he bribed us. He took us to a Switch Engine Locomotive and had us ride in the cab back and forth in the railroad switching yard a few times. Then we talked. We were taken home in a Police Cruiser, and "Patric was forbidden to play with Laura for a few weeks!" [Imagine that!]

Meanwhile, going back to the situation where neither Mother nor I was home very much—would you believe it is hard to do Homework if you are hardly ever home? I had only the vaguest idea what kind of learning I was supposed to be doing.

I did not exactly fail my grade—I did receive several D's and even an "E" (which translated to an "F",) The teachers often sent notes home to my Mother, "Patric is not working up to his potential!" [And I still have those report cards right here on my desk!]

As I neared the age of 11, and still was not earning very good grades in school, Mother was unhappy with the relationship I was developing with the local Police Department. They would do extra patrols up and down my street to see what I was doing: *Oh my God, now he is on the roof of a three-story apartment building!" This sometimes resulted in a trip down to Juvenile Court!*

But being a loving and caring parent can be defined in many ways. My mother always loved me; she was always very affectionate with me. She always made sure I had the essentials of food, clothing, and shelter. (Even when she was not able to provide dinner, she arranged for me to go to the local tavern and order myself a steak dinner—and then go to a booth to consume it. I was very well known in the tavern, Steins' Hideaway, and was always welcome. I was always polite and well behaved. Mother was always generous with her money, and more than once she provided loans to help me out of a tight financial spot.

## GOING AWAY TO BOARDING SCHOOL:
## OHIO MILITARY SCHOOL (OMI)

• • • • • • • • • • • • • • • • • • • • •

I have written about my enrolling at the age of 11 into the Ohio Military Institute---a boarding school. While in a practical sense I stopped living full time with my mother at age 11 and beyond, my mother's motivation for sending me to the boarding school was highly laudable: Educationally and academically I was doing very poorly. Behaviorally I sometimes perhaps made bad choices so there were three times I wound up in Juvenile Court for "some silly incident like breaking and entering into a vacant house 'which in my mind Nobody Owned!' Or like breaking and entering a Chauffer's automobile garage because I just wanted to borrow the tennis racket for a short time—and then return it. Socially I was often lonely. There were times when I went over to the patio behind the Stone's house and sat in a comfortable chair with their cat in my lap for an hour or more in the dark ruminating—musing—pondering; at times wishing I had some brothers or sisters—feeling my loneliness.

But when I moved to O.M.I. lots of circumstances in my life improved immensely. My life encountered a stable, dependable structure. We had good beds to sleep in, we got up every morning at the same time (at the sound of a bugle) we had a nutritious breakfast, lunch, and dinner at the same times every day, we went to bed every night at the same time (at the sound of a bugle).

And, not only did I have two wonderful roommates to relate to, but there were many other boys to play with! [ My roommate George Strayer, and I got back together 20 years ago, and are still together today!]

So, my mother arranged to provide this wonderful gift for me. Well, okay, so like in the first grade when my mother showed me how to travel to the school one time and then it was up to me to remember, I was shown how to travel on three different buses how to get from my home to school one time. Not a problem.

Ohio Military Institute was A MAJOR GAME CHANGER for me: (1) The pace of the day for me was highly scheduled: shortly after dinner, you were expected to bring your books and do your homework. If you did not understand what to do, there was always someone to teach you. For 6th graders and below grades—maybe down to fourth, Study Hall was only one hour. But for 7th graders and up, it was two hours. Lo and Behold, I started doing my homework on a regular basis. Grade reports were issued every six weeks. On the report card, were Letter Grades, Numerical Grades and Class Ranking. I will never forget receiving my first Report card from the Secretary, Mrs. Beatrice Behrens, and finding out that I was 2nd in class! I, who was usually near the bottom in Public Schools, was now ranked "Second" in class at O.M.I. Really? You are not kidding? Wow! What do you know about that!

### A MAJOR GAME CHANGER: I GO FROM BEING THE BOTTOM OF MY PUBLIC SCHOOL CLASS TO THE TOP OF MY OMI CLASS

• • • • • • • • • • • • • • • • • • • • • • •

I truly was shocked to see that I succeeded so well. I had never done that before. No one coached me to be competitive. No one said, "Why don't you try harder!" In my mind I suddenly comprehended that I could be a good student—for once. And I tasked myself with trying harder, now that I knew a goal was within reach. As I reflect, I know I never had that approach to my public-school classes, BUT I did have that approach when climbing trees, and climbing on the third-floor roof of our apartment building, and I did have that approach as I analyzed how to get inside a locked building—through the coal chute!

So, I "poured on the coal"—even did homework after taps, sprawled on the floor to read by the hallway lights. By the second report Period my numerical score was higher, but I was still 2$^{nd}$. I "poured on more coal" so by the third Report Period, I was ranked First! And I stayed first for the rest of my three years. And he who was the Academic Leader of the Class, was also the Military Leader of the Class, so I was responsible for marching our class—about 13 or so cadets—from the Drill Field up to the classroom; I brought them to "Attention" (with arms straight out perpendicular to the body, bent at the elbow to lay one on top of the other, and I reported to the instructor—e.g., Capt. Temple, that "We were ready to learn!"

That first year not only did I become the Academic and Military Leader of my class, but I was learning that good things happen when one excels at following the rules and becoming a model student. [If you are thinking about the socialization process that all tribes use to mold their youngsters into the correct tribal behavior, you are on the right track.] And I do recall beginning to feel differently about myself—being successful, not only in class but picking up the military requirements. As I sit and think, I am remembering how "unstructured" my life was the first five years of schooling. Mother worked until 5:00 P.M. or so. There was no exact time she regularly came home. Dinner was when she felt rested for a minute and put it on the table. I did not really have a strong bedtime; but I was probably asleep between 8:00 and 9:00 P.M.

As I enrolled in OMI, my clothing decisions "were all made for me: we all wore the exact same uniform—grey shirt, black tie, perhaps durable cloth pants, and black socks, black leather shoes. My height was average or taller. My weight was average or maybe a few pounds heavier. I grew at about the same rates as others. Nothing noticeable. We all received the same type haircuts—every two weeks; I believe it was on Thursdays after school.

Now, what was different, was that I was the brightest, and therefore the academic leader. Physically, I believe I was in great shape able to do what any other cadet could do.

Athletically, I was not inclined to be sports focused. I did what the gym class required, but nothing more. I recall for the baseball team, that I was the equipment manager, or the "bat-boy." I did travel with the baseball team as we traveled to Indianapolis, or Louisville or to other private schools to play.

First it was Tony Jewell leaving our apartment building and going to boarding school at OMI; a year later it was I who left the apartment building for OMI; The following year, Sydney Nathan, founder and owner of the King Record Co. and lived on the first floor of our apartment building, decided to send his son, Nat Nathan to OMI.

I know emotionally, I felt the lack of structure, and I was lonely, especially if everyone else had gone home for the evening. But the solid disciplined structure of the schedule at OMI gave me security. It was always very clear what was expected of me.

## CAPT. F. PETE DERRICK ENTERS MY LIFE

• • • • • • • • • • • • • • • • • • • • •

I learned part of this because the school had a very kind, thoughtful, loving, but also strict on the rules person: F. Pete Derrick, Captain & Commandant. He was the RIGHT person to be working in a school where several cadets did not have an active father.

Pete "took me under his wing," as he did several of the cadets, and he observed, pushed, and molded me into a fine cadet. [*My mother deeply appreciated all that Pete Derrick did for me. Not only did she send him notes and gifts, but she had him over to our home for dinner on two occasions.*]

By my 7th and 8th grade years, whenever our medical infirmary was having an epidemic—like influenza—many cadets reporting in sick—Pete would excuse me from all my other classes except his (math and American History) and I would go live in the infirmary and become the nurse's, Mrs. Stapleton's, orderly. I would carry out any errands she asked. [My mother appreciated that and sent gifts of thanks to her.] I went downstairs to the kitchen to obtain "Tea and Toast" for the patients; ran errands for the patients, learned to read thermometer's temperature readings, among other tasks. [Side note: I was in the infirmary when the first televised Presidential Inauguration was broadcast: for Dwight D. Eisenhower.]

[I remember I felt special. I knew I had responsibilities to the nurse, and I felt a need to carry my tasks out in an excellent manner. When I was not walking here and there for a task, I stationed myself in the main reception area where the nurse always knew where I was.]

## *I HAVE NEVER FORGOTTEN THAT LESSON*

• • • • • • • • • • • • • • • • • • • • • •

When the epidemic was over, I sometimes caught what it was and so stayed in the infirmary, but not always, in which case I quickly returned to my regular schedule of classes. One day that first week back, I learned a very powerful educational lesson. As the Academic Leader, I often was seated in the rear of the class. That day, Captain Derrick was passing out a scheduled math test. Pete started roving and monitoring the students' progress. He came to my desk and saw I had not written a thing on my paper! Pete asked me what was wrong! I replied that I was exhausted, and my brain was a total blank. **Now here comes the very important lesson**: Pete responded "Pat, it is OK! Go out into the woods and play; we can do the test another time, when you are rested." Wow! Thank you. And in all the years I have been a teacher/instructor **I have NEVER FORGOTTEN THAT LESSON!** And I have never forgotten that act of compassion and kindness. [See the excerpt during my college professorship.]

[Time Digression] Now that I re-printed that comment, I know often that a large part of Pete was with me when I taught.] I am remembering about five or six years back; Marissa was in my freshmen class. I found out from other classmates that Marissa had a very difficult situation at home: She had married her high school sweetheart; he had joined the U.S. Army and was sent to Afghanistan. He was driving one of those super armored trucks when it ran over an explosive device. The truck was hurled 30 feet into the air, and when it crashed back down, Marissa's husband suffered severe back injuries. Now he was home BUT, every single night he had active nightmares and he would wake up screaming. And of course, when he was interrupted in his sleep, so was Marissa. When I learned of the situation, I went to Marissa privately, and told her she could write and turn in the class assignments whenever she felt rested enough. And it was the right arrangement! Marissa was relieved, and when she did turn in a paper, it was top quality. She earned an A+ in the course.

This was probably the most extreme example of loosening the time limits, but in following years, I began saying to all my students: when you are writing our assignments, you are really writing to and for yourself. So do not turn a paper in to me until YOU are proud of your work. If it takes one or two extra days, so be it. The quality of my students' work went up. [My compassion for my students motivated me to set up learning situations where the students enjoyed their challenging work AND they would remember the knowledge long past our class. I have binders full of outstanding work my students have produced over the years.] [End of Digression]

Returning to O.M.I., for my second year I was in the 7th grade and all of my classmates, for their dorm room assignments were relocated from the Lower school Dorm in Belmont Hall, to just off campus to a lovely large old home now turned into a dormitory—Harrison Hall (named after President Benjamin Harrison who had attended the school when it was still *FARMERS COLLEGE*.)

It was a college and was so named because mostly the neighboring farmers invested their money to create the college. Across Hamilton Avenue, another college was established--the *Ohio Female College*. The community combined the two institutions for the purpose deciding to call itself *COLLEGE HILL.* The **Farmers College**, probably due to finances, kept trying different configurations. In 1880 the school opened its doors as *THE BELMONT SCHOOL FOR GIRLS.* That lasted ten years, so finally, in 1890, the school opened its doors as *THE OHIO MILITARY INSTITUTE.*

April 21, 1953. Letter from Cadet Leedom: "Dear Mom, Commissions came out today and I'm still sergeant of the First Platoon, Company C…Saturday night there's a dance called "Spring Hop!" And I will take some pictures. Pat."

George Strayer, Jerry Blankenship, and I had been roommates the year before in Belmont Hall, so we moved together. We were joined by Bill Erbeck from Eaton/Mason Ohio. Wow, I said. Roommates—fellow boys to relate to and with whom to play. That gave me daily companionship. I still see George annually in his home town of Sebring, Ohio.

I was already the Academic and Military Leader, and a sergeant of a platoon, and now Captain Derrick made me the Cleanliness and Orderliness Inspector of everyone's dorm room before we marched to breakfast over to Belmont Hall where the dining room was located on the ground floor.

## DWIGHT NELSON CHATTAWAY ENTERS MY LIFE

● ● ● ● ● ● ● ● ● ● ● ● ● ● ● ● ● ● ● ● ● ●

Also, at the beginning of my 7th grade, a new cadet enrolled in the school: Dwight Nelson Chattaway. "Chat" was four years older than I. In a short period, it was established that Chat was the most intelligent of his class. Somehow, he and I drifted together; he became like a big brother, and I was little brother. Chat got me involved the Sentinel Newspaper Staff, and the Cadet Magazine Staff. One-time Chat and I got permission (I think on a weekend) to go into the basement of Bishop Hall where all the archives of old papers were kept. Chat and I searched through them until we found articles from the 1850's and 1860's. We located where Farmer's College had been a station on the "Underground Railroad" assisting runaway slaves. And Chat and I wrote an article about it for the Cadet Magazine.

Chat's influence and encouragement helped me to grow in confidence. We enjoyed each other's company. For the Spring Break Week in spring 1954, Chat took me home with him—up to the Eastern corner of Ohio to the town of East Palestine, where I met his family. Very pleasant. One evening, Chat suggested we go for a ride in his 1951 Mercury Convertible. We headed for the back hilly roads away from town. Chat wanted to show me how fast his car could go, so soon we were flying over the tops of hills at 110 miles an hour; kind of like a rollercoaster (no seat belts of course, they had not come into use.) Then Chat pulled the car over off the road, got out, came around, and said, "OK Pat, you get behind the wheel!" "Hmmm, I am 13 years old—a month away from being 14, and I have never driven a car before. Another *I Believe I Can* moment. With Chat's instruction and guidance, I was off driving—paying very close attention to what I was doing. It all worked out and I had learned something new, and had a good time doing it. [Again, I note here, that multiple events in my life had developed a reasonable sense of confidence in myself; so rather than being afraid and unsure, I welcomed the challenge. Chat played an important role for me; so, we stayed friends off and on for 50 years.

Back to OMI I went for my third year to complete the eighth grade. I have always thought I made the right decision to finish one more year in Ohio before making a monumental change to my life's circumstances. I also participated in a Special Drill Squad, which did several fancy military steps and rifle moves. At the end of the year, I won the Best Drilled Cadet in my Division. My work on the newspaper—the OMI **SENTINEL** and **CADET** magazine continued. As a matter of fact, in order to print our newspaper, someone—me—had to take our paper stories downtown to a lithographer to have them transferred to plates to run on the school's printing machine. Pete selected me, because he knew I knew downtown well, and my mother worked a few blocks away from the lithographer's shop so I could always go up in the Crew Tower to the 22nd floor, to the offices of the Miller-Adick Co. and visit with my mother for few minutes. A nice privilege!

As to winning the medal as Best Drilled Cadet, I readily adopted the military way of life. I liked wearing a uniform, with a shirt and tie, every day. I liked shining the brass on my dress uniform, polishing my shoes, and getting all dressed up on the weekends.

I liked the discipline of the daily schedule when there was a definite stable time for each activity. You could count on it. My need for a regular, structured, organized schedule for the day what was what I needed to feel more secure and thrive. And that has remained true for the rest of my life; and probably was a big part of why I did so well in the U.S. Navy and stayed for 24 years!

While I was quite challenged with our academic assignments—I really loved learning—and I just had to earn the top grade in order to stay No. 1. When the school year ended in June 1954, I said my goodbyes to my friends, as I was not coming back in the fall. I was severing ties with the Community that had been a great "garden for me to grow in" and preparing to relocate to my Dad's in California.

[Time Digression] In terms of role-models, I did notice the older cadets, and particularly the ones who always had "a squared-away appearance." One of those students was Jay Gatchett, three years older. Another was Tom Shurter, four years older. What is an incredible coincidence, is that Jay, Tom, and I became good friends now in 2020 as we all serve on the OMI Historical Association Board of Trustees. I thoroughly enjoy his friendship, as well as Tom Shurter's and Bill McMillan. It means a lot to me. Sadly, Tom, at 84, had a severe heart condition. He waited until we had our final Old Boys reunion in October 2019—we all made a special trip to the hospital to spend an emotional hour with Tom, and he passed away the following week.

[Time Digression]: Sterling Ward was the cadet who had been Number One in class until I came and competed with him. Just three weeks ago in August 2019, I was able to connect with Sterling Ward, on the occasion of having lunch with my roommate George Strayer from OMI, who suffered both a big stroke and a heart attack ten years ago and is now confined to the medical unit of a beautiful Retirement Home, one mile from George's childhood home in Sebring, Ohio. Sterling Ward and George have agreed to meet for lunch about every there weeks and have done so for the past two years. When I arrived. We three had a loving, caring time together. I know that if I lived much closer to Cleveland, where Sterling lives, we would become good friends. I hope to see him again when I am visiting with George. [End Digression]

## *MY CALIFORNIA ZEPHYR TRIP TO MEET MY FATHER*

• • • • • • • • • • • • • • • • • • • • • •

**A life-transforming event** happened in the spring of 1953, during my 7th grade. My father, after years of giving small hints and promises that he would bring me out to California to visit with him, he finally did send me one of those old-fashioned train tickets—a yard long—a Marx Brothers movie production where every few miles, the Conductor would come by and tear off another "coupon" from the end, as we were now travelling on some other Railroad Company's trackage. The major part of the trip was on the new gleaming, all aluminum California Zephyr with new upper-level Vista Domes. There were seats for at least 40 passengers to come up and sight-see.

On a Monday morning in June when my school was ended for the year, my mother took me to Cincinnati's Union Terminal and put me aboard the New York Central train to Chicago. Arriving in Chicago, I retrieved my suitcase, hailed a taxicab and rode across Chicago to another train station where I boarded the California Zephyr—complete with "Zephyrettes" hostesses to help us.

Some people shudder when I tell them I took the three-day train ride all by myself at age 13. (They probably think of their little sheltered darlings who are still heavily dependent upon adults.) However, having carried out multiple responsibilities for the last 3+ years, I was an "Old, mature, responsible, 13-year-old." My one point of anxiety was when I was not sure I would recognize my father, nor he me. But that was on the last day of the trip.

In the main, I had a ball. My father had bought me a Coach Seat. But I couldn't see anything from there. So, I adopted the Vista Domes as my domicile. There were three to four Vista Domes on board so plenty of seats for the passengers. Each dome could seat around 40 passengers. Sometimes I sat by the window and could observe everything. Sometimes I sat next to a passenger and held a conversation. I remember one elderly woman was a close friend of Ethyl Barrymore, the famous stage and movie actress. Oh, by the way, I was dressed for an adventure: I had my "Blue Suede Shoes," yellow dress slacks, a long key chain with a watch fob—that I could twirl; a red print dress shirt, blue corduroy jacket, and a ship's captain's hat.

For meals, I followed the assigned seating time in the dining car. My mother had been taking me out to eat in fine restaurants since I was 5 years old, so handling the menu, ordering, and using my best manners came naturally. No problems. I was well treated by my fellow passengers. No one seemed to question why a 13-year-old was traveling alone. The conductor and waiters treated me the same way they treated everyone else. With having two years of military discipline behind me, I conducted myself with proper deportment, never causing anyone to be concerned about my behavior as I moved about the train, even back to the Club Car. The Zephyrettes were always on hand to courteously assist me. Reflecting back, perhaps they were extra attentive to me since they knew I was a thirteen-year-old traveling all alone. I appreciated all they did for me. In three days, there was not one uncomfortable moment. [Well, I had traveled by train before, with Mom and Grandma, so I knew how to navigate the various cars.]

At night, instead of returning to my coach seat, the Zephyrettes brought me pillows and blankets and I slept on the back-bench seat of the Vista Dome.

My whole three-day train trip was a very pleasant adventure. My father had sent me a book, ***THE SACRAMENTO RIVER OF GOLD.*** So, during some quiet moments, I read in my book, maybe more in the evening. During the day, observing out the windows was such an exciting adventure when there was so much changing scenery to view. Every state presented a different landscape. I started asking myself what is different about the desert in this state from the desert in the last state? Utah's desert had a multitude of Jack Rabbits. I remember I counted 76 of them! Ever since I was a child, roaming the neighborhoods on my own, I had had a strong sense of intellectual curiosity, and a great thirst for adventure: "I wonder what is over that hill; I wonder what might be around the bend? [Remember Laura Mac and I walked the train track for four to five hours.] I wonder what lands are on the other side of this ocean?" So, travelling, in almost any form, walking, taking a car, taking a train, taking an airplane, and later taking a submarine led me to more and more interesting places.

Having been on my own a lot and being responsible for making many of my own decisions, on the train ride I was not ever homesick, lonely, or worried. I relished in the new across-country-adventure. The train arrived in the Sacramento Railroad Station around noon on Wednesday. My father's wife, Darby, was the first to spot me. It was a brief greeting, and then we piled into Dad's 1947 Kaiser automobile and drove the 15 miles out into the country to Fair Oaks, which, in 1953, was mostly farms, ranches, and orchards. Dad was leasing a small 11 acre "ranchette." Sheep and olive trees took up most of the 9 acres, but two acres were for the house and lawn. The house was a small one-story ranch house with two bedrooms and a bathroom. Dad and Darby had spent several weeks cleaning out, cleaning up, and painting in pastel colors a former chicken coop for my BEDROOM! I thought it was really cool! Darby had acquired two kittens for me—Dagmar, and Blondie. They did like to sleep with me at night. We had a dog!—one of the very few times in my life I actually had a pet dog. It was an Irish Setter named Randy (after Randolph Scott, a famous cowboy movie actor). I was very comfortable and pleased with new abode.

Dad was a newspaper reporter and writer for the Sacramento Union Newspaper—the same one Mark Twain (Samuel Langhorne Clemens) worked on in the 1880's. So, Dad worked every day from 8:00 to 5:00 P.M. Darby would usually stay around the house. I would roam around, sometimes into the sheep enclosure—but better watch out for the ram: he likes to butt you from behind. Sometimes I climbed over the fences into the other ranches, or to the orange orchard full of fruit. Occasionally Darby would take me out for a jaunt, maybe to the store where I could purchase comic books, soda pop, and gum. Sometimes Darby took me to visit with friends of hers, like one who lived in the city with a swimming pool.

It didn't rain in California in the summer (very rarely) so we ate all of our meals outside—breakfast, lunch, and dinner. Dad and Darby had crafted these small barrels into perfect seats for the table. You might say life was a picnic.

Dad did not work on weekends. And it was on his mind to show me a really good experience coming to his home in California. So almost every weekend, he had some all-day excursion planned. Sometimes we drove up deep into the gold country and saw the little mining towns. Sometimes it was in and around Sacramento where gold was discovered at Sutter's Fort in 1849. Sometimes it was out to the lands where Folsom Prison was located. [and where a few months later, Dad was recruited to be an "extra" in a movie portraying "a newspaper reporter" of all things! The movie was *Riot in Cell Block 11;* I possess a copy of it, and Dad is on screen between the two main actors—facing one and then the other as he listened and "took notes."]

I was having the time of my life. But Dad was sad and frustrated: he could not tell if I liked what he did, or I didn't like the trips, because

I never said anything. No comments, no compliments, nothing.

The true situation as I remember it, was, having never lived with my father before, not having established a comfortable communication channel with him, I was shy around him and it was safer to keep to myself. [It took me almost three years to begin openly addressing him as "Dad" or "Father". Usually, I would walk up close to him and start talking.]

For purposes of an autobiography, I was comfortable as long as I viewed my visit as a wonder-filled vacation, and the excitement of getting to know the man who was my missing father. But I was not thinking in terms of staying an extended time. By the eighth week Dad did, one day, suggest I might like to stay with him and go to school in California. Uh, Ooops. Heart pounding. This is all too much, too quick. So, I declined and said I wanted to return to OMI.

During the ninth week, my mother, Joy, and Grandmother Daisy, came out by train. And after a few days of Mom and Dad having some good conversation (They always seemed to do well around each other, apparently no bitterness or anger lingering), we three left for San Francisco for two days of sight-seeing, then down to Los Angeles for another two days of sight-seeing. I remember we stayed at the now infamous Biltmore Hotel [where Robert Kennedy was shot.] then boarding the *SANTA FE SUPER CHIEF TRAIN* (Which was the top-of-the-line luxury passenger train, complete with a real Indian Chief as a host and guide!) back to Chicago, then to Cincinnati.

The summer of 1954 I had a relaxed and very social summer vacation. But in August, I made all preparations for moving "lock, stock, and barrel" in with my father and Darby, now in Los Angeles, South Whittier/Norwalk to be exact. This time I took the airplane west and Dad and Darby picked me up at the airport. We drove the

20 miles to their new residence—a small house in a rural part of the county. Enough land for a kitchen garden.

Here again, for the purposes of an autobiography, from the minute I arrived in my new residence, I was excited to be there, starting this brand-new adventure. I was not scared, nervous, questioning, or wishing to go back to Cincinnati. I was comfortable to be starting this new adventure.

While my mother was very supportive of my moving to California and in with my father, I was always welcome to come back and share her/our home even up through my college days and beyond. September 1954. For my Freshman year, I enrolled in California High School in Whittier—less than a half mile from our new home on 13938 McGee Avenue; so, walking to school was quick and easy. This school was sparkling new—California style with all wings a single story, with all classroom accessible from the outside. The schedule for the day was six periods, with everyone having one period of Study Hall. That lasted for just one week for me—too boring; so, I went to the office to see for what else I could sign up.

Okay, I will enroll in General Shop. One quarter of Electrical Shop, one quarter of Wood Shop, one quarter of Metal Shop, and one quarter of Mechanical Drawing. I like working with my hands, I like making things—like a large four room hamster cage. I was meeting students who were not normally in my college prep classes. And that was good. The instructors were well qualified and interested in the students' learning. Even to this day, I still clean my paint brushes the way Mr. Dave Ward demonstrated for us. It was a great experience---a break from the heavy academic courses.

I enjoyed the experience of shop courses so well, that the following year I signed up for Auto Shop. A year-long experience where partners took an old donated car, tore it apart. Removed the engine. Disassembled it completely; replaced worn parts; put the engine carefully back together, and the final exam was to push the electrical starter and see if the engine would start and run smoothly on its pint of gasoline. My partner, Meryl Clanton, and I took a 1939 Plymouth totally apart, retrieved the engine, and together we were quite successful. Meryl was kind of a shy, retiring person, but we worked well together.

***There was a very important educational lesson in this course:*** while all year long we learned about all the aspects of how an engine operates, we took quizzes on such topics as spark plug gap setting, etc. However, in the end, none of those quiz grades mattered as long as you were successful in operating your engine. That alone earned us an "A". So, I really have philosophical problems with teachers who count every little quiz grade in order to compute the final course grade. Think about this: the whole point of the class is: did the student learn the important points of the course? If so, that usually qualifies for an A.

As I moved to high school in California, I was 5 feet 4 inches at the age of 14. Average build. Not overly athletically inclined; I do remember being on the water-polo team (and wearing those funny little tie-on caps with a number on it.) I had ordinary abilities, nothing noticeable. I played Water Polo for the two years at CALHI (California High School in Whittier.) [I remember the Los Angeles SMOG. On heavy smog days, I, we, could not take really deep breaths. Our lungs would hurt!]

Socially, I was still somewhat shy. I recall that I tended to interact with the brighter male students. So, I did ask my classmate, Carolyn Watson, and she accepted. It was a pleasant time, but I was too bashful to continue the relationship. I also had this weird conception in my head that "other people didn't take much notice of me." Or that "I didn't make much of an impression on my classmates."

While I had been the academic leader in my class at OMI, I believe my mental and emotional focus was somewhat distracted by being in a very new home environment: living with my father, and his wife Darby (who was not a good stepmother at the time.) I was given chores around the house and yard, some of which I was not happy about. So, grade-wise I did OK—even making the California Scholarship Federation once or twice. On second thought, having just consulted my Annual Yearbook from CALHI, several of my classmates did comment on my "brains."

I believe it was the very first Sunday in September when my Dad came to me and explained the he and Darby always went to this Unitarian Church in Santa Monica, and he made clear that I was welcome to go with them, if I wished to, or I could choose to stay home if that is what I wanted. [My Dad, my father, was growing to be a large influence in my life. The more I knew of him the more I liked him and wanted to be with him.] Yes, Dad, I want to go to church with you and Darby. The church was 20+ miles away across Los Angeles to Santa Monica on the coast. Church service was good. And Dad said to me, "there is a wonderful church Youth Group that meets here on Sunday nights. Would you like to attend it?" "Yes." So, we went back to Whittier for the day, but in late afternoon Dad and I drove back across town in time for the LRY youth group meeting. [Dad had recently been the President of this congregation, so he had lots of friends in the area to go visit.]

## DAD INTRODUCES PATRIC TO THE L.R.Y. YOUTH GROUP

• • • • • • • • • • • • • • • • • • • • •

**Well, what happened next was another life's game changer:** In the meeting room there were perhaps eight to ten teens, some girls, some boys. I could not believe how warmly and welcomingly they greeted me; almost immediately I felt right at home as a regular member of their group! In no other situation had I ever been so welcomed and quickly made a member. As I write this and reflect, I am still overwhelmed with that miracle! Also, I am just now realizing that those high school youth were the sons and daughters of the congregation and who knew and liked my father. So, I guess I was not exactly a stranger walking into their midst.

Needless to say, I wanted to be there every time the Santa Monica LRY group met. In a few weeks, I learned they were part of a larger district—The Pacific Southwest Federation of LRY, and there was a district-wide conference coming up in November. We were fortunate in Southern California: the mountains were close by and there were plenty of camp grounds to rent for the weekend. So, I just had to go—Friday night through Sunday afternoon. Wow! 80+ youth members from all over Southern California: Pasadena, Van Nuys, Los Angeles, Long Beach, Solana Beach, and San Diego and other communities. I received the very same welcoming and feeling of instant accepted membership. [Never in my life had I felt so accepted, so warmly greeted and invited in to the events and activities. I was hooked! I became more and more active and participated more in the Federation meetings.]

In the summer of 1955, there was an experiment: let the LRY Youth have their own camp-- a brand new, first time week-long LRY Summer Camp in June—"Sky Meadows"- up in the mountains, not far from the family camp at Radford. The youth, with advisors had met once a month to plan this camp—the speakers, the workshops, the worship services, the camp fires, the activities, etc. I attended the summer camp and had a fabulous time.

I immediately joined the Summer Camp Planning Council which met once a month on a Saturday in Throop Memorial Church in Pasadena. While I was not old enough to drive, someone was always willing to pick me up in Whittier—about 10 miles away—and get me home. Then there was the Pacific Southwest Federation Council meeting on Sundays, usually the same weekend as the LRY Camp Planning Council, but the Federation Council met at First Church in downtown Los Angeles. I started attending the Federation Council meetings and took an active role. Soon, I had over 100 LRY friends all over Southern California.

Once upon a time, there was both an American Unitarian Association AND the Universalist Church of America. They were quite similar in their religious beliefs. From time to time, there were discussions about merging the two denominations.

But in the meantime, the Unitarian youth groups and the Universalist youth groups went ahead and merged in December 1953. Initially the age range was Ages 14 to 25. The new organization was named Liberal Religious Youth (LRY) [Liberal meaning we acknowledged religious truth from many other religious sources.] It was primarily the older members who wrote the Constitution and Bylaws for the organization. LRY employed ministers as consultants and liaisons---BUT LRY was its own autonomous entity. [I joined LRY in September 1954 when it was less than one year old.] Over the next three years, it became obvious that the organization could not provide meaningful programming for such an extreme age range 14 to 25.

Building on this platform, this strand of my molding of self, LRY became the central focus of my social life. Most all my time away from school, my energy, my money, went to supporting LRY activities. Consequently, I was not strongly socially involved in either of my two high schools: California High School in Whittier (Population somewhere over 3000 students) and Laguna Beach High School in Laguna Beach, California (Population around 500 students.) I certainly did socialize to an extent with my school mates, but I never belonged to a fraternity, or car club, or went to parties on the weekends.

Meetings at the National Level decided to split into two groups. Fourteen to 18 was the "High School range" age-group, and nineteen to 25 was the "College-age group." This organization change took effect in the autumn of 1957. But it should be noted that LRY was still an independent entity, where the members had the heavy responsibility of organizing, planning, implementing all of the activities, with the responsibility to make sure that all participants were safe and were following the behavior rules. Certainly adults, usually ministers were invited, consulted with us, and gave us good advice. But if the youth were not carrying out their responsibilities, no adult stepped in to save the day.

I personally, with my very strong ingrained sense of responsibility, thrived in this atmosphere. And I am given to believe that the youth continued with their responsible roles into sometime in the mid to late 1960's when society's rules and practices changed.

* * * * *

## WIFE #3, DARBY, OUT; WIFE #4, ELIZABETH, IN
• • • • • • • • • • • • • • • • • • • • • •

Marriage can sometimes present unexpected and very difficult problems. In the beginning of my Sophomore Year in 1955, Dad's marriage to Darby "went on the rocks." One reason was Dad did not like the way Darby was treating me—playing "games" on me on "Cleaning the house together" which she never did. So, Dad and Darby got into a serious argument.

Dad rented a trailer; he and I packed up our things and moved out of the house. We moved two blocks away to 9515 Gunn Ave. Whittier--a second-floor apartment accessed by a wood stair case from the back yard. That worked well through the Christmas season up until February. That was when Dad started dating a fellow newspaper reporter—Miss Elizabeth Allen. Gradually she came to live with us. A month later, we moved into a house on 1006 Inez Street in South Whittier—where we had two bathrooms instead of one off of their bedroom! When my school year ended, between my sophomore and junior year our family—Dad, Liz, and I, relocated to Laguna Beach, so I transferred to a much older and smaller school, no shop courses. But I did take typing my junior year, one of the few males in the class; and I did take Mechanical Drawing my whole senior year.

I began living with Dad when I was fourteen. I did witness and participate some in Dad's attempts to become "A newspaper owner." Why was that so important? Well, it seems that when Dad was just starting out as a Newspaper writer, his father, Chilton A. Leedom Jr., told him that he would never be successful owning/running a business. [I do not have any other details about how or why that conversation came up.] Dad, in the 1950's started answering ads in the newspaper about some small-town paper was for sale. Dad's strategy became: "I will go to work for the newspaper, just to see what is going on, and if I should buy it." I often went to work with Dad. And I remember that the newspapers Dad was considering, were for sale BECAUSE they were losing money, BECAUSE the paper's circulation was declining.

Now comes a problem: Dad's specialty was BUILDING CIRCULATION! So, within a few months of Dad exploring the community, and writing worthwhile stories, that Newspaper's circulation came back up, and the owners started making money again, and no longer were interested in selling. I remember especially the newspaper in Riverside, California. It was still using the old-fashion Linotype Machines to produce the type which was then used to print the paper. Now, this type was made of LEAD. And when the newspaper was completely printed, then all of the lead type was thrown into a large heated kettle or vat. The lead would then become molten metal. Any impurities would float to the top and be skimmed off. On the floor were metal molds in the shape of "PIGS." Not the animal pig, but a lead bar about two feet long, and a small loop at the top. When the Linotype operator needed more lead to make the letters, one of these "pigs" would be hung by chain and hook, over a small melting pot which heat the lead back into a molten form which the operator used to make the individual letters. I am very aware of this process because on Saturdays, when I was out of school, I became the person who dumped the old type into the kettle, and eventually ladled out the molten lead into the PIG forms; and removed them when they were cool and hard.

If I was home and available, and Dad was going out to cover a newspaper story in the evening, he often took me with him. I remember three occasions. 1) We went to the home of a retired German Zeppelin Captain. Zeppelins were those huge air ships filled with helium cells and carried passengers—in elegant First-Class Style in the Gondola attached at the bottom. This particular Captain usually flew the Europe to South American run, which took around four days. He was familiar with the Captain of the ill-fated *Hindenburg* which caught fire upon landing in Lakehurst, New Jersey. Our reporting Captain offered the explanation that probably a Hindenburg crew member was patrolling up in the catwalk amongst all the helium cells; and that one cell of them was leaking gas. And perhaps the crew member dropped some metal tool onto the metal catwalk setting off a spark. [Many years later, on a TV documentary, this was given as the exact explanation of the cause!!]

2) There was this Accountant—a little kooky—who loved going hunting for deer. The story was he went up into mountains alone; spotted a deer on a mountainside some distance away. He fired and shot and killed the deer—the one some distance away. But here is the serious problem: The Accountant had a very bad heart condition! And he was all alone. His story was that it took him nine hours to retrieve

and drag the deer's body back to the accountant's vehicle!! Dad (and I) were invited to come to the house for a venison dinner. When Dad rang the doorbell, the Accountant came to the door in a full COWBOY OUTFIT complete with a loaded 45 caliber pistol in his holster! The Account greeted us with the question, "Have you ever met anyone as zany as we are?" When my Dad answered "Yes" (which was quite true), the Accountant hollered to his wife, "Well honey, I guess we have to try harder!"

3) There were these two men who had lived together for years and had some peculiar habits. The first was: they wall-papered every single room in the house with magazine pictures; each room with a different theme such as—movie stars, ocean scenes, mountain scenes, animals etc. I thought it was attractive and well done. The second was, one of the men was the organist for a local church. Okay. He wore a suit and tie every day. Okay. But *he never wore the same suit twice in the same month!!* He had a calendar card in the breast pocket of each suit and would check off which day of the month he had worn it. Okay. And he **NEVER WORE THE SAME TIE TWICE!** Truly, he had racks full of ties; he would go to bargain basements, estates sales, wherever, and buy all the ties. He even reached over and handed me a couple of the ties. [And in 2020, I still have the newspaper story Dad wrote about them!]

+ + + + + + +

### PATRIC BECOMES A CONSTRUCTION LABORER FOR WESTERN WATERPROOFING COMPANY
• • • • • • • • • • • • • • • • • • • • • •

Things started changing when I turned 16. Stepping back to June 1956, when I returned to Cincinnati after finishing my sophomore year at California High School, Mr. Allen St., who sort of thought of me as his son, invited me to take a job at Western Waterproofing Company where Mr. St. was the local manager.

'Much of the work was hard physical labor. Unloading trucks, 52-gallon barrels, shoveling sand, etc. I developed a lot of muscles and a decent physique. By 16, my height was at least 5 feet 10 inches. So physically, masculinity was not a problem, in terms of a sense of manhood.

1. The cleaning, the repairs, and the waterproofing of the exterior of commercial buildings. We could clean the exterior of the building by a) sandblasting the dirt away, or b) using some strong acids applied first to the exterior, then Steam-Cleaning the dirt and soot away.

2. Interior waterproofing usually in the basement area, where our air-hammers could cut a cove-seam to join the concrete walls and floors together in a tight waterproof seal.

3. Exterior below-grade waterproofing, primarily on new construction where the foundation walls were still exposed; we waterproofed these first with a thick coat of black mastic (tar-like) and then sealing that with a polyurethane coat of plastic wrap as a "moisture barrier."

4. We also had a Gunnite Machine that had two long hoses to spray with. The lower much larger hose sprayed the dry mix of cement and sand; the upper smaller hose sprayed water. Believe or not, the two sprays mixed in midair so that ready mixed cement hit the designated area on the walls. We used this machine to build/repair animal enclosures such as bear dens at the Cincinnati Zoo; and we used it to build swimming pools.

Okay, here I am this tall 16-year-old in work clothes and work boots. Mr. Clyde Oliver was the superintendent overseeing all construction/

repair projects. In the beginning Clyde kept me with him. I drove the company pickup truck, learning all the streets and vendors. Clyde was blind in one eye, so if I was around, he preferred me to drive. Then he placed me on some of the in-town jobs, as a laborer. I unloaded trucks, carried materials to the work site. If we were making "mud" --a cement mixture to tuck-point bricks [Chiseling out the missing or rotten grouting between the bricks and replacing it with fresh grouting] or to repair cement parts of building, then I got to where I could carry one 94-pound bag of cement on each shoulder. If we were sand blasting, I got to where I could carry a 100-pound bag of white silica sand on each shoulder.

After a few weeks as an "apprentice" mud mixer, I became the mixer—it has to be just the right consistency, and you can't make it up too early because it will turn hard. After Clyde had taken me around town to meet all the vendors e.g., tools, buckets, rope, brushes, chisel point sharpeners, industrial hoses and clamps, etc. I became the "Go-For."

As a matter of fact, during my very first summer, I was sent with a crew to work in Indianapolis at night [11:00 P.M. to 7:00 A.M.] in an upscale restaurant. The restaurant was located in the basement in one of the age-old buildings flanking the famous Memorial Circle in downtown Indianapolis. When the building was constructed at the turn of the century, the foundation was of a poured concrete. The original workmen at the turn of the 1900's had placed thin wooden struts every so many feet to hold the wooden form apart while pouring. No one thought to remove the wood after the pour or maybe they did not foresee the thin wooden struts causing a future problem, so over decades, the wood rotted, so now, several feet down below the street level, there were small accesses where water could seep through the original wall and create water damage in behind the plaster.

Our job was to remove all the plaster, locate the wooden offenders, cut them out and seal the holes with waterproofing material. And here, I was up on the scaffolding with an air-hammer and chisel to remove the plaster—completely to expose the original concrete wall. One holds the air-hammer in one hand while the other hand holds and guides the chisel. Boy did my arms and hands ache after the shift during the first week or two. "And I was only a young 16-year-old!"

One very, very important piece of information about working for Clyde, was that he had watched his brother fall from a skyscraper and die. So, Clyde was extremely SAFETY CONSCIOUS. Everything we did on the job, had to be done safely. Some jobs required workmen to hang off the side of a building while doing repairs, on a scaffold operated with rope "falls"—large diameter ropes than ran through wooden block pulleys so the two workmen could raise and lower the scaffold as necessary.

Clyde had a rule: any workman who was going to put his life on the line on the hanging scaffold had the right to take the entire rig apart and rebuild it to be sure it was safe—including roof supports—either the large metal "Sky Hooks—heavy metal "question mark-shaped" supports such that the rope pullies could be attached large bottom iron ring which extended over the parapet wall; or with the 12"x 12" x 14 foot long wooden anchoring beams with a "Pad-Eye" at one end for the pullies, and several bags of 100 # sand weighing down the other end. [Generally, Clyde and I had gone down a day or two earlier to the job and rigged the scaffolding together first.]

[Note: I worked for Western Waterproofing over five years: Summer of 1956; Summer of 1957; Summer of 1958 through Fall of 1959; and Fall of 1960 through Summer 1961, These next two stories belong in the 1958-1959 segment.]

A SKY HOOK story. When lunch time came or the end of the

day, the mechanics would use the falls ropes to raise the scaffold to the very top—perhaps six stories up—and then climb **up and over the Sky Hooks back up to the roof.** I did do that one time and made it—but swore I would never do that again; **there were no safety harnesses attached to anyone's body. If you slipped and fell to the ground you were dead. The saying was "It is not the fall that kills you; it is that sudden stop at the end!" Gallows Humor.** [Occasionally I had nightmares about that event and some others when I leaped from one narrow roof to another.] Clyde never knew about this, or there would be "Hell to pay!"

This might be a good place to insert that most of the time I was not conscious of being "16." I was working pretty much like all the other men. They-the Mechanics—were far more skilled than I, but often my job was to anticipate their needs and keep them supplied with materials. So, I would count this as another "Coming of Age" passage. My knowledge and understanding of how "things are put together, and work" was expanding. And my competency in carry out the tasks was being refined.

I frequently watched closely as the mechanics applied their knowledge and skills. This was particularly true in finishing a concrete floor. A couple years later I was left alone to finish a 10' x 12' floor—I believe it was in the Pillsbury Cake Mix factory. I worked on a freshly poured concrete floor very hard for a few hours—looking for low spots or "pits". My superintendent came by, and his first words were, "Who came over and helped you?" "No one!" "Oh, come on now, who helped you?" "No one, I did it myself." It took him awhile to accept that.

I want to make an important observation: in construction work, and later in the Navy, I learned to get along with everyone and learned to respect them for the knowledge and skills they developed. This included men who had little or no formal education e.g., not able to read and write. And this has served me extremely well.

[Time Digression] A much later example was at Shawnee State University when I was elected chair of the University-Wide Facilities Committee. I became familiar with and caring of: all the Maintenance Men, all the Custodians and the Gardeners. There was one time when the University was preparing a major report for the North Central Accrediting Agency. I asked one of the Custodians—Carl W.—to write up a piece on their "Self-Directed Work Teams!" And he did, and was mighty proud, and the word got around how I showed respect for all of them. The Chairmanship was a one-year position, but the members kept "Railroading" me back into the position for 18 years! My secret: I always commenced the meeting on time. I sat right across from the clock and I always ended the meetings precisely "when the little hand was on 5, and the big hand was on 12." And, I only convened the Committee when there was something substantive to discuss and vote upon, If the vote was positive, then I took this to the University President as a "Recommendation." [End Time Digression]

One needed to be 18 years of age before riding the "swinging scaffolds", so, while I often delivered all parts of the rig to the work site, I had to wait two years before working off the side of a building. Oh, by the way, with two workmen on the scaffold, you had better really trust your partner to be able to safely untie or unhook the ropes, to raise or lower. This was a dangerous moment and other companies did suffer men falling off to their deaths if the scaffold got out of control.

The other major type of scaffolding was "Safeway" scaffolding built from the ground up with metal frames all linked together with large wooden boards laid horizontally as a support working surface for the men. Now I was old enough to work off some of the low rigs.

Early on, there was this story where I was a Helper to Joe Alexander.

He was up a ladder on a small roof, caulking windows. Gosh that looked 'so easy!' So, Joe climbed down, handed me the caulking gun and said, "Alright, it is your turn!" I climbed up the ladder to the small roof and began. Whoops! The caulking started going every which way. I didn't really know exactly how to hold the gun and put pressure on the trigger at the right time. It was a mess. And Joe Alexander had himself a good laugh. He knew what would happen; but he figured I needed to "learn my lesson." I did. I remember Joe very fondly. He was one of the older men who always cared about me, looked after me, and helped me out. Some twenty years later I was going to my classroom in Sands Montessori School to teach my kindergarten class. As I walked down the hallway, I spotted Joe and another person (his son) working out on the roof. I was pleasantly shocked to see him. I opened the window and climbed out onto the roof to shake his hand and catch up with him and try to communicate the respect and appreciation I had for him.

I will make the observation that my Problem-Solving Skills were developing right along with my abilities to carry out the construction tasks properly. For one example, sometimes our work took us back into the alleyways behind the tall buildings, and I had to figure out how to maneuver my large stake-body truck and tag-along air compressor around narrow tight spaces.

I feel the need to remind readers that this construction work was being done back in the 1950's and early 1960's when the work ethic was: if you are being paid an hourly wage, then "by god you had better be busy working and earning that wage." Sometimes this was taken to the extreme. Our company was working at the Cincinnati Zoo, sandblasting the Old Opera House. The "Mechanic" was up on the scaffold with the blasting hoses, and I was the "Hopper Tender," keeping the machine full of silica sand. So, there were periods when I was on the ground watching up for signals to me from the Mechanic. Some Official from the Zoo observed that I was "just standing there

'Not Doing Anything'." In his mind. So, my boss came to me and said, "I don't care how you do it, but you keep yourself in motion, even if you have to pick up a board, walk across the work site. Lay it down. Pick it back up and walk back across the work site!" "Yes, sir!" So that is exactly what I did!

## ROLE MODEL AND DEVELOPING MANHOOD

• • • • • • • • • • • • • • • • • • • • • •

Role models. Certainly, my father was a strong one. He was pleasant-looking, attractive, well-dressed (on purpose as a newspaper writer to command respect). I worked with a number of ministers through the LRY Youth Group, and I must say that I was well treated, and respected, as I respected them. The focus was on mental, spiritual, and theological strength. Those were the qualities I focused upon. I remember distinctly having many "arguments" (Greek-type) and discussions on "What is REALITY?" That was a theme of mine for years until I arrived at the understanding, that there were at least three forms of reality. 1) What one personally perceives to be real (related to one's belief systems). 2) Social Reality—that is, what a "group" espouses to be real; and I learned in sociology that groups can formally put forth a belief system, when in fact, no single member actually believes it anymore. And 3) What is in fact physically existent in the universe whether human beings can perceive it or not.

Thinking back, I do not remember any instance of anyone not accepting and treating me as a male. I don't remember ever having to "prove" my masculinity. What I remember is that I was "soft in terms of being sensitive, empathetic, caring, and thoughtful, and a good listener. Other teens did tell me their problems. Many of my letters that I still possess from the 1950's comment on how "understanding" I was. I am also remembering that it was not often that I felt a need to

"COMPETE" with anyone.

Going back to the concept of competing with anyone, or related concept of the "need to fit-in"—perhaps 'conforming' I was perhaps "on an outer ring" so I did conform in general terms, but I never felt the need to "dress like everyone else, or speak like everyone else." And here I am thinking of high school. But if I shift my focus to the LRY Youth group, I certainly did pay close attention to fitting in with the group. And, as time went by, I guess, as I moved up and was accepted as a leader; I was the one some of the others "looked up to."

I am quickly reminded that my liberal religion encourages independent thought. And, my father was always supportive of my thinking on my own. [My mother, on the other hand, was much more of a social conservative. For example, she fought me on my dreams of becoming a minister.]

In the Spring of 1956, my father was now reporting and writing for the Santa Ana Register Newspaper in Orange County. Not too far away was the Pacific Ocean, and an Artist Colony named Laguna Beach. As soon as CALHI high school was out for the summer, Dad, his fourth wife, Elizabeth, and I moved not only to Laguna, but to Victoria Cove on the coast where my bedroom window looked out on the ocean. And then I flew back to Cincinnati to my mother's and to work for Western Waterproofing as I described above.

Turning back to the early Days at LBHS (Laguna Beach High School), within the first week or two of school, our physical education instructor, Mr. Red Guyer, mentioned in class that the local J.C. Penney Store was looking for someone to stock shelves, empty trash and keep the store clean. My Dad was not one for giving me an allowance; his attitude was: go get a job. Just as soon as the final school bell rang, I literally took off running down the hills to get to Penney's first. I did.

And I was given the job! 90 cents an hour! Well, that was better than the student next door at Sprouse-Reitz who was only making 75 cent an hour.

## BACK IN LAGUNA BEACH, PATRIC GOES TO WORK FOR THE J.C. PENNEY DEPARTMENT STORE CO.

• • • • • • • • • • • • • • • • • • • • • •

Mr. Harold Winter was the store manager. He was a very kindly man, a strict follower of Christian values, with definite requirements for the job. It didn't take too long to learn all the tasks. And it didn't take me too long to get on the right side of all the women sales clerks (although among themselves there were conflicts). Lucy worked in the stock room and was in charge of receiving all the new shipments and placing the items on the proper shelves. She and I got along very well. I guess I worked more often side by side with her, than anyone else in the store. Lucy and I "had a secret." The stock room was actually quite dirty behind the scenes, behind the shelving units. And Mr. Winter was under a lot of pressure from the District Manager to use labor most efficiently. Mr. Harold Winter interpreted that to mean, "I was not to waste time cleaning behind the shelves but be doing something more productive!" However, both Lucy and I both agreed it would be better working space if it were cleaner. So, she would be my "lookout" and I would sneak back and clean behind the shelves. Mr. Winter never seemed to inspect behind the shelves—if he did, he never said anything—so perhaps he was or was not aware of the cleaning I did.

On an historical note: this store was still equipped with wires and trolleys running from each cashiering station straight up to the second floor and the open office window. Sometimes the sales clerks had paper work to be transmitted up to the office and back. Verda Hoffman, the secretary would reach over and retrieve the paperwork and process it.

At the cashiering station, once you loaded the trolley clip, there was a "pull-cord sling shot device" to launch the trolley up to the office. If one pulled too hard, the trolley slammed against the office window sill and all the papers came fluttering down, Oooops!

I really enjoyed this very desirable job. I worked every day, Monday through Friday, 3:30 P.M. TO 6:00 P.M. When the store closed, and every employee went home. I lived within Victoria Cove, right off of El Camino Real, also known as U.S. 101, two miles south of town. Now it just so happened that the secretary, Verda Hoffman, lived further down that highway, so she and I became a team. When it was quitting time, Verda gave me her car keys, and I retrieved her car parked a block away (a 1952 Chevrolet) and I would pick her up, drive down U.S. 101 to where I could jump out and climb over the fence, and slide down the Ice Plant flowers to my front door. This was a great kindness on her part, and it certainly helped me travel home quickly.

My father was not one to buy me clothes, so to school most days I wore blue jeans which were developing holes in the pants legs. One day Mr. Winter called me over to the Men's Department and gave me two pairs of nice slacks!!! I told you he followed Christian values. On at least two occasions he invited me over to his house so I could participate in one of their prayer services. I respected him for it; but I had my own church.

I normally worked Saturdays all day. But if I had a church obligation in Los Angeles (Pasadena) he excused me from work. He really liked me and liked my work. I was efficient and carried out tasks efficiently such as taking customers' new slacks over to the tailor two blocks away for hemming or taking an arm load of parcels over to the Post Office to be mailed.

What was a surprise was to learn that when school was out for the summer, and I was headed back to Cincinnati for my Western Waterproofing job, Mr. Winter came to me and said he wanted me back for the fall—that I should find myself a "substitute" just for the summer." I hired the school mate who worked next door.

I observed Mr. Winter, and saw how he was under tremendous pressure from the District Sales Manager. There were times when the District Manager would approach me about going into management training to become an Assistant Manager. But I knew too much and never accepted his offer. Would you believe the expectation was that Mr. Winter's daily sales receipts should always be more than the year before on that very same day??!! So, I could tell he was always under stress, I remember one time we received some bamboo window curtains from the Orient, but some of them had bugs eating on them. At first, we thought about getting rid of them, but then a while later Mr. Winter took them and put them on a table with a discounted price. He needed to make every cent he could. [At least 15 years later, I had occasion to visit with his daughter Sandy, who had been in the class right behind mine, and now living adjacent to a university in Virginia (where her husband had worked.) I stayed overnight and we talked a lot. She told me that yes, her father—the parent she really loved the most—was under a lot of stress; that after I left Laguna, Harold Winter was transferred to a store in Redlands, California, but he died of a heart attack soon after!

+ + + + + + +

[Time Digression] As I got to know my father, whom I had not lived within 11- years, I learned in his second divorce agreement he was forced to give up custody of the three sons from his second marriage. Following a year of ill health, Dad had found religion—peaceful and comforting religion in the Santa Monica Community Unitarian Church, had matured tremendously in the years following the divorce from Mom. He was very attentive and concerned about me. Whenever

I brought up a personal problem, he always found the time for the two of us to sit down, or go for a walk, and together to talk it out. Wow! I needed that! His caring was very affirming to me.

Like "peeling the layers off of an onion, the mind starts remembering one thing after another. I remember, that at 14 I went to live with my father. His parents had divorced when he was six years old. His mother up and left one day, leaving Dad and his older sister with the father. Dad never knew the true circumstances, and so, in his mind, "he felt abandoned by his mother." [It wasn't until after Dad's death that I learned the truth---that his mother had NOT willfully abandoned her children.] Dad did not always get along with his father, so there were times as a teenager, he was homeless, taken in occasionally by friends and relatives. There was one time when Dad was homeless, walking the country roads while he was very much sick (with flu maybe?) He fell over into a ditch unconscious. A farmer came along, saw him, picked him up and put him in the vehicle, took Dad to the farmer's home and nursed him back to health. Dad, in appreciation stayed several months working for the farmer. Anyway, the point I am working toward, is Dad used to tell me stories about his survival experiences *and often, Dad had to use problem-solving skills* in order to take care of himself. So, I had those messages to inform how I was to survive.

My father, Bob Leedom, became a major influence in my values, my orientation to situations, my life in general. Even today, 60 years later, I can still state that my father, was the best father I could have ever had. Even with his faults and shortcomings, he was still a terrific role-model.

Remember when I wrote that I "ran the streets" at ages 7, 8, 9—I pretty much had tremendous independence. Well, the Divorce Court gave my mother custody of me. So, when I went to live with my father at my age 14, in a legal sense, my mother was "loaning" me to my

Dad. And Dad created a scenario in his mind, that if he was not extra nice and lenient with me, that I would leave him and return to living with my mother. The reality is: I NEVER, NEVER, EVER spoke or thought of such an idea! So, particularly after I purchased my first car (1953 Oldsmobile 98 Holiday) I made up my own travel schedule. For example, one evening at dinner in our Laguna Beach apartment, when Dad had married his fourth wife, Elizabeth, I announced that I was driving to San Diego for the weekend (to visit LRY church friends—the Blackmans Ida, Dave, Barbara, Betty, and Peggy, with whom I often stayed overnight.) Liz spoke right up and said to my father, "Dear, it sounds like Patric is telling us. Shouldn't he be asking?" My Dad responded immediately, "No! Patric does not ask. As long as he tells me where he is going, an emergency phone number, a time he is leaving, and a time he will return, he tells us!"

## PATRIC AND HIS FRIENDS—THE "BROTHERS"

• • • • • • • • • • • • • • • • • • • • • •

And now my mind remembers the years when I was socializing with my African American friends in South Central Los Angeles. I was 16 to 17 years old. I had met Duane, Bruce, Donnie, Levi, Lorenzo (and his older brother El Ray) when LRY early on was ages 14-25. We became good friends even after LRY changed to 14-18. In the Black neighborhood of South-Central Los Angeles, I was always well received and well hosted by all the families with whom I would stay overnight. All of my buddies were older than I was—19, 20, 22. Duane W. and I actually owned a car together. It was a 1950 Ford Sedan that had seen a lot of heavy use. Therefore "cheap" probably qualifying as a "Jalopy."

I never knew how old Lorenzo's brother "El-Ray" was—maybe mid to late 20's. El-Ray worked in a Chevrolet car assembly plant, as did some of his friends; El-Ray owed a new, big Buick Roadmaster.

He, and his friends would sit in the car in front of his house and listen to "sides" jazz records. Whenever I appeared, the back door of the big Buick would open; I was invited to climb in. I was handed paper cup, and someone poured Silver-Satin Wine into my cup, to sip. [He may not have known how old I was.] While being the only white dude in the car, I was "one of the guys." So actually, I was quite comfortable with my "Manhood."

[Time Digression] As I reflect on these years and relationships, I need to make it clear that my behavior and adventures in South Central Los Angeles had nothing to do with "Civil Rights" nor "Integration" efforts. These were simply my good buddies that I really enjoyed being with and shared some great adventures. And I was well received by all the families.

Then there was that famous Friday night: I arrived maybe around 7:00PM The Brothers asked if I would like to go to the Track Meet tomorrow? "Yes, sure." A few hours later they said to me, "Get in the car." "What? Why?" "Oh, the Track Meet is at San Jose State College!" (400 miles away) "okay." There were six of us in a Plymouth sedan; I am the only "White Dude." We drove all night long, got to San Jose (about 60 miles south of San Francisco.) We watched the Track Meet all day long. When it was over, we drove to China Town in San Francisco, had a delicious Chinese dinner, then drove all night long back to Los Angeles. Do you think I told my father about my wild adventure? Naw, I was pretty independent, and decided my own schedules. [I am not going to write about our foray to Tiajuana, Mexico at 1:00 AM in the morning, when I crossed the border on a 21-year-old Black Driver's License. (No pictures in those days.]

Also, as I reflect, these experiences certainly were motivation during my college days for me to join the picketers every Saturday morning in downtown Los Angeles in protesting Woolworth's Department Store policy of not letting African Americans eat at their lunch counters.

Similarly, this was motivation for me at age 18 in Cincinnati to volunteer with the American Friends Service Committee to participate in their programed Work Camps to work through the Welfare Department and select families in poverty, to spend the weekend painting and fixing up their living quarters for a more pleasant environment. You can accomplish a lot when you have a crew of twenty plus helping hands. Some weekends it was all high school students; other weekends it was all college students. On a personal note, the majority of our volunteers had never had a paint brush in their hands, so I became an instructor of efficiently applying brushes and rollers—without "decorating yourself, your hair, your clothes and shoes with paint." [End Time Digression]

\* \* \* \* \*

## MOVING TO LAGUNA BEACH HIGH SCHOOL: ANOTHER GAME CHANGER

• • • • • • • • • • • • • • • • • • • • • •

It is now the fall of 1956. We live in Laguna Beach now. Digression: Turning our focus back to my experiences in high school—both CALHI and Laguna in the 1950's this was still the era when women were restricted to only a few careers e.g., secretary, nurse, teacher, home-maker. The great benefit to students was that there were some very brilliant women teachers, particularly in MATH. We received excellent instruction from very knowledgeable and skilled teachers. I remember looking forward to going to school every day, because there was plenty of interesting learning going on. May I also comment that in that era—in the middle-class schools, the students were fairly well disciplined, polite, and well-behaved. My first impression of LBHS—both the students and the campus, was that it was small, friendly, and comfortable. I felt accepted the very first week. I had transferred from California High School in Whittier (CALHI) which by comparison was huge with hundreds of students in each grade level.

Memories. Riding the school bus from Victoria Cove (Polly's Pizza Restaurant on the corner). The ceiling of the bus was so low, tall people had to bend heads or bodies. Antoinette Dietrich, Class of '57, rode with me. She was always very friendly. Sometimes I missed the bus and had to walk the two miles to school.

Red Guyer was a refreshing Physical Education teacher—no matter what your body build was, or your athletic ability was—if you put out a lot of effort and tried hard, you earned an "A". Whereas at "CALHI" in Whittier, only the strong athletic types got A's.

And Red Guyer believed that we ought to know and have some skill in all of the sports—badminton, tennis. Volleyball, as well as the usual—basketball, track, etc. I really respected and appreciated the way he taught.

* * * * *

Laguna Beach was founded in the 1920's by a group of "Plein-Air" Artists (who often usually painted outside in open air) who would arrive in the warm weather to paint the various seascapes. I believe sometime in the late 1940's someone got the idea to "recreate famous works of art using human beings to portray the various statues, and persons in the paintings. This became known as the Pageant of Masters. Sometime in the early 1950's an Amphitheatre was built with rows of seats terracing the hillside.

My father first took me to the Pageant in 1954 (two years before we moved there.) I remember food service was primitive, for example a large pot of chili on a picnic table to serve the guests. And a costumed lady walked around the picnic grounds singing opera songs.

In 1956 as I became a student in LAGUNA Beach I heard about the Pageant and they began production in January each year. And they put out the word for volunteers to help. I went down my senior year and I was cast first in an oil painting *The Liberator* and then I was cast as a statue—one of the *Eight Immortal Chinese Statues*. I was the one holding a flower basket. AND we all had to be totally white head to toe. They used white cloth costumes to cover our bodies, and then white body paint for all of our skin areas (Including my small beard.)

Since my family were "outsiders" with no social connections, I didn't think the other students took much notice of me. Let me tell you, that once I started attending LBHS Reunions, I found out how misguided I was. Others did take strong notice of me. For example, when I was taking the junior level U.S. History course, even though I was a senior, we had one of the most boring instructors. He would assign us a history chapter to read tonight for tomorrow's class, and then in class he would proceed to read aloud the same chapter to us. Now I was becoming more worldly, socially and politically, and so I would raise my hand and introduce a new topic. It was obvious that Mr. Ferguson welcomed a more interesting discussion; several of the students who had been sleeping with their heads on their desks began waking up to join in. Years later at reunions, classmates would remind me how they appreciated how I instigated more interesting discussions. Now, how could I not be aware of my personal impact on others? But I wasn't.

As I look through the yearbooks, I am aware of an important dynamic. Within myself, I was not totally at peace with myself. I was living with my father who was a very accomplished newspaperman and manager [He was the manager of the Orange County 'Fair in 1958' that many of us went to.] I had just met my father a few years back and he was "bending over backwards" to be a "Hands-On" parent—sensitive to my needs and always ready to sit down and talk things over with me. We, he had a new wife/stepmother who "had had no classes in step-mothering" and she was not very mature.

I had come from three years in an all-boys military academy in Ohio, so my skills of connecting and conversing with girls was limited. I wanted to be accepted "in the various social groups" but I was limited by several factors:

1. Basically, I hardly ever saw any Laguna Beach classmates outside of the school setting.
2. I was still somewhat awkward in my social skills connecting with groups.
3. Due to my six days a week job at the J.C. Penney Store I had limited time. Combined with I had very little money so was dependent upon my weekly wages at 90 cents an hour.
4. My father was very religious and so he got me involved in a district-wide youth group—where I ...integrated-and where the many challenges and opportunities with their group-consumed a lot of my time.

Reflecting back on my daily classroom demeanor and behavior, I can recall being primarily focused on the academics, so I could do well grade-wise; and while I was always cordial and responsive to my classmates, I was hesitant and insecure to try to connect with them beyond superficially.

However, if the other person, boy or girl, initiated the conversations and signaled acceptance, then I was glad to respond in my awkward way.

It may sound stupid, but in my introverted shyness, I didn't think other students noticed me much!

Laguna Beach High School was just the right "garden for me to grow in."….students were warm, friendly, and accepting, even if I was not smart enough to sense and pick up on the signals.

As I re-read the yearbook comments from both years, students did express friendliness, acceptance and that I had an impact upon them.

Starting with the first reunion and building further in the following reunions, to my delight, many classmates were glad to see me, and sometimes to relate some anecdote where we had done things together. It felt wonderful.

While my father's fourth wife, Elizabeth was bright, had many talents, an excellent newspaper writer, she was near totally lacking in anything like proper social skills. She could be very embarrassing. She never had any true close friends. Many years later, after my sister Erin gave birth to a totally autistic child, the family figured that Elizabeth, herself had a case of autism, and was not able to emotionally connect with others. So, there was no way I would ever invite anyone to come and visit me at home.

The complex I developed in # 1 above, was still with me. I felt "different" from my classmates, at some levels "not good enough, not quite 'acceptable'. And again, as I had just moved into town, I was not socially connected with any of my classmates' families. Combine this with a) my working at J.C. Penney's every school afternoon and most Saturdays; b) I had very limited finances; after I purchased my car (and car payments, and insurance payments, and fuel and oil for the car) I had almost no extra money to socialize. [My activities with LRY depended upon others contributing money to my travels and home visits.] and c) my very heavy commitment and devotion to my church youth group activities—all of which took place out of town. There just wasn't a strong supportive base for me to interact more with my high school classmates.

Because my mother and my father were sort of sharing "joint custody of me" I would spend the academic year with my father in California, but then I would fly to Cincinnati immediately after attending our week-long church camp in California and live with my mother and resume working for Western Waterproofing Co., and I would work right up to the last Friday before my high school classes commenced on Monday. A strange "Tug-of-War" developed. Every June as I got ready to leave, my father would always say, "Son, I hope you will come back in the fall to live with me." And every September as I got ready to leave, my mother would say, "Son, I was hoping you would stay with me and go to high school in Cincinnati." In a sense, I removed myself from this Tug-of-war because in my mind, there was no question but what I was returning to California where my life was much more exciting, adventurous, and socially freeing, and enjoying my father's parenting and friendship, than staying in stodgy "Blue Book" (Clear distinctions between social classes) Cincinnati.

My being in Cincinnati all summer led to an interesting academic situation: Registration for classes at Laguna Beach was scheduled for the middle of summer when I was not around. So, my father's fourth wife, Elizabeth, would register classes for me. However, she didn't always follow what was recommended. So, as a Junior, I was enrolled in some senior classes, particularly Physics.

By the luck of the draw, I sat right next to the academic leader of the Senior Class (Valedictorian), Joan Morthland. Now I happened to be very good at physics, so Joan and I had a friendly rivalry all year long: sometimes on a quiz or test I got the highest score, and sometimes Joan did. It was exciting competition, and helpful as I had just moved to town and knew no one, I got to know many of the seniors.

Joan wrote in my Year Book: "Hi Pat, Oh man this year has been really something. It has been a hassle especially trying to ace you out in Physics—you have sure been wiping me out recently, by the way. You have certainly been an asset to our school. Well, seriously, here is wishing you the best of luck for the future. Luck and Love. Joan M. 57'. (I had the greatest respect for Joan as very decent human being. Joan was a shining light in my school experience.)

In the realm of dating girls, I was reluctant. There was a small social circle that I socialized with, and did some innocent dating, especially with Tina Ashling. She was a kind, thoughtful, intelligent young lady and we enjoyed a number of dates together. But largely it never occurred to me that there were some of the "In-crowd popular girls" were interested in me, but those were the days when rarely did a girl approach a boy. One such popular girl was Lynne G. She was prominent in many of the academic and social activities. I liked her from a distance, but never considered dating her. As reunions started bringing us together, we became friends and enjoyed taking walks and talking together. It was about seven years ago Lynne and I were sitting next to each other at a small Reunion gathering at restaurant for breakfast. The topic of "Who had been on the 'In-Crowd' in our high school days. I remarked that I thought Lynne was one of those popular in-crowd people. She immediately responded, "Yes, I was popular—with the girls!~ But did you know I never had a date in high school?? No one ever asked me out. I'm tall. Patric you are tall; you would have made a good dancing partner. Why didn't YOU ever ask me out?" Now years later, I regret not knowing to ask her. In consulting my Yearbook 1958, I suddenly opened the page where Lynne had written , "Remember Palm Springs? Good show this year! I really know you'll always be happy—you deserve to be." Lynne.

Just this past August 2018, at another reunion in Laguna, I sat at a dinner table next to one of the other women whom I thought was attractive and popular in high school, Sally B. J. In the middle of a dinner conversation, she suddenly turned to me and said, "Why didn't YOU ever ask me out?" Sally B. J.

Again, while she and I were classmates, had served on clubs together (The American Field Service Club to bring Hanalore Egner from Germany to our school—fifteen girls and ME**.) It never once occurred to me. And there was one sort of wild weekend where a few carloads of classmates drove up to Palm Springs for a fun day—and I am remembering I drove my 1953 Oldsmobile 98 Holiday, AND BOTH LYNNE AND SALLY were passengers with me. Hmmm? And I had no awareness that they were the least bit interested in me. And I found Sally J.'s entry in the yearbook: "Pat, it's really been great knowing you. I'll never forget the trip to Palm Springs. What a Ball! Lots of Luck always, Sally." Oh my god, here it is 60 years later, and I am just realizing how we did spend time together.

[Time Digression] In later years in the 60's, having undergone some personal psychological therapy, I am aware that I am effective in developing a "public self" that interacts and functions quite well e.g., speaking up in class, negotiating normal social situations etc. while at the same time keeping my private, very emotional self" heavily protected and not available to interact with others.

The above paragraph reflectively lays the pre-groundwork for understanding my commitment to the LRY youth group: with them, I DID MAKE AVAILABLE MY DEEP INNER EMOTIONAL SELF [As much as my hidden emotions would allow.]. I did feel safe and secure with them, and my personal connections with them were much deeper. [End digression]

Now to put a bigger perspective on this dating situation, while I was super active with the LRY Federation, attending many conferences and council meets etc., and, once I moved far away to Laguna, I was hosted overnight by LRY friends, mostly female, I was always welcome, because my reputation nickname was "St. Patrick," meaning I was "safe" not focused on female dating relationships. I was totally safe in being the guest. Some of my frequent hosts were the Swanstroms, Elva and Sigrid; the Kents, Analou. Eventually, however, it was the Coleman home in Monterey Park, where Joyce Tobi Coleman lived. She was three years younger and became the perfect "Little Sister." The whole Coleman family looked forward to my visits. Tobi and I wrote to each other for over two years, even after I had relocated to Cincinnati.

"All of my leadership's skills developing…" This calls for first a discussion of my strong sense of BEING RESPONSIBLE. Going back to when I was five and six years old, I had to become responsible as I was having to get myself to school and back, sometimes by walking the twelve blocks or so. And taking responsibility as I negotiated myself going down town, learning the streets, keeping my self-safe, and returning home. Even as a 7, 8, and 9-year-old, other parents would make me responsible to see that the their children arrived back home on time.

Certainly, taking a job at age 9 at the Xavier Concession Stands was a very responsible job. Joe, the Cedar Hill Farms Milkman, certainly trusted me to be his assistant on Saturday mornings as we filled customers' dairy orders—he was servicing the homes across the street, I am servicing the homes on the curb side-not crossing the street. Certainly, Joe Shelt, my neighbor across the street—Manager of the Canada Dry Bottling Co. who "adopted me" trusted me to work at the Sharonville Gun Club setting clay pigeon traps for Skeet Shooters. (This could be very dangerous, because the device that hurled clay pigeons into the area was remotely operated and had a blade that could do severe damage. So, when needing to load another clay pigeon, there was a safety bar that had to be in place to protect the worker. Upon enrolling in Ohio Military Institute at age 11 and becoming both the academic leader and military leader of my class required maturing senses of responsibility.

So, as I moved up through the LRY ranks to leadership, I was a very serious and responsible "office holder." Added to this was a growing skill of PROBLEM-SOLVING SKILLS. I did not turn away from difficult problems but welcomed the challenge to solve it. [Of course, this involved enlisting others and seeking help from those that knew more than I did.]

Re-commencing my discussion of all of my leadership's skills developing in the sophomore and junior years, came to fruition in my senior year. By the Spring of 1958, I was Vice-President of the Pacific Southwest District of LRY. At that time our District boundaries stretched eastward to include all of Arizona, all of New Mexico, and the city of El Paso, Texas. But in all my years in LRY I never met any LRYers from east of the Sierra Nevada Mountain Range. Nianne Harris, our National Council Representative, came back from a National meeting and mentioned our district was not connected very well to the desert states.

That was just the spark I needed to get into action. It just so happened that our church's denominational executive was passing through town. From him I obtained all the names and addresses of all the churches and fellowships located in those states and city. I wrote a letter to each one of the congregations proposing that we have a meeting this Spring. Tucson was pointed out by the District Executive as probably being large enough to host such a conference, so I sent them a more detailed letter. The replies from the congregations that had youth groups, were positive. Tucson not only welcomed the chance but also introduced a new idea: why not form the desert LRY Groups into a new Federation since it was many, many hours to attempt to drive over the mountains to a west coast conference. From California, five of us from Los Angeles areas and one of us from San Diego, agreed to attend the desert meeting in Tucson. It took us quite few hours to collect everyone from Los Angeles—Elva Swanstrom, Stewart Grant, Analou Kent, and me then drive to San Diego to pick up Nianne Harris then head for Tucson. It took us until 10:00 A.M. to arrive. When all the delegates had arrived, the vote was taken, and it was decided to create a Desert Federation. We spent the weekend writing up a constitution and the paper work necessary to incorporate as a separate Federation. When I returned home, since I was one of the instigators, I wrote a report for the Pamphlet touting the New Desert Federation. May I share snippets with you?

### THE BIRTH OF A FEDERATION: A SOUTHERN CALIFORNIA VIEW BY PATRIC LEEDOM

• • • • • • • • • • • • • • • • • • • • • •

The year was but a fawn, all wet and shiny with newness. The Mid-Winter National Council meetings had just finished their initiation into the ages, and our Regional Representative, Nianne Harris, was home again in San Diego.

...one field trip in particular stood out and shouted at me—to the desert!!...I met with the West Coast Church Executive, and he gave me all the names and addresses of all the LRY groups in Arizona, New Mexico, and El Paso Texas.

Within a few days the mails were humming with communications partly to feel out the possibilities of a conference and partly to write to participants. The replies soon came back and all bearing positive answers.

I sent the Tucson Arizona Group a more informative letter for it was Tucson that had been pointed out to me as having the best facilities and a youth group capable of handling such a project as holding a conference.

On the evening of Friday, April 18ᵗʰ, 1958, I said good-bye to last sun that was to stand between me and the product of many well-spent days and nights by many well-meaning people.

The trip over was a long, but enjoyable one for me and my four companions: Nianne Harris, Elva Swanstrom, Analou Kent, and Stewart Grant. It takes at least nine hours to drive from San Diego over to Tucson. We arrived at 10:00 A.M.—a few hours after the Conference started. The day was taken up with business affairs of creating a New Federation.

For dinner that evening, we all got dressed up in our suits and dresses for the occasion. [This was the 1950's and youth were much more formal than clothing requirements today; and even now, I like to be dressed in a much more formal manner.]

Dinner was served in the Banquet Room of a Local Restaurant.... The Tucson group turned their Church's Multi-purpose room into a ballroom and was enjoyed as we all danced to records and played some games. Everyone had a great time.

Midnight came as it does every evening at that time. We wrapped up the evening in a cloak of goodwill as we all stood in a friendship circle… "clasped hand in hand; there are no words to describe that scene..."

A few of us had thoughts of a moonlight swim in a member's pool, but a note from the parents "I'd rather you wouldn't…" so we laid that dream aside.

Some of the passengers in my car were locals, and they suggested we drive up to the De Grazia Mission.…We drove up over narrow dirt roads. In a while a clearing appeared among the desert shrubs. We parked the car and started along a path. The night was dark with no moon. In a matter of minutes, we were standing before a low, mud-constructed building.

On one side of the building was a narrow wooden door and it creaked open as if it had seen Father Junipero Sierra himself! We stepped over the threshold. It was only a board a few inches high, but it made as much difference as two worlds' centuries apart. We were from a world of calm cool night air with a touch of desert fragrance added, and of fantastic displays of nature's beauty. But inside was a different matter. It was a room fifteen feet by thirty feet. The center section of the roof was open and at one end of the room was a large wooden cross which, at some time during the day, cast an inspiring shadow on the floor; but now, all was dark. At the same far end of the room stood what might possibly be conceived of as an altar that might possibly have been level at one time. And upon this pile of stones and mud rested a lone lit candle. It stood there. Materially it was made of wax and a wick, but spiritually to us it stood as a symbol of warmth, peace, happiness, and friendship, standing out in defiance against the perils of a moonless night. Its glow radiated and created a glow which placed us not so much against the night, but strangely with the night.

Written in 1958, "Today, as Mr. DeGrazia did then, he maintains it so that they of the Catholic Faith might enjoy a few moments of ecstasy. Strange, isn't it, that we of the Liberal Religions can sit and become awed and "ecstacized" through the same symbols as those so religiously different from us. But, perhaps, it isn't so strange after all, for there is a force in the Universe which binds one to all, and all to one." [End Digression]

\* \* \* \* \*

As a follow-on to my quarter of mechanical drawing in my freshman year at CALHI, at LBHS I enrolled in a year of Mechanical Drawing in my Junior Year. I had joined the ***American Field Service*** club, whose mission was international student exchanges. I was the only male in the group, but that helped with friendships. . We needed money! We decided we had to sell "Shares of Stock" to Raise that money. That became my project: to design, print and duplicate hundreds of the Stock Certificates. And I was very appreciated by the club. And yes, both Lynne G. and Sally B. J. were also members.

The money allowed us to bring Hannelore Egner from Germany to join us for the whole year. [Time digression] Hanna came to our 50th Reunion, and she remembered that I had done a lot to bring her over, and to befriend her. When I retired from teaching, I contemplated going to visit her in Germany. She was all for it; but in the end, I didn't have enough money.]

Well, as one might expect, the next year as a senior, I needed to take some junior classes such as Civics and History. And here, I got to meet and know many of the juniors. Additionally, each year I also took a few multi-grade courses such as, Latin I, Typing, and Mechanical Drawing. This gave me the opportunity to meet and know many of the lower classmen—freshmen and sophomores. [Years later, at multi-grade class reunions, I often knew more of the attendees from the other Class years than my classmates did. And at this multi-grade reunion in 1989, I re-met one of my Junior-level classmates Christine, which led to a growing friendship, which led ten years later to an attempt at marriage in 2000. While we had been great friends, it did not work as marriage partners, so we divorced two years later.]

## *PATRIC JOINS THE GIRLS' SWIMMING CLASS*

• • • • • • • • • • • • • • • • • • • • • • •

Parallel in my senior year, I was very active in my church's denomination which had a large youth group district covering all of Los Angeles County and down to San Diego. There was a week-long summer camp—"Mile High Pines" up in the mountains for the youth each June, and a council which met all year long to plan the camp. A big problem for me was—I didn't have enough money to pay the tuition for the camp. So, the solution for me was to earn a Life-Saving Certificate. Now LBHS only taught that course to the girls. So, yes, I joined the girls' swimming class and I had to wear the same rubber swimming cap! No, I didn't join the synchronized swimming group. One of the requirements for the certificate was for each participant to jump in the water to save a drowning victim, and to pull them to safety and push them up onto the poolside. I was often the "drowning victim" to be rescued. It was quite a challenge for some of the smaller girls but, using physics, and leverage they were able to get out of the pool! [Several of my "swim mates" remarked about the experience in my yearbook.]

Not only did I not have enough money for the camp tuition, but I could not afford all the graduation paraphernalia that most seniors can buy. This includes those Senior "Calling Cards" that show up in many Thank You Cards etc.

## *YEARBOOK COMMENTARY*

• • • • • • • • • • • • • • • • • • • • •

Shifting back to Graduation from Laguna Beach High School, I think it is worth quoting from my LBHS yearbook, Vice Principal Alberta Patterson:

*"I wish I knew now what will happen to you, for I'm sure it will not be anything usual, or at least I hope not. **Very seldom does one meet a truly different type of person. YOU are one of the***

**"different" thinking independently, (and) acting as you yourself see fit.** *Good luck A.D.P."*

My god, all these years later, and I am emotionally touched by reading her words, a kind of prophecy. And in that same vein:

In old boxes I found a High School Graduation Card, which I believe I MUST HAVE READ SOMETIME IN THE PAST. But when I opened it and re-read it last night, it had a deep impact on me. Here is the message:

June 13, 1958

My Dearest "Patric"

You're a big boy now. YOU KNOW HOW MUCH I LIKE YOU. I HOPE YOU DO. To me being around you inspired me to the point where I can be a full thinking person. I feel so privileged to be able to associate with you. Well, enough of my tear-jerking phrases. But even if you don't remember me, remember what I think, OK?

I wish you all the luck and I know you'll make that goal [even] if you kill yourself. I only wish to follow you as an example of being a genuine person who is so interested in everyone else, rather than himself. Well brother and truly my closest and dearest brother too!

All my sisterly love, BUTTER CUP [AKA Margie Low, Class of 1959]

Here in 2019—60 years later—I am deeply touched by Margie's thoughts and feelings toward me. In 1958, I was emotionally "locked up" and often oblivious to other people's thoughts and feelings toward me. Again, until I had some serious psychological therapy in 1967,

I had that mental mindset that I didn't make much of an impression upon my classmates.

Margie was a year behind me in school—Class of 1959—but I did take classes with her. And I remember we were friendly and did spend time together conversing. Until I just re-read her card, I did not remember she looked upon me as a brother. I would have enjoyed having her as a sister.

Laguna Beach High School was *JUST THE RIGHT GARDEN TO GROW IN* --students were warm, friendly, and accepting, even if I was not smart enough, or socially aware, to sense and pick up on the signals.

The extreme of my mental mind-set was when I started going to our Class Reunions—was *"I wondered if classmates remembered that I was in the class also!"* As I re-read the yearbook comments years later from both Junior and Senior years., I grasped how students did express friendliness, acceptance and that I HAD HAD an impact on them.

This might be a good time to describe the pageant that was our physical Graduation night. The place, the Amphitheater where the Pageant of Master's Art Show, is named the Irvine Bowl after a wealthy contributor. During the Pageant in the summer season there were always live recreations of famous paintings. Well, for our Graduation, the art directors conspired and presented us with about five "paintings" of typical scenes in a teenager's life…such as little brother listening on Big Sister's telephone calls…

Another piece about graduating from Laguna Beach. Our setting was the "*IRVINE BOWL*" where the Pageant of Master's was performed. There are three major stone or concrete stairways leading from the top bank of the amphitheater down to the stage. So Junior classmates were expected to take pliable wooden hoops, decorated them totally with flowers, and every few steps coming down the hillsides, such that the seniors, in their white graduation gowns were rhythmically walking down through the hoops to the stage area. Right in front of the stage area, a fenced off area for our wooden folding chairs had been built. When every senior had descended the staircase and taken a seat, the Juniors brought down all the flowered hoops and erected them right around the outer frame of our "box." making a marvelous display.

After all the diplomas were handed out and the ceremonies concluded, everyone went back home, changed into dancing attire and reported back to the school cafeteria. The Parents had planned for an "ALL NIGHT PARTY" within the school's Cafeteria. The parents did an outstanding job of decorating it like as Night Club. I think I am remembering that following the formal ceremonies, each family took their children out to eat. Then the Seniors changed clothes to both party and go swimming. Breakfast was served before we were dismissed to go home. Obviously, it was a safe and sane party since no alcoholic beverages were permitted. I remember that there were door prizes given out…and the largest of these was a CAR! It was approximately a late 1940's Dodge Sedan. Nice looking. And it was free to the winning Graduate!

My father had attended one of the planning meetings to organize graduation. He came home flabbergasted!! "They want to spend $100 per person on this party!! He could not believe it, nor approve of it. But the party took place, and everyone that I know of, had a great time. There were those type of beach lounges that people can lay on. So, anyone that wanted to take snooze, could. My gosh I have very fond memories of going to school in Laguna Beach!

[Time digression] Reflective commentary: As the decades have gone by, and I have attended several Laguna Beach High School Class

Reunions, I now do regret not socializing more with my classmates, because they are the ones I see every ten years, and have become good friends; whereas I hardly ever see any of the LRY friends.

After our LRY Conference back in April, Desert representatives did cross the Sierra Mountains to attend occasional weekend conferences, but definitely did attend the LRY Summer Camp in June in the mountains.

## CHAIR OF L.R.Y. SUMMER CAMP COUNCIL

That brings to the forefront my other major accomplishment at age 17. Having been a very active member of the LRY Summer Camp Planning Council for two years, at 17 I was elected to be the Chairperson. That evolved into my doing much of the "heavy lifting." With the guidance of some of our Ministerial advisors such as the Reverend Ray Manker of Riverside Church, I accomplished most of my goals.

I began to recognize that I do possess certain levels of "power—the ability to make things happen." I was also unusual in that I was pretty much in charge of my own travel schedule, so I did not need permission from anyone else. And organizing the Desert Federation emerged from our conference, and I supported it.

I contacted a number of the Los Angeles area churches that had youth groups, and I set up meetings with the parents to promote their youth to coming to our camp. And to introduce myself as the Chairperson, and almost assuring parents that nothing negative would happen. (There had been one negative rumor floating around from last year's camp, by one young disgruntled camper who had not fit in so well with the rest of the campers. Fortunately, on the face of it, the rumored action could not have been true. However, I needed to address it in my meetings, and was successful.)

For another example, to build quality into our week-long summer camp I telephoned or drove around Southern California to interview and engage Keynote Speakers and workshop leaders. One such very fortunate keynote speaker and workshop leader, suggested by Rev. Manker, was Dr. Samuel Bois, a former French-Canadian Priest, now turned into a psychologist, and his specialty was General Semantics. I contracted with him right there and then. Remember the youth were an autonomous group. We were in charge; therefore, I did not need to consult anyone else.

I and the Planning Council members had met once a month all year to plan and organize the Camp. When the camp commenced, June 21-28, 1958 at *"Mile High Pines—Barton Flats* up in the mountains, I felt an extra strong charge, that I wanted everything to work well as we had planned, and that there would be no untoward or negative problem behaviors. I was awake and up every day 18 plus hours. It does not rain in California in the summer. There was a full-sized couch just outside of the Recreation Hall. So, every night I took a pillow and sleeping bag and slept five to six hours most nights on that couch. That was after we had done a final bed check to make sure everyone was in their proper cabins Every morning, I held a meeting with our Planning Council Members to touch base and see if there were any problems I should know about. There were not. The camp ran very smoothly.

## DR. BOIS INTRODUCES PATRIC TO GENERAL SEMANTICS

• • • • • • • • • • • • • • • • • • • • •

After participating in Dr. Bois workshop for a week, I was totally enthralled with the relationships of "***words to reality***." One set of descriptions goes like this: 1. The word (name of) is NOT the thing it represents such as a map of a territory. The word does not say everything about the thing or "map" it represents.

I spoke with Dr. Bois on my wanting to study and learn more about General Semantics. He quickly advised me to attend San Francisco State College where his student, Dr. S. I. Hayakawa, was teaching. So, I did just that, but not immediately.

## SEEDS OF "I BELIEVE I CAN."

• • • • • • • • • • • • • • • • • • • • • • •

*[The following paragraphs focused on language are significant because they have had a major impact on my whole academic life.]*

An early dictionary definition of General Semantics is: *General Semantics is a philosophical approach to language… exploring the relationship between the form of language and its use and attempting to improve the capacity to express ideas.*

Dr. S. I. Hayakawa (with whom I took a course) writes in his book **Language in Thought and Action** (and I am only selecting a few excerpts):

Page 29. The Word Is Not The Thing. The first of the principles governing symbols is this: The Symbol is NOT the thing symbolized; the word is NOT the Thing; the map is not the territory it stands for.

Page 31. Maps and Territories.

- The Word is not the THING
- The Map does not describe everything that is actual in the territory being described by the map.

The "ONE Word—One Meaning" Fallacy

Everyone, of course, who has ever given any thought to the meanings of words has noticed that they are always shifting and changing in meaning….To remedy this condition, they are likely to suggest that we should all agree on "ONE MEANING" for each word and use it only with that one meaning….Such an impasse is avoided when we start with a new premise altogether—one of the premise upon which modern linguistics thought is based: words have different meanings depending upon who is using it and in what context.

This philosophical approach (acknowledging that often the meaning of a word is constructed in the listener's mind thus "definitions can vary" can be seen in the current major theory of how human beings learn is known as **CONSTRUCTIVISM** . Briefly stated: *No learning takes place unless the learner actively mentally processes the new information coming in, and seeks connections and associations with the learner's **prior knowledge.** Thus, it is the learner who constructs **the meaning of the new information.*** Thus, when we go to a lecture, etc. what we hear and understand is created within our own minds, based upon our past experiences. The meaning we take away from a speech has been created in our minds and may have only some resemblance to the meaning the speaker had in mind.

Some related thoughts: "He or she who only knows one language knows no language at all!" The way any culture's language is constructed, contains philosophical views of how the world is viewed, the purpose of it, etc. If one knows two or more very different languages, it is easier to see the construction. Some languages, like English, emphasize nouns; some other languages emphasize action and verbs.

Anyway, my beginning understanding of how words work and "Frame" how we see and talk about what is real, has been a very important strand in my thinking as I teach and as I communicate with others. I think of "Active Listening" when the listener occasionally says to the speaker: "Let me tell you what I am hearing and see if it is what you mean."

I have half of a Master's in Speech and Communication. [before it was interrupted by the five-month strike at San Francisco State College] I was first introduced to how different cultures use different language depending upon their environment at a workshop at one of the LRY Conferences. One example used: Eskimos, or more properly Innuits, have 28 words for SNOW because they are a hunting culture, and it is a matter of life and death if they go out at the wrong time.

In all my years of instructing teacher candidates, I often say, "If you ask me a question, and I answer it, but it is not what you were thinking, ask your question again, maybe using some different words." [End Time Digression]

+ + + + + + + + + +

## "YOU'LL NEVER WALK ALONE."

• • • • • • • • • • • • • • • • • • • • • •

Friday night was our very last night. Mile High Pines Camp was in the midst of constructing a new building. There was a concrete floor and 2"x 4" wall studs frame up. Our group decided to make it a "Tea House of the August Moon." Oriental looking posters were designed, painted, and affixed to the studs. The kitchen planned a Luau to be eaten in the Tea House. Perhaps there were some rugs and carpets, so we were not sitting directly on the concrete. I don't quite remember who was sitting near me as I was eating. But at the end of the meal, all 70 campers gathered right around me in a circle and sang "*You'll*

*Never Walk Alone."* I was totally surprised and overwhelmed by their love and caring. I was so exhausted from working so hard to make sure everything worked well. As they started singing, I dissolved into sobbing tears.

"You'll Never Walk Alone."

Words by Oscar Hammerstein II
Music by Richard Rodgers
Copyright 1945

*When you walk through a storm*
*Hold your head up high.*
*And don't be afraid of the Dark.*

*At the end of the storm*
*Is a Golden Sky....*

*...Though your dreams*
*be tossed and blown.*

*Walk on, walk on*
*with hope in your heart*

*And You'll Never Walk Alone*

*You'll Never, Never Walk Alone.*

Somehow, some persons, managed to lift me up and help me walk to the Recreation Hall. I remember sitting down in a chair, and campers were sharing their feelings about the camp experience with me. That didn't last very long I don't think. I possibly fell asleep sitting there. The next thing I knew, I was lying across four girls' laps and sleeping soundly. Occasionally someone needed to get up, and I woke up for a few seconds. I never knew who the girls were. I believe I slept on their laps at least two hours or more. I don't really know who they were—I was totally out of it. I am guessing that there was dancing going on, and campers were entertaining themselves. At some point, maybe around 11:00 P.M., some persons must have helped me to my couch to sleep the rest of the night.

The "jury is in." The camp was a very positive experience. I still have letters from a few of the campers.

> "Dear Pat, I've thought of you and camp and everything "a million times" if I've thought of it once, --and so—here I am, and you'd better write back. Because I'll never forget Camp LRY, and you made it the way it was...

> I just can't say the way I'd like to how we all felt and still feel about you, Pat Please don't ever forget that I think you're the "most understanding and wonderful person I've known."

> Love, Sally Mc."

> "Dear Pat, ...The Conference (Camp) was really wonderful, and I'll remember it for a long, long time...."

> "I guess it was sort of silly the way I was acting Friday night and I hope you'll forgive me. (Back in the Recreation Hall when I was sitting in a chair half falling asleep.) But the emotion was just too much and I think it helps to cry sometimes.

> "I will always have a special place in my heart for my "Big Brother" [Me] We all miss you. "Your Sister" Love Sherry

"Dear Pat, …Being at L.R.Y. (Camp) for the first time this year has been one of the most wonderful experiences in my life! I know you can understand how I feel because of your obvious attachment. Pat, I hope our next President will be as wonderful as you, in his (her) own way of course….I want to remember you as part of my first wonderful experiences at LRY. I hope you'll always get everything you want out of life. Love always, Marva M.

\* \* \* \* \*

In the spring of my senior year, I dreamed of an exciting adventure. Since "Travel" was becoming my middle name." And I was driven to explore and learn about new things, new countries, new people, I decided upon Graduation, that I wanted to sign aboard a merchant ship and sail all around the world –see what the world, the sea, is like—for about a year. Sure, seemed like a nice romantic idea.

Well, reality entered. Sam Martin was a friend of the family, and he had spent most of his adult life as a professional sailor, sailing round the world, including down in the Antarctic Ocean (complete with pictures!) Sam came down to our house to discuss my dream. Sam made several points. 1. You will not make very much money unless you sail on a Flagged American Merchant Marine Ship [If flagged American, it meant that the shipping company had to pay union wages, and carry all the required insurance, and adhere to safety practices; and perhaps it also meant that the sailors were of a higher quality behaving human beings—I would be safer.] 2. You cannot sail on American Merchant Ships unless you are a Union Member in Good Standing, and that does not happen overnight."

If you did get a job on a foreign registry ship, you probably would not be safe, because some of the crew could be cruel, and rape nice young men like you! Okay, I get the picture. Sam, you have sold me, no sailing on the sea. Plan two: drive across country to Cincinnati by myself. No problem!

When I was convinced by our sailor friend, Sam Martin, I should not try to go around the world on a merchant ship, that is when I decided I should return to Cincinnati and to Western Waterproofing Co. to continue in construction work [However, seven years later when I enlisted in the U.S. Navy Submarine Service, I did spend two six-month trips sailing to and from several Far Eastern countries.]

I had purchased my car in the fall, so this was the first opportunity I had to drive great distances, like back to Ohio. So, from my Calling Card, one of my specialties was *Have Car Will Travel.* That included a time when my friends rented my large Chrysler Imperial Crown Convertible and me, to drive around the United States to attend a College-Level Conference in Springfield, Massachusetts. [See Score Two for the Nina Tanner story.]

However, I did not think of them as great distances. I had driven all around California, and even to Arizona. So, what could be difficult about just driving for several days to Ohio. My car was in good shape, and this Oldsmobile 98 Holiday was fun to drive and powerful. So, I purchased a Rand McNally Atlas to show me the roads. Historic reminder: this was 1958 before hardly any Interstate Highways were built, and few cars came equipped with air conditioning; mine didn't. As I was crossing some of the hottest deserts, I had a jar of water and a wash cloth. So, if need be, I cold wet my hair, faced, and neck for relief.

## PATRIC DRIVES SOLO ACROSS COUNTRY
• • • • • • • • • • • • • • • • • • • • •

Having lived at the beach next to Pacific Coast Highway, U.S. 101

for two years, I was used to driving bare-footed. I still do. I recall that my body got restless sitting on the left side of the front bench seat; so, I shifted to the right side and drove with my left hand and left foot. It went well. There was one very special time when in Arizona on a four-lane highway—two lanes going in each direction, somehow my two lanes developed a "ditch" or a small "cove" where the two concrete lanes side by side—joined in the center, came together. Well, I saw an opportunity: I carefully guided my left front wheel into that cove, which then held my wheel steady as I drove along, and I was able to drive more than half a mile without touching the steering wheel!! I warned you that I was abnormally curious.

1958 in June, there was not really a lot traffic on the road, and one could see for miles. So, I drove 90 m.p.h. on straight a-ways and 60 m.p.h. on curves. I was too inexperienced to accomplish this on this trip, but in later cross-country trips I would join "Truck Convoys" ten to 20 semi-trucks running together. I would slide in between them, and very soon they understood I spoke "truckese" having been a truck driver. [In later Convoy trips I would assist the trucks in maneuvering and passing on a hill. I would slide out and hold back the other traffic.]

1958 was also a time of very few fast-food chain restaurants, other than maybe a Howard Johnson's so I either stopped at a Truck Stop to eat (always rumored to have very good food.) or look for a homey mom and pop restaurant in town.

I did not have lots of money, but I had made arrangements to stay with some of my new Desert LRY friends at night. From the very first mile, heading east on old Route 66, I was excited. [Actually, I had sold some LRY merchandise –sweatshirts, T shirts etc. at the Summer camp, so I had that cash with me; yes, I did borrow from it, and paid it back when I started working again.]

In Tucson I stayed overnight with Bob Aker; In Albuquerque I stayed with Judy Webb and had a date with her girlfriend Nancy Hord. In McKinney Texas, I visited with F. Pete Derrick, formerly Captain and Commandant at O.M.I. but who had resigned in 1955.

My travels across country took eight days with overnight stops in Tucson, Albuquerque, McKinney, Texas,…One feature that was unusual was that most nights I was hosted in a private home, had home-cooked meals, and had dates with girls on a few occasions. I am sure it wasn't like this during pioneer days. Having just written that, I will share that quite often when I am driving on a major trip, I try to visualize myself as a pioneer with a wagon and a "draught animal"—(which could be oxen, mules, or horses)—and making our way where there may be only gravel or mud roads. I remember reading that General Dwight D. Eisenhower, as a young officer in the 1920's, was part of an army convoy driving across the United States: the trip took 66 days because the muddy roads were so bad. And after the capture of Germany in WWII, and Eisenhower saw the Autobahn, he came home and initiated the Interstate Highway System.

In Memphis, Tenn., I stayed with Devere Bond whom I had met in their Tucson home in April during the Desert Federation. My trip took a total of eight days.

Upon arrival in Cincinnati, I was immediately—the first day, put back to work. Referring to earlier Western Waterproofing working days, after my second summer (1957) of working for and with Clyde Oliver, I wrote him a long letter telling him how much he meant to me and my gratitude to him for teaching me so much. I did not learn until the following summer that Clyde had died of a heart attack that Fall. I immediately spoke of the letter, and the office staff assured me that he did receive my letter, and was deeply touched and very pleased, before he died. [I still become emotional when I think and write about this person in my life, who truly was an important mentor.]

To keep my momentum in gaining an education, I enrolled in the University of Cincinnati Evening College for one year. Would you believe the first night of registration I tucked my high school diploma under my arm and went off to the University of Cincinnati to sign up for evening classes? When I got to the admission window, the clerk inquired what was under my arm. "My High School Diploma! I was told I could not get into college without it." The clerk smiled politely and notified me that my proof of graduation was already recorded on my transcript—I did not need to show the hard copy!" "Oh."

Remember I could not afford the extras in high school? But once I went to work in Cincinnati, I did create my own Calling Card: Please excuse the youthful exuberance:

Side one: "HAVE CAR WILL TRAVEL'

Side two: "LEEDOM SHALL LEAD 'EM TO FREEDOM"

Side three "Introducing…

WILLIAM PATRIC LEEDOM
Product of Human Nature
Arguer of Philosophy
Religion
Politics
Business
Women
Side four continuation of three
Lover of Life
Working
Eating

Thinking
Love Making

[Lamp of Learning symbol]

Believer of Value
In himself
And in YOU

Matthew G. Long and mother stopped dating when I was 17, but Matt stayed connected to me. When I turned 21, Matt made sure that he was the one who bought me my first legal drink—at a Dayton Ohio Supper Club where Dorothy Lamour of the Bob Hope-Bing Crosby "On the road to..." movies fame.

Within a month or so, this was when the Home Office of Western Waterproofing in Detroit ordered Mr. Stone to fire his secretary, Barbara (who made all the payroll mistakes) and put Patric in the office, since his payroll work is always accurate." This meant I was no longer on the work crews, but I was now the secretary, the receptionist, the janitor, the garnishee receiver for the men, the whatever, because there was only Mr. Stone. and me in the office.

During the day, I was working Monday Through Friday, at Western Waterproofing Company. I was 18 now and able to obtain a "Chauffer's License" which was the early form of a truck driver's license. So now I could drive the larger stake body delivery trucks to and from various work sites—some in urban sites and some rural sites-often with an air compressor trailer attached on back. We bid and accepted construction projects in five states: Ohio, Indiana, Kentucky, West Virginia, and at times like AT&T project, Maryland.

+ + + + + + + + +

## PATRIC DELIVERS A YOUTH SERMON: THE CHALLENGE TO MODERN YOUTH

• • • • • • • • • • • • • • • • • • • • • • •

In September 1958, I crossed the threshold of St. John's Unitarian Church in Clifton, Cincinnati. I quickly joined the local LRY group. I that era, our churches used to celebrate **YOUTH SUNDAY** in the spring when the teenagers took over all aspects of the Sunday Morning Service.

So, in March 1959 Mary Brigham and I volunteered to take responsibility for the pulpit by presenting two related sermons. The general theme was **ON THE ROAD TO MATURITY.** The title of my portion was:

**THE CHALLENGE TO MODERN YOUTH.** *Excerpts*

*"The first challenge is to try to make sense out of the world. This challenge is presented to all youth, but they do not all go about it in the same manner....A challenge of this sort requires a lot of deep thinking.....*

*After our young person has accepted the first challenge and found a direction for himself, he is then faced with the second challenge of committing himself and applying his knowledge toward building a better world.....*

*If we cannot develop a system of dependability and trust of one another in our communities, how then, are we to trust people farther away? If we cannot get along with persons slightly different from us, how then are we to get along with people who are at times, quite different....Therefore, in final analysis, these challenges are necessary to our future existence and our advancement.*

*In closing, I wish to point out that, although these challenges are presented to us in our youth, they have a bearing on us all the days of our lives. Amen.*

## PATRIC VOLUNTEERS FOR THE AMERICAN FRIENDS SERVICE COMMITTEE

● ● ● ● ● ● ● ● ● ● ● ● ● ● ● ● ● ● ● ● ● ●

As I reflect deeper, my ability to relate to almost anyone includes the five years when I volunteered on projects with the American Friends Service Committee. In the autumn of my18th year I joined the **Cincinnati Weekend Work Camp.** Quotes from the brochure: **LIVE in a neighborhood where there are serious problems of substandard housing, health, and morale, a situation of challenge. Live with other students of various racial and religious backgrounds. Live assuming responsibilities for the mechanics of living, sharing food preparation, cleanup, expense.**

**WORK on housing repairs with families who have asked for help, and where we can work out some arrangement with the landlord and tenant to pay for the cost of materials. Somebody (usually children) from the family works with us.**

**...AFSC's work is rooted in fundamental Quaker principles:**

**-respect for the personality of the individual, and faith in his potential for good; and**

**-confidence in the creative power of love to remove fears, bring about mutual understanding, and take away "the occasion of all wars."**

I did mostly painting and some repairs with impoverished families through the Welfare Department. But I also, in my 20's, did some weekends in mental hospitals, and finally my six weeks inside San Quentin Prison helping with Self-Reflexive Therapy for the inmates.

* * * * *

## DESCRIPTIONS OF MY LIFE FROM
## AUGUST 1959 UNTIL AUGUST 1960
● ● ● ● ● ● ● ● ● ● ● ● ● ● ● ● ● ● ● ● ●

In August 1959, I left Cincinnati driving my Oldsmobile back to Southern California—Tujunga to be exact--to my father's and Liz's home. Upon arrival, my Dad asked me what is happening? Am I going to go to UCLA this fall semester?

I told Dad, that I had applied in time, but I have not heard anything back from UCLA." Dad said get in the car, and he drove us up to UCLA, he put me in the admissions line, and then he went in to find officials he needed to consult. He came back out in about a half hour and reported, "You have been admitted; they just forgot to notify you!"

We went back home—the family now living in a different Laguna Beach Apartment. I had a room on the first floor. So, I started commuting from Laguna Beach, up the Santa Ana Freeway to the famous "Four Banger Interchange" This was where all four of the existing freeways met and intersected with each other. It was a mess. The Pasadena Freeway was the oldest one and the only complete one. I believe it entered the top level from the east and quickly transformed into the Harbor Freeway running west, but in September 1959 the Harbor only ran to 42$^{nd}$ Street and ended. Hollywood Freeway may have been on the Third Level but only went as far as the Laurel Canyon Blvd. The

Santa Ana Freeway, which was four full lanes of traffic heading toward the Interchange was suddenly forced into ONE LANE TO MERGE THROUGH THE INTERCHANGE. What a god-awful traffic jam that was. [I believe a year or so later the officials were able to widen it to two lanes. I had to leave home somewhere near 5:00 A.M. in order to try to arrive in Westwood—UCLA—in time for 8:00 A.M. classes. I also desperately needed to secure one of the free parking spots, as I had no money for parking. Well, it was a beautiful campus, and I was delighted to be a student there. I enrolled in Sociology, Astronomy, German, Physical Education (which was Folk Dancing this quarter) and there was a required ROTC course, so I joined up with the Air Force ROTC. My courses were now on track. I had also enrolled in an Anthropology Course but dropped it after three classes because the professor would never look directly at the class!!

But one also has to fill the basic needs of life: Food, clothing, and Shelter. I could not commute from Laguna forever—50--60 miles one way, and the cost of gasoline. I needed to find a sleeping room somewhere closer to the university. But my funds were extremely limited. So now my time outside of class was divided between searching for a job and searching for housing. I may be exaggerating a little, but it sure seemed like I filled out 100 job applications. I had applied at Disneyland in September, but their season was drawing down and they were laying people off. I walked up and down the Sunset and Hollywood strips knocking on doors, and if I had been 21, I could have been hired at Dean Martin's restaurant "Dino's" because I would have had to handle alcoholic drinks. I was offered a job to park cars for 50 cents an hour.

The biggest disappointment was when I took a Post Office Civil Service Exam for sorting mail, and I scored very high. I was called in for an interview. During the process I was asked if I was a student. "Yes." "Oh, I'm sorry, we do not hire students!" Big, big hurt! If only I had been able to get that job, I could have comfortably stayed at

UCLA all four years and gotten my bachelor's degree and been a happy camper. But no.

## *I BELIEVE I CAN, I BELIEVE I CAN…(EVEN THOUGH I HAVE NEVER DONE THAT BEFORE)*

• • • • • • • • • • • • • • • • • • • • • •

I am also remembering that members of the church would ask me "Can you repair broken windows?" Or "Can you re-web the old-fashioned Venetian Blinds?" Whatever I was asked, my answer became "YES!" even though I had never done those jobs! Is that some form of **chutzpah**? [Yiddish] Loosely translated, "when one is hungry, one often says yes to many challenging jobs, whether you had ever done them before or not." I might note that I had begun working in construction for the Western Waterproofing Co. when I was 16 years old. And I learned then how to use problem-solving skills. My mother had an apt saying, "**WHERE THERE IS A WILL, THERE IS A WAY!**" *I DID IT, I BELIEVED I COULD, I BELIEVED I COULD…*

When I had enrolled in UCLA but did not have steady employment to support myself, Joseph Kent, and his wife Herta, started finding odd jobs for me amongst the church members. For example, I cleaned the apartment of one of the Hollywood writers for the **Great Gildersleeve Show**. 2. I worked for one of the electricians from a movie studio. He told me that because they shot movies all hours of the day and night, that anytime he had to work After midnight he was paid *"Golden Time" which was three times Double time!!!* When you do the math, he was paid six times his hourly wage!!

Another job which lasted several weeks, was for an immigrant couple who had emigrated from Montenegro in the Balkan States. From time to time, they would argue with each other, and when they were angry, they would ask me to re-type their financial wills—cutting each other out! But then a few weeks later, they "made up," so then I was asked to re-type the wills bringing them back together! This event happened at least three times while I was in their employ.

And then, while I was still studying at UCLA, and Joseph Kent had several construction jobs being completed, he would hire me to do some of the deep cleaning work. Suddenly I am remembering some of the **ODD JOB EXPERIENCES**. But first, I want to describe Joseph Kent. He was born in Cologne Germany around 1900. As he became a teenager, he was involved in a boating club, and they needed to build a Boat House. They went down to City Hall and took out a sizable loan to build the house. Along came World War One. And after the war financial inflation grew and grew. This was when Germany started printing 1,000,000 Mark notes. Joe told me that one day, he walked down to City Hall and paid off the whole loan out of "**HIS POCKET CHANGE!**"

I finally found a sleeping room in a utility room of a large mansion in the lower part of Laurel Canyon not far from the magician Houdini's old home. A Dr. Rose and his wife and child owned it. There was not much in my facility, no stove or refrigerator, yes, a toilet. One lamp, some kind of a single bed to sleep on. Not a great situation. My father had loaned me his old metal ice chest. I was able to keep some food cold in it. However, one day, the landlady entered my room, when I was not there, bringing her dog with her, and the dog broke into my box and ate all the meat!!

"A funny thing happened to me" on my way home to Laguna one weekend. I stopped in Anaheim to have dinner with one of the church families, the Gottschalks. As dinner was winding down, Mrs. Gottschalk said to me, "Where are you sleeping tonight?" Holy crap, what kind of a question is that? "I'm going home to my family." "Oh no, dear, you can't do that! Your family is gone! They have moved to Oregon." What??? When??? Well, we didn't have cell phones, and I guess I did not have a land line, so Dad had no way to contact me. Sheldon Sackett had telephoned my father and asked him to take over management of the Coos Bay Oregon Newspaper. So quickly, the family packed up and moved to Coos Bay, or rather the suburb North Bend. The Gottschalks hosted me, and I returned to Hollywood and school.

Back to Laurel Canyon in Hollywood. Days were "short" in this steep-walled canyon: The sun did not peek over the crest of the hill until around 10:00 A.M. and then it only stayed around until around 3:00 P.M. So, five hours of sunlight. A few weeks after I moved in, Mrs. Rose bargained with me saying that if I would mow the lawn every Saturday morning, they would take $10.00 off of my monthly rent. I said yes. But after I cut the grass on a couple of Saturdays, I realized what a sucker I was. And I decided I was being taken advantage of, and I needed to find new quarters.

At the local market, there was a sign-up advertising someone was looking for a housemate. I took down the phone number, called, and was asked to come up for an interview. Well, first of all, this residence was on the very top of the canyon, and the maze of streets one needed to negotiate was quite challenging. Finally, I found this small, old white house, perched on the brow of a hill. I knocked, went in. On the first floor, there were three "would-be actors" and on the second floor, two brothers who were musicians—vibraphone. They did have a spare bedroom—quite nice really: large, comfortable and with a floor to ceiling window looking out over Hollywood and Los Angeles! Wow! Very Beautiful! So, I moved in, thinking I was settled. It probably was not two months until the two brothers on my floor decided to move home across town. The older brother had been the manager of the house. The three actors were not the responsible types.

Only one, and I do not remember his name, had been an Olympic "Diving Champion in the 1948 Olympics," and was now a serious actor. He did land a job on the TV program "Playhouse 90." The actors did not pay the utilities so then we had no gas and electric. I literally was forced to cook in the fireplace—hearting a pot of beans or so. One day, the youngest of the "Actors" came upstairs and informed me that he had to go home to Minneapolis to testify in court in a wild trial where supposedly this kid's father had come home and killed his mother's lover, who was a member of the Mafia. This kid had witnessed the killing. The kid told me he was responsible for paying the gas bill, so would I write him a check for (I don't remember…maybe $25.00?) I smelled a rat, so I wrote the check to the gas company, and not the kid. So, when I came home that night, my check was still on the table. Good call, Patric.

Back to the house that is sliding down the hill, and all the housemates are "abandoning ship." So now, I needed to bail out very quickly. Barbara Westley had been a very active member of the LRY; I had been to her home in downtown Los Angeles, and I knew there was an old trailer in their back yard. So, I telephoned the family and begged if I might be allowed to live in that trailer. The Westley's said yes, so in a matter of hours I was totally out of the old house—which actually was slowly sliding down the hill.

But within a week, a problem developed: the electrical cord which connected the trailer to the house was very old, the insulation was falling off, and a fire started. So now, the family arranged that I could sleep on the old couch in the dining room. With my sleeping bag, blanket and pillow, that works for me.

It was in November 1959 that I moved in with the Westley family. I was living with the Westley family in downtown LA on 2270 West 23rd St, L.A. 18, Calif. And I did live there until the following August.

The three older girls were in LRY, so we had a lot in common. The 16-year-old twins Kathy and Karen, loved to go cruising the drive-ins e.g., Van De Camp's Restaurant to check out the guys. But they did not have a car. So, we made deals. When I came home from work, they would have my dinner on the table, and they would have money for the gasoline, so off we went. The father, Ira Westley was a famous Jazz Base Player, currently working up in Hollywood in a Jazz Band at the Ivar Theater. He got up early every day, went off to work at the Howard Hughes Medical Company where he helped develop medical instruments. Oh yes, and Karen agreed to help me learn to sew. I was dating Kitten F. in Louisville Kentucky, so I got the bright idea to make a dress for her and a matching shirt for me. I did the dress first believing it would be the hardest to work on. But I was totally wrong…it was my shirt with a big "yoke" in back that required extra attention. But with Karen's help, I got them done. I am remembering that I spent my 20th birthday sitting on the couch in the Westley home "baby-sitting" or "Child-care giving for the younger three Westley children.

+ + + + + + + +

## *WHERE ARE YOUR WORK CLOTHES?*
• • • • • • • • • • • • • • • • • • • •

Now to return to my last day at UCLA, I happened to drive over to Joe's home construction site up on Fernwood—ADJACENT TO Hollywood. I got out of my car; Joe came to the edge of an upper floor, looked down at me and said, **"WHERE ARE YOUR WORK CLOTHES?"** I said, "WHAT?" And Joe said, "*You need a job, don't you?* I said yes, and immediately drove home to the Westley's and got my work clothes. I went to work for Joe that afternoon. . And I now had a paying job for the next six months. Again, to keep my educational momentum, I enrolled in Los Angeles City College for evening courses.

*Took Chinese I; Drama I, and Philosophy .*

Joseph Kent came to my rescue. So how did I know this Joseph Kent? Well, we all belonged to the same church, and his daughter, Analou, was a close friend from the church LRY Youth group. And, after my family had moved to Laguna Beach—50 miles south on the coast— the Kent family was often my host on the weekends when I needed to come to LA for LRY business. (I was active both on the Summer Camp Planning Council—which met on Saturdays at the Throop Memorial Church in Pasadena, and the LRY District Federation Council which met on Sundays in the downtown church. So, I was very familiar with the Kents—maybe you could say I was "a part of the family.". Their home was high on a hill overlooking Los Angeles, at 1821 Edgecliff Drive, LA 26, CA.

Returning to Joe Kent, he was a very smart person. In his young adult years, he apprenticed himself to a painting "***GRAINER.***" This is a specialty skill where the painter can take almost any building material such as plaster, or plywood, and with the help of very special brushes, and paint colors, the painter can create any illusion such as any type of wood—for example Mahogany, or stone such as Marble. Joe became an expert. He immigrated to New York City, and began working for the Federal Government. In public buildings, you see Marble walls. However, Joe explained to me that only the first 10 feet are actually Marble. Above that, the "Marble" is actually plaster "grained" to resemble Marble.

Someone from the Hollywood studios became aware of Joe's talent. They hired Joe to come to Hollywood and paint movie sets. As one of his projects, Joe did provide scenes from a castle, such as a ballroom. It was excellent work. But the studio decided he was TOO EXPENSIVE. SO, THEY LET HIM GO.

Joseph Kent then became a contractor. He had purchased a large lot up on the side of a hill on Fernwood Drive in the Silverlake District, adjacent to Hollywood. The lot was large enough that Joe could subdivide it into four housing lots. He had a very young but talented architect, Steve Siskind, who designed all of the wooden houses with roofs to have a hyperbolic parabola: the opposite ends go down, the other opposite ends go up. When I went to work for Joe, the city had just rescinded its law against building housing on a hillside that was greater than 45 degree down angle. So, our houses were cantilevered off from the hill. Half of the house was nestled back on a shelf in the cliff, and the other half extended out until it rested on large concrete pillars. Their front doors were near the cliff, with intricate stairways leading down the slope to the street.

As a part of his building plan, he used his skills as a "Grainer" for instance, to turn plywood into Mahogany. The "slope homes" we built on Fernwood Drive, all had had "Mahogany kitchens" which were really plywood. I helped Joe as a "painter's assistant" so I knew what they were. I was in the homes when customers came to look, and from their comments, I knew they believed the cabinets were Mahogany.

When I went to work for Joe, I was a general laborer, go-for, whatever was needed. Some days I assisted the plumber when the industry was still using iron pipes and solder from lead. Some days I help the glazer to hang windows. Some days I worked as a "Rough Carpenter" (As opposed to a Finish Carpenter). I helped deliver 2" x 4" x 10-foot wooden studs and, 4' x 8-foot sheets of plywood, and anything else the carpenters needed. I helped nail down floors with "Mule-Nails" the kind that have rings on the shafts so they never work loose. I helped nail wooden studs in place. Some days I was a painter helping Joe lay down a base coat on the plywood walls. (I became quite skilled with a roller as well as using brushes such that there never were "Holidays"—places that only had a thin coat or an uneven coat of paint. Oh yes, one more task: I was the Time Keeper for every one's payroll sheets.

The work crew resembled an international group. We had three carpenters: Jess, who was Caucasian European, Tom, an African American—who had spent years as a cook on passenger trains, and Frank, who was Latino. (I remember one of his frequent responses: *"Wash it, papa!" He meant Watch it Papa"* We had a laborer, Terry, an elderly(probably in his 50's) African American. One day while I was shoveling—using a No. 9 Idiot Spoon Shovel-- refuse into a dump truck (which I also drove to the dump) Terry walked over to me and said STOP! "You are killing yourself. Let me show you how to shovel. You make the shovel work FOR you, NOT AGAINST you. You create a rhythm: Put the shovel under a load of refuse, then swing back in a curved motion, then forward and up and let the weight of the load provide momentum *up and over the back of the* truck" "Wow! Thank you, Terry."I have remembered that lesson all the rest of my life. Oh yes, and Terry never had the opportunity to learn how to read and write—I had to witness his "X" on his paychecks. [I have known others who could not read and write—often they had to quit school to help earn money to support the family., So I do not think any less of them for how they have experienced life.

## *MOUNTAIN GOAT LEAPING FROM CLIFF TO CLIFF*

• • • • • • • • • • • • • • • • • • • • • •

Probably one of the most unusual jobs that I did, was to plant the 75 degree slope up behind the homes with ivy. There was a metal chain-linked fence running along the top of the slope (I think it must have belonged to the neighbors.) I took an extension ladder so I could get up the slope, take a heavy-duty rope, tie one end to the fence and the other around my waist so I could negotiate the slope. The earth was hard clay. So, I had a large electric drill with a three-inch wide drill bit. I had an electric extension cord which ran back down the slope to a power box in the home. Hanging off of my belt were two bags. One had a supply of Ivy plants. The other was filled with dark rich top soil. Starting near the top of the slope, I would drill a 3-inch hole, place an ivy plant in it; fill the hole around the ivy roots with top soil. Then move over about six inches and do it all again. I got to thinking of myself as some kind of ***"MOUNTAIN GOAT."***

Obviously, this planting was very labor intensive as I had to frequently adjust the rope and return to the homes to refill both bags. The slope to be planted was probably 125 feet wide and 35 feet tall. Now imagine a hole every six inches in both directions! Oh, by the way, often when I drilled a hole, a "***potato bug"*** would come crawling out! These bugs were large—at least an inch and quarter long, somewhat resembling a grasshopper. I began a collection in a milk carton fastened to my belt.

A second unusual job was actually at another site. Joe was remodeling a house down on Felix Boulevard and was putting in "Knotty Pine" molding around the top of the walls. Okay. But it really was not knotty Pine? Joe took plain pine wood and skillfully painted it to resemble knotty pine. My job was to take my thumb and "make those knots." At one point, the doors were off of the house, that left the house "vulnerable" at night. So, I was hired as the "Night Watchman." I brought my sleeping bag and bedding and slept in the house for several nights.

All in a day's work. But it gets better!! In the back pages of a Life Magazine in 1959, it displays a very talented Danny Millman executing gymnastics off of a trampoline. Okay. Well, Danny's father was a friend of Joe Kent, and Danny's father owned a corner lot at the corner of Micheltorena and Sunset Boulevard. He tore down the small wooden office building on the lot, cleared all the land, then had an excavator come and dig probably eight large holes---big enough for large heavy-duty rectangular trampoline covers. Okay, while the fence was down during construction, it was my job to sleep on the trampolines at night and protect the property! Yes, I could jump all I wanted to, and that was fun, but then I got a lesson in Thermodynamics: when you place your blankets and pillows down on a trampoline mat with nothing under it, the breezes blow much of the night and you are cold in a three-hundred-and-sixty-degree direction. BBRRRRR. I believe I put cardboard under me for the next nights.

When we needed a dump truck, in the early morning, I would drive my car to a truck rental agency and pick up a dump truck. Come to the site, pick up all the refuse, and take it to the dump some miles away, and return the truck to the rental agency on my way home.

One time I was driving the dump truck on the brand-new **GOLDEN STATE FREEWAY. [This later became part of Interstate 5 which runs from the Mexican Border to the Oregon Border.]** It was so new, there was hardly any traffic at all. *All of a sudden, the engine stopped running*, and I steered the truck to the side of the road. Got out and found a Public Telephone not too far away. I called the Rental Agency. They asked me what Truck Number was on my Rental Agreement. When I did, they said, "Oh, that was the truck we were still working on the engine. Go back and raise the hood and see if there are tools still on top of the engine. "We were working on the Distributor, and perhaps the rotor or some of the wires are malfunctioning!" (Really?)

So, I walked back to the truck, raised the hood, saw the tools, re-engaged the rotor and wires, and voila—the truck ran again! [I should tell you I took a year of Auto Shop my sophomore year in High School, so was well acquainted with engines.]

I worked for Joe from January to August 1960. But I realized that I was in an unstable financial position, and I really needed to abandon

California and return to Cincinnati to live with my mother, to go back to Western Waterproofing for a good paying job, and an opportunity to go back to the University of Cincinnati. My route east from Los Angeles took me first to Albany, Oregon where my father, my pregnant step-mother Liz (carrying Erin) and brother Casey.

When I arrived in Albany, Oregon, I explained to my Dad that I needed expense money to pay for gas etc. to travel across country. Dad: "Get a job!" The Employment Office told me: "Be at the corner of 6th and Main Streets at 6:00 AM. The Bean Field Picking Buses stop by to pick up workers. If they let you get on the bus, then you have a job!"

## PATRIC BECOMES A MIGRANT WORKER
• • • • • • • • • • • • • • • • • • • • • •

The third bus that stopped let me on. We drove out to the country and the string-bean fields. As I got off the bus, someone explained to me how it all works. "Here is a bucket and a burlap bag. The beans are all hanging on the fences. Only take the ripe ones. First, they go into the bucket; when that fills, empty it into the sack. When the sack is filled up, bring it over to the weighing scales. We are paying 2 and ¾ cents per pound. We will keep track of your pounds.

I looked around at my fellow bean pickers. A number of them were school children earning money to buy clothes for the school year. A larger number were migrant workers, usually a whole family: mom, dad, children, and often a grandmother. They would "migrate" from field to field, state to state as various crops ripened. They lived in the little shanty shacks at the far side of the field. There was one more population: older men who essentially picked crops in order to pay for a working man's hotel room, food, and booze. "King" was the leader of one of these clusters of men. The second or third day he came over to me and said, "Son, you are not going to earn very much money the way you are picking—a few beans at a time. You need to grab a large handful every time, pull them off the vine quickly then into the bucket." He was absolutely right. I thanked him for helping me out. I really appreciated his thoughtfulness. Soon I was earning about $10.00 a day. And in three weeks, I had enough money to make it across country. We were picking fields in the Willamette Valley. And for some reason, it rained every day in short bursts. No one paid any attention to it, just kept picking. In a while you were fairly dry. So, with the help of picking string beans in Oregon's Willamette Valley for three weeks, I was able to earn enough money for gas and food and then was able to drive back to Cincinnati, back to Western Waterproofing Co., and back to UC's Evening college. This time I stayed with my mother for a year and a half.

+ + + + + +

## ANYWAY, "A FUNNY THING HAPPENED ON DAD'S SOJOURN TO OWN A NEWSPAPER"

• • • • • • • • • • • • • • • • • • • • • •

Step One: Dad went to work in San Francisco for Mr. Sheldon Sackett, who owned 14 small newspapers around the United States, most of them included the word "World" in the title. Dad became Mr. Sackett's "Right Hand Man" to help with business negotiations. Dad lived with Mr. Sackett in a luxury apartment in one of San Francisco's high-rise buildings. They had a "House Boy" to care for the apartment and do the cooking. Dad was directed to always carry $100.00 with him-to pay for dining business guests, etc. [This was in 1960 dollars; today, probably something like $600.] Dad stayed with him for six months, BUT it was not a lifestyle that Dad was made for, so Dad quit and returned to Los Angeles where his family was living. I was not living with Dad at the time, so I am hazy on Dad's day-to-day employment. However, within months, Sheldon Sackett contacted Dad and asked him to go to Oregon and take over management of the **COOS BAY WORLD** newspaper. Dad and his family moved to a suburb of Coos Bay named North Bend, and Dad took over the management and editorial duties. The regular Managing Editor had taken a leave and moved to Washington DC to see if he could "better himself"-better job, higher pay.

In the early days, Dad would telephone Sheldon Sackett and consult him/ ask permission to carry out the management duties. Finally, Mr. Sackett said to my father, "Look , I hired YOU to manage the paper and the editorials. So, do it and stop calling me!" This important background to our story: for the next 18 months s Dad had the experience of "Owning and operating his own newspaper." He did it very well, including negotiating with businesses which advertised in the paper.

And after 18 months, the previous Managing Editor, Mr. Amundsen, came back from his leave of absence to resume his position as Managing Editor at the Coos Bay World . So, Da d 's job came to an end. However, those eighteen months of being in charge and running the newspaper taught him:

1. I really can do it; I can be successful in running a business.
2. I really do not like or enjoy doing it! So now he was happy being a reporter, writer, and editor.

+ + + + + + +

So, Dad was living in Albany, Oregon in August of 1960 when I needed to return across country to Cincinnati. Dad had answered an advertisement: The owner of Albany's radio and television had decided he also wanted to publish a weekly newspaper. So, he hired Dad to set it up. Dad worked successfully for several months. But just as they were only weeks away from publishing the first edition, Bob Smith, the owner, suddenly decided he wanted daily paper instead! Dad was incredulous! You have got to be kidding! A daily newspaper is a whole different type of creature. It requires a tremendous amount of organizational work. Bob Smith was very peculiar fellow, even a registered member of the **Flat Earth Society** those persons who rejected that the earth is a sphere! [An Oblate Spheroid to be exact.] Dad resigned on the spot. So did all of the other workers. Dad returned to Los Angeles for employment.

During the next two years, I was living back in Cincinnati. Dad eventually was hired by the **PASADENA INDEPENDENT STAR NEWS.** It seems that it was the old familiar story: the newspaper was losing money, because the newspaper's circulation had declined. It seems that most all the staff had each done the same job for thirty years or more. And they didn't have up-to-date knowledge of how to modernize. But the owners recognized that Dad was very knowledgeable and highly competent. So, the owners turned to Dad "to save them" and modernize the paper. He did. He even suffered the horrible car wreck in December 1961 [which I wrote about in detail in my first book **METAMORPHOSIS OF A YOUNG MAIDEN**], and was off work for a month or more, but the newspaper supported him, kept sending him paychecks until Dad was recovered enough to come back to work. Dad's next twelve years at the Independent Star News were the greatest in his career. He was a major mover and shaker in town.

+ + + + + +

When I first returned to Western Wwaterproofing Co. in Autumn 1960, I worked on local restoration jobs, short term out-of-town jobs, or I worked in the warehouse doing maintenance on equipment. My status was kind of as an "auxiliary worker." Many times, I was the truck driver who delivered material and equipment to the various jobs, but if it was out of town, I was often requested to stay a few days and help the mechanics out.

+ + + + + +

## PATRIC HAS A "MR. TOAD'S WILD RIDE" DOWN THE MOUNTAIN
• • • • • • • • • • • • • • • • • • • • • •

Once again, I left the West Coast and drove back to Cincinnati, and back to Western Waterproofing Co. I think I was 20, when I was working up in the mountains of West "By God" Virginy. I had a new Superintendent, named Will T. We had finished our work for the month, and we were driving back to Ohio. But early in this trip I was driving the 1953 Chevrolet Stake Body Truck with an air-compressor hooked on back. Will was in a pickup truck driving behind me. *Everything was fine until I started down a mountain road. And then-----suddenly my steering wheel was not responding properly. I would turn the wheel to the left, nothing happened for a few seconds—and then the truck would lurch to the left. I quickly pulled the steering wheel to the right—but nothing happened for a few seconds, then the truck would lurch to the right. Now I "had my hands full" as I had to quickly anticipate which direction the truck was going to lurch, and quickly turn the steering wheel in the opposite direction. The air-compressor on back started lurching sideways. This went on for several minutes. I can sort of picture what it must have looked like to the vehicles driving UP that mountain road: every one of them pulled totally off of the highway and onto the berm. That was a little comfort to me, figuring I was not going to crash into any one of them.*

The lurching and steering wheel turning kept up until I finally came onto flat road at the bottom. I then was able to guide the truck and air-compressor over to the side of the road and stop, and I probably exhaled a few "Whew!!s" and then I started shaking—what the hell just happened? Will at this point was not behind me! A few minutes later he did drive up. He said, "I just had to pull off the road and stop. I could not watch what was happening to you, the truck, and the air-compressor. I was sure the air-compressor would flip the truck and you were going off the side of the mountain!" "My God! You made it down safely!"

We climbed under the truck to analyze what had happened: in this 1953 truck, there were "Leaf-springs" in the front AND the front axle was attached to the "Leaf-Springs." And one end of the leaf springs had broken loose from the body of the truck! Therefore, the axel was freewheeling as I was turning the steering wheel.

I really would never want to have that experience again! However, I learned a personal lesson: I stay in control as the crisis is happening, I ride it out, and do not panic UNTIL I am stopped safely at the bottom. I have used this modus operandi several times in my life—to good advantage.

As this first score of years came to a close, I stayed in Cincinnati for a Year and a half before returning to California. I worked for Western Waterproofing by day and attended University of Cincinnati's Evening College by night.

**It is now the autumn of my 20th year.**

+ + + + + + + +

*PATRIC IS SENT TO A "MENTAL ASSYLUM."*

● ● ● ● ● ● ● ● ● ● ● ● ● ● ● ● ● ● ● ● ● ●

It was in the autumn of 1960 that I volunteered for another American Friends Service Committee weekend project: this one was at the Dayton State and Receiving Hospital (Mental Asylum). For Friday evening's orientation we met with the hospital's Assistant Director. Quotes from the brochure:

### Who Are the Patients?

`They are people who need help in the problems of daily living.

They are distressed people, who feel lonely, who are unable to cope with their emotions, and who are unable to communicate effectively with others.

### Some Do's… *[Excerpts]*

Be yourself. While you are fulfilling a role at the hospital, you are important to the patient as a **PERSON.**

Be sincere. Be warm and understanding. Patients are rebuilding their faith in people and things, and they build best when they can **believe in you.**

Be a friendly listener. Even when a patient asks for your advice, more than likely he is really asking for your belief in him.

### … and Some Don'ts *[Excerpts]*

Don't ask personal questions of the patient. This includes events leading up to his hospitalization, and even his name if he doesn't *want to tell you.*

*`Don't make telephone calls or mail letters for patients...*

*Don't talk about patients away from the hospital. You are as much bound by professional ethics as anyone on the staff...*

*Don't operate on preconceived notions of mental illness. Don't be afraid. Don't talk about "bad wards." There aren't any. True, people at the hospital sometimes have bad days, as people everywhere do...*

The Assistant Director had one more suggestion:

I encourage you, sometimes, just to sit down next to a patient for a while, even if the patient does not speak to you. Some patients are essentially nonverbal. However, recently there was an event with one such patient. When the volunteer who was sitting beside him left and went home, the patient suddenly spoke up FOR THE FIRST TIME IN MANY WEEKS and said, "**When is he coming back?**"

My experience. I was placed on what was described as "the most violent ward." However, when I arrived, I discovered that almost everyone was on medication such as *Thorazine.* Which is some kind of tranquilizer. So, in two days I never saw anyone acting violent. I did see many of the patients with "brown nicotine stained" fingers due to chain smoking. I did see some patients that had a need to keep moving in an intentional pattern. I did spend some time sitting next to silent patients (that was definitely a learning experience of how that can be meaningful to the patient.) I did have an extended discussion with a patient in his late teens or early twenties. He claimed to have gone to the same military school I did. I did enjoy speaking with him. However, the next day when I went back and connected with him, *we had the exact same conversation word for word!*

Now it is time for a bit of humor. I was walking around the ward observing the activities. I saw four patients sitting at a table playing cards. I walked over. I could see that they were only utilizing the ten, Jack, Queen, King, and Ace. I concluded, "They were not playing with a full deck!"

Imagine my amazement several years later when I observed another group on the outside playing the same game! I said, "Oh, why are you playing the same game they do in the mental hospitals?" They looked up at me quizzically and said: "We are not. We are playing **EUCRE!**" " Oh!"

On Sunday afternoon, we again met with the Assistant Director. He was interested in our observations from our experiences over the weekend. At one point a few of our participants spoke up and said, "We are watching some of the patients off and on over a long time. They did not seem to have any illness. Why are they here?" Then our host responded, "You are correct—many of our "patients" do ***not have any mental illness; they are just old; nobody wants them, and so they have been dumped here!***"

**AND MAYBE WE NEED SOME EDUCATION ON PARENT CARE AND YES, I BECAME AWARE OF THIS ESSAY WHEN I WAS WORKING WITH THE QUAKERS**

**HERE ARE SOME EXCERPTS:**

## OVER THE HILL TO THE POOR-HOUSE
### BY WILL CARLETON (1845-1912)

• • • • • • • • • • • • • • • • • • • • • •

### 1

Over the hill to the poor-house I'm trudgin' my weary way—
I, a woman of seventy, and only a trifle gray—
I, who am smart an' chipper, for all the years I've told,
As many another woman that's only half as old.

### 2

Over the hill to the poor-house —
I can't quite make it clear! Over the hill to the
poor-house — it seems so horrid queer!
Many a step I've taken, a-toilin' to and fro,
But this is a sort of journey I never thought to go.

### 3

What is the use of heapin' on me a pauper's shame?
Am I lazy or crazy? am I blind or lame?
True, I am not so supple, nor yet so awful stout;
But charity ain't no favor, if one can live without.

### 5

Once I was young an' hand'some—I was, upon my soul—
Once my cheeks was roses, my eyes was black as coal;
And I can't remember, in them days, of hearin' people say,
For any kind of a reason, that I was in their way!

### 7

And when to John I was married, sure he was good and smart,
But he and all the neighbors would own I done my part;
For life was all before me, an' I was young an' strong,
And I worked my best an' smartest in tryin' to get along.

### 10

Strange how much we think of OUR blessed little ones!—
I'd have died for my daughters, and I'd have died for my sons.
And God He made that rule of love; but when we're old and gray
I've noticed it sometimes, somehow, fails to work the other way.

### 13

She was somewhat dressy, an' hadn't a pleasant smile—
She was quite conceity, and carried a heap o' style;
But if ever I tried to be friends, I did with her, I know;
But she was hard and haughty, an' we couldn't make it go.

### 16

An' I never could speak to suit her, never could please her eye,
An' it made me independent, an' then I didn't try.
But I was terribly humbled, an' felt it like a blow,
When Charley turned agin me, an' told me I could go!

### 19

An' then I wrote to Rebecca, my girl who lives out West,
And to Isaac, not far from her — some twenty miles at best;
And one of 'em said 'twas too warm there for anyone so old,

And t'other had an opinion the climate was too cold.

### 20

So they have shirked and slighted me, an' shifted me about—
So they have well-nigh soured me, an' wore my old heart out;
But still I've borne up pretty well, an' wasn't much put down,
Till Charley went to the poor-master, an' put me on the town!

### 21

Over the hill to the poor-house—my child'rn dear, good-bye!
Many a night I've watched you when only God was nigh;
And God'll judge between us; but I will al'ays pray
That you shall never suffer the half that I do to-day!

**How to Cite this Article (APA Format):** Carelton, W. (1872). "Over the Hill To The Poor-House." Retrieved **[date accessed]** from https://socialwelfare.library.vcu.edu/issues/hill-poor-house/.

# CONTENTS

**Part Two: Dr. Patric Leedom's Autobiography
NOVEMBER 17—OCTOBER 26, 2022**

# PART TWO

## Dr. Patric Leedom's Autobiography

### NOVEMBER 17—OCTOBER 26, 2022

SCORE TWO FIRST HALF OF YEARS: Age 20 thru 30 Years

*THE AT&T DEFENSE COMMUNICATION PROJECT*

• • • • • • • • • • • • • • • • • • • • • •

In 1959, during the Cold War with the Soviet Union where both countries engaged in missile building races, submarine building races, and aircraft building races especially nuclear bombers, the U.S. Government became quite concerned about the security of our telephone line communications. At that time, all of the phone lines—which were above ground on poles in the air-- going east and west across the Mississippi River ALL WENT THROUGH SAINT LOUIS much like a giant butterfly with body in St. Louis, and one large wing going east, and one large wing going west. So, the Government and A T & T [I believe that stands for **AMERICAN TELEPHONE AND TELEGRAPH CO.**] Which at that time was the telephone company for the whole country—no competition--signed a 17-year contract to "spider-web" the whole contiguous country, running coaxial cable through all 48 states. The cable was about three inches in diameter.

Out in the country, especially working on the A T & T Project where Booster Stations were four air miles apart—but we often drove the truck 12 to 20 road miles to get there, sometimes the hole was up on the side of a mountain with an absolutely single dirt road leading to and from the site. So, I had two choices: drive straight up the road with my air-compressor on back, and then at the end of the work day, back down the road with the air-compressor "leading the way" down, or, in the morning, I could back up the dirt road with the air-compressor "leading the way." And the air-compressor had no way of steering by itself. Tricky. The old 1953 Chevrolet truck had a "Throttle" which one could use as an accelerator. So, believe it or not, I would pull the throttle open enough to gain "creeping speed," open the driver's door, stand up ON THE DRIVER'S SEAT AND LOOK BACK OVER THE TRUCK where I could see the air-compressor, and I would use my left foot to slowly turn the steering wheel as I needed, to keep the air-compressor going backwards on up the road! After several days of this, I got to be proficient. ***This was definitely an "I BELIEVE I CAN" "I DID IT." "I BELIEVED I COULD" MOMENT!***

A T & T's scheme was this: The cable was to be buried four feet under the soil—across many private farms, forests, and rural or small-town property. Every four air miles there was to be 'POWER BOOSTER" station, buried in the ground with only a small innocent-looking concrete block house sitting on top. Then every forty air miles, there was to be a very large three-story building to be almost totally built underground for monitoring and maintenance purposes on the coaxial cable. I started working on this project when I was 20, but I really got more involved when I was 21.

## *PATRIC BECAME A LABOR FOREMAN AT AGE 21*

● ● ● ● ● ● ● ● ● ● ● ● ● ● ● ● ● ● ● ● ● ● ●

I mention the term "air-miles" between stations—this refers to as drawn on a topographical map. However, mountain roads do not follow the air map. It literally can take 20 to 30 road miles to reach the next sub-station. This led to a very uncomfortable situation. We, Western Waterproofing Co., were the sub-contractors and were dependent upon the general contractor to inform us which of his Booster station sites were ready for us to come do the sand-blasting and waterproofing. We all stayed at the same motel. I asked the General Contractor every morning to give me a list of sites ready for us. He would. However, I would take my truck, the air compressor, and my crew and we would drive to the closest site that was ready.

However, quite often, the General Contractor "mis-spoke" and that booster station was NOT READY for us. So, we drove 20 more miles or so, to the next booster station. Sometimes it was NOT READY either. So, we drove many more miles to the third booster station, and it was ready, and so we went right to work. This scenario happened about twice a week. Our boss, Mr. Stone came up to see how we were progressing. Once he found out how much driving and "wasted time" we were accruing, he got very angry saying things like, "I am not paying you to drive around these mountains all day!" It is the closest time in my life to **developing an ulcer!** I was being criticized for something totally beyond my control. I certainly could not say to the General Contractor, "you have lied to us!" or questioned him in some such fashion.

I was busy working on the A T & T Defense Communication Cable Project. Actually, I was a "Labor Foreman" with my own crew when I was 21 years old!! I could hire and discharge workers as I needed them. Bob W. was my laborer from Cincinnati. At one point in Clarksburg,

West Virginia, I lived with Bob, his wife and son in an apartment. I remember arriving back at the apartment at the end of a heavy work day. I was totally exhausted. I just walked in the door, lay down on the couch and went right to sleep! I think his wife did wake me up when she put supper on the table.

Two stories involving Bob. We were working down inside one of the booster stations. We had to first sandblast the fresh concrete, remove the grease left on the concrete from the wooden pouring forms, and then cut a cove joining the walls with floor, putting waterproofing Ironite cement mixture in to the cove. It was daytime; I came up out of the hole to retrieve something from the truck. There must have been eight or more bulls lined up around the hole staring at what we were doing. Bulls! Aren't they dangerous? Bob was "an old country boy" so I called him up to help me. He came up the ladder, took one look, and simply walked out on the walk-board (from our hole back to solid ground) and said, "SHOO!" and all the bulls ran away! "Hmmm, so that is how you do it! How would I know that?"

A second story, this time it was nighttime. We had a gasoline generator operating to provide electric lights so we could see to work down in the hole. [The hole was the concrete room maybe 8 feet by 12 feet where eventually the electrical booster equipment would be placed. There were tube-like openings in the front wall and in the back wall such that the coaxial cable would arrive from the west's last booster station four miles distant, be fed in from one side, receive a boost in power from the equipment, then be fed back out to continue its journey east four miles to the next booster station.

Well, all of a sudden, the lights went out. The generator had run out of gasoline. I sent Bob up to refill the generator. After a number of minutes Bob called me up to help him. It was a dark night. We did not have any flashlights. Bob had been trying to fill the generator in the dark, where he could not see well. So, I struck a match, so he could see what he was doing. When my match burned down to the end, I threw it back over my shoulder. "KAWHOOM" All the ground where we were standing exploded into flame! Bob had accidentally poured gasoline ALL OVER THE GROUND! Everything was on fire including the generator. Fortunately, there was a big pile of sand and two shovels right next to us. So, Bob and I hurriedly shoveled sand all over the generator to put it out, and next shoveled sand on the ground that was on fire. Wow. Now the fire was out. The generator was ruined. There was nothing for Bob and me to do but get into the truck and drive back to our motel for the night.

The next day, we picked up the generator and took it to a repair shop. We lost a day of work time while they fixed it. The company lost money because we were not accomplishing any work.

## A SAD PARTING FROM WESTERN WATERPROOFING

• • • • • • • • • • • • • • • • • • • • • •

I worked for Western Waterproofing until late summer. There was a crew of us working up in Maryland. Somehow the conversation got started about our pay. We were not given any extra money for hotels or meals. The men started comparing notes and came to the conclusion, that once we paid all of our out-of-town bills, there was hardly any money left to send to our families back home. The men then decided to walk off the job, get in the car and drive back to Cincinnati to complain to Mr. Stone, who now owned the company. They strongly urged me to join them, because I was also treated as badly as they were. So, I did join them. When we arrived, Mr. Stone refused to offer us anymore money. The men, along with me, we went to the Union Hall and complained. The Union Boss called Mr. Stone and threatened to shut down every Western Waterproofing job in town unless he paid us.

Mr. Stone finally did, BUT we were all out of a job. And that ended my "Father-son relationship" with Mr. Stone. My mother was shocked at Mr. Stone's poor treatment of me. Looking back, Mr. Stone was taking advantage of us, for his own benefit. I was never sorry I left.

I want to turn now to a different narrative. I was living in Cincinnati, working for Western Waterproofing Co. when I turned 21. Matt Long, while no longer dating Mom, still loved me, and wanted to be the first person to buy me my first "legal drink." He took me and Mom, up to the Dayton Supper Club for dinner and a floor show. Dorothy Lamour, of the Bob Hope, Bing Crosby "Road" movies (e.g. "Roads to Mandalay") fame was the main entertainer. She was dressed in her famous sarong dress. And sang some of her famous songs. Thank YOU, Matt.

## PATRIC'S DEVELOPING LIFE'S PHILOSOPHY OF MANHOOD

• • • • • • • • • • • • • • • • • • • • • • •

In our culture, when one turns 21 years old, that is considered entering adulthood. So, I want to take some time to explore this concept because it is a significant building block in my confidence and attitude that *I BELIEVE I CAN.*

What, EXACTLY does ADULTHOOD mean? What are the roles and responsibilities? Well, on the face of it, I have just asked an ignorant question...

- Think about the 8,000,000,000 plus human beings that inhabit our planet.
- Think about the 180 countries that claim territory in 2020.
- Think about the even far more numerous cultures that exist in those countries.

- Think about the socialization processes used to "Inform" the young human beings into that culture's version of adulthood.

Now I need to rephrase my question. Born and raised in a variety of cultures in the United States, all within the classification of "Middle Class," how have I developed and grown into the adult male that I am?

During each phase of growing and experiencing caregivers, one is surrounded by philosophy. Even the language one is taught to speak contains a very specific philosophy about how the outer world is organized. English, for example, is very NOUN or THING oriented. Some other languages are VERB or ACTION oriented.

When we discuss how children are raised to become functioning adults in that particular culture, and if we want to **UNDERSTAND** what that process is, we can not avoid a discussion of that culture's philosophy. [And this becomes an ABSTRACT quest rather than a CONCRETE quest.]

A short hand definition of philosophy is "A Philosophy of life is—a philosophical view or vision of the nature or purpose of life, or the way life **SHOULD** be lived.

One dictionary definition of philosophy is: the **RATIONAL** investigation of the **TRUTHS** and principles of being. [So now we have three abstract terms to guide us…]

Returning now to my quest: How have I developed or grown into the man I am? If I had spent my entire existence encapsulated in one narrowly focused culture, I could easily respond to the question. But I have been exposed to and often participated in a variety of cultures. For a quick example, my mother was an "Eisenhower-Taft Country Club

Republican" [Back in the 1940's, 1950's, and 1960's when Republicans were comparatively much more moderate and fiscally conservative in their political views.]

My father was a Liberal Social Democrat [Back in the 1940's, 1950's, and 1960's when Liberal was a co-equal term with Conservative, and Social meant concerned with the political needs of the Common Man (Person.) Having lived quite closely with each of my parents, I have adopted strong segments from each of them.

Now that I have begun this discussion, now is the time to ask: **What is REALITY?"** I do not remember when I first became fascinated with this question. I do remember I was around ten or eleven when I began mulling over "What is the meaning of life?" and "Is there a heaven and a hell?" When I began living with my father, who often thought and spoke philosophically, and some of our church services discussed historical philosophies, is probably when I took up the challenge. At age 16-17 I do remember engaging some of my LRY friends in discussions of reality.

## PATRIC ENROLLS IN UNIVERSITY OF CINCINNATI EVENING COLLEGE

● ● ● ● ● ● ● ● ● ● ● ● ● ● ● ● ● ● ● ● ●

In the Autumn of 1958 when I entered the University of Cincinnati Evening College, one of the first courses I enrolled in was Philosophy 101. And in that course, I was introduced to what I view as a powerful metaphor that I have alluded to all my life.

## PLATO'S ALLEGORY OF THE CAVE

●●●●●●●●●●●●●●●●●●●●●●●

Plato's Cave serves many philosophical purposes. Perhaps one of the most useful is to illustrate man's relationship to Reality. As a big picture start:

1. Reality is happening along the road which parallels the mouth of the large cave.
2. Inside the cave are people who have always lived inside the cave and have never been allowed to observe outside.
3. There is a wall maybe five to six feet tall built Athwart ships or completely across the cave floor but parallel to the road outside.
4. The "Cave People" are sitting inside the cave, butts flat on the floor, chained to the wall such that none can get free and stand up in order to look over the wall toward the outside.
5. Outside, vehicles and people are traveling along the road which is directly outside of the mouth of the cave; the people are talking, laughing, conducting business or whatever.
6. These people's voices coming from on the road and other noises are echoed into the cave and appear to sound like they are coming from the back wall of the cave.
7. A large fire is built on the opposite side of the road, but directly in front of the cave.
8. The fire thus causes shadows to be projected on to the back wall.
9. The people chained to the floor have never viewed the actual objects, so they truly believe that what they are observing with movement and sounds of the shadows on the back wall of the cave ARE THE TRUE REALITY!

10. It isn't until one day, one of the persons manages to break free, goes over the wall and out into the road.

That person, after their eyes become adjusted to the bright light, observes, and comes to realize that reality is really outside of the cave, and not the shadows on the back wall.

[From here the Allegory of the Cave Story has several endings as to what happened when the free person goes back into the Cave to share the news that reality is outside. Some endings have the people killing the messenger because they cannot cope with having their "original conception of reality" challenged or disproved. That can be very threatening to one's whole belief system.]

One does not need to go far to encounter persons whose versions of reality resemble the shadows on the wall; and they become intensely upset if one suggests that they are mistaken.

I believe I should start with Plato's Allegory of the Cave. Since, in my mind, I do carry a strand of philosophical thinking. And I found Plato Allegory highly enlightening. I think one lesson is: people tend to believe REALITY is what they think they are observing i.e., shadows on the wall when the existent reality is something far different. And in my mind, "the wall" can be metaphorical for belief systems, whether they be religious, political, economic etc. If a person mentally "locks on" to certain concepts—be they true or not, then those concepts become their "wall." I am thinking too, of isolated tribes down through historical and pre-historical times when the tribe held to a certain set of beliefs, and all members of the tribe were expected to accept those beliefs as "the truth" or "the way things are." And there was no room for questioning. The person who did was somehow removed from the tribe either by shunning, exile, or death.

Now, it is important to note that not all persons "hold their beliefs" in the same way. Some persons appear to have a very powerful need to "lock down" or be "absolutely certain" that some things are true for all times. I believe this is a good place to insert Sam Keen's quote from his book Fire in the Belly P. 126. "Most people remain relatively unconscious, unaware of the forces that shape their lives." I believe this concept is related to people who are discouraged from ever questioning philosophical beliefs. I am aware also, that in society there are social groups who have rigid requirements if one wants to be accepted as a member of that group. I can envision members always being careful to utter thoughts and ideas that are congruent with that particular group's orientation to life.

**In a book of philosophy, and in the section on INTEGRITY Comes another of my over-arching life's philosophies:**

### *IT MATTERS WHAT WE BELIEVE*

• • • • • • • • • • • • • • • • • • • •

Some beliefs are like walled gardens.
They encourage exclusiveness, and the
feeling of being especially privileged.

> *Other beliefs are expansive and*
> *Lead the way into wider*
> *Deeper sympathies.*

Some beliefs are like shadows,
Clouding children's days with fears
Of unknown calamities

> *Other beliefs are like sunshine*

*Blessing children with the Warmth of happiness.*

Some beliefs are divisive, separating
The saved from the unsaved, friends
From enemies.

*Other beliefs are bonds in a*
*World community, where sincere*
*Differences beautify the pattern.*

Some beliefs are like blinders, shutting
Off the power to choose one's
Own direction.

*Other beliefs are like gateways*
*Opening wide vistas for*
*exploration.*

Some beliefs weaken a person's self-hood.
They blight the growth of resourcefulness.

*Other beliefs nurture self-confidence*
*And enrich the feeling of personal*
*Worth.*

Some beliefs are rigid, like the body
Of death, impotent in a changing world.

*Other beliefs are pliable, like the young sapling, ever*
*growing with the upward Thrust of life.*

**By Sophia Lyon Fahs**

This particular offering of philosophy has especial meaning to me. In March of 1959, when I was delivering a Youth Sermon in my church, Sophia Lyon Fahs, famous for authoring a children's curriculum for our denominations, was delivering the sermon at another of our churches across town. She was my competition!

In the 1980's I was visiting an elderly cousin in a Nursing Home in Hamilton Ohio. The subject of religion came up, Georgiana Harr asked me what religion I was. I told her, and she said, "Oh, one of your minister's lives here by the name of Sophia Lyon Fahs!" I thought to myself "Yeah, right! How likely is that?" So, when I finished visiting with my cousin, I went to the Nurses' Station and inquired. "Yes, she is here, she is 100 years old, she lives right across the hall, knock on her (open) door and go in!"

So, I did, and it was Sophia Lyon Fahs! We had a good time laughing over our "competition" back in 1959! She may be 100 years old, but her mind was sharp as a tack. She was living in Hamilton because her son was a professor at Miami University just up the road in Oxford. What an honor I had getting to spend time with her!

Now focusing back on her philosophy, as you read about my employment adventures, you might realize that I could not have been successful if I didn't have and utilized those "***Other beliefs…***" that allowed me to shift and reframe my understandings of what was required of me such as being a construction worker, a labor foreman, Business Manager of a small private Montessori School, a Kindergarten-First Grade teacher in a public Montessori School, a substitute Command Master Chief of the submarine Admiral's Operational Control Center, an Assistant Navigator guiding our submarine up into the Arctic Ocean, a doctoral student in the Department of Curriculum and Instruction, the creator of the Academic Student Advising Center for the entire College of Education, playing "Vana White" in a Fernald Nuclear

Plant helping Project Engineers catch up with the latest government requirements, a developer of curriculum for the workers in the United States Shoe Corporation, a professor of Teacher education, an employee of the Ohio Department of Education etc., etc.

Many of these jobs and responsibilities fit within *I BELIEVE I CAN,* when I had never done any of these tasks before.

## SAM KEEN IN HIS BOOK FIRE IN THE BELLY ALSO ADDRESSES THE VIRTUE OF COMMUNION

• • • • • • • • • • • • • • • • • • • • • •

That leads me to remember that I am bi-cultural: my mother was a "conservative Eisenhower-Taft Country Club Republican." Which implicated she held to a certain set of political, economic, social beliefs. My father was a "liberal social Democrat and defender of the common person" which again implicated that he held to a certain set of political, economic, and social beliefs." And I had the philosophical advantage of learning from both of them.

Page 175-176. The superficial answer is that we don't do anything except talk about the things that matter the most to us and listen to each other. We laugh a lot. We challenge each other. But a more profound answer is that almost by accident we discovered the missing ingredient that is as necessary to the health of the male psyche as Vitamin C is to the health of the body—the virtue of ***community.*** Medicine. What I found was that men in our culture share a common experience of growing up male and as a result I no longer feel alone in my struggle.

P. 176 Within the community of men, I have learned that men's loneliness is a measurement of the degree to which we have ignored the fundamental truth of interdependence. In devoting ourselves to getting, spending, and being entertained, we simply forget that we inevitably feel alienated when we do not live within a circle of friends, within the arms of the family, within the conversation of a community.

## *SEEDS OF "I BELIEVE I CAN."*

● ● ● ● ● ● ● ● ● ● ● ● ● ● ● ● ● ● ● ● ● ● ●

Step 1. Here is one well-known theory of 'Identity Development'. We construct the concept of our SELF: Structural Symbolic Interactionism by Sheldon Stryker. As humans, we develop a sense of who we are by the ways others treat us, speak to us, interact with us, think of us, respond to us. Not to get too far into academics, our care givers by natural processes instill certain values, beliefs systems, orientations toward our environments. So, who our care givers are, our immediate families, our community are very important because they influence the development of our self and identity.

So, it is important to know something about where did we come from. What messages were transmitted to us? What expectations did they have of us? And so on. So, I spend some time describing my "tribes."

Returning to the question of "How did I become the man I am?" I am thinking of a multitude of role models who informed my manhood.

## *ROLE MODELS IN MY LIFE*

● ● ● ● ● ● ● ● ● ● ● ● ● ● ● ● ● ● ● ● ● ●

I am thinking of a multitude of role models.

1.  My grandfather, George Robert Shelhouse, how he looked, acted, and treated me. And was known as a very KIND

person. (I was encouraged to "be like my grandfather—very kind.)

2. My mother's boyfriends such as Matt Long. College-Educated, Debonair; Masterful, and Congenial. They demonstrated roles of masculinity and caring.

3. Going to OMI and observing the men who worked with us and taught us.

4. Pete Derrick in particular was a strong person, definite clear values; forceful in carrying out his responsibilities. At the same time very sensitive, caring, compassionate. He stayed my mentor until the day he died.

5. Byron Dann, my surrogate "grandfather." Who gave me new ways to think and took me "under his wing." I even had a key to his apartment for me to stay when I came in from Scioto County.

Role models. Certainly, my father was a strong one. He was pleasant-looking, attractive, well-dressed (on purpose as a newspaper writer to command respect). I worked with a number of ministers through the LRY Youth Group, and I must say that I was well treated, and respected, as I respected them. The focus was on mental, spiritual, and theological strength. Those were the qualities I focused upon. I remember distinctly having many "arguments" (Greek-type) and discussions on "What is REALITY?" That was a theme of mine for years until I arrived at the understanding, that there were at least three forms of reality. 1) What one personally perceives to be real (related to one's belief system). 2) Social Reality—that is, what a "group" espouses to be real; and I learned in sociology that groups can formally put forth a belief system, when in fact, no single member actually believes it anymore. And 3) What is in fact existent in the universe whether human beings can perceive it or not.

Thinking back, I do not remember any instance of anyone not

accepting and treating me as a male. I don't remember ever having to "prove" my masculinity. What I remember is that I was "soft" in terms of being sensitive, empathetic, caring, and thoughtful, and a good listener. Other teens did tell me their problems. Many of my letters that I still possess from the 1950's comment on how "understanding" I was. I am also remembering that it was not often that I felt need to "COMPETE" with anyone.

And now my mind remembers the years when I was socializing with my African American friends in South Central LA. I was 16 to 17 years old. All of them were older—19, 20, and 22. I was always cared about, respected, and included. Not once did I never hear anyone refer to me as "white."

My need for a regular, structured, organized schedule for the day what was what I needed to feel more secure and thrive. And that has remained true for the rest of my life. Probably a big part of why I did so well in the U.S. Navy and stayed for 24 years.

### *HERE I HAVE INSERTED MY DISCUSSION OF MANHOOD AS I INTERPRET IT*

• • • • • • • • • • • • • • • • • • • • •

Above I have listed a number of philosophical concepts from which I will utilize in building my vision of my manhood.

"We don't work just to make a living. Increasingly, the world of work provides the meaning of our lives." (Sam Keen, Page 55)

It is certainly true that in my youth I engaged in several jobs because I needed the money to live on. But over time, and with a lot of commitment and perseverance, I was able, with the help of college degrees, to create a career for myself which allowed for passion and inspiration, and did exercise many of my natural inclinations, talents, skills, desires, whatever which resulted in my becoming a teacher, first of elementary grades, and then with a doctorate, a college professor of Teacher Candidates. And truly, since taking my first step into my classroom in Children's House Montessori—where I first taught a Kindergarten-First Grade Combination—I have never ever regretted my choices. I have never had a day when I wished I was somewhere else or doing something else. My career of working closely with students of whatever age has been the primary meaning of my life.

P. 154. Modern manhood is a work in progress. It's too soon to see who we are becoming. We can catch glimpses of a prodigal man who has taken a journey into the depths of the self and a new heroic life, and how he might act on his return to this familiar and strange world.

Aha! It pays to be a "Pack Rat." I found among my college papers, one that I wrote for a course at University of Cincinnati titled *SELF-CONCEPT AND ACHIEVEMENT,* 11 February 1986. "…I found only two articles that related directly to the area of my *SELF-INVESTMENT.* The first is Kenneth Gergen's *SELF-CONCEPTION AND PERSONAL ASPIRATIONS:*

"We have already seen that aspirations may bias self-conception. Wanting to be something can influence one to see himself as he wishes to be. Yet, one's conception of self can also affect his aspirations—what he chooses to do and how much effort he expends doing it. The primary reason is that people aspire to do that which will yield success and shun activities which may lead to failure. Self-conception is central to this process in two ways.

"The first is implicit in our earlier discussions of esteem needs. 'Success' in the above formulation usually involves gaining social approval, either real or implied, and thus feeling enhanced esteem for self....

"Second, in order to gauge the probability of succeeding at a given activity we must have some idea of our own capacities. Whether we play bridge with experts depends on how we appraise our sophistication at the game, and whether we choose to attend college depends in part on how we estimate our mental capacities. Our aspirations thus depend on our estimates of self."

I am reminded of Dr. Sheldon Stryker's theory of how one develops a **sense of self**: "Structural Symbolic Interactionism." ** There are two main themes in this theory:

1.  *We gain a sense of "who we are—or our sense of SELF depending upon how the significant others in our lives treat us and speak to us.*
2.  *The second theme is to what groups does one aspire to become a member? Then one observes carefully and imitates: How do they walk (gait)? How do they greet each other? how do they dress? And How do they engage in conversations?*

3.  **Think of Dorothy Law Nolte's Poem 'Children Learn what they live."**

### CHILDREN LEARN WHAT THEY LIVE
### BY DOROTHY LAW NOLTE

• • • • • • • • • • • • • • • • • • • • • •

If children live with criticism,
They learn to condemn.
If children live with hostility,
They learn to fight.
If children live with ridicule
They learn to be shy.
If children live with shame,
They learn to feel guilty.
If children live with tolerance,
They learn to be patient
If children live with encouragement,
They learn confidence.
If children live with praise,
They learn to appreciate.
If children live with fairness,
They learn justice.
If children live with security
They learn to have faith.
If children live with approval,
They learn to like themselves
If children live with friendship,
They learn to find love in the world.

Some person took this poem and expanded "Children" to read "a person." The rest is identical except for the very last PRECEPT:

"If a person lives with acceptance and friendship
He (they) learn there is love in the world and learns to give love in return."

[Digression] Reflective commentary. I have been aware of the implications of this poem starting in my twenties. Coupled with that I became a Montessori Teacher with the philosophy that we always try to phrase "Re-directing (correction) a student's unacceptable behavior in positive terms. Example: student is running around in the crowded environment of the classroom. Teacher says, "Ronnie, running is for outside; walking is for inside."

I carried this same philosophical strategy when I have taught college students. I tried very consciously to phrase things in a positive way. For example, I am grading a student's paper and it is not the quality I expected and had demonstrated. So, I write on the second or third page: "I am ceasing to grade this paper because it does not resemble the exemplar I placed in your hands (for a brief ten minutes or so.) Would you like me to show you the exemplar again, and would you like to rewrite your paper again?" That is all I ever communicate to the student. It is then up to the student to choose.

In 25 years of college teaching, the worst thing I ever said—to two immature young men was, "Go home and Grow UP!" Would you believe that a year or two later one of those students came back to me and said, "Now I understand what you meant by that comment." [End digression]

Reflective commentary. I am remembering it was not until I was eleven years old and enrolled in Ohio Military Institute and had received my first report card showing I was "Second in Class Rank." That was the very moment I realized I was capable of being a smart student, and then I aspired to be First. As I have written elsewhere "I poured on the coal, and by the third grading period I was FIRST in Rank, and with intentional effort, I stayed First for the rest of my three years.

I am remembering when I joined the church youth group, LRY,

and began receiving strong validation and affirmation from fellow members, that I felt inspired to move toward leadership. As a junior in high school, I was voted to become the Vice-President of the Federation which led the following year to my conceiving of connecting with all the LRY groups in Arizona, New Mexico, and El Paso, Texas. I wrote to every group and suggested a conference to get us all together. (This led to the formation of the Desert Federation, April 1958).

After a wonderful experience in the one-week LRY summer youth camp in June 1955, I immediately joined the Planning Council for future camps, and by the autumn of my senior year, I was elected Chairman of the Planning Council, and I devoted hundreds of hours and miles of travel to the churches in the Los Angeles area to plan the best camp ever. From this, my self-conception included a *form of power—the ability to accomplish responsibilities for the benefit of others.*

I am remembering my strong commitment to obtaining a bachelor's degree from college. There was no extra money in our families. I did not clearly understand what scholarships were, so I never applied for any. I literally worked myself through college. Over the six and a half years, I attended five colleges and universities. But I stuck with it—starving sometimes with very little money for food.

I am remembering that when I joined the U.S. Navy Submarine Reserves, and came to understand the promotion system, I once again, "poured on the coal" and made sure I was prepared to compete for the next higher rate. I was promoted to E7 Chief Quartermaster in 7 ½ years. It helped tremendously when I was invited on to the staff of the Commander, Submarine Force, U.S. Atlantic Fleet. I was honored and thrilled to be working "at the top." My personal commitment was to never be idle. If there was not enough work at the front desk, I went around to see who else needed my help. I was rewarded both by being kept on the staff for eleven years, and by obtaining excellent evaluations so I was promoted to Senior Chief in 1975 and Master Chief in 1978—fifteen years after I had enlisted!

+ + + + + + + + + + +

I am remembering in 1970 when I began volunteering with the brand new alternative New School. I had just come from eight years in San Francisco during the Flower Child, Hippie era where there was impetus to try and make our country and society a better place. And schooling was a segment that needed improvement. I readily bought into the New School's philosophies—Montessori in the Pre-school Kindergarten down stairs, and an alternative "Summer Hill" type upstairs.

I volunteered part of the year during the school's first year. And after my divorce from my second immature wife, Shelley, I began volunteering full time. Toward the end of the school's second year, a "Blue Ribbon Panel" of parents created a Personnel Committee to put a firmer, more successful staff structure in place. From this event, I was asked to become the Administrator-Business Manager, (along with Building Manager, the Answering Service for the Cincinnati Montessori Society, Public Relations both with incoming families and city inspecting officials.)

At the same time, I recognized that the Montessori philosophy and practices were a winning combination, so I enrolled in Xavier University's Montessori Teacher Education Program (Graduating in May 1976.)

In 1975 I was asked to be the President of the Board of Trustees of the Cincinnati Montessori Society.

I remember when I was working on my doctorate, I was asked by my Curriculum and Instruction Department to become an Academic

Advisor for persons who had a bachelor's degree not in teaching, and what would they need to obtain one. By my records, I met with 1200 persons. At the end of the year, The Dean of the College of Education invited me into his office and said, "Patric, I hear that you are very good at Academic Advising. We have dreamed for years of creating an Academic Advising Center for the whole college. Would you do that for us, and we will hire four people to work for you?" "Yes, sure, I can do that." And so, I did. I was able to visualize how I would go about it. I was able to visualize Self-Investment.

Okay, okay. Enough of the philosophical "Rabbit Hole." Except, in terms of **"I BELIEVE I CAN"** there are one's beliefs about the reality of the "I". Who am "I"? What beliefs and dispositions must I have before I proclaim, 'I BELIEVE I can'?

## LESSON I INHERITED FROM "MY TRIBE"

● ● ● ● ● ● ● ● ● ● ● ● ● ● ● ● ● ● ● ● ● ● ●

- What did I glean while living with my family members?
- Here is a beginning list of things I believe I inherited from my "tribe."
- The world is a safe place for me.
- I am wanted and celebrated in this world.
- Love and affection do come to me from my mother, my grandmother, my grandfather, my father, and other care givers.
- Basic Needs: Food, clothing, and shelter are provided:
  o Food security—there would always be a meal for me; I wasn't going to starve.
  o Clothing security—I always had adequate clothing whether in the summer time or winter time.
  o Shelter security. I always had warm, protected place to

live, bathe, and sleep. Safety security. I was protected from harmful threats:

- A sense of place—where did I come from, from whom did I come.
- I had a sense of family history going back several generations.
- I learned the importance and excitement of learning; I was strongly encouraged.
- I learned that I had mobility and could walk or run over to the object of my curiosity.
- I learned a sense of wonder and curiosity. Truly, at the age of three and four, my grandparents used to drive me out into the country on Sundays just to see—trees, fields, flowers, streams, etc. and so I could see the cows, pigs, sheep, chickens, horses, barns, farms, and nature.
- And in my 20's I learned I can be comfortable and function well not only in the higher levels of society' but all levels of society.

+ + + + + +

Here is where I would like to share one of my sources: the concepts that author Sam Keen proposes in his book, ***FIRE IN THE BELLY.***

*SAM KEEN'S BEGINNING OF A*
*FRAMEWORK OF MANHOOD*

• • • • • • • • • • • • • • • • • • • • •

**SAM KEEN FIRE IN THE BELLY *FIRE IN THE BELLY: ON BEING A MAN* by Sam Keen Bantam Books 1991**

**BEGINNINGS OF A FRAMEWORK OF MANHOOD**

**While it is certainly true that a person's issues with manhood (womanhood) begin somewhere during one's teen years, for purposes of this** autobiography, I decided I would address these issues in my early twenties.

"Neither manhood nor womanhood is ever experienced in a social vacuum. Manhood is not an eternal essence that men acquire by their own doing, but A CULTURAL CONSTRUCT THAT KEEPS CHANGING. P. 84 We take our definitions and our assurance that we are men from a community, from the audience before whom we enact the drama of our lives. We see ourselves as others see us.

"Modern manhood is a work in progress. It's too soon to see who we are becoming. We can catch glimpses of an introspective man who has taken a journey into the depths of the self and a new heroic life, and how he might act on his return to this familiar and strange world. (p. 154)

Page 89. And definitions of virtue and manhood also evolve and change.

Virility involves life in communion; when we try to discover the principle of manhood within the isolated self, we will end up not fulfilling the self but destroying it. Manhood can be defined only in relational terms. How large and generous we may become depends on the size of the Other we take into ourselves. (P. 103)"

Okay, let us write about my development of "manhood."

"If the changing ideals of manhood have always been shaped by historical challenges, we must assume that modern manhood will also be defined by the problems and opportunities emerging today. Virility has always been measured by a man's willingness to hear and respond to the calling of his age." (Keen, 1991)."[End of Fire in the Belly.]

Because I was born Caucasian in the War Years, 1940, in the United States to parents from the Middle Class, and we lived primarily in urban areas, "the calling of my age" "Sounded very different than what some other male born into very different circumstances would hear."

Here is some of what I heard:

- Going into the Armed Forces was one of society's expectations.
- Being aware of your "social class" and always dress and act properly. One does not go to school wearing blue jeans and tennis shoes. One wears corduroy type slacks and leather shoes. Blue jeans are for play time, and tennis shoes are to be carried to school for the gym class. One spoke proper Standard English: "I do not have..." Instead of "I aint got..." "Please pass the biscuits..." instead of "Gimme some of them biscuits."
- I heard one needs to obtain a good education, including college, if one wants to have a worthwhile career and earn ample money. When I was born, my mother's father started a "College Savings Account" in the Seven Mile Bank. (It never held a lot of money, since Grandpa died when I was four, but the message was clear: I needed to do whatever, in order to obtain college degrees. This expectation was actually quite strong in my goals. Student scholarships, grants, loans, and other sources of funding were not plentiful. My family(s) did not have a lot of extra money, and I misunderstood how scholarships worked, so I never applied for one. I had grown up around older men who exclaimed, "No one ever helped me, I made it all on my

own!" I absorbed that attitude. Consequently, my college career is quite a "patchwork."

+ + + + + + + + +

In our philosophical (physiological) pause, my mind is nagging me to speak about "receptors." Usually, we think of receptors as specialized nerve endings to receive sight and sound and touch. I want to argue for mental and emotional receptors. As we grow and develop our brains are trained to become "selective" hearers, and selective see-ers. We need this capacity to make sense of all the possible stimuli coming at us from the outer world.

Returning to Sheldon Stryker's Sense of Self: And 2) The second theme is to what groups does one aspire to become a member? Then one observes carefully and imitates: How do they walk (gait)? How do they greet each other? How do they dress? How do they engage in conversations?

While I am not a psychologist, it has been my observation of people that when a child is raised **without a strong, stable, consistent input of healthy love—not only for the self, but for the other persons in their world,** when that child becomes an adult, they lack the ability to love others in a healthy, wholesome way. (No "gaminess', no manipulation, etc.)

Again, I am not a psychologist, or neurologist etc., but I would make a similar argument for the development of a rational, reasoning mind. Some parenting environments "teach" children, youth to "think" thoughts only in a narrow, absolute way, and don't make trouble. Other parenting environments "teach" their children, youth to explore thoughts, and entertain different viewpoints etc.

[Academic Digression] Dr. Melvin Kohn from Sociology is famous for his world-wide studies of Parent-child raising. If the parent works all of his/her life at a job where they are paid to use their hands and not their minds, to follow the rules and not make trouble, then they use an authoritarian form of child-raising—"do what you are told to, use your hands but not your mind, and don't make trouble." On the other hand, parents who are paid to use their minds for work, similarly raise their children to use their minds and do analytical thinking. This is from my doctoral studies. [End Digression.]

And what I have observed is that how a person displays outwardly their thoughts and feelings, the same is somewhat true inwardly toward that person's self.

The question can be, "To what are we open to receiving?" The Buddhist saying comes to mind: "When the student is ready, the master will appear."

## *PATRIC BECOMES A TRUCK DRIVER FOR THE UNITED PARCEL SERVICE (UPS)*

• • • • • • • • • • • • • • • • • • • • • • •

Having departed from Western Waterproofing in September of 1961, it was not very many weeks until I read in the newspaper Want Ads that **United Parcel Service** was looking for Christmas help to drive and deliver packages. I applied and was accepted. **What followed was another Game Changer:** UPS put me through one of the finest truck driving schools—far better than any ordinary car driving school, and I have attended eight of them! No, I was not a bad driver; but every time the US Navy offered a National Safety Council Driving Program, I volunteered to go—it was kind of like collecting stamps and coins. But I will state---none of the eight schools included the material that

UPS offered! United Parcel's major goal was to **NEVER have any of its trucks involved in an accident!** So therefore, the driver training was comprehensive, and focused on what the driver could do, by constantly "reading the traffic" and watching for potential problems. They taught us:

> Keep your eyes moving checking your mirrors and all around you such that you tried to keep "a doughnut of a safety zone" around the truck. Do not drive too close to any other vehicle.[When I took Driver's training in High School, the Rule of Thumb was to keep back one full car length for each ten mph of speed e.g., 40 miles an hour—you should be back four car lengths. Boy, almost no one follows that rule today; and consequently, Ohio has thousands of rear-end crashes every year. I know that often drivers become very impatient with me because I am "not right on top of the car in front of me."

> Do not drive "side-by-side" next to any vehicle for any distance if you can help it. Pull forward or drop back so no other vehicle is right next to you. Concept: try as much as you can to keep maneuvering room around your vehicle in case of emergency and you need to swerve or do some other avoidance effort to prevent collisions.

When Rosie, the United Parcel Service driving supervisor, approved my driving and gave me a route, it was a split route. In the morning, UPS gave me my old neighborhood of Avondale/North Avondale to deliver packages, usually from a Department Store. That was interesting. One day the lady, who answered my knock, looked at me and said, "Aren't you that blond headed kid that used to run across our lawn on Marion Avenue?" "Yes." "Well, I am one of the Sitron sisters, and I remember you!" "Oh, hi. It is nice to see you again."

Some of the packages came C.O.D. which translates to Cash-On-

Delivery, meaning I needed to collect money from such customers. And I remember at noon, when I switched from delivering packages to an industrial route when I picked up packages to take back to the truck barn. I would always carefully count the money to be sure I had exactly the right amount. At the end of the day, we would drop our envelope of cash into a slot in the safe. But weekly there would be reports that I was short. My assumption was someone was taking money out of my envelope to balance their own envelope.

I really enjoyed the job and became friendly with all my industrial customers. One day, at least two customers reported to me that my boss had been there to check up on how I was doing. Both customers gave me a good report. The week after Christmas UPS laid off most of its Christmas Help Drivers, including me. Ok. A few weeks later, just as I was packing my car to drive to California, the telephone rang, and UPS was offering me a full-time job! " Thank you very much, but I am on my way to California."

[Time Digression] Ten years later, I was back in Cincinnati, and needing a job. I telephoned UPS; they looked up my record and hired me back!! Although this time I was a "Furniture Helper" riding in the large furniture trucks, rather than a delivery driver. [But remember: leaving a good record behind one is a great idea.][End Digression]

Commentary: I have actually driven across the United States over 30 plus times. And I have observed so many drivers that appear to be oblivious to any other vehicle. I particularly become irritated when, let's say I am driving at 70 miles an hour. And another vehicle, coming up from behind me-- is going around 72 miles an hour. They appear in my left rear quarter. And they creep, and they creep. They move and pull ahead along side of me at the rate of ten feet every 4 to 5 minutes. Sometimes I look over and see the driver just chatting away with the passenger, totally seemingly unaware of my car, or that I am approaching slower traffic and I need to get over. Sometimes I slow down to get the car away from me, but more often I step on the gas and quickly move ahead.

A similar irritation occurs when, let's say I am driving 75 miles an hour, and I approach and pass a car that is driving 68 miles an hour. Suddenly I look in my rearview mirror, and that car is now driving 75 miles an hour and is fairly close behind me (tagging a long.) Oh, no you don't. Sometimes I will increase my speed by a few miles an hour and check to see if the car behind is keeping up with me. Then I do speed up and move quickly away.

+ + + + + +

## WAIT A MINUTE, DAD, WHEN DID YOU JOIN THE JOHN F. KENNEDY ENCOURAGE
• • • • • • • • • • • • • • • • • • • • • • • •

I had returned to California and was visiting my father. We always shared a bed so we could continue talking.

So, I am lying there listening to Dad, when he turned and asked me, "Did you ever wonder where **Life Magazine** got all of those excellent pictures?" "Gee, Dad, no, I never have." "Well, when the Kennedys came to visit, they brought a **Life Photographer** with them, and he just started snapping away taking multiple photographs. I had my photographer with me, but he only had one roll of film. So, the Life Photographer gave him some more…"

"Wait a minute, Dad. WHEN did the Kennedys come for a visit? I never heard about this!" "Well, yes, and they came twice…"

In 1959 and 1960, my father was the editor of the largest newspaper in Southwestern Oregon, the Coos Bay World. And when John F. Kennedy was running for the Democratic Nomination, he, Jackie, and Bobby (Robert) Kennedy came to Coos Bay to do "the political thing," visit major industries—e.g. lumber, fishing, etc. meet the workers, make speeches. In the evening, my father and stepmother joined them for dinner.

By some coincidence, I was present at the Los Angeles Sports Arena—where the Democratic National Convention was being held—I was part of a group outside marching, supporting Adlai Stevenson; but somehow, we had one or two passes which allowed the possessor to enter the Sports Arena. I just happened to take my turn to be in the Arena when John F. Kennedy received the Democratic Nomination!

So now, the Kennedys needed to comeback around the country politicking, and coming back to Coos Bay for a repeat performance, and, once again my father and stepmother joined the Kennedys for dinner. Years later, my-stepmother commented that they liked Bobby the best—he was friendly and easy to talk with. I still have the newspaper that has my father's front-page story along with a picture of the Kennedys.

This story contains an accidental circumstance: my father was a very modest person, and never bragged about who had met and interviewed. So, I never knew about this connection with the Kennedys until 1968 when I was living in San Francisco, and my now-divorced father was living alone in the Tujunga house. Occasionally I would fly down for a weekend visit. And we always slept together so we could talk on into the night. [End of digression.]

Dad did not return to California from Oregon right away. Months later now Dad and his family returned to the Los Angeles area. During the next two years, I was living back in Cincinnati.

Dad eventually was hired by the **PASADENA INDEPENDENT STAR NEWS.** Dad's next twelve years at the Independent Star News were the greatest in his career. He was a major mover and shaker in town.

+ + + + + +

In January 1962, I drove my 1957 Chrysler Imperial Crown Convertible to Tujunga, 7419 Summitrose Avenue to my father's home. I had been accepted to San Francisco State College. When I arrived, however, I discovered that my father had been in a terrible automobile accident in December. That was the seventeen-car pile-up; the car of teenagers that slammed first into the back of Dad's car—who had his wheels turned to go around the truck; consequently, Dad's car went flying out into a farmer's field, so then the teenagers slammed into the back of a flatbed truck, and had all died. Dad's body was in pain. On a Sunday, with tears in his eyes, he begged me to stay living with him (and Liz, Casey 3, Erin 1 1/2; Liz was pregnant with Kilian.) Okay, so on Sunday afternoon, I made the heavy decision not to go to San Francisco, but to live with Dad, Liz, and the children, at least for several months.

Memories from living in Tujunga. There was a young high school girl from just down the street, and she came regularly as a baby sitter. Over time, she fell in love with me. And began writing some short love letters to me. I believe she was a senior at Verdugo High School, and for their graduation party, they went to Disneyland for a special all-night High School Celebration. Carol invited me, so I went. I did enjoy myself. I recall always being a gentleman around Carol—being pleasant but not "leading her on." I do not believe I ever kissed her; I really was not interested in a romantic relationship.

He was a major mover and shaker in town. [I dreamed about when I complete this book and publish, I would then write writing a book about my father titled **THE MAN WHO KEPT PASADENA FROM BURNING. (However, I have stressed my body "over the line" so doctors have advised me to stop writing. AWWW!0** My father, a newspaper man, was closely connected to the two dissimilar African American communities—"the House Hands" who arrived in the 1880's, and "the Field Hands" who arrived right after World War II in Pasadena. These two communities were not speaking to each other BUT they both were speaking to my father, whom they both recognized as "their Ally." When the neighborhood of WATTS in Los Angeles went up in flames from a riot in July 1965, the Pasadena city political leaders—both Black and White-- commissioned my father to do what he could to keep the city from burning. And he did.

## *PATRIC ENROLLS IN GLENDALE COMMUNITY COLLEGE*
● ● ● ● ● ● ● ● ● ● ● ● ● ● ● ● ● ● ● ● ● ●

Now, in February 1962 I needed to continue my education, so I enrolled in Glendale Community College. I took, Economic American History (which for the first time assisted me to make sense of the Common Man's need to move westward-covered wagons etc.) I took Ceramics including melting glass; I took a non-laboratory Biology Course. And I took a physical education class in Bowling. That is important to mention because it was in that class that I met one of my life-long friends: Howard Landau.

I needed an income. So, I answered some advertisements, and gained two jobs. The first was delivering paper products for the De Hater Paper Co. Rolla De Hater was the owner. It was a very small company. They had a 1941 Dodge Stake-body truck. Would you believe it came complete with a wind-out windshield? You turn the crank and the windshield opened from the bottom. Not that that was any great help on a bad **smog** day. [L.A. coined this word from a mixture of smoke—often from cars, mixed with fog.] The company and warehouse were in Glendale, a separate city within Los Angeles County. But the customers were spread out in several communities, so I spent a lot of time driving, which I didn't mind since I was a truck driver; I had just finished driving for United Parcel.

### PATRIC BECOMES A DELIVERY TRUCK DRIVER FOR DE-HATER PAPER CO. AND ALSO BECOMES A DOOR-TO-DOOR SALESMAN FOR FULLER BRUSH

• • • • • • • • • • • • • • • • • • • • • •

My second job was delivering Fuller Brush Company products in the La Canada, La Cresenta and Glendale areas. I don't remember the names of the husband-and-wife team that went door to door selling. But they, out of their home, bagged the items customers had ordered and gave me the addresses. I forget now how much I was paid, but the two jobs supported my car, and going to college.

[Time Digression] CBS SUNDAY MORNING recently in 2020 was reminding us of the Civil Defense era when people were scared the Soviets were going to rain down nuclear missiles upon us. Buildings began having signs posted outside that "This is a CIVIL DEFENSE SHELTER. In the Basements of many/most/all of the "SHELTERS" there were stored barrels of water, and barrels of food. I know that a few had biscuits; I do not know what the rest contained. I do know *that SANDS MONTESSORI SCHOOL*, when we moved in in 1979, still had those barrels in the Basement!! No doubt everything inedible by then. Radios were produced that had the CD LOGO printed over the two radio stations that could be counted on to broadcast instructions if we were attacked. And, yes, some people did in fact, build Fall Out

Shelters in their yards. When I delivered Fuller Brush Products in La Canada, and La Crescentia to customers' homes, I did see Fall Out Shelters in some of the yards! And I also remember the philosophical arguments around "Just who will be allowed in, to take shelter?" The big example was, if the missile attack took place during the day, the father would be at work; the children would be at school; perhaps only mom was home in the house. The sirens go off. Who does mom allow to go in the Shelter with her? The neighbors? Strangers? This problem was never resolved satisfactorily. [End Digression]

In the early spring months, I, we, decided it was time I had my own bedroom. Dad's house had an extra-large garage—big enough for two cars, but also there was an additional 8-9 feet beyond the length of the cars. However, Dad and Liz parked their cars out in front. Liz, a reporter, and writer for the Glendale News Press, had won $100 for her news story about being trapped in a forest fire. (Along with the firemen, so with their help, she was able to escape.) She offered the $100 to me to build a bedroom in the back of the garage. So, Dad and I did that. It only accommodated a single bed, dresser, desk, lamp, and chair. But it was adequate. Two windows looked out on a view of the mountains, and undeveloped land. That was pleasant. The main house had two bathrooms, so I was able to use the same one that the children used.

When my courses in Glendale College were over for the semester, I was asked if I wanted to have my own Fuller Brush Route? Okay, yes. The company assigned me to Sunland, which was a small community adjacent to Tujunga. These were the days when sales people did walk the blocks, knocking on every house door. And often the wife was home in the daytime, occasionally a man. So, I peddled my wares with moderate success. We were supposed to give out small samples of some of Fuller Brush Products—lotions, perfumes, miniature vegetable scrub brushes. Ok, but the sales person, me, had to buy them for at least a penny a piece. That got expensive. I was encouraged to push the idea of selling two or three containers of product, rather than just one. There were quite a number of aerosols can products like foot spray. [What I know is that an aerosol can is an expensive way to buy—not as much product as you would receive in a plain bottle of the same liquid.]

In short order, I connected with the Avon Lady who was also walking the same territory. She and I conspired that I would not sell the type of products she was selling, and she would not sell the same type I was. And we would refer customers to each other. It made our two lives much more pleasant.

I had one male customer who liked me to stop and have a drink with him. He was the manager of all maintenance for "Flying Tigers Airline" which was started by one of the original Flying Tigers pilots of the World War II China Theatre. The Airline in the 1960's was strictly a cargo carrying operation.

He was fun to talk with, so I put him at the end of my route for the day. We got to be buddies. *I mentioned that I was getting ready to drive around the United States,* so he asked me to play a joke on his secretary: As I would stop in various cities and states, would I please write a postcard to his secretary and sign it "Your Lover, Pete." Which I did. Upon my return to Tujunga, my friend took me to his office so I could meet the secretary and introduce myself as "Your Lover Pete." It was a good laugh all around.

When I discussed with my friend that I was moving to San Francisco to attend college, he offered to get me a job with the Flying Tigers Maintenance Facility at the San Francisco Airport. He was good to his word, and they did offer me a job. However, it was only twenty hours a week, and the pay was not great. I figured that if I took the job, I would have to keep my car, keep making payments, and basically just break even, with little extra to support me with rent and college expenses.

So, I thanked them for the offer and left.

Memories of the time period. I remember that Marilyn Monroe had been found dead in her apartment—they suspected alcohol and sleeping pills or some such drug. I mention it because Marilyn—whose birth name was Norma Jean Baker—had a mentally ill mother, who was a patient in a Glendale Sanitarium. Since Liz was a reporter for Glendale News Press, Liz had the assignment of interviewing Marilyn's mother! [My understanding is that with Norma Jean Baker growing up with a mentally ill mother, Marilyn had difficulty ever being really contented and happy.]

My sister, Kilian [Jeanne] was born on May 25, 1962 in the Glendale Hospital. I was there when Liz and Kilian were being released from the hospital, so I drove down and picked them up. I was the one who carried Kilian [nick named Kelly] as a new born infant across the threshold into the house and I laid her gently down on the bed in the corner of the living room. A comment that I would make, is that Kilian's personality was evident even as a newborn, and I have observed that same personality orientation her whole life.

+++++++++++++++++++++

What did I mean that I was getting ready to drive around the United States? Well, that will be my next story.

## NINA TANNER'S INSPIRED TRIP ALL AROUND THE USA IN 1962

• • • • • • • • • • • • • • • • • • • • • •

**Okay, here is the story.** I spent most of my summer as a Fuller Brush Door-to-Door Salesperson. My territory was Sunland which is adjacent to Tujunga. So, it was very easy for me to stop home for lunch. One day while I was home having lunch, the telephone rang. It was my LRY close friend, Nina Tanner, with a very strange request. She informed me that there was a group that wanted to travel to Springfield, Massachusetts, for a College-age Church Conference; and could they borrow my car---a 1957 Chrysler Imperial Crown Convertible, so wide that four people could sit side by side on the front seats. Hmmmm. Well, yes but, I come with the car. Could you and your friends pay my way? Nina said, "I will check and call you tomorrow." Nina called the next day and said, "You're on!" I quit my jobs. And on the following Wednesday, the four of us piled into my car and we were off on our adventure AT 4:00 P.M. Pacific Daylight Savings Time. The four were Nina Tanner, Frank Buell, Helmut Manteuffel (from Germany), and me. There were three drivers, so we all took turns. When I was not driving, I could take a pillow and blanket and stretch out in the well where the convertible top rested when it was in the down position.

We drove "straight through." We only stopped for gas, bathrooms, and food. It was the fastest time I have ever traveled across the U.S. by car: we arrived at my mother's house at 4:00 P.M. Cincinnati time, which was 1:00 P.M. Los Angeles time, which calculates to 45 hours. As I recall, we had dinner with Mom; we only visited for two hours, then we drove to Columbus Ohio where Nina had relatives. I remembered taking a seat on the sofa in their living room, but it seems I fell sound asleep until it was time to travel on. We arrived in Springfield, Massachusetts in time for the start of the conference. There were International students there as well. I recall spending time with Kay Smith from England. We corresponded for a while afterwards. When the conference concluded, suddenly we had six persons to ride back in my car. One woman was from Atlanta, Judy from Dallas, Texas, Doug Stevenson from Washington State. We were not in a hurry on our return trip. We had an invitation from one delegate to stay overnight in Boston one night. We had an invitation from another delegate to visit New York City and stay overnight. As we departed New York City, our next planned stop was Washington, D. C. Our highway planned route took us down the New Jersey Turnpike. The tires on my car were re-treads and were subject to going bad. So, we are driving in the high-speed lane when the right front tire went bad. I was driving. Traffic was quite heavy; so, I immediately pulled over on to the left berm. I got out the spare tire and the jack, **only to discover that the Imperial needed two separate jacks**—one for the back bumper, and a very different one for the front bumper. And to discover I only had the jack for the back bumper, which was useless to use on the front bumper.

## LEPRECHAUN IN THE GRASS

• • • • • • • • • • • • • • • • • • • • • •

My father's paternal grandmother, Lydia Chamblin, came directly from County Cork in Ireland; so that makes me part Irish; so, do not tell me there are not Leprechauns who sometimes come to your aid: I walked down the grassy berm 300 to 400 feet, and what do you think I found laying the grass? **Exactly! The rare wheel jack that is only used for Imperials and WAS A FRONT BUMPER JACK!!**

So, we were able to continue our journey to Washington D.C. where Doug Stevenson had an uncle and aunt. The uncle worked for the U.S. Census Bureau, and following dinner, he wanted to take us to his office to see their new Unifax Computer. Well, I will tell you, 1962 was in the early, early days of business computers. These business computers required over 100 feet of equipment! They were so big, that Admiral Grace Hopper, the Navy's top computer specialist, started speaking of "BUGS" in the computer, and she meant real live bugs that would crawl into the electrical equipment and cause short circuits! (And become "dead" bugs.) At the very front of the computer, there was one small desk with a typewriter-like device that actually punched holes in cards. And the cards—when fed into the computer, provided directions and commands to the computer.

The next day our group decided to tour the White House. But before I tell you about that, I need to explain that new tires for the Imperial were over $100 even back then. I could not afford that. So, in those early days, there were "Rubber Welders" who would take a worn-out tire, and mold [glue?] new rubber tread onto the casing. That I could afford. However, if one drove many hours at highway speeds, the glue or adhesive would begin to come loose, and the tire would develop "bubbles." I believe had to replace all four tires during that trip. But on this particular day, I dropped the group off at the White House Tour Entrance, and I drove off to the "Rubber Welder store" for another to replace the tire that had gone bad on the New Jersey Turnpike. And would you believe that while I was so engaged, the group was waiting in line to enter the White House when President John F. Kennedy came out onto the lawn, and on his way to the Marine Helicopter which would take him to Hyannis Port, Massachusetts, the President walked over and shook hands with some of those waiting, including our group! (But not me.) Thanks, guys.

Back to our cross-country adventure in August 1962. When we left Washington, D.C. we headed to Atlanta, Ga. To deliver—I think her name was something like Deanna, home to Atlanta. She invited us to stay over a couple of days, and she would take us over to meet Rev. Dr. Martin Luther King—as her youth group participated in activities with him. We discussed it, and decided we were needing to move on, so I told Deanna something like, "Thank you very much, but we are pushing on; I will try to meet him on my next time through." [Okay, so I never got to meet him, but I was almost at the March on Washington the following year.]

Returning to our trip around the USA. From Atlanta, we decided to head toward New Orleans, where most of us had never been. I strongly recall that we had dinner in the French Quarter, at the famous **Court of Two Sisters Restaurant.** We ate outside in the patio; it was hot, and the mosquitoes were flying. And shortly waiters came around with some sort machine that put out a mist or fog that would kill the mosquitoes. After dinner, I don't believe we stopped anywhere to sleep, but pushed on to Dallas, to deliver Judy home.

From Dallas, we journeyed straight to Los Angeles, so Nina and Frank could go home. Doug Stevenson needed to go to San Francisco. So, he came home with me, while I packed up my things, and we were off. Doug had some friends in San Francisco, on Carl Street, in a Flat, so that is where I started my new life in San Francisco.

*PATRIC MOVES TO SAN FRANCISCO WITH ONLY $6, AND ENROLLS IN SAN FRANCISCO STATE COLLEGE, FINDS A PLACE TO LIVE, AND FINDS A JOB IN THAT ORDER! (REALLY?)*

● ● ● ● ● ● ● ● ● ● ● ● ● ● ● ● ● ● ● ● ● ●

At the conclusion of that trip in 1962, I had again been accepted by San Francisco State College, so I packed my bags and moved to San Francisco. But there was a big problem in moving to San Francisco: *I had no money! I know I had six dollars in my pocket. Literally! But I managed to get myself admitted to San Francisco State College, a place to live, and a job in that order!!*

Really? How did you manage that magic trick? Well, I spent a few days hurriedly applying for a job, with no luck. I recall walking up Market Street, with growing desperation, and figuring, that if nothing else, I would join the Armed Forces. May I quote from a letter I wrote to my mother on September 25, 1962: *"Even at 3:00 P.M. on the very last* *day of SFSC Registration, I didn't know how I was going to make it. The story briefly is that Tuesday morning I had gone to my father's former boss (Sheldon Sackett) here in San Francisco who owns quite a few businesses (14 newspapers) is worth a few million dollars, and is fond of my father. I had met him about two years ago when I passed through (From Christmas with my family in Coos Bay, Oregon, back to Los Angeles and UCLA). Anyhow I explained my problem to him, and he explained that he wasn't doing too well and had debts of his own and had also made a number of loans to people who hadn't paid him back. Finally, he said that he didn't have the $250.00 (which I must have asked for.) but if I could talk them (the Registrar at SFSC) into letting me be a resident, he would loan the local fee.*

*Later that day while I was still looking for a job, some man explained that there was no difference between a resident and a registered voter. It so happens I had registered here in California. So, I went back to school and was able to talk to somebody that had some sense. She asked me if I had paid California income taxes for 1961. Of course, I said no since I was in Ohio. Then she asked me if I would be willing to pay them, because if I did, they would allow me to be a resident and they would give me more time to pay the taxes. I agreed to pay and ran to the telephone and called Sheldon Sackett who agreed to pay, and so I made it in…..Registration closed at 5:00 P.M. on Tuesday September 18th. I handed them my money* **at two minutes of!!! (Totally true.)** *The actual Registration fee was $48.00. But I asked Mr. Sackett for $60.00. That way I would have $12.00 for food and gasoline.*

That next weekend, I was invited up to Santa Rosa in Marin County, where a family, the Minnemans, from Cincinnati had just moved. I went. Spent the weekend; and on Sunday night, Kathy asked me if I needed any money—"I'm working and living at home with no expenses, and I have savings." So, I borrowed $100. I then answered an ad in the newspaper for a housemate to join a Flat, 71 Buena Vista

Terrace—just off the famous Haight Street. I did join and was given the large bedroom in the front of the Flat. My rent was $37.50 a month!

Now for a job. I kept answering ads, going to businesses, filling out applications, but no luck. Finally, I went to an Employment Agency. But they wanted $25 just to speak to me—which I did not have. As I was leaving, a nice young African American woman, walking out at the same time too, asked me what I was looking for? I told her a job so I could attend college. She quickly said that the Bank of America often hires students. I said great, "where are they?" She pointed south down Market Street and Van Ness Ave. and said the bank was about eight blocks down. I practically ran down the eight blocks and was able to get right into the Personnel Office and fill out an application. They didn't have a job to offer at the moment, but they would keep me in mind.

Years before, my father, who grew up during the Depression of the 1930's, told me how he wanted to become a newspaper man—as his older friend Ralph Woodward was. Dad went to the Cincinnati Enquirer Newspaper and applied. No job. BUT he kept going back to them once a week and asking; and after several weeks-maybe two months—they did give him a job on the Copy Desk.

## PATRIC IS SENT TO THE BANK'S VAULT TO BECOME A COIN AND CURRENCY VERIFICATION TELLER

• • • • • • • • • • • • • • • • • • • • • •

I remembered this story, so every two days, I either telephoned the Personnel Office, or I went down in person. And after eight days, the Personnel Manager said. "Come on down and see me!" I forget what he initially offered over the phone, but when I arrived, he explained they had an opening on the Evening Shift, downstairs in their Central Cash Vault. I would be Bonded and be counting money! And I could start tomorrow. (Thank you! Thank You!) But I had to promise that I would stay in their employment for at least two years. Okay. [I actually was employed by the San Francisco Cash Vault—where the Armored Cars deliver all their locked money bags-- for seven years 1962 to 1969. Then I left to go to graduate school in Chicago. That didn't work out. I came back to Los Angeles, and they called me to work on the Day Shift of their Cash Vault—at a salary higher than when I left! But that is another story.]

And as soon as I received a paycheck—no—Bank of America was probably one of the first employers to use "Direct Deposit" so I received a "Deposit Slip." And I quickly paid Mr. Sackett and Kathy Minnemum back.

Within a few weeks, it appeared that after four years of wandering back and forth from California to Ohio, enrolling in other colleges, that my life was becoming stabilized. Oh, Thank Goodness! "I am so tired mentally and emotionally from changing my life every year from California to Ohio. Ohio to California back and forth; back and forth. And from this college to that college."

Please understand, my mother in Ohio provides a quiet stable place for me to live and go to school. The West Coast was often a "Gypsy Life" changing apartments every few months.

As I recall, SF State gave me credit for all of the courses I had taken at other schools, so I had a year under my belt. Okay, so what major should I choose? Hmmm? Gosh, wouldn't it be glamourous to work around the world in some United States Embassy or Consulate? Yes. Alright, I will major in government—Political Science. [I will have to consult my school records to see exactly what courses I took.]

## *PATRIC ENTERS THE SUBMARINE NAVY*

• • • • • • • • • • • • • • • • • • • • • •

In October 1962 as I was walking across the big lawn at San Francisco State College heading toward the Commons (Cafeteria) I suddenly encountered one of my old high school classmates from Laguna Beach—Noel Tilden. "Noel, hi! Let's go out together this weekend and visit." "No, I can't" "Why?" "I have Submarine Reserves all this weekend." "Submarine Reserves? Tell me all about it."

[Time Digression:] Commencing when I was 18 years old, I volunteered for participation in the American Friends Service Committee projects, such as helping welfare families fix up their homes, spending the weekend in a mental hospital, letting patients know someone cares, and my last project was spending time in San Quentin Prison—but that is another story. See page #192. Anyway, spending a lot of time with Quakers, I entertained the thought of being a Conscientious Objector and not participating in war. However, I decided I could not, because if someone was attacking and killing my friends and family, and the only way to stop them was to take a gun and kill them, I would. And the current Armed Forces Drafting Age was 22 ½, and I was 22 ½.

I became very interested in what Noel was explaining to me. I ended by saying, "Noel, take me with you!" Noel was descended from a wealthy family in New York see Tilden Park in Manhattan, and Noel's Ancestor, Samuel Tilden, ran for U. S. President in 1876. So, on Saturday morning, Noel came to my house in his Mercedes 300SL Gull Wing car. We drove with the Gull Wings wide open. And that is how I arrived at the Base and began my career in the U.S. Navy Submarine Reserves.

[Historical Digression]

## *SAMUEL TILDEN: CANDIDATE FOR U.S. PRESIDENT*

• • • • • • • • • • • • • • • • • • • • •

**Candidate:** <u>Samuel Tilden</u>; Thomas A. Hendrich...

**Campaign:** <u>U.S. Presidential Election, 1876</u>

**Affiliation:** <u>Democratic Party</u>

As the Governor of the most populous U.S. state, New York, Tilden was an obvious choice and the front-runner for the 1876 Democratic presidential nomination. ... Hayes won the Republican nomination as a compromise candidate after front-runner James G. Blaine failed in his nomination bid due to his corruption scandals.

**People also ask**

What was Samuel Tilden known for before he ran for president in 1876?

Samuel Jones Tilden (February 9, 1814 – August 4, 1886) was an American politician who served as the 25th Governor of New York and was the Democratic candidate for president in the disputed 1876 United States presidential election.

Who did Samuel Tilden run against for president?

The 1876 United States presidential election was the 23rd quadrennial presidential election, held on Tuesday, November 7, 1876, in which Republican nominee Rutherford B. Hayes faced Democrat Samuel J. Tilden.

Search for: Who did Samuel Tilden run against for president?

What is the Hayes-Tilden compromise?

Through the **Compromise**, Republican Rutherford B. **Hayes** was awarded the White House over Democrat Samuel J. **Tilden** on the understanding that **Hayes** would remove the federal troops whose support was essential for the survival of Republican state governments in South Carolina, Florida and Louisiana. [End Historical Digression]

+ + + + + +

As I came into the Reserve Building, in Hunter's Point Naval Shipyard, I was welcomed with open arms. Later in the morning, a Third Class (E4) Torpedoman—I believe his name was Williams-- came to me and said, "let me take you down to the pier and we can go aboard the Reserve Training Submarine, (USS Dentuda (AGSS 335). Wow! This sure is neat. By the end of the day, I said to the Officer-In-Charge, "Sign me up!"

It took a few weeks to get all the enlisting papers ready, so it was in November when I signed. A week or two later, they had me come to the Center and take the Entrance Test. (At that time, the test was known as ARI-GCT. It was a combined form of intelligence test plus achievement test. Chief Eini administered the test to me. I took it; he went into the back room to grade it; a few minutes later he came out and exclaimed, "I have never seen such a high score before! Can we send you to the Naval Academy?" I had heard horror stories about the hazing, and since I was 22 ½ I thought I was too old, and I really was not interested.

*PATRIC CHOOSES TO STRIKE FOR QUARTERMASTER WHO DOES NAVIGATION—STAR SIGHTS-PILOTING AND COMMUNICATION SUCH AS FLASHING LIGHT*

• • • • • • • • • • • • • • • • • • • • • • •

Digression, when I joined (which was immediately after the Cuban Missile Crisis) I still had over two years of college courses to go, and the Navy deferred my active-duty requirement until I graduated. During that time, I chose to become a Quartermaster—because they worked with charts, navigation, flashing signal lights, celestial navigation—real sea-going jobs. I was able to study and take the test for Third Class Quartermaster (E4) just before I went on Active Duty in April 1965.

Yes, I want to be a **QUARTERMASTER**: Some explanatory description is warranted. While a Quartermaster in the Army deals with supplies and logistics, a Quartermaster in the Navy is in the Navigation Department—ensuring that the ship "steams" on its intended track. Therefore, the quartermaster takes frequent "fixes"—lines of bearings from known objects on land such as lighthouses, smoke stacks, radio towers IF the ship is "piloting" within sight of land. When the ship is out in the open ocean, the quartermaster relies on Celestial Navigation, taking bearings from the stars and the sun; utilizing LORAN [Long range Radio Navigation] signals if they were available in your part of the ocean, and finally "Dead Reckoning" where you estimate where the ship is Based upon mathematical calculations using courses and speed changes recorded in the Quartermaster's Notebook. [That was in the 1960's. Nowadays, Satellites and the Ship's Inertial Navigation System tells the quartermaster what is the ship's position.] [I do take a very dim view of this new method: Quartermasters today DO NOT NEED TO DO ANY DEEP THINKING—the machines tell them everything they need to know; therefore, the quartermasters have no mental understanding of the mathematical calculations involved. If this were a Celestial Star fix, there are at least 18 steps! Would you believe that the U.S. Navy stopped teaching the Art of Celestial Navigation with a Sextant for 12 years or more!! How dumb is that! Finally, some bright officer raised the question: "If we lost all of our electronic equipment, how would we know where we are?" Duh. So now two years ago the U.S. Navy has re-started teaching the art of Celestial Navigation.

The quartermaster keeps a time log of all course and speed changes; the quartermaster is responsible for reading and understanding visual communications such as sending and receiving flashing light Morse code, semaphore flags, and flag hoists on other ships "yard arms." And many other tasks.

+ + + + + +

### PATRIC MEETS HIS LIFE-LONG FRIEND MARVIN WARKENTIN

• • • • • • • • • • • • • • • • • • • • • • •

[Time Digression] In the Autumn of 1962, I took a Physical Education course in Handball. In that course I became acquainted with fellow student Marvin Warkentin, from Dinuba, California—down in the Central Valley about 200 miles away. We liked each other immediately. We started going to coffee or lunch together. In a while I talked Marv into moving in to the flat at 71 Buena Vista Terrace. We stayed in contact together. I talked Marv into joining the Naval Submarine Reserves. He went to Submarine School with me. He earned his "Dolphins" onboard the U.S.S. Ronquil (SS396) with the assistance of that famous officer Lloyd "Pete" Bucher of U.S.S. Pueblo (PER 03) Intelligence Gathering fame. I talked Marv into to going to Officer's Candidate School (OCS). Marv graduated from SFSC a semester before I did. He came back and told me that if I wanted to stay with submarines, I should not go to OCS because I did not have an Engineering Degree. So, I didn't go.

Marv went on Active Duty as a "Forward Observer" flying in a small plane over enemy territory in Viet Nam. Then he was transferred to a Destroyer, operating drone helicopters carrying two torpedoes against submarine targets.

There was a time when my ship, the U.S.S. Rock (AGSS 274), was the "target" for Marv's Destroyer. There were four destroyers practicing sending exercise torpedoes our way. Marv's ship was the only one that was successful. When the FXP Exercise was over and we surfaced, I came up on our Search Light and tried to communicate with Marv's destroyer, but no luck. When we returned to port, I sent Marv a letter. Would you believe Marv wrote back saying "He was the helicopter Controller on that successful run!!!

Oh, by the way, Marv's father Leonard was a medic in World War II and landed on Iwo Jima a few days after the invasion, and set up the medical facilities similar to that recent movie of the Medic saving all those lives, lowering injured men down a cliff.

In June 1964, Marv was the best man in my wedding, and in 1970 I was the Head Usher in Marv's wedding! We have stayed close friends all these many years. We just spoke on the telephone in May, 2021 for my birthday! [End Digression]

## PATRIC RECEIVES A VISIT FROM THE FBI

• • • • • • • • • • • • • • • • • • • • •

Well, that brings up another story. J. Edgar Hoover, the head of the FBI, did NOT like Dr. Martin Luther King, nor did he like Civil Rights activists. Back in 1959 in downtown Los Angeles, I participated with a collection of individuals known As *Independent Student Union.* However, to my knowledge, I was not aware that there were any formal meetings. We picketed downtown Woolworth Store because in the Deep South, the store would not permit African Americans to eat at the Lunch Counter. We did this most every Saturday Morning. Well, wouldn't you know it (and I certainly did not) that there were FBI Agents photographing each one of us as we marched.

Now moved ahead four years and 400 miles. In the Autumn of 1963, in San Francisco, two FBI Agents knocked on my apartment door!! And yes, like the record of Arlo Guthrie's song **"You Can Get Anything You Want at Alice's Restaurant"** the FBI Agents had "8 x10" Glossy Photographs with circles and arrows and a paragraph on the back!"

The two agents sat with me and questioned me for over an hour. They would present scenarios and then ask me, "Well, what did the Communist Party think about that?" My response was, "I have no idea. I do not know any Communists. I have not heard the word mentioned during all of hours of picketing. I have heard no discussion of politics during the hours of picketing." The conversation went on and on in similar vein. The two agents came back a week later. They had tape recorded everything I had said and typed out a transcript. I had to read and approve every word and sign my name to every page. Then it seemed like they were convinced I was not a Communist. BUT, a few of the picketers were later identified as Communists, and that group had now migrated from Los Angeles to Berkeley and had founded a "W. E. B. Dubois Marxist-Leninist Study Group." And now the FBI wanted me to infiltrate that group, get the members "To show me their Communist Party Membership Cards, and then I could arrive in court and provide 'State's Evidence' and testify against them!" My response was, "No, I really am not needing to do that!"

However, in those days, one feared the FBI. It was the age of McCarthyism, and many innocent people (and probably a few guilty people) lost their jobs on the basis of rumors." I was not ever a Communist nor a Socialist. But for forty years, I quit signing any kind of political petition, because I was aware the FBI was able to access them.

Yes, I liked being a member of the government; one time I ran for the office of Treasurer of the Student Body on the Independent Ticket. One day I discovered that another member of the ticket was a Socialist. I immediately telephoned the local branch of the FBI, to report my situation on the ticket to Agent Jack B.

This saga does have a happy ending: eighteen years later, FBI Agent Jack B. approved my Navy Top Secret Clearance!!

## PATRIC BECOMES PRESIDENT OF THE COLLEGE YMCA
• • • • • • • • • • • • • • • • • • • • • •

In the autumn of 1962, I joined the College YMCA on Campus, and became a very active member, which led to me becoming selected to be the President by early summer 1963.

But back in May 1963, the YMCA sponsored a trip up into the wine country of Marin Country; we visited three or four wineries, one of which was Berringer Brothers. That is significant because that was the beginning of my relationship with Jeannie LeCount (the older sister of Rosalie, one of the YMCAs' most active members.) Jeannie and I dated for maybe a month, and then I had other obligations to attend to. It was going to be a busy summer. * I had to step away from my Part Time Job-- Monday, Tuesday, and Friday evenings at the Central Cash Vault.

My mother married Mark Mitchell Jr. in Cincinnati on June 15th. I flew back to be in attendance. In June 1963 Mark Mitchell Jr. and my mother, Joy, got married, and I, age 23, gained stepsiblings: Sally 21, Mark III 19, and Elizabeth 15. [That has been a great gift to me all these years.]

And as a Submarine Naval Reservist, I was required to attend Submarine School located in Hunters' Point Naval Shipyard, San Francisco. At the Submarine School, the curriculum was divided into two sessions. The first two weeks were designated "Submarine Preparatory School" and taught the big picture basics of how a submarine works. The very first week, five of us cadets were called into the Training Center's Office and told that the follow-on school—Submarine Graduate School (lasting four weeks) was all filled up—no seats for us. However, the Navy Chiefs offered an alternative plan: we were to go down to the training submarine, the USS Dentuda (AGSS 335), and spend three weeks "Assholes and Elbows" crawling all over the physical equipment and tracing each of the 20 plus systems—air, oil, water, electric. Then making detailed drawings of each system showing each and every valve and so forth. Okay, we can do that.

The Dentuda, (AGSS 335) was a decommissioned submarine, with its propellers removed, and the 252 battery cells removed, so the ship was "welded to the pier." But all of the systems were identical to those on active-duty diesel electric submarines, so we could learn a lot. [Of historical note, the USS Dentuda participated in the nuclear bomb tests at Bikini Island in the 1950's. It was positioned several thousand yards from the explosion site, and it was placed at a depth of 150 feet. Still, when the nuclear bomb went off, its shock waves managed to bend the ship into an arc! However, the arc was very slight, and one normally could not tell the difference by sight.]

During the second week of Submarine Preparatory School, all five of the above-mentioned cadets were called back into the office and told that now there were enough seats for us in the "Submarine Graduate School" (reason being at least five of the other cadets had flunked out.) Three of us agreed to take those seats, but, John Lilly and I said we were keeping to the original contract: three weeks on the Dentuda, then for two more weeks, assigned aboard an active submarine at the San Diego Ballast Point Submarine Base.

## PATRIC GOES TO SEA ABOARD THE USS RONQUIL (SS396)

John Lilly and I were a perfect team with our flashlights and notebooks for drawing systems. We were very efficient and completed all of the systems during our three weeks. I was sent aboard the USS Ronquil (SS 396) which was scheduled to go to sea during both weeks. Great. As I came aboard, the leading quartermaster, Chief Dick, came immediately to me, acknowledged that I was 'Striking" (becoming an apprentice) for Quartermaster. Chief Dick explained that he was very short handed of personnel and wanted me to immediately become a working quartermaster, "Standing four-hour watches" in the Conning Tower—that funny little compartment just below the bridge, that houses the periscopes, radar, Fire Control Equipment, and the ship's primary steering stand (helm). If I would help him out, he guaranteed he would help me obtain all of the qualifying signatures I need to graduate from submarine school! What a deal. I would be glad to help you and learn all I can. The two different week cruises out in the Pacific Ocean were very exciting and rewarding; the final step in qualifying for graduation was a meeting with the ship's Executive Officer—[Second in Command behind the Captain] Would you believe that that officer was Lieutenant Commander Lloyd "Pete" Bucher, who in a couple of years would become famous as the Captain of the USS Pueblo (PER 2) an intelligence gathering ship which was captured off of the coast of North

Korea. The Captain and crew were imprisoned, and tortured some, for a year, then released. (That ship is still on display in North Korea.)

[Time digression] In May 2019, our local United States Submarine Veterans held our traditional Memorial Day Service. Our Chaplin, John Barker, who was sitting one chair away from me, got this long cardboard box out of his car, opened it, and placed an expensive model of a World War II submarine. It just happened to be: U.S. S. RONQUIL (SS396). After the ceremony, and the model submarine was still sitting there, I asked John "WHAT IS WITH THIS SUBMARINE?" He immediately replied, **"I am just about to give it to you; you will not own it, but you will have the custody, because you are the one that does a lecture on the *HISTORY OF American Submarining. AND, in September, I attended the USS Ronquil Boat Reunion in Cleveland.* I took the model with me; and I delivered my lecture on submarines. [End Digression]

Following my successful summer in Submarine School, I "poured on the coal" and learned the rest of the curriculum—especially since I was living right there among all of the submarine systems, and the active-duty station keeper sailors tutored me. In November 1963, when the U.S.S. Sterlet (SS 392) steamed into port to take the Reservists out to sea for the weekend, I requested to be examined for qualification. It just so happened that there was a Navy Publicity Photographer on board. So, there are photographs of me explaining to the examiners some of the systems. I passed. And as was the old tradition, when someone qualified, they were "thrown over the side into the ocean" there is a picture of me flying in midair toward the water.

Meanwhile, back at the ranch, all of us as housemates in the flat at 71 Buena Vista Terrace, scattered for the summer, giving up the flat. Rosalie LeCount arranged for me to store all of my belongings in the LeCount House Basement. That was indeed a large favor.

## PATRIC IS SENT TO SAN QUENTIN PRISON

• • • • • • • • • • • • • • • • • • • • • • •

In November 1963, I attended an American Friends Service Committee (Quakers) weekend on a ranch where we had workshops in helping to rehabilitate prisoners in San Quentin Prison. While both men and women attended the workshops, only men were allowed to go into the prison to participate in the therapy program. The concept was: "Self-Reflexive Therapy: what could a prisoner—no—the correct expression is a person who happened to be in prison—could change about their lifestyle so they could "stop doing life-in-prison-on-the-installment-Plan!" Meaning serve one sentence for one crime, getting out of prison, then a year or so later, committing more crimes and landing back in prison [Recidivism Page 1610 in my Unabridged Dictionary 1. Repeated or habitual relapse, as into crime.] Certain prison guards volunteered to be trained as therapists. Men in prison could volunteer to participate in the therapy sessions. Each session one or two men would volunteer to have their lives discussed to find ways to change and stay out of prison.

Meanwhile, back inside of San Quinten Prison….what? what did you say? Oh yes, I needed to prepare for this. Since I was not working most night in November and December, 1963, I accepted an assignment from the American Friends Service Committee to work on a project to help persons who were incarcerated, to carefully examine their life's behaviors, and to change them to more acceptable behaviors in society and to "**STOP DOING LIFE IN PRISON ON THE INSTALLMENT PLAN: Serving time in prison, bring released to society and within six months to a year, they commit a crime—often the same one- and thus back in prison.** I was a concerned person to try and help. So, every Thursday night, I was let into the prison; escorted across the "Big Yard" and escorted to the library where eleven or so inmates and one guard were seated around the table... All labels were left at the door.

The guard WAS TRAINED AS THE *Facilitator; AND AS A RESULT OF RECOGNIZING EACH OTHER AS HUMAN BEINGS, THE INMATES STARTED PROTECTING THE GUARD WHEN HE WAS IN the big yard.*

On Thursday nights I took a bus to San Quentin Prison, signed in at the Guard Station. I was escorted across "The Big Yard" to the Library, where the guard-therapist and about 12 men were meeting. I joined them for the whole meeting. The first night or two, the men inquired why in the world was I there? But then they accepted me, and I was comfortable being with them. I even recognized one of the men who was a well-known radio disc jockey. I was never informed what he or any of the men did to be placed in prison. It was none of my business. The sessions were productive. At the end of the session, the men returned to their cells, and the guard and I went to the canteen to have coffee and discuss the experience. I learned, for example, that the Guard-Therapist said that his role as a guard---especially when he was supervising in the Big Yard—changed for the better. That the men who were in the therapy sessions spread the word "You don't mess with this guard—he is helping us!" That as an outcome of the weekly sessions, everyone recognized that each other was a human being, with feelings, with families, with needs. They saw each other as "persons" rather than as prisoners or the Screw (guard). Similarly, I also learned to see the men as persons, who happened to have done something to land them in prison. I spent six weeks participating. I only stopped because the Bank of America Cash Vault offered me a full-time evening job. I have always been glad I was fortunate to have had that life's experience. I have never forgotten the lessons I learned, and they have been useful in other contexts.

So then, the last night the gates opened and let me out of the prison, I went immediately to the telephone booth—which was immediately located within a few feet up close to the tall stone walls-- and called my mother to arrange to fly back to Cincinnati for Christmas. "Hi Mom! Guess what: I am calling you from San Quentin Prison!" "My God, what?" "It's alright, I am not an inmate…"

## SAN QUENTIN PRISON FROM THE INSIDE

• • • • • • • • • • • • • • • • • • • • • • •

I was interviewed by the University's newspaper—***Golden Gater,*** December 5, 1963.

### S.Q. seen from inside

"Several weeks ago, an SF student entered San Quentin for the first time. He was immediately put in a room with eight prisoners, and a corrections officer. The group had an amiable discussion for two hours, after which the student left, a free man….."

"One of the chief objects of the program is to let the prisoners know that someone outside cares they exist."….

"When I finally met them, they looked, talked, and acted just like you and me. According to the corrections officer I worked with, the average cross section of San Quentin society is just like that of the outside world, even as far as education is concerned."……

The corrections officer whose primary job is to rehabilitate prisoners, is the discussion leader…anyone could ask questions of anyone else. No one had to answer, but most did.

Once the discussion started the prisoners showed no signs of bitterness.

*Most of the bitterness seemed to be hostility toward everything in general, although some expressed bitterness toward society...*

*"He added, "It seems to that if a man can adjust to society, he can be rehabilitated. He may have felt justified in his own crime, but if he can accept society's rules, he can fit in."*

*Leedom said "the corrections officer agreed with him in this and also agreed that the present system of rehabilitation is inadequate."*

*But the officer added, "We can only help the prisoner to adjust to society. Rehabilitation isn't something that happens to a prisoner, it's something he does to himself."*

## *ASSOCIATE JUSTICE: ASSOCIATED STUDENT GOVERNMENT COURT*

● ● ● ● ● ● ● ● ● ● ● ● ● ● ● ● ● ● ● ● ●

In this same edition of the Gator, I was a part of another article:

### Court rules again; nullifying rep election

*"For the second time this semester as the Associated Student Body Judicial Court has declared an A.S. election null and void.*

*The physical education representative election of November 19 and 20 was nullified by a court decision submitted by Chief Justice Keith Mackie on December 3.*

***Justices Pat Leedom,** Phil Plotkin, Rick Davies and Dean Dorothy Wells concurred in the decision...."*

Yes, I was active in the Associated Students Government. I was a justice on the court for two years. I was also a member of the "Academic Review Board" we monitored students' grade point averages. The rule was, if a student's GPA fell below 2.50, then they were no longer permitted to serve as an officer of any student organization on campus. There were some screams and tears, but we held to the rule.

## PATRIC CONVINCES HIS FATHER TO JOURNEY BACK TO OHIO AND RECONCILE WITH HIS MOTHER

• • • • • • • • • • • • • • • • • • • • • • •

After Submarine School and my incredible two weeks at sea aboard the USS Ronquil (SS396) I returned to San Francisco. Shortly thereafter I was asked to attend a YMCA Presidents' Conference in Lake Geneva, Wisconsin. I was given a nominal amount of money. At the same time, I had convinced my father to drive back and visit with his mother, whom he had not seen in 26 years. So, he and I, Stepmother Elizabeth, and three-year old Casey, packed into Dad's French DS Citroen automobile and started our trip from Los Angeles to Southern Ohio. As we reached the town of Liberal, Kansas, the car broke down; the long periods of overheated engine had warped the engine head. So now it was a crisis because there were only two Citroen car dealers in the United States: Hollywood in Los Angeles, and Philadelphia, Pennsylvania. So, a local car dealership had to make the arrangements of order and receiving the required parts from a long distance away. The family was stuck in a motel for days at a time.

But I could not stay that long. I needed to stop by Cincinnati and visit with mother and her new husband, Mark Mitchell, and then I needed to scurry up to Lake Geneva for the Presidents' Conference. About two days after the Conference began; there was talk of Rev. Martin Luther King's "famous March on Washington" which would conclude with his famous "I Have-A-Dream-Speech." The majority of delegates voted that we should rent a Greyhound bus and go to Washington and be there for the March and Speech. I telephoned my father to let him know my potential plans to go.

OOOPS. My Dad and his fourth wife did not have smooth luvvy dubby relationship; it was more like fencing and sparring. So, he was very upset with me, because he felt I deserted him in Kansas and left him alone with his wife, Elizabeth! (And 3-year-old, Casey) *That was the first time that I was aware of his upset-ness. He essentially said to me, "If you are not at the college in Lake Geneva, Wisconsin when I drive through, you can just find your own way back to California!" Big ouch. I had no extra money. So out of fear and anxiety, I declined to take the bus to Washington. [I have regretted all my life that I came so close to being there at that famous moment in United States History.] As it turned out, our delegates had travelled all night long to attend the March and Speech, and then immediately drove all night long back to Wisconsin, arriving a day or two before my father did.

I arrived back in San Francisco in late August. But now I had two major problems: My part time job at the Bank of America Monday, Tuesday, and Friday nights counting money in the cash vault had been suspended since I was not a full-time employee. Now I was "on call" if they needed extra help. And that turned out to be somewhat less than once a week. So, my money was ultra-minimal. Problem number two: I had no place to live, and of course without money for rent, there was no point in looking.

## PATRIC, WITHOUT A JOB, IS INVITED TO LIVE
## RENT-FREE ON SHIPYARD SUBMARINE

• • • • • • • • • • • • • • • • • • • • • •

But then "my guardian Leprechaun came to my rescue." We had a Naval Reserve Weekend, and we were down on the Dentuda Submarine for training. In charge of the submarine was an active-duty Chief Engineman. He and I began discussing my predicament of no place to live. He then suggested "Why don't you just move aboard here on the submarine—rent free?" "Really? Are you serious?" "Yes!" "Alright, then, I will." And I did. In exchange for rent, I had two assignments. Help hold "Field Day" on Fridays (help clean and scrub belowdecks,--keep the ship presentable for tourists.) And number two, provide explanatory tours for anyone wishing to go through the submarine. Okay. No problem. I remember that I took over the Captain's State Room for my stateroom. I might need to explain a couple of things. Most of my possessions were still stored in the LeCount's Basement at their home on the corner of 32nd Street and Clement. So, I really only had minimal possessions on the sub. Second, I was actually the only person living on the submarine. Now since it was still classified as an Active-Duty Training Submarine, there was always one active-duty Station Keeper sailor who came down to spend the night. It depended upon who had the official 24-hour duty.

This living arrangement "saved my life." Oh yes, Hunters' Point was an active shipyard, and so there were always two to three submarines on blocks in the dry docks, undergoing an overhaul. There was a Navy chow hall located just a few feet from the dry docks for the convenience of the various ship's crews. Again, my finances were minimal. I did have enough money to pay the 15 cents it cost to take the street cars and buses to school and back; and in the late evenings there were "Jitneys." [Page 1030 in my Unabridged Dictionary jit'ne 1. A small bus or car following a regular route along which it picks up and discharges passengers, originally charging each passenger five cents.] The Navy Jitneys ran along Market Street and picked up sailors at specific corners. I forget what the cost was—maybe 25 cents, but I did have enough. When we got to the Naval Base and Shipyard, we each had to show our Identification cards to the guards at the gate. And I did have my Reservist ID card. However, it was not exactly legal for me to be living on the submarine, but no one ever questioned me.

Nor was it legal either for me to eat in the chow hall. But there were evenings when I was hungry and had no food nor money. I put on my dungaree Navy uniform, with a big thick Foul Weather Jacket. I got in line with the other sailors; I guess they all assumed since there were two to three subs there, that I must be a member of some other boat crew. But no one ever asked. Good. With my big heavy jacket with big pockets, I went through the chow line stuffing my pockets with apples, oranges, milks, juices, and cookies, for future consumption. I took my big metal tray full of food, found a table by myself, and "ate the fastest I have ever eaten in my whole life, before or since." And hurried out of the door!

As an historical note, I was living aboard in November of 1963 when our President, John F. Kennedy, was shot and killed. We had a television set on board, and there were three full days of televised events. I chose to skip school and stayed on board all three days, watching.

*PATRIC HAS MOVED TO SAN FRANCISCO STATE IN ORDER TO FULFILL HIS DREAM OF STUDYING GENERAL SEMANTICS*

• • • • • • • • • • • • • • • • • • • • • •

This was the semester that I was enrolled in Dr. S. I. Hayakawa's course on General Semantics. My desk was by the windows near the front. Maybe that explains why, when I appeared for the next scheduled class, Dr. Hayakawa confronted me and wanted to know why I had been absent! Two related stories. #1. I turned around in my seat one day and observed that the middle-aged woman seated behind me was wearing a miniature set of Gold Submarine Dolphins! I inquired if she was related to anyone in the submarine service? She responded, "Yes. My uncle—Admiral Hyman Rickover!!" [The father of the U.S. nuclear Navy!] "Wow! Thank you."

Story # 2. Small-world-ism: Dr. Hayakawa's wife, whom I never met, was my mother's mother's first boyfriend's brother's daughter! My mother told me that when the family came to Hamilton, Ohio, that she, my mother, entertained the daughter, often in card games. And, it was the daughter's brother, who married Svetlana Stalin when she immigrated to this country.

Shifting gears, the LeCount family somewhat adopted me. Knowing that I was living on a deserted submarine during the week, they often had me come and stay the weekend and holidays in their home, and sleep on the bed in the Basement. That was very nurturing. I know I was visiting there the weekend I "Qualified in Submarines" and earned my silver dolphins.

When I joined (which was immediately after the Cuban Missile Crisis) I still had over two years of college courses to go, and the Navy deferred my active-duty requirement until I graduated. During that time, I chose to become a Quartermaster—because they worked with charts, navigation, flashing signal lights, celestial navigation—real sea-going jobs. I was able to study and take the test for Third Class Quartermaster (E4) just before I went on Active Duty in April 1965.

+ + + + + + +

Referring to that period in 1963 when I stepped away from my bank job to attend my mother's wedding, and to spend a few months in the Navy, and consequently did not have a steady income up until January 1964, I offer the following: A humorous occurrence. The Bank had telephoned me in early December 1963, offering full time. I said I would be glad to accept; but may I postpone starting until January 1st? Yes.

I am remembering that that fall semester at San Francisco State, I was taking a physical education course in skiing. And our instructor owned his own small ski business. He hired me and a girl named Gail Sears to come up and be his assistants and work for a week. We would be loaned ski equipment, be given ski lessons, and allowed to use the "Tow Cable" up the slope after hours. What a treat. I had never skied before. But I learned quickly. Riding the tow cable was an interesting experience: the cable ran continuously from the engine shack up the ski slope, around that large pulley wheel and back down. You had to walk in your skis up to the tow, point your skis up hill and with your hand and arm, grab on to the tow cable and let it pull you up the slope, and it was up to you to figure when to let go of the cable.

Christmas with the MITCHELL family in Cincinnati was delightful…my first Christmas with my mother and her new husband, and my new stepsisters and brother. "Grampy" Mitchell—Mark Jr.'s father—was still alive. Mark Sr. had gone to Yale for college. He had an outstanding singing voice and joined the Yale Glee Cub and was a founder of the "Whiffenpoofs." He also was an excellent Yodeler. And in 1961 when Mark Sr. was in his 80's, he was invited back to Yale to provide Yodeling on a new Yale Glee Club record album [which I still have.] Anyway, on New Year's Eve, it was a family tradition to play "penny-Ante" Poker. And we did. At around Midnight everyone had gone to bed except me. And then I heard a loud car crash! It had been snowing for a few days and the roads were slick. I saw that a person had crashed their car straight into a Utility pole. I went downstairs and out into the street. The driver as an African American who was a driver for Pepsi-Cola. He was all shook up—and I think crying. I went and got my borrowed car and I drove him back home downtown in the West End. He was so very grateful and couldn't stop thanking me.

San Francisco State College (Later University) had formerly been a "Normal School" or Teachers' College. [The word "Normal" actually comes from the French, with a very different meaning than in English.] Our campus was primitive compared to most other colleges. Many offices and organizations were housed in Quonset Huts, as was the YMCA. Also, SFSC did not have an Administrative Division "Host" for guests on Campus. So, our YMCA was asked to be the host for whomever. This included Anthropologist Margaret Meade; the Mayor of Paris; Norman Thomas, who as a Socialist Candidate, had campaigned for the Presidency of the United States six times, and had been a consultant President Franklin D. Roosevelt; the Kirov Ballet from the Soviet Union; and the Original U.S. Peace Corps Staff: Nan McAvoy, Coates Redman, and a gentleman whose name escapes me. They were recruiter for their boss Sargent Shriver (brother-in-law to President John F. Kennedy). They were successful in recruiting; my sister-in-law, Rosalie LeCount signed up for two years in Ecuador.

## JEANNIE AND PATRIC "GET HITCHED"

• • • • • • • • • • • • • • • • • • • • •

Now it is early 1964. Jeannie, the oldest of five siblings, and I had not dated since last June. She was dating other men, and I had occasional dates with other women. Or maybe Jeannie was between dating other men. There was that night when I was visiting in the LeCount home. Jeannie fixed a wonderful dinner; I thanked her and went off to date someone else. And apparently Jeannie and her mother began discussing that I would be "a good catch" because in the weeks that followed, Jeannie mounted a campaign to attract me to her. It worked. Jeannie and I were married June 13th and set up housekeeping in an apartment just south of Golden Gate Park, overlooking the Great Highway and Pacific Ocean. Since January 1st, I was working five nights a week in the Bank of America Central Cash Vault—4:30 P.M. until 12:45 A.M. Our daughter, Julia, was born late that year.

I was finishing my senior year in college, so I was taking courses in the daytime; that left the weekends to enjoy being husband and wife. But, oh yes, one weekend a month I spent all day Saturday and Sunday as a reservist at the Naval Base. I was still President of the College YMCA, which sponsored a weekend of hiking in the mountains. Jeannie was pregnant but we didn't think she was that far along, so we joined the hikers. Our guide related to us specifically that on an earlier trip there had been a pregnant woman, and upon her return home, her water had broken, and her child was born the next day. Hmmm, interesting story, but let's keep hiking. We arrived home Sunday evening. In the middle of the night, Jeannie's water broke, flooding the bed. We did not own a car, so we called her parents and her father took us to the hospital "to have a miscarriage." No? [We had not known how far along Jeannie's pregnancy was.] Eighteen hours later we left the hospital with our daughter Julia in our arms. On the way out the door, the administrative clerks stopped us "because they wanted to see our "miscarriage" that we had told them we were having as we checked in.

Finally, after three extra months of academic writing, I graduated with a bachelor's in political science. Why Political Science? Well, as a diehard romantic, I thought it would be great to work in the United States Embassies and Consulates abroad! [In the days before the book, **The Ugly American** was published cataloguing Americans' poor behavior abroad.] I had become bored with my major—it didn't seem much like a science; the articles and chapters were so abstract and difficult for me to comprehend. I remember the cartoon in my mind: "A political scientist is someone who climbs up a tree to see into someone's second floor window, and even though the window is shut, the scientist takes notes and writes a theory about what is going on inside!" I asked the Navy if I could continue my deferment from Active Duty if I changed my major. "No. Either finish your current degree or go on Active Duty right now!" "Okay, I will finish my current degree." I turned in my last required papers in early April 1965 and reported to the Navy two weeks later. Also, the Bank of America was required by Federal Law to hold my job open while I was on Military Duty. As a matter of fact, they gave me two extra pay checks with a letter explaining "Since you will be earning a lot less money in the military…"

## PATRIC IS CALLED TO ACTIVE DUTY ON SUBMARINES

• • • • • • • • • • • • • • • • • • • • • • •

Step one was to report to Treasure Island Naval Base—the island that is located in the Bay between San Francisco and Oakland. The Bay Bridge runs right through it. My first set of Orders were to an aircraft carrier, the U.S.S. Hancock (CV 19). I walked up to the Orders window, pointed to my Submarine Dolphins, and literally said, "Do these look-like wings?" "No?" "Then I don't go on aircraft carriers!" One week later they gave me Orders to the U.S.S. Capitaine (AGSS 336) in San Diego. [AGSS designates an "Auxiliary General Submarine—too old to go on War Patrols, but good enough to service foreign navies.]

I was sent by train to San Diego, then by bus to the Submarine Base at Ballast Point. Arriving at the Sub Piers, there were around 10 to 12 submarines in port tied up together in nests. I asked where is the U.S.S. Capitaine? And they pointed to the farthest boat out from the pier, and it was quickly obvious that it was the "oldest boat in the fleet." It had the original "Shears"—a metal open-air support structure which contained the periscopes, and their housings, radar masts, and assorted antennas. The bridge was old style, there was a "Cigarette Deck" at the back of the bridge—where the 20-millimeter canon used to stand, and no Snorkel Equipment.

I thought "Oh No. I wanted one of those new upgraded subs with the North Atlantic High Sails on them—like on the U.S. S. Ronquil (SS 396) which I had ridden the year before." Ugh. However, "perhaps one should not judge a book by its cover, nor a submarine by its topside appearance!" Three weeks later, I discovered I was on one of the best boats.

### PATRIC IS FORTUNATE: HE BYPASSES SIX MONTHS OF MESS-COOKING AND DECK GANG SCRAPPING AND PAINTING, AND GOES DIRECTLY INTO THE QUARTERMASTER GANG

• • • • • • • • • • • • • • • • • • • • •

The normal routine for a new seaman (E3) reporting aboard, is to be assigned both "Mess Cooking" (helping prepare, serve, and clean up after meals) for six months, and be a part of the Seaman Gang in port to scrap and paint the ship and assorted duties; After six months, THEN one could be assigned to the "gang" of one's choice e.g., radio, torpedo, engine, sonar, etc.

But I was far more fortunate. Within the first hours aboard, Bill Baise, the Chief Quartermaster, found me and said, "You are a quartermaster—I need you NOW in the gang." So, I never did mess cook, nor spend more than a few days in the Seaman Gang. Instead, Chief Baise was a wonderful boss, and I immediately started classes when Chief Base began to instruct myself and my partner and fellow third-class quartermaster, John Q. Perry how to do celestial navigation.

This skill is normally reserved for First Class Petty Officers and Chiefs, not Third-Class Petty Officers.

Chief Bill Baise was one of those very intelligent sailors who is excellent in his knowledge and skills of quartermastering—he had been in the Navy pushing 20 years, but he seemed also to have a personality that got him in trouble with the officers; consequently, he had been promoted to Chief, demoted to First Class, promoted to Chief demoted to First Class; when I went to work for him, he was on his way back up to Chief. John Perry and I quickly learned the long complicated mathematical procedures for calculating the exact angle of the stars. Without stopping to consult my Navigation Text book, it took at least 15 steps. Normally one chooses seven of the brightest navigation stars (from the Rude Start Finder—templates etc.) available to your sky at the time of observing. Each star can take 20 minutes to calculate the final reading, so to lay down a star fix takes in the neighborhood of two hours.

Oh yes, before reporting for Active Duty, I had taken the test for Quartermaster Third Class and passed. So, two weeks after reporting aboard, I "sewed on the Crow" (actually the American Eagle) the uniform left sleeve insignia. [And, I had been in the Navy over two years, so my monthly pay was considerably higher than someone with less than two years. And since I was married with a daughter, this was an excellent benefit.]+

Above, I stated that this ship was one of the oldest. Well, sort of. During World War II, American submarines carried Army Artillery pieces mounted on the deck for both sinking merchant ships and for defense. However, right after the war, the artillery was removed from the subs on Active Duty, and all traces removed. The Capitaine had been built in 1944, so was fairly new, and after the war ended it was "mothballed" in 1945. It was recommissioned in the late 1950's but with no updating of ship's equipment. We had the mounting for the canon, the Gun Access Trunk that came straight up from the Control Room—such that gunners could be at their stations, armed and ready in less than three minutes. We had the Ammunition Pass-through pipe, which led directly from the After-Battery Compartment where most of the ammunition was stored below decks; and we had the JA Sound-Powered Gun Firing Circuit still in place. Literally, the only thing new of the ship since WWII, was the crew!

After a few weeks, I was able to go back home to San Francisco and pack up my wife and daughter and move them to my parents' home in Tujunga (a suburb of Los Angeles.) My parents had "contracted" with Jeannie that she would live on the premises –in the garage room that I had built a few years before—rent free BUT she was expected to help take care of the children—Casey, Erin, and Kelly as well as our daughter, Julia, and do some kitchen cooking and cleaning.

This arrangement was necessary because the U.S.S. Capitaine was scheduled to leave the United States in early July and sail to the Western Pacific—known as a WEST PAC tour to last six months.

Indeed, we did just that. I need to pause the story and explain that World War II Diesel Electric Submarines were essentially "surface ships that had the capacity to submerged for short periods of time—usually 30 hours or less but in extreme emergency, the ship could stay down around 48 hours.

*THE FOLLOWING SECTION IS HEAVILY FOCUSED ON HOW WWII SUBMARINES ARE CONFIGURED AND OPERATE. IF YOU ARE NOT INTERESTED IN THESE TOPICS, JUMP AHEAD TO THE NEXT SECTION PAGE 225.*

• • • • • • • • • • • • • • • • • • • • • •

**I have been thinking, what is the attraction to submarines for me.** Why I have I so readily given so much of my life riding on submarines both below the surface of the ocean and on the surface? The mental emotional attraction to submarines probably comes from that same space in my brain, that had attracted me to the SEA LAB IIi.

*WHEN THE SEA LAB III WAS IN DRY DOCK AT THE HUNTER'S POINT NAVAL SHIPYARD, AND MY ATTRACTION TO WISHING TO SERVE ON SEA LAB III*

• • • • • • • • • • • • • • • • • • • • •

*The Sea Lab was an experimental underwater living environment to see how well humans could work and survive when living under water 400 feet, moored to the Continental Shelf.* Divers were able to enter and depart the Sea Lab at will as the air pressure inside kept the water out of the open hatch, on the deck of the diving space. [I toured the Sea Lab for a few hours when it was manned by an all-submarine sailor crew. There were three compartments: a small compartment for suiting up in diving suits and departing and returning to the lab through an uncovered cylindrical access hatch; a medium sized compartment which was the primary living space when scientists were not in their bunks. But were carrying out daily tasks eating, carrying out scientific experiments, washing their clothes in a set of Kenmore Washer and Dryer. The third compartment was the crew's sleeping space. There were maybe twelve bunks as I recall and PORTHOLES that one could look out and see the sea life, the fish, and the sea.

So, what is that part of my brain thinking that creates these attractions?

I can visualize a whole recipe of ingredients:

1. Almost insatiable curiosity about the world and what is in it.
2. A desire to be a part of a structure where everything has a clear-cut purpose and makes logical sense.
3. A wish to be a part of a team where everyone is qualified to carry out their assigned tasks and can be counted upon to do those tasks not only during regular routines, but in times of crisis and emergency.
4. Where there is a need and purpose for each crew person to be there. There is "no dead wood" or "or persons who are not contributing to the successful mission of our expedition of exploration.
5. Where there is a clear and competent structure of command; outstanding leadership, using positive motivation rather than negative threats.`

I *read Jules Verne's 20 Thousand Leagues under the Sea* on a submarine named *NAUTILUS*--especially while I was serving aboard the United States' First Nuclear Submarine: *U.S.S. Nautilus (SSN 571)* and was quite taken with the possibilities of undersea exploration. In the 1960's when I first starting sailing on submarines, and as a quartermaster, I was quite often on the bridge where I could see the ocean swells and waves go by. And the awareness that our small 'can of people "—(*That is what the Baby Sardine said to its mother when a submarine went by)*- was all out there alone on the sea, but yet our craft is built to survive and protect us. It was easy for me to imagine the two-mile depths of the ocean and millions of gallons of water that surrounded us, even as we would submerge down several hundred feet.

*Submarines are one of the most efficient fighting machines. There is no superfluous equipment or space on board. This includes the crew. In the 1960's, all crew members took at a test to support that each had an IQ "Above Average—Above a score of 100; I am thinking that actually it was above 110."*

As a quartermaster, if I was on Watch, then it was my job to "dog the hatch shut as we submerged, and undog the hatch when we surfaced, and I was the first person to leap up onto the Bridge and yell out 'No immediate contacts, sir."

## A TOUR OF AN OLD DIESEL-ELECTRIC
## SUBMARINE WITH COMMENTARY

• • • • • • • • • • • • • • • • • • • • • • •

So, as we transited first to Hawaii and then to Yokosuka, Japan, we did so on the surface. Also, the old Fleet Type Boats were configured with eight compartments in a line plus the Conning Tower over top of the Control Room [The old diesel-electric submarines could withstand flooding in two of the compartments and still survive.] in a straight line from Bow to Stern: Forward Torpedo Room where there were sixteen racks for enlisted sailors, six torpedo tubes and a load of 18 torpedoes. Forward Battery which had 126 Battery Cells down below the walking deck, and "Officers' Country" above. This is where the Captain had his separate quarters, and all the other officers shared three-man staterooms. There was a Wardroom where the Officers took meals, watched movies, and had conferences. There was the Ship's Office where the Yeoman (Secretary) worked. And finally, there were the Chiefs' Quarters where six chiefs each had their own rack to sleep in. Traditionally, aboard Naval Ships, the Chiefs' Quarters are referred to as the "GOAT LOCKER." I am not quite sure of the origin of the term, BUT, having been a "Fire Watch" in a Chiefs' Barracks with open dormitory sleeping rooms, the SMELL of old men sleeping without using deodorant can be fierce. May I quickly note, that in the 1960's there were many sailors that stayed on active duty into their fifties and sometimes sixties. [Those days are long gone and older men do smell more. [Those days are long gone—life on board the modern nuclear submarines if very rigorous and demanding, and the military often pushes enlisted men out in their 40's, let alone 50's and 60's].

Tour continued. I am going to shift to the Radar Pickett Submarine for it has an extra 30-foot compartment immediately adjacent to the Forward Battery. This inserted compartment is designated the COMBAT COMPARTMENT. When the sub was active as a Radar Pickett boat, this compartment was crammed full of radar equipment. When the Radar Picket program was disestablished, this compartment left one Radar monitoring station in the corner and converted the rest to Crews' Sleeping Quarters above the walking deck, and below the walking deck were storage and work spaces for various Gangs such as Store Keepers, Electronics Technicians, and Quartermasters. [In 24 years, The USS Rock (AGSS 274) was the only submarine where I had a decent 24-hour work space in this special compartment!!]

The fourth compartment in line (bow to stern) was CONTROL. This was a major command and control type space. Starting in the upper Port Corner, was the Chief of the Watch, who controlled the valves in opening and closing the Ballast Tanks. The physical control of the ship is controlled primarily from this compartment: Surfacing and submerging the ship. Moving water either fore and aft, or port to starboard, to trim the angle of the ship; the hi-pressure air valves for expelling the water out of the ballast tanks in order to surface.

Control Compartment has the secondary Steering Stand (Helm) in case the Conning Tower is lost. Control Room is the home of the Bow and Stern Planes, which—like airplane wings and ailerons-- assist the ship to dive deep or come up.

Directly below the Control Room is the Pump Room containing the high-pressure air compressors, the Low-Pressure Blower. The Trim Pump for moving good water in and out of various tanks; and the Drain Pump to move waste water overboard. There are also hydraulic pumps, for the periscopes, helm, bow and stern planes.

Directly above the Control Room is the Conning Tower [5th Compartment—8' wide x 13' long], where the periscopes are, radar station, fire control equipment for firing torpedoes; the main steering (helm) stand, the three alarms and the Command Center during battles. Directly above the Conning Tower is the Bridge. The hatches and ladders almost line up in a straight line, such that Bridge personnel, on the command to "Clear the Bridge" can be down into Control; e.g., for the Lookouts to man the Bow and Stern planes in less than one minute of time.

Point of Information. When a submarine is out on the open ocean, there is only one authorized access in and out of the ship. And that is from the Control Room, one climbs up the ladder to the Conning Tower. From the Conning Tower one climbs up the ladder to the Bridge.

All four of the additional hatches are closed and dogged down. This is especially true of the After-Battery Hatch. This access tube is about eight feet long. When a ship is loading up food for a long, long deployment, the "Doubler Hatch" is bolted to the lower end of the tube. Then several hundred pounds of potatoes are loaded into the tube; the upper hatch is sealed and "Dogged Down" (the three articulated clamps that seal the hatch cover to the interior lip of the ship, are known as "Dogs.") With a moment's thought you will understand that when the cooks need more potatoes, yep, we have to surface the ship!

In the rear of Control, is the "Radio Shack" where all radio messages are sent and received. Would you believe when I went aboard in 1965, the radio transmissions were done with a telegraph key using the Morse Code. To speed up the process, our Chief Radioman Price started tape recording the radio traffic, then transcribing the messages. Outside the Radio Shack door was the deck (floor) hatch for the "Dry Stores" for much of the food that did not need refrigeration or freezing.

Then as we continue aft on our ship, we climb through the 'Watertight Door" into the After-Battery Compartment. As one steps through, immediately is the deck hatch for the refrigerator and freezer. I make note of this because once I saw the mail petty officer come down the After-Battery hatch from topside, turn forward, not looking where he was going; the Refrigerator Hatch was open, and he fell down into the Refrigerator. He climbs back out, stepped through the Water tight Door where the Dry Stores Hatch was open, and he proceeded to fall down into the Dry Stores!!! I kid thee not; it really did happen that way!

So now we are in the After Battery. The Compartment gets its name from the huge 126 cell battery below the walking deck. Above deck is the Galley (kitchen) where all of the food is prepared—for enlisted and officers. Just beyond the Galley is the "Crew's Dinette" containing four tables each seating six persons. It took it three evolutions of serving and cleaning to feed the whole crew.

When meals are not being served, the Crew's Mess with its four tables becomes the place for recreation. Off-watch sailors can play card games, such as Cribbage, or Acey-Deucey. Some crew members read books; some write letters home. There is a tape recorder that can be used to play music—that is if someone took the time to record music on tape. The evening movie for the enlisted men is projected here.

This space is also the largest assembling space when the Captain wishes to speak with the crew. Now with 80 plus men on board, they all cannot fit in at one time. So, the Captain needs to address each Watch Section, one at a time. And this space is used on Sunday mornings for Catholic Services, and Protestant Services for those who wish to participate.

The After-Battery Compartment is divided into two distinct areas, with a bulkhead (wall) and somewhat soundproof door to pass from one to the other. This second area is the largest crew's sleeping quarters on the ship. There are 36 bunks with 12 vertical configurations of three bunks each.

Then this area is further divided between the sleeping quarters and the "Head" or bathroom. It contains two toilet stalls, four sinks, and two showers. Special note: our ship had a minimum capacity of distilling water from the seawater. We could maybe process 2000 gallons a day if both stills were operating correctly, but the primary use of this limited water was 1) 252 Battery Cells; 2) All of the Galley's water needs for cooking and related uses e.g., coffee urn, the scullery sink (dish washing facility and 3) the four large diesel engines. There is very little water left over for the crew. Therefore, only the following personnel are permitted to shower daily: the cooks, the mess cooks, the corpsman (Medical person), and very occasionally a crew member who was involved in an extremely dirty job such as rebuilding an engine.

Given that only a few were allowed to use the ship's showers, when it was raining topside on the USS Capitaine. [only this ship and one other in the squadron had a large enough Bridge deck so sailors could wash off in the rain with soap and towels.] Now if it did not rain for days, and the smell got fierce, then the Captain would order a **SWIM CALL** and require every sailor to jump in with salt water soap.

Thus, more than ten off-watch sailors could come up, take a seat, read a book, smoke a cigarette, cigar, or pipe; or just enjoy talking with friends. The closer we came to the equator to more brilliant were the colors in the evening clouds. Water temperature ranged in the 80's. Come to think of it, good water for swimming!

Our Commanding Officer, LCDR J. D. Hovater, was a kind and fun-loving skipper. He was game for interesting activities. Please note: that when a submarine (or maybe any Navy ship is transiting across the ocean, they are assigned a "Navigation Search Box," that is, the ship is required to stay within an imaginary rectangle that is 50 miles length, and 10 miles wide. Within that framework, the ship is allowed to be as much as 30 miles ahead or twenty miles behind; and only five miles off to either side of its intended track. Theoretically, if the ship was exactly in position as delineated in the ship Movement Orders, then that ship's position would fit right on top of its PIM—Position of Intended Movement. That is reference point when we say 50 miles ahead (of PIM) or 30 miles behind (of PIM). Under normal conditions, our sub would steam around 10 to 12 knots per hour.

Here comes the fun: The Captain would order the Officer of the Deck to speed up until we calculated that we were 50 miles ahead. Then we would come to "All Stop." And slowly flood down such that the main deck was about two feet above the surface of the ocean. We would declare a "Swim Call" and everyone who wanted to could jump over board and swim. Naturally there had to be a duty section on watch control the ship and keeping it safe. For example, we always stationed a "SHARK WATCH" a crew member who was good with a rifle. And would station himself high up on the bridge to better have a better view a view of the surrounding sea. The Captain made sure that the watch sections were rotated, and everyone had a chance to swim. One trick several of us like to do, was to swim down to the limber holes that lead to Bow Buoyancy Tank Number 1. The openings were big enough to swim in; we would sit up on some of the interior struts while the Bow of the ship rocked forward and aft; forward plunging the bow down into the water, and the rising water compressed the air we were breathing, and you guessed it—we were all talking like Donald Duck with high squeaky voices!

After about an hour, the ship's cooks brought out charcoal grills—created from vertically sawing 52-gallon drums in half. And not long after the crew was treated to steak dinners, the fun-loving Captain even "Spiked" our punch with some of his medicinal alcohol. As we neared the back end of our navigation box, we would crank up the engines, inflate the boat back up to its normal position, and speed up to our normal PIM position. Those were not our only surfaced adventures. Early in the Viet Nam War, there were incidents where American Submarines in the Gulf of Tonkin came under fire from North Vietnamese Junks, (small wooden sailing vessels, often used for fishing.) using 50-caliber machine guns. In retaliation, the Americans dug out the old-World War II submarine gun stantions and welded them back up on the bridge where they had been during that war. Then we were issued two WWII 50-Caliber-Machine Guns, four-gun barrels, asbestos gloves, and boxes and boxes of WW II Ammunition. We were taken up the coast to the large Marine Base at Camp Pendleton, to a gun range, set ourselves up, and commenced practicing and firing. Now for the uninitiated, every fifth round (bullet) was an incendiary tracer designed to light the way, so the gunner could aim the gun better on the target. But I said this was old WWII ammunition, and so, without warning, some of the tracers would explode shortly after leaving the barrel. When that occurred, the Command was "Duck and Hold."

Back out at sea, we would mount the guns on the bridge and practice firing usually at some large metal containers that would float for a while.

Now I mentioned that we were given four barrels and asbestos gloves. 50-Caliber Gun Barrels get hot quickly. One does not hold down the "Butterfly" trigger for a long spray of bullets; too much heat. Instead, one pushes the trigger down for a very short burst of three to six bullets. And pause. At appropriate times the gun handlers would put on the asbestos gloves and change out the hot barrel for a cool one.

Now we are heading aft again toward the Forward Engine Room. We are at sea so all the Water-tight Doors are either dogged shut or "on the latch." This is a good time for a survival story. All of the American World War II Submarines were built in such a way as each and every compartment could be sealed off and isolated from every other compartment. So, if during a wartime battle the submarine took damage such as flooding in a compartment, that compartment could be isolated not only by the Water tight Door (which weighed 450 pounds!) but also by the "Bulk Head Flappers" which sealed off the air system. These submarines could withstand flooding in two compartments and still survive to make it to the surface. These Fleet type boats were constructed with a 'Safety Tank" which held the equivalent amount of water that would be contained in a flooded compartment, and the Safety Tank was normally full of water. So, if a compartment did flood, the crew could then "Blow the water completely out of the Safety Tank and maintain stability.

The Forward Engine Room contained two 1600 horsepower diesel engines. These engines were each directly linked to a large generator directly behind the engine. The engine's primary job was to create electricity. A secondary job was to assist with ventilation such as when one wanted to evacuate smoke-filled air. Also in the Forward Engine Room were the two large 1000-gallon water stills. These operated by taking on sea water, heating it up until it made steam, then siphon off and condense the steam into fresh water, and expel the salty brine overboard. Continuing aft is the After-Engine Room, much like the Forward Engine Room. Once the engines were started and running normally, then the "Speed Control" was given over to the Electricians in the Maneuvering Compartment.

Brief comments. A submarine could be propelled by any combination of these four engines. One reason being the 252 battery cells needed charging daily (or maybe nightly when the enemy was unlikely to detect the presence of the submarine.) So sometimes the sub did operate one engine on propulsion, and three on battery charging; as the batteries became charged, then an engine could be switched over to propulsion.

Continuing aft through the next Water-tight Door, is the Maneuvering Compartment. This is where most all of the electrical systems of the boat could be controlled and monitored. However, the primary function of this compartment was to control the ships' movements both forward (Ahead) or backward (Astern) or Stop. These orders to Maneuvering are generated by the Officer of the deck who is in administrative control of the ship. Located in both the Conning Tower and Control Room there are sets of "Motor Order Telegraphs" that can select both the direction and speed requested. The Officer of the Deck directs the Helmsman to operate the Motor Order Telegraphs by turning a knob. As the Helmsman does this, a bell rings back in Maneuvering Room. The Electricians in Charge observe the request ordered speed and then the Electricians carry out the orders first and then can respond to the Helmsman by turning Maneuvering's knob and arrows to match what was ordered. Each Motor Order Telegraph has two sets of arrows or indicators linked to the knobs. One set indicates what is requested—for example "All Ahead Two Thirds" "All Ahead Standard" "All Ahead Full" "All Ahead Flank" "All Back One Third or All Back Emergency." The old-World War II submarines had two propellers: Port (left) and Starboard (Right). They were able to send separate orders to each; for example, "Port Ahead One Third, Starboard back two thirds."

[History Lesson Digression.} In ancient times with Greek, Phoenician, Egyptian ships, the rudder was not all the way aft but lashed on the right side back quarter. Since it was used for "STEERING," the right side of the vessel became known as the **Steerboard"** and over the centuries it changed to **Starboard which was easier to pronounce.** Still in ancient times. The left side was known the **Lard Board,** because that was the side of the vessel where food supplies, as well as passengers came aboard. But during heavy seas and storms, it became very difficult to distinguish between Larboard and starboard, when orders were being hollered out. So, in more recent times, the name was changed to **PORT.** [End of history lesson.]

**The final or** last compartment is The After-Torpedo Room. This Compartment only had four torpedo tubes, whereas the Forward Torpedo Room had six. For crew's sleeping, they only had twelve bunks instead of sixteen. This compartment also housed our Signal Flare Ejector to send up to the surface to signal some important message to the ships on the surface.

One quick story: The USS Rock (AGSS 274) [my second submarine home] was in the San Diego Operations area. We were conducting War Games with an Aircraft Carrier Task Group—USS Kearsarge (CVS 33). We would each open out about 20 miles "to our boxing ring corners." And then begin. The aircraft carrier was protected by a ring of Destroyers. So, the submarine's task was to penetrate the defenses and "torpedo and sink the carrier." We did that successfully the very first night, but the Admiral on board the carrier denied that we had been that successful. So, the next night, our Captain Kennedy had a plan. Again, we penetrated the defenses and headed toward the carrier, and as we "sank the carrier" we fired a green flare that flew up and landed on their Flight Deck. Our Captain's comment was "Deny that, you Son of a Bitch."

Diving and Surfacing. The WW II boats were on the surface most of the time and being spotted by an enemy aircraft could be very dangerous. So, the old submarines had the capability of going from completely surfaced to completely submerged in less than 60 seconds! I know the record on my submarine was 49 seconds! Technically, what the ship did was to open the tops of the Ballast Tanks allowing the high-pressure air—which was supporting the sub on the surface, to quickly escape and allow water to quickly enter the Open Flood Ports at the bottom of the tanks, and quickly fill, making the ship very heavy. The sailors who had been the two Lookouts on the Bridge, upon the Command "Clear the Bridge! Clear the Bridge" instantly dropped down from their Lookout perches, drop quickly down the Bridge hatch ladder into the Conning Tower. Turn to their right two steps, drop down the Conning Tower hatch ladder to the Control Room and within seconds man the Bow and Stern Planes Control Stations. This is all done in less than 30 seconds. Usually on the sound of the Diving Alarm, the Chief of the Watch hits the switch to Rig out the Bow Planes from their vertically folded positions, such that the planes are fully out by the time the lookout needs to take charge and assist with the dive. [The Stern planes are permanently "rigged out." Actually, they are built in their horizontal position as they are constructed as part of the Rudder assembly.

Surfacing is naturally a slower process. Typically, the submarine has been below periscope depth, so the ship can only hear other ships and sea noises but cannot see anything yet. The Captain orders Sonar to do a careful sound search to see if we can detect anyone close by. When Sonar reports all clear, the Captain orders the ship to ascend to periscope keel depth about 60 feet. As the ship is ascending the Captain is 'waltzing" the scope round and round to quickly see if there is any danger above. [Note: a submarine sits low in the water, and the periscope only comes out of the water two to three feet, and with the earth reported to be round, the periscope can only see or observe four miles away on the horizon. ] [Modern submarines no longer have "Periscopes" because they are so easily detected by the Enemy. While a periscope is above the surface 10-12 seconds, the new Electronic Masts are only up maybe several seconds less than that.] If it is all clear, the Captain orders the ship to "Surface." The Quartermaster "stands by" the upper hatch to the bridge ready to follow commands. Captain calls out "Crack the Hatch." "Crack the Hatch, aye sir." Turning the wheel that undogs the hatch which allows any high-pressure air in the boat to escape out safely. Then the Captain orders, "Open the Hatch." The quartermaster repeats back as he is opening the hatch and scrambling up the ladder and instantly scanning the horizon to see if there are any contacts in the air or on the surface. And reports the results to the Captain.

## CONCLUSION OF SUBMARINE TOUR

• • • • • • • • • • • • • • • • • • • • •

Back to May 1965, life on board the Capitaine turned out to be pretty pleasant. I was berthed in the After-Battery Compartment, inboard middle bunk on the Companion Way between compartments. Our ship only had two Three-Ton Air-conditioning Units—just enough to cool the electronics, but not the crew. There was an electric fan mounted high up on the bulkhead [wall] which could be set to rotate. Our bunks were just a thin mattress on a canvas support structure. These racks could be "Triced Up" raised up to almost vertical position by moving the chains which held the racks. While we did have "Bunk Bags" strapped to the outer bar of the bed, they were only big enough for toiletries and a few clothes. Our main personal storage area was behind a little square door built into the bulkhead (wall) that provided one to two cubic feet of space.

Our working day was divided up into four hour "watches" twice a day; so, I might have the "Four to Eight" meaning I would report to my Quartermaster Station at 3:45 A.M. and work until I was relieved by the next watch stander at 7:45 A.M. I would repeat this process in the afternoon for four hours. The Navy believed that "A well-fed watch stander is a more alert and competent watch stander" so the ship provided six meals a day—one before the beginning of each watch. These were the regular Breakfast, Lunch, and Dinner, but in between there were three "Soup-Downs or Mid-Rats = Midnight Rations. A sailor could get a cup of soup and a sandwich before watch. Meals on submarines have always been some of the best in the Navy as a means of compensation (along with the "Hazardous Duty Pay") because of our hazardous duty assignments.

I personally preferred the "4 to 8's" because, since I worked in conjunction with the Bridge of the ship, I got to observe sun rise in the morning, and sunset in the evening. These were also good "Star Times" meaning for Celestial Navigation, the 33 designated navigation stars (the brightest in the sky; the first stars to "pop-out" during twilight in the evening and the last to fade out in the morning dawn.)

My quartermaster work space consisted of 1) the Conning Tower—that small cylinder 8 feet wide by 13 feet long affixed on top of the main line of compartments, and just below the bridge. If the ship was operating on the surface—which was most of the time—the quartermaster, with the permission of the Office of the Deck—could be up on the bridge as often as needed—training and supervising the young sailor Lookouts.

[One normally uses just the naked eye to spot contacts. Then when you see something, then you use the binoculars! On a dark night, one keeps the eyes slowly moving because you do not detect ships etc. with the center of one's eyes; you detect contacts with the sides of your pupils.] I would often compete with the lookouts to see who could spot the contact first. Another interesting phenomenon occurs in certain parts of the ocean. You might be searching for an island and before you see the land, a large mass of low hanging clouds can indicate the location.

Oh, I just have to tell this story. When the old submarines were submerged but to only periscope depth—60 feet—or Snorkeling depth—57 feet, looking out of the periscope with one eye can be fatiguing. So, the Conning Officer and the Quartermaster take turns. Mischief a foot. Sometimes the Quartermaster would yell out, "Oh my god, here comes a GU11!" And the officer would grab the scope and say "Where, where?" Well, a GU11 is a Seagull! And sometimes I would say, "What submarine do you know has three periscopes?" And once again the Conning Officer would grab the scope and say, "Where, where?" Me: "Oh, I was just thinking about one." Actually, when Fleet Ballistic Missile were first built, they did have three periscopes: the third one was an experimental "Star Scope" for Celestial Navigation. But later they removed it.

When the old Diesel Electric Subs were on the surface, quartermasters were required to take weather reports—temperature, due point, direction of wind, waves, swells, description of the percentage of cloud cover and exactly which type of clouds e.g., cumulus, stratus, cirrus etc. consulting with the Officer of the Deck concerning future scheduled course and speed changes.

This is not the place for a detailed discussion of how one fixes the ship's position using a "star fix" or "Sun Line fix". But I will provide an elementary description. A sextant is a complex instrument with which measures the angle obtained between the height of a designated star and the horizon. Each angle represents a "Circle of equal Altitude" meaning that there can be a circle on the earth's surface, and everyone standing on that circle and observing that star will all obtain the exact same angle above the horizon. Now if you "Shoot" a second star (measure the angle from a star to the horizon—actually, with a Correction, it is assumed to be the Center of the Earth) now you have identified a second Circle of Equal Altitude. Where the circles intersect, defines two possible locations on the earth where the ship might be located. Now if you shoot a third star, hopefully the three circles will intersect very close to each other—may be even "Pinpoint" and thereby you have an approximate fix (position) which is said to be accurate to within five miles of your actual position.

Observing the Sun yields some different type data. If one measures the height and bearing (direction) of the sun when it just has arisen, it will yield a vertical line perpendicular to your ship's track; then the routine calls for measuring the sun's height at the exact point of "Noon." This is accomplished by the navigator (or sometimes one of the quartermasters—I did it as an (E4) Third Class) beginning to shoot the Sun a few minutes before noon is thought to happen; he shoots the sun every few seconds and calls out the angles from the Vernier (a small adjustment wheel on the sextant.) A quartermaster is recording every single angle, and this goes on for ten minutes, and during that time an ARC will be displayed, and it is the highest point on the arc that is "Noon". This will give you a line Parallel to the equator and indicates your **exact latitude.** So, there is a quick look at the process.

### THE IMPORTANCE OF DETERMINING LONGTITUDE

• • • • • • • • • • • • • • • • • • • • •

[History Lesson Digression] While the determining of Latitude has been known from Ancient-Times. But the determining of Longitude was not known until an English Clockmaker, John Harrison, produced a highly accurate sea-going clock in the 1770's. Before that there were numerous disasters at sea: In a single such accident, on October 22, 1707, at the Scilly Isles four homebound British warships ran aground and nearly two thousand men lost their lives. Page 8, [***The Illustrated***

*Longitude, Dava Sobel and William H. Andrewses 1995, ISBN0-8027-1344-0 Walker Publishing Co.]*

Sometime in the late 1940's, the Navy was able to create some specialized radio transmitters around the habitable earth. This creates the system of LORAN=Long Range Radio Navigation. By being able to receive at least two varied radio signals on your Radio equipment you can get an approximate fix. Three stations would be better. To quickly summarize, the Quartermaster of the Watch [QMOW] is responsible for knowing the ship's position at all times, and to be sure the ship is not "standing into danger."

Other quartermaster tasks include visual and radio communication. Visual includes Flashing LIGHT using the Navy Morse Code system of dots and dashes. America would be spelled:

.-    --    .    .-.    ..    -.-.    .-

A    M    E    R    I    C    A

Semaphore Flags, sometimes referred to as Wig Wags, but these can transmit all the letters. And when submarines are operating with surface ships, these ships have several different flag hoists that they raise up the yard arms to communicate Identification, commands, Situations on board.

On the old diesel-electric submarines, the quartermaster was expected to know how to operate all the equipment in the Conning Tower such as the Main Steering Stand (Helm) with its three redundant hydraulic systems for power; the radar equipment for taking electronic bearings and ranges, the Dead-Reckoning Tracer to plot the ship's progress, all the Fire Control Equipment for firing torpedoes [The quartermaster was only responsible for lighting off (energizing) the equipment and in-putting basic bearings, course, and speeds until the officers can take over.] The quartermaster's primary job is to utilize his charts and fixes so as to guide the ship and stay on track and to stay safe.

Quick story of navigating using only Radar Ranges and Bearings: in the autumn of 1965, we were operating with the Republic of Korea (ROK) naval forces. This morning we were alone steaming up the north coast of South Korea. The Captain and Navigator had given us orders to watch for a small island (or maybe a very large rock) which was calculated to appear on our Portside (left). We are maintaining a 20-mile distance off from the coast for safety reasons. So, all the personnel on the Bridge are straining their eyes to locate this assigned island or rock. We are steaming along and steaming along ["Steaming" is a generic term any time a ship is traveling even though our ship was on diesel engines.] and we are steaming along, and no such island appears. One of the Lookouts happens to turn toward the Starboard side and hollers out that he sees such an island BUT it is on the Starboard side!!(right)! "What??" "All Stop. All back Full! Then stop!" so we are dead in the water. "Where are we? And why are we off-track?" It took some time to figure it out. When we did, we found that on the coast of Korea there is a coastal set of mountains to navigate from, BUT 20 miles behind them there is a second set, and they had higher elevations: Our Radar was detecting only the second set of mountain ridges!! Our ship was 20 miles closer to shore and possibly steaming into dangerous waters! No one was to blame, but it was good lesson about what you assume when you only have the radar scope to view.

+ + + + + + + + + +

In June 1965, I was active in the NAVY at Ballast Point Submarine Base in San Diego. My family and I were living at Dad's house in Tujunga, north of Los Angeles. We didn't own a car; so, my Dad loaned one of his. Every morning I had to drive 140 miles down to the Submarine

Base. And return every evening unless I had overnight duty.

*[I KNOW THE FOLLOWING IS A HUGE DIGRESSION; BUT IN JULY 1965 IN A SECTION OF LOS ANGELES, NAMED WATTS, THERE WAS A GINORMOUS RACE RIOT WHERE MORE THAN 100 PEOPLE WERE KILLED AND 200 BUSINESSES BURNED TO THE GROUND. I NEEDED TO INSERT THE FOLLOWING REPORT]*

## MY FATHER IS REQUESTED TO KEEP THE CITY OF PASADENA FROM BURNING DURING A SEASON OF RACE-RIOTS

• • • • • • • • • • • • • • • • • • • • • •

Now don't go away: my father, Bob Leedom, reporter, writer, editor of the Pasadena Independent Star News, was a MAJOR CIVIL RIGHTS WORKER! If you have read the book or seen the movie, **The Grapes of Wrath** by John Steinbeck, you have a sense of "The Common People" in the movie is the line "God must love us because he has made so many of us!"

My father, his whole newspaper career, was a champion of the people, whatever race or ethnic group they belonged to. Pasadena was a city founded in the 1880's by very wealthy families from the east coast. They wanted a warm winter retreat. They brought their Black "House Servants" with them to Pasadena. House Servants were like "members of the family" who often raised the white children as well as other house duties. The former House Servants were able to send their children to school and to college where their sons and daughters became teachers, social workers, business men etc.

Along came World War Two. And the Troop Trains brought to California the "Field Hands" from the Deep South. These persons had not been a part of white families, they had not had the opportunity to gain much schooling or ever go to college. And upon observing that life in Pasadena was far better than living in the segregated South, they began moving into Pasadena. Even though both populations were "Black" they had very very little in common and resented each other. There was more Black upon Black violence in Pasadena than Black upon White.

My father was highly skilled in getting along with any group; and so, he was quite familiar with both groups. Now this is July 1965. I don't remember the causes, but there was a horrendous riot in the community of WATTS, California. Hundreds of businesses were burned to the ground; over 100 persons were killed. It was riot!

Pasadena was maybe 20 miles or so up the freeway. The city leaders—Black and White- got scared. They summoned my father into a secret meeting. They knew my father was friendly and accepted by both Black groups. They literally instructed my father to "Keep Pasadena from Burning!"

They said "We will give you all the power you need to make changes in the way our city operates; The Pasadena Independent Star News managers said, "Bob, we will just keep giving you your paychecks; write articles whenever it is important to you in your work." This WAS a secret meeting. There was never any mention of it. Truly, Dad went forth and made changes, many, many changes! Too many to go into depth with all of them.

He caused the Police Chief to be fired! He helped re-write the Constitution of the Police Department. He organized and "educational program" where members of the Black Community held classes to teach the mostly white Policemen how to enforce the law in the Black Community WITHOUT causing a riot. Further, he helped create, when tension got really hot, a "citizens police force within the Black communities, that had the power to tell the uniformed police "Leave now! A riot may be starting, and we will handle it!" and the uniformed police did pull out.

Dad was heavily involved in a very friendly respectful way with the Pasadena Police Department. Occasionally, when they were doing a "Line UP" for the witness to identify the criminal, they would put Dad up on the stage in the Line Up (he was never "fingered" as the culprit.)

My father got the Real Estate businessmen to stop "RED LINING" neighborhoods so the Blacks were not confined to living in special segregated communities. He got the Small Business Administration to begin making bank loans to qualified Black Businessmen; he got the Rose Parade Commission to give over their huge hangar type building, which they only used two months of the year to build Rose Parade Floats, and was located within the Black Community, so the Black Community could use the building for the community's identified needs, whether it be recreation or classes. He got a local manufacturing corporation to loan an unused warehouse to be converted into an educational center.

He got Pasadena City College to give him $500,000 to set up short term training sessions WITH A GUARANTEED JOB AT GRADUATION! These were often eight-week training like cashiering, simple electronic repair, etc. The students were often persons who had not ever held a job. Social workers were brought in to partner with the trainee, helping them to understand the world of being an employee—e.g., arriving at work on time, being appropriately dressed for work, learning how to socialize with fellow employees. [20 years later, I took my daughter Julia camping up in the mountains of Southern California; we got to talking to the camper across the campfire. He remarked that he worked for McDonnel-Douglass and they still hire workers from Dad's program!]

Occasionally the NEW Police Chief would travel somewhere with Dad in Dad's car. Okay. But the car was a French 1960 Citroen DS with many peculiar features. One was that it rode on air shock absorbers, but when one started the car, you had to be patient while the car pumped itself up. The Police Chief dubbed it "The Getaway Car!" (You are supposed to laugh.)

+ + + + + +

## USS CAPITAINE (AGSS336) DEPARTS FOR THE ORIENT

• • • • • • • • • • • • • • • • • • • • • • •

The July date for departure was now a few days away. Using an "ALL HANDS CHAIN GANG FROM THE PIER—where the boxes of food were piled high- TO THE AFTER BATTERY HATCH" we loaded the ship with food for 90 days to feed 85 men. The "Fuel King" had already taken on 120,000 gallons of diesel fuel; and filled all the Fresh Water Tanks. I believe it was July 5th. The crew hugged and kissed their mates and children, and the USS Capitaine was underway across the Pacific Ocean on our great six-month adventure. It took eight days of steady steaming to reach Pearl Harbor, Hawaii. Once we were moored alongside a submarine pier, we were in port at least a week. Those crewmembers not already qualified, had to undergo training in the 50-foot Escape Training Tower. In our bathing suits, we were instructed how to put on a rescue "Steinke Hood", which when inflated would assist us to rise to the surface from a "sunken" submarine. A small group of us –6 to 8, were placed into a High-Pressure Air Chamber. High Pressure air was then admitted to the chamber. We were to all fill our lungs with it. Then the chamber was flooded full of water and until the pressures with the Escape Tank equalized; then we opened the outdoor to the Tank. One by one, each of us ducked our heads under the hatch rim, entered the Escape Tank and began rising toward the surface. With high pressure air in our lungs, we were required to exhale continuously—yelling "HO, HO, HO" all the way to the 50-foot away surface---we did this for possibly two minutes without INHALING—a very unnerving experience. There were life guards stationed every few feet along the walls observing each of us to be sure we weren't in danger of exploding our lungs. All of our group made it safely to the surface; however, what a very strange experience to be exhaling your breath continuously for around two minutes! One never forgets it.

During our off-duty time, I remember a small group of us sailors rented two convertible cars and took off to drive around Oahu Island. One of the points of interest was the Polynesian Cultural Center at the village of Leie. I believe it was the Church of Seventh Day Adventists who had erected a college at that location, and had gone around to many of the island cultures in the South Pacific, and enrolled some of their young people to come and be students, but they also bring with them materials to construct a typical living dwelling from their island, and, for the interest of tourists, put on a show with dancing and singing. They also had samples of their food, and souvenirs for sale. I do not remember all of the different cultures there, but they included Maoris from New Zealand, Fiji Islands, Tonga Islands, Samoa Islands, as well as Hawaiians. We had a marvelous time and I still have some Tapa Cloth—bark of a certain tree that is beaten into soft cloth-like material and painted with burnt umber designs. It was a very pleasant sightseeing adventure.

In the evening we were allowed to frequent Waikiki Beach and all the entertainment businesses. One Night-club was the Duke Kamonamoku Floor Show starring Don Ho, famous at the time for his song *TINY BUBBLES.* The show also featured groups of Hawaiian dancers, and Tahitian Dancers, and Samoan Fire Dancers, each with their own rhythms and styles. At one point Don Ho invited any armed forces personnel in uniform to come up and dance with the girls. So, I did!

The day came when the ship was totally resupplied, and the crew rested (and maybe out of money too.) so it was time for us to depart for Japan. This was a much longer trip—two weeks. Again, being the quartermaster of the watch, being on the bridge from time to time was part of my routine. And I must tell you, I found it to be very relaxing observing the waves and swells of the sea, the birds that flew close to the waves, and the dolphins who took delight in having a companion "Iron Fish" (which happens to be exactly what the Navajo Code Talkers in WWII used to designate a submarine.)

Remembering that our Bridge, Shears, and deck areas were strictly left over from World War II. The iron railing that used to provide safety for the 40-millimeter gunners on the aft Bridge deck, was now converted into a topside "crews' lounge." Bench-Seats metal frames were welded onto the railings, and the San Diego Sail Loft manufactured Naugahyde covered cushions for us. Thus, more than ten off-watch sailors could come up, take a seat, read a book, smoke a cigarette, cigar, or pipe; or just enjoy talking with friends. The closer we came to the equator to more brilliant were the colors in the evening clouds.

+ + + + + +

## THE RETURN OF 50-CALIBER MACHINE GUNS

• • • • • • • • • • • • • • • • • • • • • •

Early in the Viet Nam War, there were incidents where American Submarines in the Gulf of Tonkin came under fire from North Vietnamese Junks, (small wooden sailing vessels, often used for fishing.) using 50-caliber machine guns. In retaliation, the Americans dug out the old-World War II submarine gun stantions and welded them back up on the bridge where they were in WWII. Then we were issued two WWII 50-Caliber-Machine Guns, four-gun barrels, asbestos gloves, and boxes and boxes of WW II Ammunition. We were taken up the coast to the large Marine Base at Camp Pendleton, to a gun range, set ourselves up, and commenced practicing and firing. Now for the uninitiated, every fifth round (bullet) was an incendiary tracer designed to light the way, so the gunner could aim the gun better on the target. But I said this was old WWII ammunition, and so, without warning, some of the tracers would explode shortly after leaving the barrel. When that occurred, the Command was "Duck and Hold."

Back out at sea, we would mount the 50 Caliber Machine guns on the bridge and practice firing usually at some large metal containers that would float for a while. Now I mentioned that we were given four barrels and asbestos gloves. 50-Caliber Gun Barrels get hot quickly. One does not hold down the "Butterfly" trigger for a long spray of bullets; too much heat. Instead, one pushes the trigger down for a very short burst of three to six bullets. And pause. At appropriate times, the gun handlers would put on the asbestos gloves and change out the hot barrel for a cool one.

During my two years of Active Duty, I was sent to two schools: 50-Caliber Machine Gun School for the USS Capitaine; and 50-Caliber Machine Gun School for the USS Rock. The Captain of the USS Rock (AGSS274) Nevin Kennedy III was much more aggressive. He ordered me "if we get into a shooting event with some North Vietnamese Junk (sailboat), I want you to grab the Ensign (American flag) jump down on the main deck, run back, and put up our flag so the enemy will know who is shooting back!" (In my mind: "You have got to be kidding me: with 50 Caliber bullets flying all around—right through our fiber glass sail (the part of the submarine above the main deck)—50 Calibers are the guns you see on top of Army Tanks. The bullet can travel quite accurately for thousands of yards) and I am supposed to run back and haul up the flag?? "Please, Mr. Custer, I don't want to go."

The USS Capitaine (AGSS 336) had not been updated with new more powerful equipment and electronics. We were not utilized for active war patrols and intelligence collecting (spying). Instead, we were a component of the US Military Assistance Program (MAP). Our assignment was to operate with various foreign navies and train them on anti-submarine warfare-(teach them how to track, locate, identify, and kill an enemy submarine. We carried a special publication on board designated Fleet Exercise Publication-1 (FXP) in the book it would identify different types of exercises that surface ships and submarines could use for the training. The two ships would communicate over the radio as to what the surface ship wanted the submarine to do; for example, what depth, what compass direction, and what speed. Many times, it was the quartermaster that handled the radio communications for the exercise.

During our six months, we conducted these "War Games" with the Republic of Korea Navy (South Korea); with the Nationalist Chinese who occupied the island of Taiwan (also known to the world as Formosa); the Royal Thai Navy (Thailand also known as Siam), and operated with our own forces from the Philippines. Lots of stories.

Story Number One: The Nationalist Navy gave us a very specific assignment:

- Submerged the submarine to a keel depth of 150 feet.
- Steer a course of 000 degrees (or in Chinese Dung, Dung, Dung).
- Set a speed of 2 ½ knots.
- Do this for nine hours.

We followed orders and steamed that way for nine hours. Then they told us we could surface. We did. Logically and mathematically, we should now be 22 ½ Nautical miles north of our Diving Posit. But we were NOT. Chief Bill Base struggled and struggled. Nothing seemed to be fitting into place. "Alright, who has been the 'wise' guy?" Over an hour later, we finally, finally figured we were located 5 miles due east of our Diving Posit!! We had not moved forward a single foot!! What happened? There was an under-ocean river traveling Southeast at 2 ½ knots; the river pushed us sideways! And the old WWII Boats had no instruments to detect sideways motion.

Story Two. This takes place during the exact same FXP exercise. Originally, submarines did not have air-conditioning. The Navy only started to equipping subs with air conditioning when the Navy placed electronic equipment on board. The Capitaine, somewhat fresh from Mothballs, only carried two small 3-ton air conditioners. Early that morning before the exercise commenced, the first Unit ceased to work. We submerged. Just a little over an hour, the second Unit ceased to work! Can you imagine? The heat in the compartments rose to over 90 degrees. The humidity rose to 100%. A "Rain Forest" was created where all of the metal overhead pipes began to drip continuously. The crew stripped down to a pair of short shorts and sandals. Any one not on watch could go to their rack—but then that created puddles of body sweat. As I recall, the cooks prepared no hot meals, just cold sandwiches. Some of the crew chose to sit in the Crews Mess, with trickles of black body dirt running down their bellies. I don't recall anyone playing cards; most crew members took on the appearance of a coma! [Remember: it was 8 long hours before we were allowed to surface and obtain cool fresh air!]

Story three: In 1965, the USS Capitaine (AGSS336) provided several different weeks of War Games with the Nationalist Chinese Navy. Commander Chong of the Chinese Navy came aboard to translate English into Chinese over the radio, and vice versa. He and I spent a lot of time together discussing social life among the Chinese, among the Americans, and other assorted subjects. We got to enjoy each other's company.

In December 1965 the U.S.S. Capitaine (AGSS 336) returned to San Diego, and three months later, the ship was Decommissioned and sold to the Italian Navy (where it was renamed the Alfredo Cappellini). I assisted in the Decommissioning Ceremony in Hunters' Point Naval Shipyard. On my Dream Sheet, I was allowed to choose three other San Diego homeported submarines as possible new homes.

I chose all three of the former Radar Pickett Submarines: The USS Rasher (AGSS 269); the USS Raton (AGSS 270); and the USS Rock (AGSS 274). Why because I had ridden all three ships out to sea; I liked them and felt comfortable. But probably a primary reason was because they all three had that extra Combat Compartment—formerly filled with radar equipment, but now provided excellent sleeping compartment above the walking deck and storage and work spaces including one for quartermasters. I was assigned to the USS Rock (AGSS 274). I became the "Leading White Hat Quartermaster." This was during the Viet Nam War and promotions were sped up. I was promoted to (E5) Second Class Petty Officer in ten months! There was a Quartermaster Chief on Board for Celestial Navigation and Administrative Duties, but I was in charge of the lower rated quartermasters. I made up the Watch Bill of who stood which hourly watches.

A somewhat related story. When we were operating out of Taiwan, General Issimo Chang Kai-Shek was the President or head leader. One day, his Number Two son—who was in charge of all the Taiwanese Military, boarded our ship for the day. And where do you think he spent most of the day? Right next to me as I worked on the Plotter! He was very friendly, so I spent a good portion of my time teaching him about the operation of a submarine. When we returned to port Kaohsiung, Number Two son got on the ship's General Announcing system to thank all of us. Would you believe his English was better than anyone of us? He had been educated in the United States—I believe Cornel University.

Story Four. The following story can apply to any of the old Diesel-Electric submarines. "A Depth Control Party." Sometimes a brand newly minted junior officer would report aboard with an "Arrogant Attitude" toward the Enlisted men. When the sub was submerged and that young officer was the "Diving Officer"—overseeing the Bow and Stern Planesmen which control the depth and attitude of the submarine, the Off-Duty crew would meet in the After Torpedo Room and start slowly walking forward toward the Bow. In the Control Room this Passage Way was behind the Diving Officer where he could not see what was happening. The crew kept quietly walking forward to the Forward Torpedo Room. These subs were so small that a weight change of 20+ men can have a strong impact on the depth and attitude of the sub. Thus, the Diving Officer would have to constantly give orders to the Bow and Stern Planes men, and perhaps pump some water from some forward tanks to the Aft tanks. Then the off-duty crew would reverse course and slowly walk quietly back to the After-Torpedo Room. This was a 'DEPTH CONTROL PARTY" to teach the young officer a lesson. It did not take too many of these Parties, before the young officer shifted and learned to respect the Enlisted men. In case you are wondering all the rest of the personnel—Captain and officers alike with the Enlisted knew what was going on-but was not about to stop it!

Oh, those were the great "Old Days" when submarining was so much fun! Now-a-days it seems like "fun" is against the Operating Regulations. In 2018 I toured a very late model submarine, and even the Control Room seemed dull and boring.

[(Depth Control Parties do not work on Nuclear Submarines because they are much larger, much heavier, so human weight does not have an impact.)

Let's go back to our arrival in Japan at the Port of Yokosuka. During World War II, Yokosuka had been a major Japanese Naval Base. But after the war, the Americans took it over as a major operating base in the Far East.

Yokosuka is located on the Southern side of the island of Honshu. It is located inside of Tokyo Bay, about 60 miles west of Tokyo. In between Yokosuka and Tokyo is the large city of Yokohoma.

## *LOCATING MY FULBRIGHT SCHOLAR HOUSE-MATE IN TOKYO*

• • • • • • • • • • • • • • • • • • • • • •

Story. Back in the Autumn of 1962 at San Francisco State College, I became active in the International Students Association. We welcomed students from all over the world. One special group that we hosted were the Fulbright Scholars; these were high school teachers from around the world whose specialty was teaching English language. SFSC encouraged our students to take home and host these students, so they could get a more intimate experience in the United States. I was now in charge of our four-person flat at 71 Buena Vista Terrace, and we did have an open bedroom, so I invited Toshiro Hyashi, from Tokyo to live with us, and he accepted. He spent the whole semester with us, and he and I were the main friends.

So, when I took myself on the train to Tokyo in 1965, I went looking for Toshiro. [I had not kept in touch, so did not have his address. Ooops.] First, I went to the American Embassy, and they directed me to the Fulbright Commission Building a couple of blocks away. I went in and started inquiring if anyone could tell me how to find my friend Toshiro. I was not having much luck—no one seemed to have heard of him. Then Lady Luck smiled: I suddenly looked to the back of the very large office, and I spied Mrs. Itsuko sitting at a desk!!! She had been at SFSC and did know Toshiro Hyashi! I kept calling to her, and finally some nice clerk went back and got her for me. She was very surprised if not shocked and pleased to see me! She immediately came to my counter, I explained I was trying to connect with Toshiro. She immediately said she did know exactly where he lived, and she would take me there!! WOW! [How many Americans would go to this extended trouble for a foreign visitor?] We immediately left the Fulbright Commission and commenced to take one bus after another, one train after another, until we arrived in the village of Higashi Mura Yama [East Mountain Village]. Mrs. Itsuko knew exactly where Toshiro's home was and took me straight there. Fortunately, Toshiro and his family were home. And you can imagine how surprised and shocked he was to see me!! He immediately invited me in. and invited Mrs. Itsuko to please come in. However, she declined; we said some very polite thank you's and she was on her way back to the train station. Wow. What a gift she gave me! This trip had taken at least 45 minutes or longer. Toshiro and I began a great series of visits. It was so good to be back together.

The USS Capitaine made several stops in and out of Yokosuka. In between we were servicing other navies. And make a Rest and Recreation visit to Hong Kong—which is the name of the colony not the name of the Island. The island is Victoria. When our ship first pulled into port, I had the Duty to stay and protect and service the ship. But the next day, I had Liberty. We were required to wear our White Navy Uniforms. I had borrowed ***Fielding's' Guide to the Orient*** so I knew of the major tourist sights.

## YOU MEET THE DARNDEST PEOPLE
## IN THE DARNDEST PLACES

• • • • • • • • • • • • • • • • • • • • • •

I decided to take the Tram up to the Top of Victoria Peak. When I reached the top, I noticed there was an open-air restaurant a few feet away. As I walked through to tall stone pillar entrance, I immediately heard a voice, **"Hey sailor, come over here!"** I looked up and saw two tables full of American students having lunch. I walked over, they invited me to join them; they introduced themselves and explained they were all part of a private Peace Corps, from New York City, which was deploying to Laos the very next day. This was their last night of freedom, they were celebrating and wanted me to be a part of it. The apparent leader waved some credit cards in the air and said, "My father gave me his credit cards to go have fun! And so, we are and want you to join us. **"That is very kind of you, and yes, I will join you."** After lunch we returned to the Hong Kong Hilton to rest before the big Banquet planned for the evening. As I entered their rooms, I inquired if I might be able to take a bath? At first, they looked at me strangely. I explained I had had showers, and swims in the ocean, but I had not been in a bath tub for months!" They laughed and said sure, Go Ahead! Oh, I can't tell you how great that felt. The evening hour came; everyone got all dressed up and we took the elevator to the *Eagles Nest Restaurant* on the 25th floor of the Hong Kong Hilton. As we walked in, the Maître Dee, escorted us to our beautiful banquet, over near one of the walls. I slid in and sat with my back to the wall. We began to eat and drink. In a little while, **I look over to the front entrance and whom do I see walking into the restaurant?? The Captain of the USS Capitaine, Commander J. D. Hovater; the Executive Officer Lieutenant Commander Mike Myers, and my boss, the Chief Quartermaster, Bill Base. It was like a Hollywood movie set: They sauntered in, scoping out the scene, when all of a sudden, they spotted me! "Leedom, what are you doing?" "Hello**

**Captain, please come on over and meet my new friends." "But we just got into port last night!" "I know but come on over anyway." And I introduced everyone.**

Well, I will tell you, for the rest of the trip I was teased about the incident. When we would reach a port, and they saw me, they said, "We are not sure we are going to let you leave the ship, because we don't know what you will get into next!" (Humor; yes, I did go on Liberty.) 1965 was when the Viet Nam War was heating up—President Lyndon Johnson dispatched 500,000 troops to Viet Nam in July. Over the next five-years fighting was fierce—even into Cambodia and Laos. I have often wondered if those delightful, well educated, dedicated young persons, dedicated to making the world a better place, survived. I have no way of knowing; they certainly helped me to have a wonderous experience.

A Hong Kong Story. Back in Pasadena at the Pasadena Independent Star Newspaper, there was a young Chinese reporter who was a friend of Dad's. I don't know if I ever knew his first name, but his family name was Wong. His father, many many years ago, went to work for Standard Oil Company which owned oil wells in China. Mr. Wong's job was to walk on a regular basis (kind of like patrolling) to all of the wells and check to make sure all the pumps were working properly. I do not know the "in between" story, but over time, Mr. Wong became very rich. By the time I met him, he owned at least one bank, a couple of Peugeot Car Dealerships, and… Anyway, Dad told his Mr. Wong that I would be visiting Hong Kong where his father lived. So, he asked his family to host me when I arrived. I telephoned the house when I arrived, and we made arrangements for a visit. The sons came down to the quay—in a Peugeot naturally and picked me up. First, we went back up to Jarden Drive—the expensive part where wealthy Chinese had their mansions, so that I would have the privilege of meeting and speaking with the elder Mr. Wong. I was escorted into his bedroom, as he was old, frail, and in bed. I had very pleasant time meeting him, thanking him for his hospitality, and chatting for a little while. Then his sons took me on a tour of the island. Eventually we went to a very fine restaurant and had dinner. One of the sons had been an officer in the U.S. Navy!! So, we got along just fine. And then they took me back to my ship.

And would you believe when I went to Hong Kong the following year aboard the USS Rock (AGSS 274), the Wong family came back down to the port again and hosted me for the day? I even went to a business men's luncheon where they were discussing the upcoming event in 30 years of the British ending its lease on the Colony, and the People's Republic of China (Communist) would be in control. Wow. Okay, so now it is September, 2019, Hong Kong has been given back to the Chinese Government and there are major demonstrations—at least a million people have filled the street in protest of a new law that allows Peking to arrest and try Hong Kong Citizens who are supposed to be under semi-autonomous rule.

Another Hong Kong story. Our ship was moored in the quay on the island. We took a water taxi over to the city of Kowloon. There they offered a tour of the city and environs. Around eight signed up and climbed in an eight-passenger van. A very knowledgeable retired business man, Mr. Lee, was our diver and tour guide. And he knew his stuff. He took us to a Buddhist temple, a Walled City with fifteen-foot stone walls for protection. Apparently historically there had been warfare between competing neighbors. All the villagers lived inside the walls—where there were only small houses and concrete walkways. All of their gardens were outside the walls. They wore huge woven sun hats to protect their faces and necks. [I bought one off a man for $1.00 American Dollar. And I still have it 50 years later!] Our guide, Mr. Lee, took us to an Upper-Class Cemetery where the concrete entrances were shaped like a woman's vagina. There was some theology involved—we are born from a woman and to a woman we return in death. He took us up to the border between British Hong Kong and The Peoples Republic of China (Communist.)

It was a great learning experience, and we really appreciated Mr. Lee. I tell this story in detail, because the following year when I sailed on the USS Rock (AGSS 274) and we came back to Hong Kong, I encouraged my shipmates to take the same tour. OOOPs, when we climbed into the van, the driver was a very young person, and as he drove to the same landmarks—he knew NONE OF THE STORIES! OK, *I BELIEVE I CAN, I BELIEVE I CAN* So, I took over as the Tour Guide because I had remembered them all. The driver was in shock that a western sailor knew these stories! *I DID IT! I BELIEVED I COULD!*

At one time in our sailing schedule, the ship pulled into Sasebo Naval Base on the Island of Kyushu. If one looks on the map, the city of Nagasaki—the second city to have an atomic air burst during World War II is just a short train ride away. Naturally, I was drawn to an historical event. Like Hiroshima, Nagasaki also has a Peace Park and a museum detailing the events. I felt a need to show my respects. I was in my white Navy Uniform. Everyone was polite and respectful, and I was respectful to them. It was a powerful and somber experience. Another main attraction is the Scottish Lord Sir Thomas Glover's home, built on a cliff overlooking the ocean. The story I heard was that in the late 1800.s The Emperor invited Sir Thomas Glover to come to Japan and help to modernize it, for example, build railroads on all the islands. Sir Thomas Glover accomplished many feats and was honored by Japan. But there is another solid reason to visit is home: The opera Madam Butterfly by Puccini is based upon a true story which took place in Sir Thomas Glover's home. While I was there a group of Japanese students came. They asked me if they could practice their English with me. "Why, yes, of course." So, we enjoyed each other's company and had our photograph taken in front of Sir Thomas Glover's Statue.

Getting back to Sasebo, our Captain thought it was a good time for a ship's party, so we rented the Black Cat Night Club, AND engaged two Strip Tease Dancers. The Captain bought the first round of drinks for everyone. Great, thank you. After a few more rounds of drinks, no one was feeling any pain, and we wanted to show our appreciation to the Captain J. D. Hovater. Torpedoman First Class George Brundage was a very big and strong man. He picked the Captain up, placing him on George's shoulders, and everyone started the chant "Hip, hip, hooray for the Captain." And then they raised their glasses in toast. The Captain joined in and raised his glass too. I would say he had had two, three or more drinks. The crew kept cheering him and raising their glasses and the Captain followed along.

## WHO ARE THE STRIP TEASERS? MY, MY?

A little while later the Strip Tease entertainment started. We all formed our chairs in large circle, while these two Japanese girls stepped out in to the center. The Strip Music started. The girls began what they understood to be strip Teasing with one's clothes. But somehow, they didn't quite have the right spirit and movements. Finally, two enginemen jumped up and shouted, "Stop the Music!" Next, they told the girls to go sit down. Then they said, "Start the Music" we will show you how a strip tease is done!" And true to their word, they put on a performance that everyone who was there still talks about!! (I have left out the names to protect the guilty.")

The next morning, it was time for the ship to get underway. We are sailing out into the ocean; the Maneuvering watch has been secured. We are sailing smoothly along. And the Captain came up into the Conning Tower and sat right next to Dead Reckoning Plotter as he often did, sitting next to me as I was plotting our track. He kept inspecting his hands. I looked over and I could see that the top of all of his fingers were bloody and scabbing over. Finally, he said to me, "You know, I must have had my hand last night where it did not belong!" (And our Captain, whom we all loved, did make sure he enjoyed himself in liberty ports.) Finally, out of pity and sympathy, I said, "Captain, if you really want to know what happened to your hands, I can tell you." "Okay, Leedom, tell me what I was doing last night." "Well sir, you had bought drinks for all of us last night, and so then we started buying drinks for you; and we wanted to honor you, so George Brundage lifted you up on his shoulders, and we all started singing, "Hip, Hip, Hooray for our Captain, and raised our glasses in toast, and you did it too—BUT YOU HAD A LARGE ROTATING FAN OVER YOUR HEAD, so every time you raised your hand, it was hit by the fan blades!"

Before I go any further, I need to "set the stage." John Perry, my Third-Class Quartermaster partner, had had a nasty divorce from his wife a few months before we departed CONUS Continental United States. And as we came into a port, John would beg me to give him "a Stand-By-Chit." That meant I agreed to stay on board ship another 24 hours taking his duty, while he found himself a "Girlfriend for the night." I agreed and gave him a Stand by in Hawaii, Yokosuka, Japan, Chinhai and Pusan, Korea. However, on the second half of our trip when we went to Hong Kong, Bangkok Thailand, and Brisbane Australia, I collected. In Hong Kong, I stood one duty day instead of two; In Bangkok I stood no duty days, and in Brisbane, I stood one duty day instead of two! It certainly worked out to be a very fine arrangement for me.

From our R & R visit to Hong Kong, we steamed into the Gulf of Siam and began conducting exercises with the Royal Thai Navy, in anti-submarine strategies. In 1965, Thailand was not that wealthy, and they had a very small navy. We operated with three small patrol boats. They were so small that at lunch time they would all cluster together and tie alongside each other and only one boat kept its engines running to steer the assemblage! We worked several days, even during the night time. I mention that because the Gulf of Siam was known to have poisonous snakes who lived on top of the water, and the folklore was that when a submarine surfaced under them, the snakes would drop down onto the quartermaster who was opening the hatch. I heard that rumor. So, I had a flashlight all "rigged for red," so when the Conning Officer commanded "Crack the Hatch"—to let the pressure of air equalize, now commanded "Open the Hatch" I took my red flashlight and was peering around through the crack to see if I saw any snakes. The Captain was too impatient so he "Goosed me—and said, "Up that Hatch, Leedom!" "Yeeess sir!" I think I did spot some snakes down on the main deck, but none on the Bridge.

One day, the Thai Navy gave us permission to moor in this small fishing village, called "Sattahip." There was not much there…one open air beer bar, so naturally most of the crew headed for the bar, threw down a pile of American Money and planted themselves on the stools. I had one or two beers with them, and then I got up to go exploring. There was not much to the town, so I just started walking down this dirt country road. There were farmers in their fields with their Water Buffalo pulling the plows. The farmers waved to me first, and I waved back. Probably a quarter of a mile later, I encountered a Buddhist Temple alongside the road. So, I knocked on the front door. The Head Monk answered the door, spoke English, and invited me in! It was a fairly large open-air room with a nice couch at one end. He invited me to come sit with him. The monks served us both iced coffees. I do not remember the Monk's name, but we sat and discussed many things for over two hours! The Monk wanted to know all about the United States, and I wanted to know more about the Buddhist religion. As we sat talking, there were three young monks across the room from us "pasting Thai Baht (money) on this construction of wood and string in the shape of a tree." I inquired, and sure enough, they were making a "Money

Tree!" In Thailand, Money Trees are a common sight. Sometimes the monks place a tree on the side walk of the town, and the citizens would come up and paste some money on the tree as they walked by. It was the people's way of financially supporting the monks in the temple. Which reminds me of story.

In the Buddhist Religion, it is expected that every young male will spend two years serving as a monk in the temples. These young monks carry a bowl with them as they walk around the village or town. Inhabitants often come out of their homes and deposit food in the bowls so the monks will have something to eat. Foreigners label them "Begging Bowls" but the monks do not see it that way. 95% plus of the Thai Society is Buddhist, and they are devout. And it gives the people pleasure to be able to contribute the food.

A few days later, we had completed our work with the Thai Navy, and now we were invited to steam up the commercial ship river to Bangkok (or in the original language Krung Thep). Also, originally, Krung Thep was very similar to Venice Italy: The whole city was built on "KLONGS" or canals. Transportation was strictly by boat. I don't know the exact time period but somewhere in the late 1800's, someone had the idea to fill in all the Klongs on the Eastern side of the river. [Thailand was another port where John Q. Perry stood all the watches.] I had a delightful time. Several of our officers and a few enlisted men (me) took the Klong Tour sightseeing much of the Western side of Krung Thep. There are many Buddhist Temples to visit. One has a solid gold Buddha—3 to 4 feet tall. It, and maybe a few others were made back in the 600's or so. Then a century or two later they were going to be invaded by the Burmese army. So, the Monks went out and covered every Buddha in concrete. Now the majority of the statues had been already concrete, but now the invading army could not tell which was which. It seems centuries went by and the memory of the gold buddhas faded away. It seems this one Buddha was living outside with no roof. A big windstorm came up—maybe a Tsunami?—and knocked our Buddha over on its side. When the monks went to right it, they saw a chip in the cheek, and under it --gleaming gold. They got permission from the head monk and chipped all the concrete off revealing this magnificent statue for all to see.

There is a second temple which known for the "Emerald Buddha". It is beautiful, in a secure case. Stands maybe 24-28 inches high out of one piece of gem. There is some controversy as to whether it really is Emerald, or probably Jade. Either way, it is a feast for the eyes.

There was a third "Temple of the Morning" but I could see from the boat that the steps leading to the top were extremely steep and dangerous. So, no go. What I also observed was that in Thailand's wet jungle climate, the Temples mold and have other stuff growing on them. They take constant maintenance.

What I know about religions in general, is that when they invade an existing culture, the religion subsumes some of the existing beliefs and practices. I do not know what the previous major religion was, but there was/is a very strong belief in Spirits, some of which are evil. So, most homes of consequence have a miniature temple displayed on the property to keep Evil Spirits away. And large public buildings have these huge 12-foot-tall YEAKS (pronounced "YAKS") which are fierce warriors to guard the entrances to the buildings.

Another observation I made, was that Thailand was one of the few Asian countries that was not over populated. I did not witness huge crowds except on "King Chulalongkorn Day." The play, movie, **THE KING AND I,** was based upon a true story, where an English Lady came to live in Siam, and wound up marrying the king—who was **KING CHULALONGCORN.** that day is celebrated once a year; it is a big festival, to which the King and Queen of Siam appear in public in the vintage **YELLOW ROLLS-ROYCE!** I was there, I did witness the appearance of the King and Queen. It was a thrill. A strange custom is that only the King is allowed to have a Yellow car!! I do not know why. And, would you believe apples are forbidden in Thailand! At least in 1965. Our sailors used apples to barter to good advantage. Bangkok is a land of gold. There are numerous jewelry stores selling pure gold jewelry. I bought my wife Jeannie a solid gold charm bracelet with jade dangles. However, their gold is soft—I think 18 carats?

And so, one has to use harder gold for the clasps. A long time custom in Thailand is to make "RUBBINGS" of famous works of art. Some artists use rice paper, some use silk, or maybe they use some different material to make the rubbing and then transfer the art to rice paper and silk. I bought four of each. I have carried them around for years, thinking someday I will frame them. I have slowly given some away. I just this minute checked: I have two gorgeous silk rubbings left. Okay, so when am I framing them, Patric? One night I did splurge and treat myself to the Sabibong Restaurant, which not only had outstanding food, but theatre to watch: the historic Monkey people and devil? Spirits; exquisite dancing. One must lay down on the floor, drape one arm—the left arm over a velvet support and eat with your right hand from a wide variety of little dishes full of good things. An evening I will never forget.

Alongside the wall where we were moored was a Seamens' Club— there were quite a few ocean-going merchant vessels that could sail right up the river to Bangkok. The dinner was unremarkable, but the desert: Thailand is the home of very sweet pineapple, so I had one very large slice each evening with my coffee.

Final note: our visit was in the summer of 1965. The Viet Nam War was in progress, but Bangkok had not yet become a destination for American servicemen to relax. Formally it is known as Rest and

Recreation, but informally it is known as Intoxication and Intercourse. I understand that within a year, the whole atmosphere, ambience of Bangkok changed for the worse. In 1965 there were very few gasoline vehicles—mostly Pedicabs—bicycled by the driver. On TV a few years ago, *I* sadly saw that Bangkok was over-run with cars and trucks and the air was foul—smog-like in L.A.

## *A DEMOCRATIC VOTE TO TRANSIT TO AUSTRALIA*

When the USS Capitaine had fulfilled its Military Assistance Program (MAP) our Captain, LCDR J. D. Hovater, who was liked by our squadron back in San Diego, requested that we be allowed to travel southward to Brisbane Australia. The squadron concurred with his request. The Captain then called the crew together for a vote. He explained that if the majority of the crew voted YES GO, it would mean we would not be back to homeport before December 29th. But if the majority voted NO, then we would be home for Christmas. The crew voted and 75% voted YES LET'S GO!

So, off to Australia we sailed. We couldn't have arranged a better sea voyage! The closer we got to the equator the more brilliant and deeply colored the clouds and sky became, especially at sunset. The water temperature was in the 80's. Anyone one who knows "Sea Lore" knows that when a ship crosses the Equator there must be an initiation held by the old "Shellback" sailors to initiate the "Lowly Slimy Pollywogs!" And so, it was. And about 10 of our crew were Shellbacks, so they constructed the activities.

We Pollywogs had to all wait down inside the Forward Torpedo Room until individually summoned by His Majesty King Neptune, the Royal Baby, and other attendants. Station One: get all of your hair shaved off bald! Station Two: Kiss the Royal Baby's naked belly smeared with grease! Station Three: Crawl slowly through the Royal "Garbage Chute" which was a canvas tube ten feet long filled with several days of stinking, slimy garbage saved by the cooks for just this purpose. Station Four: Kneel before the Royal Cook and allow him to squirt a baster full of guaranteed awful "medicine" into your mouth! Yuk. Station Five: Walk the Royal Gang Plank Blindfolded until you fell off into the ocean! (Actually, that was the best part!)

As we approached the port of Brisbane, our ship received a radio message inviting the whole crew to join the ***JUNIOR-AUSTRALIAN-AMERICAN FRIENDSHIP ASSOCIATION for a "BARBIE."***

During World War Two, the American Navy purposely created submarine bases in Australia (and other U.S. Military bases) to assist American Forces to fight the Japanese Military BUT ALSO to protect Australia from a Japanese Invasion. So many, many years thereafter, The Australians were deeply grateful to the U.S. Submarine Force. Therefore, the invitation to a steak bar-b-que. Sadly only 40% of the crew accepted the invitation, but boy, did we have a fabulous festive occasion! The Australians were generally young professionals in their 20's and 30's. We were in Brisbane for six days, and for six days we partied with our new friends. The picnic was only the beginning.

They drove us to Aborigine towns of Maroochydore and Mallulaba— both were about 60 miles one north, one south of Brisbane, right on the coast was excellent surfing opportunities. [Suring originally started in Australia]. We had dinner with our friends almost every night at a restaurant. That is where I learned not to ask the waiter for a "Napkin" but to ask for a "Table Cloth." [Napkins are what women use.] I also learned that in Australia, a PIE is an American TART, and an Australian Tart is an American Pie.

One night there was a house party. And about as soon as I came through the front door, I requested from our host to go in the bathroom and run some water in the bathtub and then pull the plug. "Why?" "Because I want to observe the "Coriolis Effect" the water circling clockwise, instead of counter clock-wise as in the Northern Hemisphere.

Everywhere in Australia, we submarine sailors were welcomed with open arms. Everything was free. If we entered a Beer Garden, the owner invited to order whatever we wanted! Public transportation was free to us. I did journey out to a Museum to see how the Aborigine had lived over time. I learned they used human hair to construct ordinary utensils like baskets. I learned that what we Americans think of as Boomerangs—the slightly curved ones that are supposed to come back to you, are really children's toys! The real Boomerangs are long—maybe three feet or so, are flat and have sharp edges. They can be hurled tumbling toward a kangaroo, or other prey and bring them down to kill.

I, and our ship's Executive Office, Mike Myers, took a car to **Lone Pine Sanctuary** a type of zoo that specializes in Australia's unusual animals like **Platypuses, and Koala** . I got to hold one briefly and have my picture taken! They are warm, soft, and furry, but they do particularly like being handled by people.

Our new young friends could not have done more to keep us company and keep us entertained. I remember Hellen Jolly, was one of the women who came aboard the Capitaine and did our morning announcement over the 1MC—the all boat announcing system— imagine waking up in the morning to the sounds of a soothing female voice saying, "Alright mateys, it is time to rise and shine!" I was fond of her and kept her name in my wallet for a year or two. I always dreamed that I might have some opportunity to visit in the future, but that never came. But at the time, every country I visited, I said in my mind, "This may be my only opportunity to visit this country, so let's make the most of it. And I am pleased to report that I have fulfilled that orientation.

Okay, it is time to go back to San Diego and home. We could plot a fairly straight course from Brisbane to San Diego; however, we would not be passing close to any country where we could refuel. When fully tanked off, we carry 120,000 gallons of diesel fuel. But is that enough so we can make it straight through? LT. Saxon was our engineer, and he spent a couple days of very close mathematical calculations. It would be very close, but we could make it.

We left Brisbane on December 8th, 1965. We were using British Admiralty Charts, first constructed in 1895, and had over 100 corrections registered along the bottom. Several of the charted islands had notes written next to them: *"Caution: This island has been reported to be five miles northeast of its charted position!"*

## *A MAJOR GAMBLE ON WHICH WAY TO NAVIGATE HOME*

• • • • • • • • • • • • • • • • • • • • • •

*Our trip home was calculated to be 21 days sailing to get home. We were scheduled to travel through parts of the ocean where rarely any other ship travelled. And I will witness that we travelled for nineteen days without seeing a single ship or airplane, and to make matters more complex, there were no LORAN Radio Beacons operating in the whole South Pacific. There were no landmarks or island to use for radar ranges.....and many days the skies stayed overcast 24 hours day, so truly we were left with "Dead-Reckoning" calculations we made inside the ship based on the courses we were steering, and the speeds we had rung up first on the "MOTOR ORDER TELEGRAPH" which then the Electricians transmit to the engines, and also taking into consideration the ocean swells, waves, and wind. It just so happened that on the evening of the fourth day of an over-cast sky I came on Watch at Midnight I jumped up to the Bridge and lo and Behold,—the sky was clear! And the stars were brightly shinning! So, I jumped back into the Conning Tower, got out the Sextant, and calculated the location of some "Navigation Stars" [These are the 33 brightest stars in the sky—the last ones to disappear at Dawn and the first to "pop out" at Twilight. However, one can "Shoot Stars whenever one has a clear horizon . I shot my stars, went back down to the plotting table and laid down my fix. And do you know after four solid days of no fixes—our Dead Reckoning was not that far off!*

Within weeks of arriving back in Port in San Diego, Jeannie and I first bought a car—a 1962 VW Beetle. Good. Now the Capitaine did not stay in San Diego very long, it was ordered to San Francisco Naval Shipyard at Hunters' Point. The Capitaine was to be refurbished and sold to the Italian Navy. So, Jeannie, Julia and I were assigned a half of Quonset hut to move into. So now we are back in San Francisco.

## PATRIC TRANSFERS TO THE USS ROCK (AGSS274) FORMERLY A RADAR PICKET SUBMARINE

• • • • • • • • • • • • • • • • • • • • • •

I was assigned to the USS Rock (AGSS 274). And it was located back at the submarine base at Ballast Point, San Diego. So, then I left Jeannie and Julia. And went south to San Diego. At some point, my very close friends the Blackman's offered that we could move into the mother- Ida, her father's house. So, as George Carlen described it, we took a smaller version of our stuff and moved in. Eventually we were able to locate a two-bedroom apartment on Ascot Circle right off of El Cajon Blvd. And we finally collected all of our things in one place. But happiness was not around the corner. Once I was integrated into the USS Rock's crew, we found out the ship was due to deploy back to the Western Pacific in October six months down the calendar.

I became the "Leading White Hat Quartermaster." This was during the Viet Nam War and promotions were sped up. I was promoted to (E5) Second Class Petty Officer in ten months! There was a Quartermaster Chief on Board for Celestial Navigation and Administrative Duties, but I was in charge of the lower rated quartermasters. I made up the Watch Bill of who stood which hourly watches.

In September 1966, the USS Rock was given orders to conduct another Western Pacific (WEST PAC) six-month deployment. We loaded up the stores and departed. [This event also ended my first marriage, because my wife was tired of being home alone.] I will tell one related story then return to life aboard the USS Capitaine. When the USS Rock (AGSS 274) arrived in Kaohsiung Harbor, Taiwan, once again Commander Chong of the Chinese Navy came aboard to render translation services. We headed out to sea for a week-long series of Anti-Submarine Warfare (ASW) exercises. However, during a break when we were on the surface, Commander Chong requested I come into a back corner of the Bridge with him. "Leedom, I need to check with you: my Chinese Navy vessels head back to port every evening. Your Captain wants to stay out here at sea all week long. What do you think your crew members would like to do?" "Commander, I think they would like to return to port every night!" "Good! I will take care of it!" And yes, with the Captain fuming, the USS Rock returned to port every night, and the Captain never knew I had a hand in it!"

+ + + + + +

## THE END OF A MARRIAGE

• • • • • • • • • • • • • • • • • • • • • •

Married life was not all bliss. Jeannie, who basically was an angry person, was angry that the ship was deploying for six more months, and she was bitter that I had not tried to transfer to a ship that was staying in the states. We got along "ok," but it was not high quality. I remember that I was pleased to be going back overseas.

Halfway through THE USS Rock (AGSS274) tour of the Far East, Jeannie sent me a "Dear John Letter" that our marriage "was over; we were going to get a divorce." These were still the days when I was still "intellectualizing my feelings" rather than being truly in touch with my deep-down emotions. Jeannie's letter caught me totally by surprise, I had to be relieved from duty for three days while I got my thoughts and emotions back in order. I remember writing Jeannie a letter suggesting maybe we could go to counseling, but Jeannie slammed the door on that suggestion.

The WESTPAC tour of the USS Rock was quite similar to that of the USS Capitaine. It lasted from October 1966 to March 1967. We operated with some of the same navies such as Nationalist Chinese. We did not go to Australia but we did spend more time in the Gulf of Tonkin—adjacent to Viet Nam We did "Plane Guard for aircraft flying off of the carrier; and we did Exercises with Destroyers attached to the Carrier Group to keep their anti-submarine skills competent. On the first day at the completion of our assigned exercise, the Destroyer, on the UQC Underwater Communication device, told the USS Rock that it was safe to surface. Well, as the Captain was on the Periscope as we came up all he saw was "Grey, Grey, Grey Emergency Deep—We are right close to the Carrier! The Captain then spoke to me and said, "Leedom, don't you ever let us get that close to a carrier. I will give you the secret location codes so we can know at any one time where all four of the Carrier Groups are in relation to us." He also gave me the procedures for calling in our location to "Yankee Station" if we were able to transmit.

Instead of completing 24 months of my required Active Duty, I requested to be extended two more months "because it was inconvenient for me to be released in April (due to divorce proceedings with my wife, and my plan to return to graduate school at San Francisco State College.) The Executive Officer stated he had heard of the government extending a person's active duty for the good of the government; but he had not heard of a person's active duty being extended at the request of the service member; but he did submit the paperwork and it was approved!

## *RELEASE FROM ACTIVE DUTY AND*
## *RETURN TO CIVILIAN LIFE*

• • • • • • • • • • • • • • • • • • • • • •

When I arrived back in San Diego, Jeannie and I had agreed to a divorce, but we also agreed I could live in the apartment with her until I was released from the Active Duty in the Navy in June. I took my 2 ½ year old daughter Julia and in July flew back to visit with my mother first in Cincinnati, and then we three drove down to Bat Cave North Carolina to spend a week in the Mitchell Cabin. Great time. I made several repairs to the house that Mrs. Sally Mitchell, my stepfather's mother, was hoping I would make one—the Garbage Disposal, and I did several more: I re-wired every lamp in the house and the kitchen exhaust fan because the 1930's insulation was cracking off and exposing bare wires. [I then became a favorite guest in Mrs. Mitchell's home during holiday celebrations.] In July, Julia and I flew back to Solana Beach where Jeannie had moved. I said my tearful good byes to Julia.

I headed the car north to Half Moon Bay where my stepmother Elizabeth's parents lived. They had invited me to come and stay on my way back to San Francisco. I arrived just as the sun was setting on the waters. We had pleasant meal. Toward the end of the meal, Grandmother Dorothy Milnor looks over at me and says, "And where are you spending the night?" "What? What? Aren't I staying here because you invited me?" "Oh NO. Your father and Liz had a fight, and we are angry at your father. So, you can't stay here!"

It wasn't the first time, nor the last time, but my guts just instantly curled up in a tight knot, my heart was racing, my breathing quickened. I could feel my whole-body slip into shock. I thought to myself, "My God! It is ten o'clock at night, I have little money, and now I am not welcome to stay here—and I just have to go out into the night—alone—and confused—and angry—and I have to think of something. As I drove over toward U.S. 101, I finally thought, "Well, I do know where Karmindther and Sharon Chohan live in San Jose. I have no idea if they are home, or on a trip, or… but I will park in their driveway and sleep in my car. At least that will be some comfort. No sooner had I made myself comfortable, and the headlights of a car came up behind me. It was them!! They were thrilled to see me. They hugged me, kissed me, and welcomed me to come in…not just for the night but how about staying and living with them full time??? Oh my God. I am saved. I am wanted! I am loved! By some very dear friends. (Karmindther had been the Head Usher in Jeannie and my wedding June 13, 1964. We were very close friends. And I wound up living with them for over a month!!! Talk about true friendship…..Talk about a night when my emotions did all kinds of circus tricks from being shot out of a cannon, walking the tight rope, swinging on the trapezes and being safely caught!

I returned to San Francisco State College and began work on a master's degree in Speech in pursuance of a degree in General Semantics,

And I had returned immediately off Military Leave and back to Bank of America's San Francisco Central Cash Vault, working and counting money five nights a week. A somewhat humorous story happened one night when I pulled a $20 bill out of a customer's deposit and wrote it up as being counterfeit. I called the Assistant Manager, Stewart over to sign off for me. He balked stating it was a good bill, not counterfeit. So, I called the Manager, John over to sign me off. Same story: "Pat, this is a good bill, not counterfeit." I then said, "John, when I was hired, I was told I could challenge any bill. I challenged that bill!" When I came to work this next afternoon I said, "Well?" And John said, "Pat, you were right! It was counterfeit!" [I don't know that I smirked, but it certainly was a deep sense of satisfaction. And, as I reflect, it may have had something to do with me being immediately hired at the Los Angeles Central Cash Vault a year later when I returned from Chicago to California.]

I lived with Karmindther and Sharon for a month. I used my construction skills. First, I built a fair-sized bookcase, then I orchestrated building a concrete patio. The drive on U.S. 101 from San Jose to San Francisco and back each day was 100 miles. So, I did search for housing in San Francisco. So, I started searching the San Francisco Chronicle Want Ads for a place to live. I spotted an Ad to share a penthouse apartment in San Francisco. I telephoned and made an appointment. The next day, I found the apartment building way up on Corwin Street in the "Lower Twin Peaks" area. Frank Chimera had taken an hour off of work to meet with me. The apartment was simply gorgeous with an outstanding view. We had a pleasant interview conversation, then I went off to work at the Bank thinking "Oh, they probably wouldn't want me because Frank is 43 years old, Andy is 41 years old, and I am only 27 years old, and a college student." BUT I was wrong! Frank telephoned the next day and invited me to move in! What an incredible piece of luck.

## FINALLY—A "FAMILY" AT LAST!

• • • • • • • • • • • • • • • • • • • •

What happened after I moved in was a ***Game Changer in my life!***

***Frank, Andy, and I became a "family"!*** I really, really mean that! Frank had been born and raised in San Francisco of Italian heritage; he was a very kind, and caring person but for whatever reason had not gotten married. Andy was born and raised in Sydney Nebraska but immigrated to San Francisco and had hooked up with Frank five years before. It was amazing how we three just connected with each other, always trying to do something nice for the other person. For example, when it was one person's birthday, the other two would "conspire" to treat that person to an upscale dinner, and then to a show of some kind. For Christmas, we three went together to pick out a very nice tree. No one had any ornaments, so we went to a hobby shop and bought Styrofoam balls and all the materials to decorate them. I brought home a box of money straps—different color for each denomination. We sat together and made chains of colored straps for the tree. And we bought a nice gift for each other. Frank gave me a pair of expensive ***Suppose Knee-Length-Support-Stockings.*** He said to me, "Once you put these on and wear them, you will never wear anything else!" How very prophetic! He was absolutely right. Here it is 54 years later, and all I ever buy are knee length support stockings! They are wonderful. The stocking massage your feet and legs as you walk, and you never have tired feet. And they don't smell! I gave Andy a Bonsai Tree because he loved to grow flowers and plants. My father, who was divorced at this time, loved to come up from Los Angeles and spend a few days with us "because it was such a loving, caring, atmosphere."

In my situation of going to school full time and working at the Bank full time in the evenings, I only saw Frank and Andy on the weekends. However, may I tell you that every night when Frank prepared a delicious dinner for Andy and himself, Frank always prepared a third plate of dinner for me, and placed it in the refrigerator so when I got home around 1:00 AM, I had something decent to eat before going to bed. How is that for a true family-feeling? Saturday night was usually "Date Night" for me. But Sunday nights were "Family Nights." Frank was a tremendous skilled cook and would whip up an outstanding meal. Andy was the desert maker and dishwasher. I contributed wines and special coffees and helped out. Our dining table was right in front of a big picture window where we could see the city and Bay. We chose to have candle light. It was quite special to be a part of that.

Our apartment, which was very beautiful to start with—paintings on the walls, plants inside and outside on the roof deck, was always neat and clean. Every so many months, we would declare a "Cleaning Saturday" and we three worked as a team to clean every room. Our bathroom had a skylight in it, and on occasion, I took a ladder and cleaned it. Our shower-tub combination had sliding glass doors. I would take the doors completely apart and off of the tub, and scrub everything. Our apartment was always very presentable. My stepsister Sally Mitchell, and her cousin Judith Mitchell lived in town, so we had them over for dinner once in a while. We had Frank's family over often—his father, his sister, and her husband.

Andy's small family lived back in Sydney Nebraska—too far for visiting, except, one time, his 90-year-old mother did come. And brought fascinating stories! Her mother and father were Danish. Her father was a merchant seaman, sailing the oceans to make enough money to immigrate to America. When he thought he had enough, her married his sweetheart and sailed to America. They bought a Conestoga Wagon and headed across the United States for California. The time period would be late 1870's. They travelled as far as Sydney Nebraska—on the far western edge of Nebraska, and they ran out of money!~

## *FOR A HOME, THEY LITERALLY DUG*
## *A HOLE IN THE GROUND*

● ● ● ● ● ● ● ● ● ● ● ● ● ● ● ● ● ● ● ● ● ● ● ●

***Literally, they dug a hole in the ground for a home and used the canvas top of the wagon for a roof!*** That winter, Andy's mother was born. She reported that her mother was so devastated at being stranded out in the middle of a prairie that she cried herself to sleep for three years! Andy's mother said it took many, many years to make their farm successful and profitable.

I lived with Frank and Andy two full years. A major event changed their lives: Frank developed Multiple Sclerosis! Slowly at first. Because he started falling at times; when he and Andy would walk down the three flights of stairs, Frank would have to put his hands-on Andy's shoulders for support. And after I moved away, Frank lost the ability to drive a car, and Andy, who had driven in his early adult life, but had had an accident and decided not to drive anymore [and San Francisco was definitely a city where one did not need a car—the public transportation was so available and affordable—15 cents anywhere you wanted to go] now had to re-learn how to drive and take over from Frank.

So, my mind was very fertile, and life was so exciting, here in the Land of The Summer of Love, the Flower Child Era, followed by the Hippie Communes. So, I will start with the essay about my 29th Birthday and then the discussions of painting come afterwards during the summer months.

## *MY 29TH BIRTHDAY...MAY 13, 1969 BY WILLIAM PATRIC LEEDOM RE-TYPED AUGUST 29, 2019*

● ● ● ● ● ● ● ● ● ● ● ● ● ● ● ● ● ● ● ● ●

I woke up this morning to the sound of the phone ringing. It was 7:45 AM and Sonja Ellingson was calling to tell me that we couldn't have breakfast together at her house on the beach as we had planned. She had to get her young niece to school at nine, which would give us no time, and wouldn't it be possible to meet her at school instead, say about 9:15? [Sonja was my co-instructor for the Speech Course: **Interpersonal Communication.**]

I agreed to the plan and slipped quickly back into bed to grab a few more winks. Besides, it was a grey day outside anyway; wouldn't even be as nice as the breakfast we had had together on the beach two weeks before. I managed to sleep until 8:30. I got up, took my usual shower, looked into the bathroom mirror and said, "Happy Birthday, Patric!"

I stuffed the bag full of doughnuts which I had bought for the planned breakfast into my brief case and headed off to school. I parked in my usual area on Junipero Serra Boulevard, crossed over to the street below routinely, and commenced my morning ritual of admiring (smelling) all the flowers in bloom that grow in the yards of the many houses along my path to school. [San Francisco State College.] This ritual always puts me in brighter spirits for facing the day's tasks and events.

At the table [In the Commons (cafeteria) where we were having coffee] we started with the small talk; that's seemingly easy enough to do. For whatever reason of her own, Sonja at one point phrased the question, "How is it going?" I took immediate advantage of that entrance, dropped the small talk, and told her that not only was today my Birthday, but that I was sinking deeper into a depression. And that was no lie. Right there at the table, if the wrong thing had been said,

I felt like I would burst into tears!

Dear Sonja, beautiful Sonja, in spite of some of her flippant ways, she has several redeeming graces. She decided right then and there that the thing for me to do—since it was my Birthday, and particularly since I was feeling so blue, was to take off from school, and spend the day by myself down at her house, on the beach in Pacifica. [On the coast twenty plus miles south of San Francisco.]

I just about ran back to my car. I could sense inside of myself that the downward spiral was arrested; and if anything, beginning a slow ascent. I couldn't very well enjoy myself at the beach if I was wearing some of my best clothes, so I headed home for a fast change. [Home was the penthouse apartment overlooking San Francisco and the Bay, that I, 27 years old, was sharing with Frank Chimera, 43 years old, and Andy Davis, 41 years old—who had become my caring "family."]

[Down at Sonja's home in Pacifica] At a place where the path widened, and a grassy-weedy part sloped back away from the cliff, I lay down and looked out over the sea. The air was fragrant with flowers, the sun popped through the overcast warming my body, and all the insects I could see went about their normal activity. This was becoming indeed, a very Happy Birthday.

In a little while I got up and moved farther down the path. I came upon a place where the rock was crumbling away from the geological pattern in the wall that rose up and away to my left. And in the midst of the fallen rock wild flowers were blooming—so I am witnessing destruction and creation! One follows the other; one needs the other; how right it somehow seems! And I was pleased.

Every now and then I prodded my mind to contemplate the meaning of all of this, and to take advantage of the creativity that this seascape could encourage. Slowly but finally, it came to me: "You have to be in possession of your own soul in order to really live and experience life!" And when the full import had come into my consciousness, I raised my arm in a quick semi-violent fashion to the "closed fist Strike Salute position," and I uttered aloud, "And by God I am snatching (retrieving) my soul back from all the many places others have taken it to!!!"

That is plenty for anybody to wrestle with in one day, so I quit the thinking game, and just soaked up some more sun, and wind, and fragrance of the flowers. How I love the smell of flowers, and the sounds of birds! They comfort me and make me whole again. And below, the sea was playing with the rocky coast in rhythmic patterns.

I was sitting on the bench on the back porch eating when the telephone rang. It was Sonja inquiring if I was enjoying myself well enough and, was I planning to stop by school on my way home? She had a package in her office for me—one from one of our students. A present for me? Oh WOW!

I found the package and looked inside. Among the incongruent articles that stared back at me, I saw a fuzzy stuffed monkey, and a notebook that I recognized as being a "journal" that was part of the course's assignments. Dianne Cantor, one of my students, was turning in her journal to me, as I had requested a few weeks before; but she was also sharing more with me.

At any rate, the cute little monkey was holding a note between its paws: "Dear Patric…Happy Birthday!! I want you to have this lovable furry monkey. He is quite beautiful. You can talk to him endlessly and he will never answer you back. He shows his character by the movement of his hands and legs. This reminds me of you. YOU show much of yourself through your non-verbal actions! To me the monkey is a HE, but if you prefer you can make it a SHE."

Back to Dianne's **Journal**. On the second to the last page, my eye caught on a few words: "**I feel the closest to Pat. He, like myself, shows and exposes the inner conflict that he has dealt with in an effort to become what he is at this very moment.** He is a very beautiful person. His blushing—facial expressions always tell so much about him. He really can't hide behind his face."

[On my way to work in the Cash Vault] Oh yes, since it was a special occasion, I picked a dusty pink rose from our apartment garden and put it into a slender necked vase I had brought from Japan. [Andy Davis, with Frank Chimera's help, and the Landlord's permission to plant the whole hillside behind our building, kept us in fresh flowers all the year around! And inside the apartment as well!] The rose came with me to work, so that I might be reminded of all the thousands of flowers that had made my day so happy.

My partner in the counting cage—no one person was allowed to be alone with the money---Babe was one of the finest human beings I have had the pleasure to associate with. There was one night when, in the money I was counting, came up a one-dollar bill that was signed by all four of the Beatles!! I kid thee not! The Beatles had just been in San Francisco giving a concert during the past month [And I never thought that they would become THAT famous!] I knew that Babe's fourteen-year-old-daughter was crazy about the Beatles, so I asked Babe, "Do you think your daughter would like to have this bill?" And so, I gave it to her. And I have never regretted doing that. Babe had been through a number of serious surgeries—she said she had so many scars on her abdomen that people could play a good game of Tick Tack Toe on it! And yet Babe was one of the most caring and giving persons on the night crew.

As the clock on the wall neared the 9:53 PM mark, I stopped work and began preparing myself for the ritual. This was really it: in a few moments I would never again be 28 years old or any age younger than that. For a moment I felt a twinge of hesitancy, almost fear, but then the philosophical part of me took over and I began telling myself, "What has this whole past year been about if it has not been to prepare myself for the coming years?" And then I thought of my aging process as a kind of pyramid: each lower year becomes the base platform upon which the higher years rest and look out over the landscape (***Life-scape??)*** from their elevated position. With that concept in mind, I began to see the different years of my life being friends with each other; and further than that, I began to think that if I failed to move into each new year with a square grasp and an air of excitement and expectation, that it would be a big disappointment to all the years that had gone before, and had worked so hard to get me this far.

As a final minute made its way around the numbers, I visualized the two years "holding hands" for a brief moment, and when the second hand passed twelve, they grasped extra firmly and then parted. The imagery changed and I saw the 29th year as a brand-new ship being launched down the shipping ways into the sea, setting sail for new and different adventures. For a moment I heard an inner voice saying, "Say goodbye to 28, Patric, and say hello to 29!" And then it was accomplished and all over. Well Done, Patric!

+ + + + + +

## PATRIC IS INSPIRED TO TRY HIS HAND AT WATER-COLOR PAINTINGS

• • • • • • • • • • • • • • • • • • • • • •

1968-1969 were very powerful years for me. I wrote many letters, some stories and after seeing a professional exhibit of some of America's great water-color Artists—Thomas Moran, Grant Wood, Andrew Wyeth et al., I decided to try my hand at it. *I BELIEVE I CAN! I BELIVE I CAN!* I spent the summer of 1968 painting in water colors—first I tried the Dieffenbachia Plant in our living room. Okay; not bad at all. Let's try the interior of the Living Room view of our Pent House Apartment overlooking San Francisco and the Bay. On my God, I love it. Now we take the art easel out onto the roof deck and let's paint the San Francisco Sky Line. "What? Are you crazy?" Well, I can try, can't I?" "Well, okay but it won't quite match the painting of the interior." "I can live with that." I even painted with toothpicks for the building under construction. As a Navy person, I included the USS Enterprise CVN 1, the United States's first nuclear-powered aircraft carrier, which at that time was homeported in Alameda across the Bay. When first constructed, the Enterprise had a conical or round "island"—that part of the carrier that protrudes above the Flight Deck. I recall having the opportunity to climb up in the top of it to see where the Look Outs (sailors watching for danger) were stationed out of the weather. *I DID IT! I BELIEVED I COULD! I BELIEVD I COULD!* Those three paintings are now hanging on my false wall, here in my "Man Cave" at Twin Towers Retirement Center in Cincinnati.

Everything was fine until the autumn of 1968 when the campus erupted into a five-month student, and later joined by the faculty, a strike that lasted until mid-April 1969. But in the Fall of 1968, there was a *BLACK Student Union* Strike to create a Department of Black Studies.

## *SO LONG SAN FRANCISCO; HELLO CHICAGO AND NORTHWESTERN UNIVERSITY*

• • • • • • • • • • • • • • • • • • • • • •

**That was when three caring speech professors** of mine, who had all gotten their doctorates at Northwestern University in Evanston,

Illinois, made arrangements for me to transfer there. Over the summer my friend Marvin Warkentin took a leisurely sojourn across country with me.

While I had moved away to Chicago in August of 1969, whenever I was in the Bay area, I always lived with Frank and Andy. Many years ago, Frank had bought a small modest house in San Leandro, across the Bay, for his father to live in. But the father had grown old and passed away. So, Frank and Andy moved into the house. They had taken on another housemate, but they were not terribly happy with him. He did not meld into the family I had had.

## LETTERS FROM FRANK AND ANDY
• • • • • • • • • • • • • • • • • • • • • •

October 27, 1969 [Frank:] Dear Pat, Well!! When are you coming back home? Your letter gave me the impression you just about had enough of Chicago. I purchased a new mattress for "your bed" *So get yourself back home....*

How is your Dad feeling these days? I trust he is feeling well and is still making history with his newspaper reporting. **It is an honor to know him.**

**My sister…misses you also. Write soon . Frank**

[**Andy**] Dear Pat, …Yes, we did have a wonderful two years while you were with us; and we miss you. Sure wish you'll come back to S.F.— you can always have your room back.…Don't know if we will bother with a [Christmas] tree this year or not. If you were here, we would for sure. Why don't you come back home to your old San Francisco?… As ever your friend Andy.

By September 1969, I was enrolled in Northwestern's Speech Department, and teaching *Interpersonal Communication* (the same course I had taught at SFSC for two years.) My teaching went well, but my personal life had had some emotional trauma, so I was not successful as a student. I withdrew at the end of the quarter.

I visited in Cincinnati off and on, and by January 1970 I was engaged to be married to Shelley, the younger sister of an old flame. [See my book *Metamorphosis of a Young Maiden* for that story.]

It is now 53 years later here in 2021, and I have kept that same philosophy of greeting and accepting each new year. I have never wished to be a day younger than what I am, nor a day older. I have lived a good life. Patric Leedom

[Time Digression] Maybe now in the 2000's plus I regret some of this day after day being in the warm sun for hours: now I am frequently having surgery on my face to eliminate basal cell, and squamous cell skin cancer. I go to an outstanding Skin Cancer Surgery Center; but I have an absolute requirement: the doctors are not allowed to cut on me UNLESS THEY PLAY MY MUSIC— *"IF YOU'RE GOING TO SAN FRANCISCO, BE SURE TO WEAR SOME FLOWERS IN YOUR HAIR"* by Scott McKinsey. Dr. Coldiron calls me "the Hippie from the 60's in San Francisco" because I did live there from 1962 to 1969. It was the Flower Child-Hippie Era, (but I never was a Hippie, but I am not telling him that. Dr. Coldiron is now very fond of the song, my requirement is now boldly written into my chart! [It makes the surgery less painful."][End Digression]

# CONTENTS

# PART THREE

## Dr. Patric Leedom's Autobiography

### NOVEMBER 18—OCTOBER 23, 2022

SCORE TWO SECOND HALF OR YEARS: Age 30 thru 40 Years

*SHELLEY AND I MARRIED JUNE 13, 1970*

• • • • • • • • • • • • • • • • • • • • • •

**Where did that come from?** This story begins back in September 1969 when Sally (Shelley's older sister by nine years) whom I had dated for a year in 1959, invited me to meet in our former church, and then join the family for Sunday Dinner. Shelley was now 19, a student in a Music Academy. Following dinner, Shelley was requested to get out her 12-string guitar and play and sing some of the songs she had composed. I was very impressed. The mother, Stella, then asked me if I was coming back from graduate school in Chicago for Thanksgiving. Yes. "Well, you must come here and join us for Thanksgiving." "Okay." I did. Once again Shelley got out her 12-string guitar to play and sing. "Wow! More beautiful music, thank you." The mother then asked me if I was coming back for Christmas Vacation. Yes. "What Day?" "December 16th." "Oh good, you are just in time to escort Shelley to a Christmas Chorale where Shelley is the guest soloist singing Ave Maria on the 17<sup>th</sup>!" I choked and wondered if it was socially proper that a 29-year-old man should be involved with a teenager? Well, okay, she was 19. Shelley seemed interested in the arrangement. So, I agreed.

Following our visit in September, Shelley wrote in her diary and told her sister, Sally, "If he would ask me to marry him, I would!" And then there was all the contrived guitar playing for me. So, on December 17<sup>th</sup>, I was totally naïve, ignorant, and gullible—knowing nothing of Shelley's intentions.

But on the evening of the seventeenth, and almost every day or night thereafter "lightning struck! And the "vibrations" between us became intense." The two of us did connect something like "nuclear fusion." Within a few nights I was telling Shelley I loved her. On January 1—at 2:00 A.M. I was asking Shelley to marry me.

I was in the process of moving from Chicago back to California to live with my father in Los Angeles, so Shelley and I began writing letters and making a few telephone calls over the next six months. Thus, we married in June 1970. This entire story is written in my first book *METAMORPHOSIS OF A YOUNG MAIDEN* now on the market.

I took Shelley on a HONEYMOON TRIP through Indiana (Wedding night), Illinois, Iowa, (Amana Colonies) South Dakota (Mount Rushmore), Wyoming (Cody—the Irma Hotel) (Yellowstone National Park—Old Faithful Inn two nights), cousin Ruth Thom in Reno, Nevada, into California via US 395 down the east side of the Sierras to Los Angeles and Tujunga—Dad's Home and mine. I went back to work at the Bank of America Central Cash Vault, 11<sup>th</sup> and Flower Streets, Downtown Los Angeles. Barely three weeks later, Shelley's life time companion, Sarabel, takes seriously ill. I put Shelley on a plane back to Cincinnati to be with her dog. Eight days later, Sarabel—having serious cancer, has to be put down. Shelley is devastated, holds dog for three hours until stone cold.

**After Patric gives up his Bank Job in L.A. at the end of August-and returns to Cincinnati; Shelley and Patric take a nice one-bedroom apartment. Patric takes a job as manager of a Pizza Inn Restaurant, and Shelley continues with her music education.**

## *SHELLEY WAS JUST TOO YOUNG FOR MARRIAGE AND WE PARTED AMICABLY*

● ● ● ● ● ● ● ● ● ● ● ● ● ● ● ● ● ● ● ● ●

Sadly, the roles and responsibilities and need to communicate when problems arise were too overwhelming for Shelley. Patric and Shelley limp through several months of marriage. Patric takes Shelley to counseling but she refuses to change. Patric loses 28 pounds from stress, and finally decides to divorce Shelley. They part amicably. Patric does not consider the institution of marriage for 29 years!

[Time digression] Serendipitously Shelley and I reconnected 18 years later! I was working on my doctorate in education at the University. I had been tasked with meeting and advising anyone who possessed a bachelor's degree not in teaching, but now wanted a bachelor's of Teacher Education.

Shelley had remarried three to four years later after our divorce, and now had three daughters, was now helping out in the classroom, and decided to pursue a teaching degree. She made an appointment and came in in November 1989.

Guess who the designated Evaluator was? Me, of course. [We re-kindled our friendship, which was not that hard since we still cared about each other.]

I advised Shelley pretty much what I advised most of my advisees—it would take two more years of education courses and practicums. Shelley decided that was too much. She and her husband had been offered staff positions at a church conference center in a Southern state, and now they accepted and moved down there.

Now it just so happens it was the same conference center that I attended occasionally. So, Shelley and I would always take some time together. In the beginning we took time to re-examine our failed marriage. Shelley's frequent response was, "I apologize for mistreating you; I was just too young. If we had met and married at an older age, it might have worked." But then during future visits we moved on to just being friends for the next 20 years discussing current experiences and situations.[End of Time Digression.]

As soon as I divorced Shelley, I immediately quit my job at the Pizza Inn. Now my calendar was open for new adventures. My mother was employed as the Secretary-Treasurer of the Miller-Addick Co, a mineral brokerage firm that utilized the river Union Barge Lines that hauled ore from Mexico up the Mississippi River to the Ohio and thence to Pittsburgh and the steel mills. I was aware that Mother's boss had taken some short-perhaps day rides on the towboats. So, I asked my mother to arrange one for me.

## TOWBOAT TRIP DOWN THE OHIO
## AND MISSISSIPPI RIVERS

• • • • • • • • • • • • • • • • • • • • • • •

Mother telephoned the Vice President who made all the arrangements and understood that I wanted to travel all the way to New Orleans. On a July day, I was placed aboard the Union Barge Lines Towboat *Western* at Bill Kinsler's Southern Harbor across from Cincinnati. I was a guest of the company, so had no work duties, and I had access to the "High Bench" at the back of the Pilot House. On the second day out, I was talking to the Master (captain) Claire Carpenter. I mentioned that I had an uncle that spent most of his life working on the Tows. Claire: "What was his name?" "Richard Rader." "You don't mean old 'Q-Ball Rader?" "Yes, I do." "Oh, I know old Q-Ball, he used to work for me! Alright Patric, that makes you "Family" so come on over here and get your hands on these sticks!" [Towboats do not have steering wheels or helms. Instead, they have three steering sticks each for the port and starboard motors/propellers. The propellers are housed in a "Korte Nozzle" with wire net doors at each end to protect the motors and propellers from all the driftwood and jetsam and flotsam in the water. When the tow is moving forward, one just uses the single steering stick to control the forward rudder, which located aft of the Kort Nozzle. When one is "backing down, one uses the two backing steering sticks because there are two backing rudders just forward of the Kort Nozzle.

Okay, so I am expected to get off the High Bench, come over and sit in the Captain's chair and take control of the steering sticks as well as the engine controllers. Really? *Yes. And I Believe I Can.* I had been navigating submarines for several years; I did understand rudder responses in water, and that each ship has its own pivot or turning point in rudder changes. Okay, I got it! Claire stayed by my side coaching me along, but after a few hours I got the hang of it. And drove several more hours successfully.

Now towboat companies that travel the entire system from Pittsburgh down to New Orleans, have an efficient system: On the upper Ohio, they use a smaller powered towboat: 3200 horsepower. Their barge loads are usually not that big—fifteen barges at most. In the middle, lower Ohio and upper Mississippi Rivers, the companies use medium sized towboats: 4500 hundred horsepower. And for the lower Mississippi, where there are no locks, and the barge loads can expand to upwards of 25 barges—five across and five long. The companies use the large towboats: 6400 horsepower.

The sum of the above discussion meant that I would be transferred from the **Western** to the middle sized *Northern*. And finally, to the largest *Mariner*. All along the captains kept passing the word. "Give Patric driving lessons."

I have forgotten the name of the *Northern*'s captain, but he knew my grandmother Bessie Olive Leedom Rader—my father's mother, in Manchester (a town that provided many sailors for the river trade.), and even had a few beers with her at the Eagles Club. So, he certainly treated me as family. On that stretch of the river the tow boat needed to pass through the Louisville Locks. As the boat first nosed the first six rows of barges into the lock and unwired the rest for the second locking [the old locks were 110 feet wide while three barges across equaled 105 feet wide. The entire tow was 1200 feet in length, but the lock could only handle 600 feet. So, we had to "break tow": nose the first six hundred feet of barges into the lock. Then un-wire or un-cable all the barges behind those 600 feet, back off, let the gates close, and the Lock Master would lower and pull out those 600 feet of barges, tie them off downstream, then repeat the procedure with the back half of 600 feet of barges and Towboat.

The Captain invited me, and we left the boat, walked up over the flood bank and down to this conveniently located tavern. The Captain bought me two "Boiler Makers" A beer combined with a shot of Maker's Mark Whiskey! Whew! Okay back to the boat. I was only on the *Northern* for two days until we met up with the *Mariner* coming up the river. Understand this: there are barges full of commodities that are destined to keep traveling down the river, while another string of barges is destined to be delivered somewhere up the river. The **Western** takes its barges down the river until it meets the *Northern* bringing a string up the river. The two tows tie off to the bank of the river. The Western unties itself from its "down-river" load, drives around toward the "upward bound string," while the **Northern** does the same thing in reverse order and takes charge of the down bound tow. The process is called "Turning Tow." My task, as a passenger, was to make sure all of my belongings were in my Navy Sea Bag and that bag was placed on the deck of the down-bound barge. Once that has been completed, both tows continue on their way.

The **Mariner's** Master was named "Meryl 'Preacher' Clausing" because during World War I, Meryl's father placed him, at his age of 6, up on a wooden crate at the corner of Canal and Royal Streets in New Orleans to sell War Bonds. Preacher had been working on the Mississippi River for over forty years, and he was "full of river tales" which I loved to hear. The Pilot (the person who captained the boat during the alternate shifts—six hours on and six hours off) was named John. He was a nice pleasant person, but "he did not know any stories" so was not as interesting with whom to stand watches. One day I asked Preacher why John did not know any stories. Preacher answered, "Because he never asked me." A few of Preacher's stories were telling about the real early days steam-powered tow boats who could only "push" one or two barges up river. [I didn't ask Preacher, but I assumed that in the early early days, the tow boats actually towed a barge behind them, providing the name 'Towboat."] Preacher also explained that in the early days, the Army Corps of Engineers had not yet taken responsibility for controlling the path or "river bed" of the Mississippi River; therefore 1) there was no dredging of the river, therefore no guaranteeing a ten-foot depth in the mid channel for the tows. Consequently, during dryer weather spells, steamboats and tows had to "Puddle Jump" meaning travel as far as the channel would keep you a float but once you ran out of deep water, you had to wait until it rained again.

Well, lo and behold, we had that experience-sort of. The **Mariner** was still navigating in the lower Ohio where there were still locks and the use of the old Wicket dams (a gate by which a flow of water is regulated; these are individual large wooden beams (perhaps 16" x 16") that were anchored very close together on a threshold at the bottom of the river. There was a lock boatman that could reach down with a hook of some type and raise the wickets one by one when there was not sufficient water for boats to pass by the lock; then the boats had to go through the locks to continue their travels. And the lock boats could lower each wicket when there was sufficient water (a minimum ten-foot depth because a fully loaded tow-barge drew 9 feet of water) for the tows to bypass the lock gates.

There was this one afternoon when the Mariner, with its 6400 horsepower diesel engines was chugging merrily along. But then Preacher spotted this upbound tow dead still in the water—"AGROUND", and it was IN THE MIDDLE OF THE CHANNEL! Preacher radioed down and found one of the wicket dams had broken and let too much water flow out. So, we tied off to the north side of the Illinois Shore. While we were "Waiting for Water" I got the bright idea I wanted to go over and explore the shore. So, the deck hands placed a ladder horizontally so I could climb over. After a few minutes I realized that I was limited to walking on the tops of fallen logs, and all around them the thick weeds were three feet high!! Did I want to put my feet down where I couldn't see a thing and take a chance there was some creature crawling around down there, such as a snake?? –No, I will not take a chance! So back aboard the *Mariner* I went.

We waited twelve hours for the water to be restored. Preacher supplied me with a large thick book of maps of the Mississippi River which every page portrayed around 40 miles of the river. I needed this book in my lap as I was doing the driving and needed to see what was coming up. It is remarkable that from the pilot seat that it is extremely difficult to perceive a bend in the river until you come right up on it, because all the trees blended in and camouflage the bend. Radar does help identify the bends. [I still own that large thick book 50 years later!]

Preacher also explained that historically, the Mississippi River is a meandering river with a generally sand bottom, such that strong river currents could eventually cut right across the "neck" of one of the meandering "tongues" of land and thereby not only cut through farmers' fields, but to leave towns formerly fronting on the river, now 20 miles inland. AND since the neighboring states had already declared their state borders, now parts of each state were located on BOTH SIDES of the river. Preacher also related that before the Army Corps of Engineers installed the Revetment Program [Dictionary Definition: Page 1648 revetment n. 1. A facing of masonry or the like esp. for protecting the embankment.] and the Army Corp also used old cars, metal wiring and whatever.] the river changed it banks regularly to the point that there had to be Pilots who lived locally and "knew" the river for a certain number of miles stationed along the river to guide the tows, and rode the boats just for those miles.

Even in the1970's the river still changed frequently enough in places that the Coast Guard had to keep placing buoys to indicate the channel course.

So needless to say, I stood most all my watches with Preacher, and it was with him I took my everyday driving lessons. With my submarine driving experiences, I really caught on to judging when to start the turn and how much rudder to use (an angle of just so many compass degrees to use), and when to take the angle off. Bear in mind, now that we are in the lower Mississippi River where it is wide and there are no locking systems. Tows could now add additional barges, so instead of three barges wide giving us 105 foot wide beam, now we had five barges giving us 175-foot-wide beam.

Bear in mind that while the square footage surface area of the "Farm" (collective name for all the barges) compares similarly to the square footage of an aircraft carrier landing deck; these barges were all "wired together" (hopefully securely, but it depends upon each deck hand doing his/her job properly.) And the effect was that the head of the tow did not turn quite as neatly as a ship would. So, turning was tricky, needing sharp eyes and quick decision making. But I conquered it.

## *I BELIEVE I COULD—AND I DID IT!*

• • • • • • • • • • • • • • • • • • • • •

During the last two days of the trip, I actually drove four hours straight commencing as we were passing through Baton Rouge. I drove under bridges and around bends. It took 10 days to travel from Cincinnati to New Orleans. [The Barge Lines offered to take me back up to Cincinnati BUT that would have taken three weeks, which I could not afford.] But I did I begin entertaining thoughts of going to work for the company and taking a career on the river.

## *MY TRIP TERMINATED IN NEW ORLEANS*

• • • • • • • • • • • • • • • • • • • • •

When we landed at a shipyard near New Orleans, I was driven into town and dropped off on General Robert E. Lee Circle, where I was to stay in the YMCA. But the big story I want to get to, is when I spent several hours speaking with the guards at both the Cabildo Museum and the Presbytery Museum. These gentlemen were heavy duty history buffs. This trip gave me the historical knowledge that the Ohio Valley settlers did consider becoming a Spanish Colony. STORY:

The guards took time with me to explain that while the French had founded New Orleans, the Spaniards gained governmental control during the Queen Anne's War [Here in the U.S. known as the French and Indian War] in the 1770's. So, it was to the Spanish Governor that the settlers from the territories of Ohio, Kentucky, Indiana that they appealed to for permission to unload and sell their wares. The Spanish Governor was all in favor of the trade; Spanish money was now being one of the currencies used in the settlements. The Spanish Governor put forth the invitation for the settlements of Ohio, Kentucky, and Indiana and others to secede from the United States and become part of the Louisiana Spanish Colony. He argued that once the settlers came over the mountains to the Ohio River Valley, the people no longer had any direct connection with those states over the mountains to the East. He did have a point. The U.S. Congress heard about the invitation, got scared, and quickly started the building of the National Road from Cumberland, Maryland straight across Ohio, Indiana and into Illinois. (Interstate 70 today follows its route. And there is a diorama museum just outside Zanesville depicting the building of the road.)

## THE NATIONAL ROAD

• • • • • • • • • • • • • • • • • • • • •

The National Road was a way to have stronger communication with the settlers in the Ohio Valley and the original 13 colonies that formed the United States. And so, history records that the settlers never did become a Spanish Colony. Of course, not too many years later, the French won the territory back again, and then in three days, sold it to the United States.

In summary, I had a delightful Towboat experience; I got along well with all of the crew and cooks. I slept well; and I ATE well—I gained ten pounds in ten days!! Of historical note there was another Apollo Space Launch while we were on the river. My ability to drive the towboat did inspire me to travel up to the Pittsburgh Union Office and apply. Fortunately, the Union Official was honest and blunt that I did not have a chance to be hired, when so many other men were waiting in line. He told me, "Keep your money, and go home."

While the Barge Line Offered to transport me back up the rivers—a trip of three weeks, I had a house painting job waiting for me, so I took the bus back to Cincinnati. Upon arrival in Cincinnati, I immediately went back to painting this large old house for Kit and George Buquo. I am a very conscientious painter, but the house had not been painted in many years so there was a lot of preparation work to do. My friends were not prepared to pay for that."

## FAMILY ROOTS ON MY FATHER'S SIDE

• • • • • • • • • • • • • • • • • • • •

[My Family Roots Digression] Since the Leedom family was one of the first three white families to found Adams County, Ohio, and the town of Manchester, Ohio, this is an appropriate time to present my family on my father's side. The eldest founder was my great, great, great great (to the fourth) grandfather William Leedom. He is written up in the History of Adams County for a number of accomplishments. I have already written that he, and fellow farmers constructed a Flatboat—200 feet long and 20 feet wide in which to haul all over their farm produce and animal furs etc. William Leedom accomplished 15 of these trips over a 23-year period. With no means of boating back up the rivers, the farmers sold everything including the FLATBOAT made of hardwood (which was then used to build many of the fine homes in New Orleans) and walked back up to Ohio, utilizing the Natchez Trace part of the way. I was told that after a trip or two, the farmers got smart and bought a horse. The first farmer would mount the horse and ride for an hour, get off, tether the horse to eat grass and relax, and the farmer would take off walking When the next two farmers arrived at the horse, the second farmer would mount the horse and ride for an hour then tether the horse and take off walking. And so forth.

I do not have a strong grasp of exactly how long these trips took, but I would guess somewhere in the 40-day range. I did read in **THE HISTORY OF ADAMS COUNTY** that there was at least once when William was quarantined in New Orleans due to an outbreak of Yellow Fever. During the War of 1812, William served as a Captain in the US Army.

One of William's other notable accomplishments, when the U.S. Congress awarded funds to build the NATIONAL ROAD [From Cumberland Maryland straight across country (the current Interstate 70) to mid Illinois.] and in addition, there was a divide in the road outside of the settlement of Zanesville, sending off "Zane's Trace" which came down in a South by Southwesterly direction to hook up with what is now Route 68 going across the Ohio River at Aberdeen and Maysville, Kentucky. Well, Great Grandfather William took a job on Zane's Trace helping to build the road [breaking large rocks with mallets or hammers, into smaller pieces as measured by an iron ring. William's father-in-law Mr. Edgington bought himself some acreage near Bentonville and built himself a Tavern and William operated it, along with his older sister, Almira and her daughter Tacy (who was now William's wife) Not only did it serve as an Inn for travelers, but it was the only public building around, so it was also used a church, a court, and any other public meeting needs.

So, for many years, the Leedoms owned a lot of land, built businesses such as sawmills, grain mills, and a Livery Stable. Third Great Grandpa Joseph drove a stagecoach from Ohio, down route 68 to Lexington, Kentucky for several years even including snowy winters. Joseph also represented counties Brown, Adams, and Scioto in the Ohio House of Representatives for two terms—1848-1850.

Focusing on my roots, William Leedom (my fourth great grandfather) gave birth to my father's direct lineage to Joseph Leedom 3rd who gave birth to Thomas Meek Leedom (2nd Great) , who gave birth to Chilton Alexander (1st great grandfather) , who at age 16, married an Irish Lass, Lydia Chamblin, straight from Ireland, at a time when the English forbade marrying any Irish. Thomas Meek forced an annulment, but Lydia was already pregnant with my grandfather also named Chilton Alexander Jr. or just C.A. born in 1888. The Irish family bitterly resented the annulment and loss of financial support, so they abused the child.

C.A. Jr. later married Bessie Olive Hines, daughter of a schoolteacher also in Manchester. They had two children: Mary Elizabeth who was born November 4, 1911 (but later succumbed to diphtheria in 1924.) And then my father, Robert William. Born July 21, 1914 (and passed away August 26, 1974.).

An "Appalachian Incident." Sometime in the early 1970's my grandmother, Bessie Olive Hines (formerly Leedom) Rader, reported that after her marriage to C.A., her mother stated "Bessie, you just married your third cousin!" Bessie tried to tell me that that was "news to her."

But she should have known because her mother's maiden name was Leedom! The mother was descended from one of William's other sons, **Elijah!** *So, I have a double dose of Leedom-"ness"*. Another family story: Grandma Bessie's Uncle John Peter Leedom, was the Sergeant of Arms in the U.S. Congress from December 6,1883 to December 2, 1889—Forty-eighth, Forty- ninth, Fiftieth, and Fifty-first Congress. So, I would judge them to be middle-class—with a lot of intelligence making its way through the family.

So, while all the branches of the family tree are solidly middle class, my mother, Joy, was able to accomplish joining the "Blue Book" society of Cincinnati. Mother's long-time boyfriend, and my surrogate stepfather, Mathew G. Long, living at the Cincinnati Country Club, was solidly upper class and took Mom everywhere with him, and introduced her to everyone, and she was well accepted.

My mother, Joy, was super-bright, college-educated, had been her cousin Edward J. Hancock's chauffer and co-host at Governor's affairs at her age of 16, she had an encyclopedic knowledge of Classical Music and Poetry, spoke three languages, and played in two civic symphony orchestras. Through her many social experiences, developed a skill in offering stimulating conversations. So yes, mother comfortably fit in and was accepted. [End of Family Roots Digression]

[Of a historical note in July 1971: Musician Trumpet player Louis "Satchmo" Armstrong, from New Orleans, had just passed away, so there were many tributes to him around town.]

As I drove home from the Pittsburgh Seamen's Union Office, I asked myself a very important question: "Now that you are recently divorced from Shelley, and somewhat "flapping in the breeze without a clear life's plan (or source of income) What shall I do? Go back to California, maybe?" After some deep philosophical thought, I decided to return to this new exciting educational experiment that was taking place in the **NEW SCHOOL** over in North Avondale (my childhood neighborhood), a block off of Clinton Springs and Mitchell Avenues.

## NEW CAREER VOLUNTEERING WITH
## THE NEW SCHOOL MONTESSORI

• • • • • • • • • • • • • • • • • • • • • •

But now it was summer of 1971, and my mother took me over to meet Great Aunt Monica Mitchell Hoppe Fenton-Lawson. She and I became rapid friends. In small-world-ism, it was Aunt Monica Mitchell who had sold the Mitchell Mansion to the Catholic Archdiocese in 1927, and it was the archdiocese that rented the mansion to the New School!! So, I was "distantly related to this building; many of my stepfather's relatives had grown up in this building. From 1933 to 1965 the Archdiocese had conducted St. Thomas Aquinas Elementary School in the mansion, and since my neighbors attended there, I was occasionally a guest in the St. Thomas Aquinas school. Aunt Monica also loaned to me a set of photographs that the family had taken when they were trying to sell the house.

I took these photographs right over to the New School in August to compare what the rooms had looked like. There were several staff members and parents there that day and they heartily encouraged me to come back and be part of their community. Okay. Before Shelley and I got our divorce, we were living together in Norwood. But after the divorce we gave up the apartment, and I moved in with my mother and Stepfather in the ultra-modern apartments of Kulla Viken in Lower Price Hill. However, once I was anchored into the New School Community, I moved into the Mansion! There were not really any real bedrooms left, and when we re-wired the school, we were told not to re-wire the Third Floor. So, while I moved a dresser and a closet up to the Third Floor for storage, on the Second Floor there was a lockable Mirrored Closet in the far back bedroom which I used. [This bedroom had been my step-grandfather, Mark Lincoln Mitchell Sr.'s bedroom when he lived in the house, and then later, it was used by Aunt Monica's step-daughter Elizabeth Hoppe (later Briggs and one of my very best friends).

By September I was involved in founding a brand new alternative private school which a few years later became all Montessori. During the Academic Year 1971-1972 I was a full-time volunteer (living in the mansion.)

## WITH VERY LITTLE INCOME, I TOOK UP RESIDENCE IN THE MANSION

• • • • • • • • • • • • • • • • • • • • • •

I lived in the old Mansion—which my stepfather Mark Mitchell's great, great grandfather Robert Mitchell, a millionaire in the 1880's had perhaps the largest furniture company in the United States with Sales Offices not only in Cincinnati, but in Memphis, Natchez, Little Rock, and New Orleans. He owned thousands of acres in North Avondale from Reading Road to near Vine Street, from North Crescent north to near Paddock Road. He had the Mansion built not for himself, but for his daughter-in-law Mary Pearl Lincoln Mitchell and her growing family of eight children which grew to 11 after they moved into the Mansion in 1891.

I lived in the Mansion for five years because I did not have enough money to do otherwise. And I was not afraid of any possible ghosts: I figured since I knew many of the living and passed on Mitchells, that I could hold interesting conversations. At least **I Believed I Could! But no ghosts ever made their presence known.** Again, there were no longer bedrooms as such, but there were some very large bean-bag chairs that made nice sleeping pallets. I had a sleeping bag, sheets, and pillows so I was comfortable. Eventually one of the parents, Judy Bissmeyer, donated couches, so then I wound up be sleeping in the office only a few feet from my desk. There were still old-fashioned bathrooms on the second floor, so a tub bath was very nice. There were two kitchens, so I could store and cook meals. I paid no rent, but this was compensation for no salary in 1971 to 1972. I mention all this because I am written into the school's history lore as the person who lived in the house for five years!!

[Time Digression] I had been recruited two years ago in 1970 by Tom Corbett and Carol Lee—the head teachers at the New School, so I was in fact, at the front door in September 1970 when the school commenced. [Historical note: I am still in touch with Tom and Carol in 2021. Carol is 94; Tom is 93, and their son Sebastian is 48] I was not a paid staff member, but an enthusiastic volunteer. That first Autumn Season, I primarily worked with the building manager finishing painting the classrooms, cleaning the floors, transporting children to various field trips. Etc. During our first year—1970-1971, I was married at the time and my wife was taking classes at the Conservatory of Music at UC.; my paying job was managing a Pizza Inn Restaurant in Fairfield, Ohio. There, I worked a mixture of some days and some evenings. The owner decided he would run the weekend evenings. Great. So, I was free during some of the daytimes. Eventually, my wife, in tandem with her mother decided I had no business "volunteering away from home" so after the Christmas Holiday, I ceased volunteering. [End Digression]

At the conceptualizing of the school and curriculum and culture, the community was to be "Participatory Democracy" every member of the parent-staff community and provide input to any and all decisions, and **NO One was to have "more power than anyone else!"** We had a COW! Or more properly a C.O.W. which was the Committee of the Whole, which met twice a month in the beginning. And here all purchases, business issues, and academic issues were discussed and voted upon. By the end of two years, a deeply concerned group of parents who loved the school and wanted it to survive, created a committee to restructure the organization somewhat. For example, it was decided that the school ought to have one person to run the office and business affairs. And another change was that in the elementary program there would be regular classes daily to teach the basic subjects—reading, writing, math, English etc. [Throughout the past year there had been an academic disagreement between the staff of the First Floor all Montessori Program (who did not have mandatory classes as such) and the non-

Montessori Elementary Staff that was losing students because they were not learning, and the staff wanted to institute mandatory classes.]

At any rate, in the Spring of 1972, those of us who desired to stay working full time at the New School had to survive a grueling interview process before the whole Personnel Committee themselves and we had to promise to obey the new rules and parameters. The next day I received a telephone call from Judge Jack Sherman, of the committee, explaining that, first of all, I did have a job. Secondly, since I had more administrative and managerial experience than anyone else who had applied, would I please be in charge of the business affairs. "Yes!"

## HIRED AS THE BUSINESS MANAGER, BUILDING MANAGER, PUBLIC RELATIONS, ETC.

Well, a pragmatic way to describe the employment situation was to say, everyone else in the building was teaching except me. I was in charge of EVERYTHING ELSE. I was the Business Manager, The Building Manager; I was the Public Relations Officer, not only meeting with current and prospective parents, but all of the city officials such as the Board of Health, and Day Care Licensing Bureau. And, oh by the way, I was the Answering Service for the Cincinnati Montessori Society—using a separate telephone. I'm tired just listing all those. Truly, taken together it was far more than a forty hour a week job; I sometimes worked late to eight or nine o'clock trying to keep up with everything. And every once in a while, I broke down in tears from exhaustion. As I recall, my annual salary was $2,700 a year!! As a salary committee we divided up the salary pot depending who had how many dependents. And I was all alone.

But even with paying no rent or utilities, it was not enough. I was still a drilling Naval Reservist driving to the submarine unit in Cleveland once a month. My stepfather, Mark Mitchell, worked for the Cincinnati AAA Club, and he got me a job as Holiday Help on the Emergency Answering Service Telephone Board. This was an interesting experience: there were 14 telephones all "hooked up in series": The incoming telephone call came to phone #1; but if that phone was busy, then it rolled over to phone # 2, if that phone was busy then it rolled over to phone #3, and so on up the line. Now if operator on phone number #1 hung up, then the very next call came to # 1. It did get lonely at phone # 14 where I was assigned. So, the next night I was assigned phone # 11; and the night after that I was assigned phone # 8, and the night after that I was assigned phone # 3, and the night after that I was assigned phone # 1 !! And I stayed on phone # 1 through the season. But before the season ended, I was called into the office and offered a regular job coming in on Saturdays every weekend. "Yes, I'll take it." But before I made it to my first Saturday, I was asked to do Sundays also. Okay.

Sometime in those days, a parent, who was a medical doctor and drove a big van came up with the idea that we could have a "Food Cooperative" on our back porch every Friday. We could purchase wholesale food at much lower prices such that our staff, parents, and neighbors could buy very fresh food reasonably. And the Sweet Heart deal was that the large Cincinnati Food Coop agreed to take all of our left-over produce for the price we had paid. Whoopee! In addition to vegetable and fruit, we had access to dairy products, cheese , yogurt. Our coop ran for over a year, and that parent moved out of state. Eventually, I took over management when we were losing money, and I turned it around with careful shopping and 20% markups. Certainly, I was able to eat better at lower costs.

*ALSO IN SEPTEMBER 1972, I ENROLLED
IN XAVIER UNIVERSITY'S MONTESSORI
MASTERS DEGREE PROGRAM*

• • • • • • • • • • • • • • • • • • • • • •

After working around the New School and spending time as a teacher in the Downstairs Montessori Environment, I decided I wanted to become heavily involved in the Montessori Philosophy and Methods. Xavier University was just down the street six blocks on Dana Avenue, so I began my four-year adventure in the evenings and on Saturdays.

+ + + + + + + + + +

My father, DURING his whole newspaper career, was a champion of the people, whatever race, or ethnic group they belonged to. Pasadena was a city founded in the 1880's by very wealthy families from the east coast. They wanted a warm winter retreat. They brought their Black "House Servants" with them to Pasadena. House Servants were like "members of the family" who often raised their children to go to college and become teachers, business men and other careers.

*DAD HAS A HEART ATTACK!*

• • • • • • • • • • • • • • • • • • • • • •

***In early 1973 "A Funny thing happened on the way to the Forum.'*** (Performed by the actor Zero Mostel in the PLAY and the Movie,) My father was social friends with one of the local firemen. The firemen picked up dad in the fireman's car to go to a nice restaurant. But as they are travelling the streets Dad notices they are not using the correct street. He inquired why not? The Fireman responded: I am taking you to the hospital because you are having a **HEART ATTACK! Dad said, "what do you mean?"** The fireman said look down at your fingernails, Bob, they are all blue for lack of oxygen! And so, they were; and so, when they arrived at the hospital the doctors and nurses took dad in immediately and began working on him. It was a serious heart attack! That was in early February 1973. That was the end of Dad's Newspaper writing career. The serious heart condition prevented Dad from doing any serious deep thought reading and writing, because the heart was too weak.

A few years back, Dad had help form the ***BAMBOO WRITERS CLUB FOR SERIOUS WRITERS.*** These were serious published writers who wanted to learn more and be a support group to fellow writers. Every person in the group had published a few books or published serious journal articles on some worthwhile topic. If I was in Los Angeles, I would go with Dad and attend the meetings. Usually at a meeting one person had pre-distributed the chapter or journal article he or she wanted criticism and feedback on. Lois Dean was a prime member. When Dad had his serious heart attack, she immediately invited Bob to go live in her home and she would take care of him. Wow! Thanks! My young brother Casey, 13 years old was living with Dad at the time, so Casey was welcome to move in also. Dad and Casey lived with Lois's family for well over a year. When I went to California to visit, it was at Lois's house. She and her family were very good to Dad and Casey.

She helped him, drove him to all his doctor's appointments. In Spring of 1974 Dad and Casey felt strong enough to move back to Tujunga. I was not living in California at the time, so I do not have a tight grip of how things worked out. In late July/Early August I had picked up Julia for a few weeks visit, and we did go to Dad's. The local Los Angeles Opera was performing a famous opera in English in our neighborhood Tujunga theatre. Dad took all of us down to enjoy it. Julia was nine years old at the time, but she has strong memories of the performance. The next day, I took Julia and Casey down to Disneyland in Anaheim to spend the entire day. We three always loved going to

Disneyland in California (and Disney World in Florida.) It was a long day. While we were gone, my mother telephoned Dad's House to inform me of a cousin's sudden death. But since I was not home **Dad and mother spoke to each other for three long hours!!** When Julia, Casey, and I arrived home late that night, Dad was all a glow: With a deep all-around smile, he reported that that was the best conversation he had ever had with my mother (whom he divorced in 1944); He said they discussed many of the times and places where they did not understand each other, and now how did that person explain what had happened! I have never seen him so happy. I am glad I wasn't there so the three hours conversation could take place.

A day or two later, I was in Dad's bedroom--where he spent most of his time lying quietly in bed resting. I walked in and sat down. Dad started saying to me what a failure he had been to me as a father. I got very upset with him! This was early August 1974. And in the summer of 1961, he and I had had a deep heart to heart discussion this very issue and I stated "Dad, I forgive you for whatever had happened in the past. But now, you are the best Dad I could have, and I need you now, and I love you very much." So, I thought all those negative thoughts and feelings had been settled years before. So, I started to argue with Dad. He grabs his nitroglycerin and grabs is heart. "Oh. My heart!" So, I stopped dead. I didn't say another word, but I thought "You dirty fighter—you start something but then when I push back, you play dirty and grab your heart. That is the last time I will ever argue with you." And inside I was very sad to see him mentally and emotionally "Dumping negative thoughts" on himself. And that was the very last time. And when Julia and I left the next morning, that was the last time I ever said good bye to my Dad. We left on the 6th of August, and he died of a massive heart attack while in the hospital and in an intensive care unit on the 26th of August.

## *DAD PASSES AWAY AUGUST 1974 (BIG OUCH FOR ME!)*

• • • • • • • • • • • • • • • • • • • • • •

Dad's death was a major trauma for me. I was so close to him. I was in my New School Business Office when I got the telephone call from Dad's neighbors --the Clark family—who were taking care of Casey—that Dad had died in the hospital the day before. Immediately, I felt my heart pounding in my chest! And I felt my heart beating for the next two months!! It took me two years to finally adjust to his being gone out of my life.—Remember I had only met him when I was 13 years old and commenced living with him on a daily basis when I was 14. And, I believed that my father was one of the finest men I ever knew! And in 2020, I still believe that!

## *RITES PLANNED FOR BOB LEEDOM*

• • • • • • • • • • • • • • • • • • • • • •

*August 28, 1974*

*Memorial services were in the planning stages Tuesday for Robert Leedom, a 40-year veteran of the newspaper business and former Star-News reporter....*

*His concern for race relations in Pasadena resulted in several landmark developments benefitting black citizens and earned him the compliment of being considered "an ally" in efforts of black reformers to improve the Northwest (of Pasadena).*

*His participation in community affairs related to community and human relations far exceeded that of a reporter in that he became personally involved in efforts to improve the quality of life for all citizens of Pasadena," said William H. Boone, human relations administrator for the City of Pasadena.*

*Mr. Leedom was instrumental in persuading Pasadena City College to open the Adult Training Center in 1968 which provides instruction for completion of high school credits.*

*He also persuaded Tournament of Roses association to permit the use of a large building for a recreation center for the northwestern area youngsters 10 months out of the year, Boone said, adding it was the first effort to respond directly to the needs of the northwestern youths, initiating the neighborhood youth center approach which resulted in Jackie Robinson and Villa-Park centers.*

*Mr. Leedom began his career as a reporter for the Cincinnati Enquirer where he gained notoriety for his exposes on the high rate of venereal disease and graft in the county.*

*A bullet fired through the window as he worked late one-night persuaded him it was time to seek employment elsewhere and he went to Albuquerque, N.M. where he became good friends with the later famous war correspondent Ernie Pyle...*

Note: When I was notified that Dad had died, I flew immediately from Cincinnati to Pasadena. Upon arriving at Star-News, I was directed to go see the same Dr. William Boone, at the Martin Luther King Recreation Center. I had my 12-year-old sister Kilian with me—I took her everywhere I went to make Memorial arrangements. She was my emotional support. It was 10:00 A.M. when we met Dr. Boone. He listened to me, looked at his watch, and then said, "Son, can you be back here at 3:00 P.M.?" "Yes Sir, I can."

We came back at 3:00 P.M. Dr. Boone's office was quite large—I think maybe it was also used as a Conference Room—anyway, the room was packed—literally Standing Room Only! Both Black and White men filled the room. Dr. Boone said to me, "Son, just tell them what you want for the Memorial." I did, and they provided it! The City of Pasadena paid for my father's Memorial Service. The congregation that came to Dad's Memorial Service at the churh was like a small United Nations with people from a wide variety of ethnic groups. The Service was on Labor Day Weekend, so some people sent me their regrets. It a beautiful service. I had wanted to engage a Scottish Bagpiper but couldn't find one that quickly. So, I had a Harpist and Flutist play Bagpipe music.

Special note: Dad had been seriously ill with his heart condition for two years. He had not been able to do anything with his financial affairs and Federal Income Taxes. I turned to one of his friends, the Director of the Legal Aid Society who directed me to the President of the Tournament of Roses Association, who had a very large law firm, Mr. Fred Solwedle. He was kind and generous, and his firm took on the many shoe boxes full of papers. It took several months to process everything. When all was said and done there was only $1900 available. And the Rose Parade law firm charge me $0.00! I believe that happened because of their respect for what Dad did for the City of Pasadena. That's when I learned that I was NOT the executor—in the past year he had appointed my stepmother, Liz! But she took the check and said, "I think your father really intended for you to have this, so she split it with me. Thank goodness because I had spent about $900.00 on my flight, rental car, etcetera, and as Business Manager of a "Start-up" private Montessori School, my annual salary was only $2,700.00!!

Personal note: I had become very very close to Dad. I idolized him. I thought he was one of the greatest men I ever knew. Even Liz in later years said he was the greatest man she ever knew! I strongly believe that I had become Dad's closest friend. And I sadly know that none of his last four children ever really knew him well. It took me two years to fully accommodate myself to his passing. I will forever give thanks that I was smart enough to move in with him when I was 14-years old. It was and is **one of the largest game changers in my life! Thank you, thank you, thank you Dad! I love you very much.**

**[Time Digression]** Like "peeling the layers off of an onion, the mind starts remembering one thing after another. I remember, that at 14 I went to live with my father. His parents had divorced when he was six years old. His mother up and left one day, leaving Dad and his older sister with the father. Dad never knew the true circumstances, and so, in his mind, "he felt abandoned by his mother." [It wasn't until twenty some years later after Dad's death that I learned the truth from my First Cousin, Charla Ann Striblen, who had been given the real story by Grandma---that his mother had NOT willfully abandoned her children. The father had threatened to beat her up if she tried to take the children.]

Dad did not always get along with his father, so there were times as a teenager, he was homeless, taken in occasionally by friends and relatives. There was one time when Dad was homeless, walking the country roads while he was very much sick (with flu maybe?) He fell over into a ditch unconscious. A farmer came along, saw him, picked him up and put him in the vehicle, took Dad to the farmer's home and nursed him back to health. Dad, in appreciation stayed several months working for the farmer. Anyway, the point I am working toward, is Dad used to tell me stories about his survival experiences *and often, Dad had to use problem-solving skills* in order to take care of himself. So, I had those messages to inform how I survived.

After Dad's Memorial, I returned to Cincinnati. As my father had requested, I took Dad's Cremains out to Manchester, Ohio and buried the box on top of his father, Chilton Alexander Leedom Jr. who was buried next to his father, Chilton Alexander Leedom Sr, who was buried next to his father, Thomas Meek Leedom. Dad's mother, Bessie Rader, was in attendance. (She passed away three years later.)

+ + + + + + + + + +

## *RETURNING TO MY JOB AT THE NEW SCHOOL*

• • • • • • • • • • • • • • • • • • • •

Returning again to when I took over as Business Manager of the New School in September 1972, I also became the Answering Service for the Cincinnati Montessori Society. Essentially the phone would ring when new people in town would call to locate a Montessori School for their child. At that time, we had 43 Accredited Schools in the Greater Cincinnati Area! I had a brochure which listed all of them. People would ask which is the best? And my answer was: Ma'am find the schools geographically that would be convenient to you; call the school and ask to come observe for a few hours. Find one whose philosophy fits with your family's. Little by little I became more and more involved with the Society, I attended Board of Trustees Meetings, and teacher-oriented events. There was a separate sub-group for school administrators, which I joined. But to continue my educational career, I enrolled in Xavier University's Masters in Montessori Program.

Kathleen Duvall was the President, and I worked more and more with her, in a supportive manner. She arranged for Cincinnati to host the National American Montessori Society Convention in 1976. She needed to be a full-time Chairman, so she talked me into becoming the President of the Cincinnati Montessori Society Board of Trustees for a two-year term.

At the same time, I took charge of all the physical facilities for the

National Convention which was held at the Omni-Netherland Hotel. I took a very close look at our daily needs for meeting rooms, then I sat down with the Hotel Management. I arranged for the hotel staff to set up a meeting room with all the tables and chairs that would be needed for the morning, the afternoon, and the evening meetings that would need that specific room. The concept was: during the day, the hotel staff had only to come in, change table clothes, provide fresh ice water and glasses. And that was all: the chairs and tables required were already in that room. I did this for all of our rooms. I also made it clear that I was the only one to communicate with the hotel staff. "If you need something, you come and communicate with me, and I will communicate with the hotel." The hotel very much appreciated this. In terms of audio-visual equipment, I ordered twice as much as we needed: if one projector or microphone was not working correctly, I could have it replaced in about five minutes! Our convention ran very smoothly. The Banquet Manager came into our dinner with tears in his eyes: "I have never had such a wonderful, cooperative group to work with! Thank you so much!" The Hotel was so delighted, the hotel subtracted $2,000 off of our bill, because we were so easy to work with. I was awarded the Maria Montessori Medal. [As a follow on, I was invited to the 1977 National Convention in Philadelphia to be the Assistant Facilities Manager.]

## PATRIC BECOMES THE PRESIDENT OF THE CINCINNATI AMERICAN MONTESSORI SOCIETY BOARD OF TRUSTEES

• • • • • • • • • • • • • • • • • • • • • •

As President of the Board of Trustees, it was my responsibility to call meetings and set an agenda. One might say I am a Control Freak or possibly OCD or maybe not any of those BUT when it comes to calling meetings: I make sure there are important matters to be discussed and decided. The meeting starts right on time. The meeting adjourns right on time! Some of our members told me they would not serve on our Board if it was not so organized. One of our major accomplishments was to join forces at the local level with the other Montessori organization—American Montessori Internationale. Yes, there were two competing nation-wide groups, but we decided to not compete, but to cooperate closely. We used one Calendar of Events to coordinate all the activities, speakers, etc. It worked very well.

Parallel to my work with AMS, I was enrolled in Xavier University's Montessori Teacher Training Program. I had enrolled in the fall of 1972 as I took over Business Manager of the New School. Fortunately, Xavier was about an eight-block walk from our school. Most of the courses were taught in the evening and on Saturdays. It took me four years to complete. I graduated in May 1976 with: A Master's Degree in Education; A Montessori Certification for teaching three- to six-year-olds; AND an Ohio State Teaching Certificate Kindergarten through Third Grade. Wow!

## *NANCY MCCORMICK RAMBUCH COMES TO TOWN*

Meanwhile, "back at the ranch" the Cincinnati Public Schools entered into an agreement with Xavier University to sponsor Nancy McCormick Rambusch—to oversee the organization and development of a new Public Montessori School Program.

[Historic Digression] [Nancy McCormick Rambusch was also the person who went to Europe in the late 1940's; learned all about Montessori Philosophy and Practices and brought "the Message: back to Connecticut, in 1950. Montessori herself brought her Philosophy and Methods to the United States in 1908-1910 timeframe-and there are a few Montessori Schools still operating that Founded, but then

World War I interfered. So, Nancy Rambusch was re-introducing Montessori to the U.S. While Maria Montessori passed away in 1949, I do not know if Nancy ever met her.]

In addition to her regular required work, she was available to consult with several of the private Montessori schools, such as the New School. Now, it so happens that I, as President of the Cincinnati Montessori Society, and Business Manager of the New School, I worked closely with Nancy Rambusch.

And that leads to a humorous story. The Cincinnati Montessori Society had brought in a big-name speaker: George Leonard who wrote a book ***EDUCATION AND ECSTASY*** which was all the buzz in the country. We had a VIP Luncheon and I sat right next to George Leonard. And I consumed two "Golden Cadillac" drinks.

*WITH NANCY'S INSTIGATION PATRIC IS HIRED BY THE CINCINNATI PUBLIC SCHOOL: CHILDREN'S HOUSE WEST TO TEACH A KINDERGARTEN-FIRST GRADE COMBINATION*

• • • • • • • • • • • • • • • • • • • • • •

Immediately after lunch, I had an interview with the new public Montessori School Principal, Ron Staggs. I had known Ron Staggs for a few years because he had been the Principal at North Avondale Elementary School—four blocks from the New School where I was the Business Manager, and he and I went to joint meetings.

So, we were familiar with each other. Now Nancy Rambusch also attended my interview for hiring. The scenario went like this: Ron would ask me a specific question. Before I could speak, Nancy would answer it for me!! Then all I had to say was, "Yes, that is what I think!"

The Golden Cadillac were still influencing my thinking, so at the end of the interview, I spoke up and said, "Well, you might as well hire me this year, because you will get me next year anyway!" (Oh boy! Did I really say that? Yes!") Suffice it to say, four days later I received a phone call from Ron stating I was hired!

The Cincinnati Public Schools had already opened one site in Mt. Adams in 1975, called **CHILDREN'S HOUSE** in honor of the first school Maria Montessori had opened in Rome Italy in 1906 *CASA DE BAMBINO.* Now for the fall of 1976, CPS opened a second site on the third floor of Oyler School on the west side of downtown, and so we were labeled **CHILDREN'S HOUSE WEST.** There were eight classrooms and teachers at the original school—now Children's House EAST—and eight classrooms and teachers at West.

A couple of notable events: Cincinnati Public Schools did not make any provision for us to have "an ART Teacher; nor did they provide for a MUSIC Teacher." However, among the Montessori teachers hired, was Georgi Gross—a well-known Art Teacher, and Cathy Carletti—a well-known Music Teacher. The teachers from both schools had a joint meeting and decided: each site would disestablish Georgi's and Cathy's assigned classrooms; each of us would increase the numbers our classroom students by three. That freed up Georgi to teach ART to the students at West, and Cathy to teach Music at East, and then the two specialists would switch schools at the end of the semester. This plan worked extremely well.

A second minor event was that I helped all the other teachers at C.H. West to move furniture and help each to organize their classrooms as they saw fit. Suffice it to say, I was the last one to construct my classroom. You might say I played a form of "Paper Dolls." I used graph paper and penciled in where I thought various tables should go, and where various bookcases or "Shelving Units" should be placed. (And

Montessori classrooms have many book cases for the manipulative materials; I had eight Bookcase-like-shelving-units.) As I did so, I became aware that I really had no space for a Teacher's Desk. And then I asked myself, "Do you REALLY need a Teacher's Desk?" NO! I was going to be working with the children the whole time. I had a closet and some other shelves for my things. My Assistant Teacher did have a small round table by the front door for occasional administrative; otherwise, the table was used for reading lessons. So, in all my seven years, I never had a Teacher's Desk.

I remember I was very excited and honored to be a part of the forefront of improving public education. Once again, my career teaching became the all-encompassing focus of my life. I put in hundreds of extra hours making manipulative materials and learning activities. [All of the newly hired faculty did.] I wanted to provide an excellent learning environment and experience for all of my students.

The first three years in our original site, the classrooms were pretty "squared away" so we teachers did not have to make too many modifications. However, when we moved to our second site in the summer of 1979, the classrooms were in disrepair with "rippled floors"—the humps being where the desks had all been fastened to the floor, and the valleys where the students had walked up and down for over 60 years.

When we relocated our Children's House sites into the one building—Sands Montessori School, we teachers were allowed to go over in June 1979 when school was out and choose the classroom we wanted for our personal room.

## PATRIC REMODELS—PAINTS HIS CLASSROOM

• • • • • • • • • • • • • • • • • • • • •

The Kindergarten Team was the first group to visit Sands and to begin the process. I chose Room 102—The school had a "Ground Floor" and then a "First Floor." 102 was on the First Floor overlooking what was to become our playground. The building had been built in around 1908, so it was old and outdated. The walls were ugly and had not been painted for many years. The fluorescent light fixtures—high up on the ten to twelve-foot ceilings—were filthy: I could literally see that the dust was almost an inch high, and a goodly number of light bulbs were burnt out. The windows, which had large metal screens fastened over them, had not been washed on the outside for years. This was summer time so we had a month or so to prepare our classrooms. I went into "hyper-warp." I brought Charles, the custodian, a quart of Gin. In return he brought me a tall ladder and boxes of new light bulbs, and buckets to wash with for the lights and walls. I cleaned and repaired all the light fixtures. I got the school to provide buckets of cream-colored paint. I provided the brushes and rollers. In the middle of my painting work, the Principal came to my door to see if I was willing to accept one more student into my classroom, even though I was already above the Contract number of 25 students. I said, "Send the parent in to see me." It was Mr. Ken Tulley (owner of a pie factory) who wanted to enroll his son Brandon. We talked briefly, and I said I would welcome him. Then Ken Tulley said to me, "I have just the right equipment to paint your ceiling; how about if I go home and get them?" "Fantastic!" Within a half hour, Ken was back, with painting clothes on, and we went to work. As I remember it probably took two or three days to paint the ceilings—in the Cloak Room as well, and because it took two coats of paint to cover the old ugly paint.

Typical of old-fashioned schools, the desks had been screwed into the flooring for decades. And just before we came for a visit, the desks were removed; this left a very rippled floor with "Hills" where the desks had been, and "Valleys" where the students had walked up and down the aisles for years. The wooden floor was an ugly brown, not having been refinished in decades. So, when the painting was completed, I went to a Tool Rental Store, and rented a large 80-pound belt sander, and began the ritual of going back and forth at a 45-degree angle across the wooden floor—to smooth out the ripples. That took a few days, and our Cloak Rooms were large maybe 7 feet wide by 15 feet long, so we included it in the painting and the sanding. (Would you believe I utilized the Cloak Room as an additional instruction space? Yes, at one end I could use a projector for language lessons.) Would you believe I usually had a four-year old on my lap to also learn? She was in our classroom most days because her mother, Annamarie, a very dedicated "Room Mother" was in attendance most days.

At the other end of the Cloakroom—past the large Storage Closet which effectively blocked the window light, was our Art Easel next to the window. Once the floor had been stripped—sanded off all of the old worn varnish, it exposed a beautiful hard wood floor.

When the administration originally conceived of our new classrooms, they visualized covering all of the floors with in-door-out-door carpeting. But I had a better idea: I only wanted half of my room's floor covered with carpeting. The other half I wanted my beautiful new Polyethylened wooden floor. Why? Because that was where the children's tables and chairs would be, and that is where daily we served a snack such as of milk and graham crackers—where children sometimes spilled their beverage and sometimes where we might be doing some messy work such as papier Mache pinatas—and mine were always huge such as a Space Shuttle, or a giant SUN with long arms of "Sun Rays" or a very large elephant with long tusks. Our pinatas started with a base of balloons, carboard, string and tape to create the basic shape, then we started dipping strips of newspaper into pans of Stay-Flo Starch, wiping off the excess with our fingers, then applying the paper to make the outside walls of the pinata. Once upon a time we three kindergarten teachers used to get together after school to make our pinatas. But since I always chose to make a very complex one, I needed to finish it during the daytime when the students were in class. But then, several students kept coming over to me to ask what I am doing; then they asked may we do that too? And I thought to myself, "Why Not!" so, I had the children bring old adult-sized shirts to use as smocks. Did it get messy?? Oh yes! For several days. Anyway, a plastic-coated wooden floor is a lot easier to mop us, clean up, than carpeting. I told our Vice Principal in charge of the carpeting that I did not want full carpeting. She replied, make us a drawing of exactly what you do want. I did. And the excess carpeting that was not used for my classroom exactly fit the Teachers' Lounge floor!

I was hired as a teacher of First Grade & Kindergarten combination. At the end of the second year, I consulted the Principal and said that the Kindergarteners were being dragged along in a "watered-down" First Grade; and I wanted to separate them. He agreed. I took full-day Montessori Kindergarten for five more years. I taught with Cincinnati Public Schools for seven years. After the first three years, all three sites of Children's House got merged into one building named George F. Sands. So, our school was renamed *SANDS MONTESSORI SCHOOL.* We were located in the West End of Downtown Cincinnati at the corner of Poplar and Freeman Streets. We were a "Magnet School" meaning we drew students from all over the Cincinnati School District. Magnet Schools were conceptualized in the early 1970's in response to being sued by the NAACP for having school populations that were too segregated—that is schools that had population of all Black students or nearly so, and all white schools or nearly so. One legal solution was to have "Magnet Schools" which by design could have 70% of one racial group and 30% of the other racial group. Our school took our mission very seriously. I was on the Admissions Committee. Our ideal goal was to have 25% Black boys, 25% White Boys, 25% Black Girls, and 25 % White Girls. We may not have been 50% and 50%, but we came close to 56% and 44%.

By Teachers' Union Contract, the ratios in the classrooms were 25 students per teacher. The Administration could not force teachers to take more. However, the individual teacher could choose to take additional students, and I always did…usually 27-29 students. Here, I admit to something some people would label "Selfishness." I always took more than 25 students because 1) I had good classroom management and could handle more students successfully. 2) I had fewer behavioral problems than the women teachers maybe because being a man, the students could not play " a gamey Mom Manipulation Game" with me. Example: one student would come up to me crying about something she wanted. I would say to her, "Jane, I really want to hear what you are saying. But would you step out into the hall and finish your crying, then come back and talk to me." She would not even make it to the classroom door and her tears "would magically dry up!" On other occasions, Alex and George were close friends. George would come up to me and request permission to go to the bathroom down the hall. I gave him permission. Suddenly Alex would come running up to me holding his crotch and "dancing" and request permission to use the bathroom. I would respond, "Alex, didn't I just give you permission 15 minutes ago?" Alex would pause, reflect, and admit "Yes." And he would walk away---no dancing, no crotch holding (and therefore "No Game.")

The second reason I always took more students than the limit was because, if a student left our school, I still had more students than 25. Teachers who kept to exactly 25, if they lost a student, then they were a target to add in a new student—a go through the process of orientation to the Montessori requirements which sometimes took weeks.

I deeply loved what I was doing. Teaching was my calling. In 45 years in the field of Education, there has never been a single day that I have awakened and thought or said, "Oh crap! I have to go to school today!"

## PATRIC'S MONTESSORI CURRICULUM

• • • • • • • • • • • • • • • • • • • • • •

I was very proud of the academic structure of my instruction. The Kindergarten Faculty arranged with the Principal to stagger enrollment the first week. For example, the very first week of school, only one third of the class came the first day. I was able to individually test each one on their letter recognition, letter sounds, numerical recognition, numerical counting, identification of colors and shapes. The second day, only the second third came, and so on. Based upon my test scores I organized three levels of reading groups, and three levels of math groups. BUT group membership was never "set in concrete!" Why? A big reason is that some children have had two to three years of preschool before they enter kindergarten, so they did know quite a bit. And some children never had the opportunity to go to pre-school, so they didn't know too much the first days.

Now as a good observant Montessori teacher, you observe each student's progress as you provide lessons and do reinforcements. Within three weeks or so, it becomes obvious that some of the ones who knew a lot on the first day, did not have the cognitive maturation which allowed them to remember the previous day's lesson and to be able to apply it. And some who appeared not to know so much the first day, demonstrated strong cognitive maturation and were able to absorb a new lesson every day, remember them and apply them. So occasionally, a student who may have started in the advanced group might succeed better in the Middle Group. And some who may have started in the low group, may make it to the advanced group within four to six weeks.

Additionally, I often observed a "mid-year rocket launching!" where a student was doing well in the middle level group, but suddenly the "light bulb goes off" and the child really understands how words are put together, and now fits quite comfortably in the advanced reading group.

For the educators among the readers, my lower reading group typically could absorb one lesson a week where they could remember and apply the letters and sounds, occasionally maybe two lessons that week. The middle level reading group could handle at least two reading lesson per week and sometimes three. The advanced reading group could absorb a lesson a day, so we might do four or five lessons that week, and usually did not have to do much reinforcement the following week. From the academic year-long perspective, the advanced group could master all 40 phonics books by the end of the year. The first ten books introduced all five short vowel sounds—cat, bed, sit, hot, tub. The second ten books built on the short vowels and introduced the long vowels sound cake, street, high, boat, unicorn. The third set of ten books built on the vowel sounds and introduced blends—flag, bread, creek, store. The last set of ten introduced digraphs—church, shook, thick, plus punctuation. Any kindergartener who mastered all 40 books was now reading on the Second Grade Level.

So, to compare, my advanced readers always finished all 40 books. My middle level readers might achieve somewhere in the 20's to 30's. My lower-level group actually split into two groups: By January, the more advanced might be reading three or four books, but the lowest group was not cognitively mature and could hardly remember the sounds of the letters. (Some of these students I requested to retain for another year.)

On a typical reading day when I was providing tutoring and reinforcement, I and five students sat at a six-seat table. I would sit in the back middle seat (where I could still keep an eye on the classroom.)

The student who needed the most help sat directly across from me where I could reach across, maybe with a notched index card, so I could isolate the word we were focusing upon. The next most needy students would sit to the left and right of my focused student. The two students who were close to being competent sat to my left and right. Each child may be on a different book. I could actually use my mental radar and listen in on each child, and if I heard an error, ask them to take a second look. I truly became very adept at reading upside down and backwards. My assistant teacher, and a few of the Parent helpers began to be able working with more than one child at the same time.

Other than daily calling for each level reading group to come to me for our regular weekly lessons, I placed no pressure or requirements on a child. Montessori teaches that each child has their own developmental timeline. It was the adults' task to carefully observe when a specific child was ready for the next challenge.

[A "Visitor" digression] Cincinnati was the first city to provide a major public system of teaching using the Montessori philosophy, methods, and special manipulative equipment. So, we attracted visiting educators from all over the country. Many of my colleagues request a day or two notice that Visitors would observe be in that teacher's classroom. I did not have any issues like that. I told the Principal she could send visitors to my classroom any hour of the day, any day of the week. I told the Principal that if I was having a good day, they would see "a good day." If I was having not so good day" they would see that. Consequently, many visitors came to our classroom. If I were sitting on the floor—with my back to the classroom door, I never knew whether we had visitors in the room or not. They would stand quietly against the front Chalkboard. My students were trained just to continue doing their work. So, the students never made any sounds or motions to indicate we had visitors. Bless you children. I told the Principal that if I had time, I would go over and speak with the visitors.

But most of the time I didn't. By the way, a very strong component of the Montessori System is teaching Concentration. And after school had been in session for a month or two, my students were excellent and stayed focused on their work even with strange adults in the classroom. A particular activity which required two full days of concentration was math—for example--the "Thousand Cube Bead material. There was a solid cube with a thousand beads wired together. But then there was the "Thousand Bead Chain" which needed to be laid in the hallway from my classroom door down to the next teacher's classroom door. Students had to count every individual bead and put a Ten's marker—10, 20, 30, 40...each time they counted up the chain. [Janitors were instructed not to disturb any work in the hall.)

Usually, students worked in pairs to do the counting. And yes, often it took two or more days to count and mark all the beads. So yes, five and six-year-old students can concentrate for hours at a time. These students acted as Role-Models for the other students. [In fairness, children who have a disease or physical condition which does not allow them to concentrate, will not do well in a Montessori classroom.]

A lot of reading was accomplished in my classroom, but not because of me alone. First of all, our Phonics Books—Modern Curriculum Press were inexpensive--$5.00 for a set of ten. I encouraged families to buy the books and buy the accompanying workbooks. Many families did. I had a number of parents, usually mothers who would come in one or two days a week and work with readers. AND a few of my advanced kindergarteners were willing to work and teach the slower readers!

An "accidental" motivation: I had to make a cardboard matrix of all 40 phonics books and all 29 students. If a student mastered a book, then an appropriately colored dot was affixed to that box. So, when parents, or the advanced students looked to see who needed help they could identify the next book to be the challenge for that specific student.

However, among the students themselves, some would walk up to the matrix and count how many dots their friend had on the board "1, 2, 3, 4, .........15!! Well, how many do I have? "1, 2, 3, 4,....8!" "Mr. Leedom, Mr. Leedom, I want to read a book!" "Only if you are good, kid." (Smile) And so reading was alive in our room. One of my greatest stories about reading was during the Blizzard of 1977 when the temperatures dropped below zero for 25 days, the Ohio River Froze over, the school buses stopped running, downtown office workers lived in their offices Monday through Friday.

Our school remained open, but the only students were those whose parents could transport them. Typically, I had five students a day. Well, this one special day, four of the students who arrived were my advanced students, so I gave them the responsibility of deciding what materials or activities they wanted to do. Willie Richardson was my fifth student. And Willie was normally in my beginning reading group just practicing the sounds of letters.

## ON ONE SNOWY BLIZZARD DAY—PATRIC TEACHES WILLIE R. TO READ IN ONE DAY
• • • • • • • • • • • • • • • • • • • • • •

I decided to spend my whole day with Willie. We refreshed the sounds of the vowels and the consonants (maybe not everyone) Then I got out the "Pizza Cardboard Wheels" which had a vowel written in the middle, and appropriate consonants written around the rim. We started slowly with reviewing the sound of each letter. Then I said, "Willie, watch my finger and say the sound I am pointing to." I would point to the S and we would start saying that sound then slowly my finger would slide toward the vowel in the middle and our mouths would shift to "ssssaaa" and then rrrrraaa. Then mmmmaaa, then lllaaa." I would stop. And say to Willie, "Now we are going to start with the vowel sound and slide out to the rim." Aaammm aaatt aaaapp aaaagg

Okay, now we are going to start on the rim, slide briefly into the center and back out to the rim" "sssaaammm Sam rrraaatt rat ffffaatt fat lllaaapp; lap. By the end of the school day, Willie was able to read the very first eight-page phonics book by himself!!! "I exclaimed, Willie! **You are reading!!! Take this book home tonight and show your mama!"** There could not have been a wider grin on Willie's face. And there could not have been a wider grin on Willie's Mama's face when she came in a few days later to thank me.

One short story. Stephanie E. was one of those who rocketed to the top in February or March. On Monday I handed her Workbook Number One. She was done by the end of the day. On Tuesday I handed her Workbook Number Two. She was done by the end of the day. By Friday, she had completed all five workbooks and every answer was correct!!

The following year, Stephanie was promoted into the First, Second, and Third Grade Combination Classroom. (Montessori believes in grouping students in three-year spans.) Well, it was around November the following year, and early one morning there was a knock at my door. I looked up and it was a delegation of third graders whom I had taught in years past. "Yes, Maria, what may I do for you?" "We need to talk to you!" "Yes, what about?" "What did YOU DO to that Stephanie E.??" "What do you mean what did I do to that Stephanie E.?" "Well, we are all third graders. And SHE IS A FIRST GRADER! And every week our class has Spelling Bees, and every week SHE BEATS US!! And we don't like it!"" "Oh, I see. I sorry!" Smile, smile ("Go! Stephanie, GO!")

The joy of teaching Montessori in those days was 1) I had a very competent Teaching Assistant, whom I treated as a co-teacher, and respected her for her knowledge and wisdom. We were a team.

Montessori has the concept: "The Shepherd and the Sheep Dog." I was the Shepherd and I spent the majority of my time in academic instruction with the children. My Assistant was the Sheep Dog: she watched over the classroom, re-directed students who were having difficulty choosing meaningful work. She was the person to whom most students turned to if they needed a bathroom trip—by themselves. She did most of the administrative work—collecting lunch money, making out the lunch orders, responding to notes from parents, unless it really needed my attention.

In order to minimize TRANSITION TIME between academic events, I trained my students to respond in 90 seconds. I would dismiss the first reading group and call for the second reading group. Those students had 90 seconds to leave their work, walk over, sit down, and be prepared for our lesson.

I always had respect for my students and their needs. One big example: Our students arrived early to our school because the buses were on double duty. They would make an early round, pick up students, bring them to school, drop them off; go back on a second round and pick up more students and bring them to our school. The majority of teachers did not want the students arriving at the classroom until 9:15. School officially began at 9:20 A.M. So, this meant that the students who arrived at our school between 7:30 and 8:00 A.M. would have to sit in the cafeteria until 9:10 UGH! Early on, I informed our Principal that I was always in my classroom by 7:30 A.M., so that my students were NEVER to sit in the cafeteria, but come straight up to our classroom, put their coats and things away, deposit lunch money on the round table, then they could choose work to do—read a book, talk with friends, do a puzzle, lay out some major math material whatever they had been shown what to do. The students knew it was my preparation time, so, I would acknowledge their presence, but I could not sit and work with them yet.

Further, sometimes a bus or two would be late arriving to our school. So, I created a flexible schedule: as each child entered the room, she or he could choose some interesting work and continue with it until I called "Group Time." And then they would walk over and sit on the carpet tape that outlined our group space. The point I want to make, is that I would not Call "Group Time" unless I knew all the buses had arrived. So instead of officially beginning class work at 9:20 A.M., I might not officially begin until 9:40 or 9:52—whenever those buses arrived. Now, notice that there was NO LOST WORK TIME. The students commenced working from the minute they walked into the classroom. So, if I called Group Time at 9:52, some students who had arrived around 8:00 A.M., had already been at work for almost two hours!!! **NEVER** were my students just sitting around waiting and waiting until I was ready. That is disrespectful! A similar situation existed both as we approached lunch time, and as we approached the end of the day. I trained my students to keep working until 5 minutes before lunch or ending, and they would quickly put their work away, clean up the floor. NO WASTED TIME!

And another feature to my classroom management: The first weeks of school my assistant, Mrs. Irene Linfert, and I trained our students how to request a "Bathroom Necklace," get permission from an adult, leave the classroom, go directly to the restroom, use the facilities properly, and promptly return to our classroom, and return the necklace. For the boys, it was no problem because their restroom was only a few feet away from our classroom door. For the girls, they had to walk clear around our large building to the other hallway. But they managed it well. Discussion: I am never inside a child's body. I do not know exactly when they needed to use the toilet. So, each child had the opportunity to use the bathroom as they needed to. This saved those massive wastes of time when the teacher only lets the students go to the bathroom when the whole class takes a bathroom trip. So inefficient. Often taking 17 minutes, (of lost "ACADEMIC TIME") because indeed, I timed them as a university observer. The only time my class used the whole class bathroom trip was right when we all came in from recess after lunch.

My modus operandi after recess was to have all of the students lie down on the floor and rest. I turned off all the classroom lights. I gave the students about 20 minutes to lie quietly. Some chose to go to sleep and that was fine. After 20 minutes I turned on one overhead light, and I began reading a book of children's literature. While I did show the pictures after each page, I explained to the students that "I know you cannot see the pictures clearly from where you are sitting; however, you know this book 'Lives right here in the Library Box', so when you have time, you may choose this book and read it to yourself."

[Special note: in the Montessori System, students are not 'kept busy all of the time." Instead, they have assignments to do but can choose when to do them; consequently, students can move about the classroom and observe what others are doing, or maybe join others in some activity—so they do have independent time.] This arrangement worked very well in connection with the art easel: There was a painting easel in the corner of the cloak room. My students were assigned to one of five different tables as their individual work spaces. Each day, a different table was chosen to have the opportunity to paint. That meant that only six children would have the opportunity to paint that day. But students from other tables could come over and observe the artist at work and absorb ideas of what they might want to do when it was their turn. Over seven years I observed a very striking phenomenon: at the beginning of the year, as I demonstrated how I might use the art easel, I ALWAYS painted something abstract—free form—"I feel like some red here, here, here, Okay, now I am feeling about painting yellow in spots. I feel like blue maybe in stripes." My whole purpose was to free up the students so they could use the paper and paint anyway they wanted to—to be creative. The paper was like

14" by 18". Yes, the students could paint every square inch if they so choose...even running off of the paper onto the oil-cloth easel. My students were "free—unhampered" to paint to their heart's desire; to use as much paint as they wanted. And sheets 14" by 18" provides a lot of space for creating (often museum quality work!) No Problem. When they were finished painting, an adult would lift the paper over to the drying rack, AND THE STUDENT would take the bucket of water and sponge setting under the easel and clean all the paint off of the easel in preparation for the next person. [When I prepared the paint jars in the morning, I put a few drops of dish-washing soap in them to make clean-up a little easier.]

Now what I found very interesting over seven years, was that the students would choose to do the abstract painting—just feeling what colors they wanted to put where. A lot of experimentation! Toward the end of the year, I believe that some students were painting museum quality work! One of my hard rules: I always kept the student in charge of evaluating their own work! The student would come to me and ask me if it was a good work of art. I would defer by saying, "Tell me what you were feeling or thinking when you painted this part?...that part...etc. Then finally I would say to the student **"WHAT DO YOU THINK OF YOUR PAINTING?"**

### *PROVIDING A COMFORTABLE CLASSROOM FOR THE STUDENTS*

I did report that the school building had been built around 1908. Well, each classroom had these huge windows that commenced three feet up from the floor and soared another six plus feet up. And they were encased in old wooden frames. You can see where I am going: over a seventy-year period those wooden frames became loose to the extent that wind could blow in where the upper and lower window joined, and around the edges of both windows. In winter this became a problem. The temperature inside some classrooms dropped to where the teacher and students were wearing their coats! But NOT in my classroom.

[Digression:] In the summertime I had brought in a ladder and was able to wash the insides of the windows; then I unscrewed the metal screens which could swing out on a hinge, and then crawling out on the ledge, I was able—with the help of a sponge mop, to wash all of the outsides.

The heavy black shades that had been used to darken the room for seventy years, were in very poor shape with rips and tears and holes. So, with a ladder. I wound them upward and secured them so you could barely know that they were there. Then I bought long curtains with animal designs in light brown on cream material. And, with the help of a ladder I installed the curtains on every window. [With my five years of construction work experience, I was adept at using ladders, even tall ones.]

Now back to the cold chill winds coming in the windows. A very old solution was to take newspapers and take a sheet and keep folding it until it was one to two inches wide, and these I stuffed into all the cracks of the wooden frame. One of my colleagues came into my classroom wearing her winter coat, complaining how cold it was in her classroom. I called her over and showed her how I was folding newspapers and stuffing them. Her response was, "That's NOT my job!" (Well, it was NOT my job to go to her room and do it for her!")

But that is not the end of the heating story. One day I was observing the old-fashioned metal heating "Registers" that filled up with steam when the boiler was running. I observed that the hot metal was exposed so that a child could get hurt. So, then I visualized how I could not only cover over the register with a screen, but I could build two shelves on top. And I did that for both registers. As I constructed the horizontal board that was to be the top of the safety screen—and be three inches above the hot metal, I lined the bottom of that board with aluminum foil. Now, when the registers were filled with hot steam, instead of the heated air going straight up to the ceiling, my boards pushed the heated air out into the room first. Truly, my classroom was at least ten degrees warmer than the other classrooms! My students were always comfortable and safe.

And oh yes, the building was NOT air-conditioned. So, in the warm weather. I installed a rotating fan on top of my new shelves—about five feet off of the floor and firmly secured it so as not to fall off.

## *A MONTESSORI PREPARED ENVIRONMENT*

• • • • • • • • • • • • • • • • • • • • • •

I learned throughout my courses in Montessori Education, that the attractiveness, the beauty of the Environment was a major pillar of a successful Learning Environment.

In my first year of teaching, a parent who worked for the National Cash Register Company in Dayton, Ohio, donated an electric grocery store cash register to our class. The National Dairy Council sold packets of laminated photographs of all kinds of foods and beverages. I went to my local grocery store and they gave me sheets of price tags. I put prices on each item of food. I created small Styrofoam cafeteria trays. I had "Menu Worksheets" where a student would choose a meal from the "Buffet"—e.g., Salads, entrée, vegetables, fruits, beverage, and deserts. Then the student would have to write down the item and its cost on separate lines on the Menu. Go to the Cash Register, punch in the costs, Punch "Total" and then go to the "BANK" of money—on a separate shelf-- which had currency--$1.00 bills, $5.00 bills. All the coins from pennies to half dollars and choose or "count out" just the exact amount of money and place it in the Cash Register!

You are thinking correctly: I had to have quite a few math activities to teach the students the values of the coins and currency. I did have a large chart with 100 actual pennies glued into a matrix with an Equals sign at the top and then real $1.00 bill laminated. I had stamping worksheets where students could practice creating varieties of ways to display the number and type of coins necessary to equal the value of a large coin; for example, how many ways are there to total the value of a quarter? 25 pennies, 20 pennies, one nickel; five nickels; one dime, two nickels, and five pennies. Etcetera.

YES, the Cafeteria activity was only for the students who could satisfactorily demonstrate that they understood the values of various denominations of coins and currency and their equivalencies.-Talk about motivation to learn math and money! Obviously, the students in my Top Math group could do the activity, but the students in my Middle Math Group were also able to practice learning all the money, demonstrate their proficiency to me or one of the teachers, and then they choose the Cafeteria Activity. [Montessori has "CONTROLS" on many of the manipulative activities so the student would learn how to correctly use the materials. I had a "Control" on the Cafeteria Activity: it was located in its own small work area at then side of the room. There were only two "Necklaces" available to put on to show who was permitted to use the activity—only two students at any one time, inside the Cafeteria area; so, there was no crowding, pushing, shoving or competing. Each student with a designated necklace, could take their time.

This was similar to the painting easel: on any given day, only one "Table of Six Students" was permitted to choose to paint. So, there was no crowding, no pressuring; the artist had plenty of time to create her or his "Masterpiece." [And I do not use 'Masterpiece' facetiously: by springtime several of the students were capable of producing high quality use of color and abstract designs. Students certainly were permitted to paint pictures of "Things" houses, dogs, sunsets, people, whatever. But over seven years I observed very few students choosing this option. I think they enjoyed the freedom to experiment with colors and designs; over the years, I did observe one student (A) observing another student's (B) ideas, and then on a day when it was Student A's turn, they could try out similar designs.

I was invited to one home and saw the boys' bedroom walls just covered with many paintings that the two brothers—when it was his turn to be in kindergarten, had produced over the years!

## MY CLASSROOM BECOMES A "FAMILY LEARNING CENTER"

• • • • • • • • • • • • • • • • • • • • • •

Also, in the spirit of a Family Learning Center, I told parents, "If you have a three or four-year-old sibling, bring them along to the class: my 'old Five-year olds' love to teach the younger children." And parents did. My last end of the year Class Photograph has a three-year-old and a four-year-old sitting in the front row!

Early on, I decided to turn my classroom into a "Family Learning Center" so I frequently had parents in my classroom most days, helping out mostly with the academic learning, but sometimes a parent would bring in an arts and crafts idea like making puppets, or using Plaster of Paris (or Dental Plaster) to make "Hand Prints" for Mother's Day. Actually, I made one of my hand print and had all the children impress their thumb prints all around the edges. We left all the deep imprints the natural white plaster color; but painted the rims with bright red, the surrounding surface a greenish-gold, and purple on the border. Another parent had my handprint professionally mounted and framed for me; I can see it now on the wall as I sit here and type. Another parent had was Japanese and had been born in Japan. She and I worked up a Social Studies Lesson on Japan, and she came in several days to instruct the students in Japanese culture. (She used grains of uncooked rice to compare the population density of Japan,

I did live in San Francisco during the Flower Child Era, so I am a bit radical at times. Every school has "Parent-Teacher Conferences." But often that signifies there are some problems. So, I decided to change the concept, and I renamed them "Parent-Teacher Sharing Times" The school only required us to meet for 20 minutes, but I always made 30 minutes available. And I would start the conference by asking the parent to tell me what they have observed at home vis-à-vis their child in our classroom.

In the same spirit, I clearly remember the very first time I filled out official report cards—which went home four times during the year. I was finished in 45 minutes! The vast majority of grades were "S' for Satisfactory, "VG" for Very Good; "O" for Outstanding, and an occasional "N" for Needs improvement. But I turned and asked myself, "What have I really communicated to the parents about their child's progress in school?" My answer quickly was "Not much." So, I sat right down and created my own Report Card with 20+ categories rather than 5 or 6. I told parents how their child interacted with the other children, and with adults; I told how the child could handle responsibilities, how the child dealt with frustration, I told parents: your child is on grade level developmentally; your child is above average developmentally, or your child is young developmentally and may need a second year with me. I was not allowed to label it a Report Card, so I had to label it "Patric's Feedback Report." And it was popular with the parents.

## PATRIC WRITES A PLAY "IN ONE HOUR!"

• • • • • • • • • • • • • • • • • • • • • • •

Time for a wild and funny story. During my very first year of teaching, as the time approached Spring Break, I wrote a letter home on Monday to all parents inviting them to come to school Friday afternoon as we were having a Play, and would they sign up to bring punch and cookies. That was Monday. On Friday morning I woke up and was preparing to come to school when I suddenly realized: ***I had not yet written the play!*** Panic time, maybe. I had an adult assistant. I told her that she was to run the class because I had to sit in the corner and write a PLAY! Well, fortunately I had taken classes in Modern Interpretive Dance, so, I wrote a Play titled the ***COMING OF SPRING.***

I had multiple body-movement parts for the children. I had four children become "TREES." I had four children become "SEEDS." I had four children become—wind, snow, rain, woodland creatures. I had one child become the SUN. The auditorium was free. I went to the kindergarten next door and asked Bridget if I could borrow 12 of her students. She said, "Honey, take all of them!" But she was joking. I took 12 of her students, 13 of mine, some chalk, and I took them all onto the stage in the auditorium. I used the chalk to mark out their stations on stage. We rehearsed for an hour before lunch. We rehearsed for another hour after lunch. And when the parents arrived at 2:00 P.M. we were ready! I did all the speaking—the narration and the students quietly carried out their roles. The four TREES were already on stage in their assigned positions (chalk marks). Now in the process of rehearsing, I had the students line up in four columns off stage (behind the curtain. The first child was the **wind** and was responsible for delivering each of the other children to their proper places. All I had to do was turn my back to the audience and raise a finger: One finger meaning wind number one please deliver the Snow children. Two fingers—line #2, and so forth; when one was finished, I raised three fingers for Line # 3; and so on. When all of the trees and seeds were "covered with snow" I did the narration of the plants surviving through the cold winter protected by the snow. Then I signaled the wind to bring rain to melt the snow. Then I signaled the **SUN** to go to each seed and each tree and **SHINE** warmly on them so they would grow and blossom. When that was completed, all of the SNOW_Children became woodland animals of their choice and came scampering back on stage. Then I would face the audience and say, "We are proud to Announce that **SPRING IS HERE!**

The play was a success, and I produced it for the entire school—700 students—utilizing two performances for the next six years. Oh yes, I always had two extra students sitting during rehearsals to observe all of the parts in case someone was not able to do their part, so then I used a substitute. In seven years, I only remember using substitutes once or twice.

At the beginning of my third year of teaching, I decided to write another Play for Kindergartners. This was a Halloween Play titled "*A WALK TO CASPER'S HOUSE*" In this play—you do remember that Casper was a Ghost-The play began with me reading a Postcard from Casper to five children who were "taking a walk with me." Casper's card told us that he was lonely, and he would like us to come visit him at his house. Intermittently, black cats would come scurrying across the stage, skeletons would come scurrying across the stage, Pumpkin Head persons would come scurrying past us and ghosts......oooohh. All the while I had my assistant off stage with a large bag of dried leaves and a large electric fan blowing the leaves across the stage toward us, and the lights of the auditorium turned almost off.

But I have two more stories. They are related. I did very much respect my students as individuals, and I did teach them to dialogue and "argue" with me. For example, each year when it got close to Thanksgiving, just "out of the blue" I would say to my students, "You know, when the Pilgrims were coming across the Ocean, they really had a Florida Vacation in mind. But then they had a "***BIG MAC ATTACK***" and that is why they landed at Plymouth Rock, got into their cars, drove to McDonalds, and got themselves some Big Macs!" [We had NEVER talked about this before!]

My sharper students would say, "I don't think they had cars back then, Mr. Leedom." And I would say, "Alright, they got on their horses and rode to McDonalds." But the students responded, "I don't think they had McDonalds back then!" and I then said, "Alright, they rode their horses to Kroger's!" Students, "I don't think they had Kroger's back then!" Me, "Alright then kids, HOW DID THEY EAT?" Students, "I think they went into the woods and shot animals and collected berries and nuts!" "OOOOOHH!"

## GENEROSITY AND CHARITY

• • • • • • • • • • • • • • • • • • • • • • •

At the elementary school level, I was in charge of the Annual Boat Luncheon Cruise in late May for the entire school-some 700 students or more. The Tour Boat Company charged a per person ticket cost of $3.00. I purposely charged everyone $3.25, so I could build up a fund to make sure everyone could afford to go on the trip. [ Commentary: an interesting situation developed: throughout most of the year, a few of the families that were entitled to either free or reduced lunches would complain about paying instructional fees or other required costs and would argue that since they qualified for free or reduced lunch, "shouldn't they receive everything else free?" I made it adamantly clear that the only money I had for boat tickets came from parents and came from nowhere else—suddenly for the boat trip money came out for tickets for several of the family members. "Interesting!"]

A Pinata Story. No, actually two. The first story is that we found out what joy the children had playing with pinatas, that I decided we would make one for Valentine's Day, and another one for Easter. The second story is about taking the students up to the gymnasium to hoist the pinatas on ropes and letting the blindfolded child swing at it. Now the night before, we three kindergarten teachers—Julie Valen, Bridgette Kennedy, and I-- decided that each student was allowed to have five pieces of candy. So, as we loaded the pinatas with candy the night before, we counted out five pieces for each student. So, when the pinata broke, we reminded the students to take only five. Which is exactly what they did. Now there were three kindergarten classes who participated, and I was in charge, so I was the one sweeping up the floor. My Assistant teacher was walking the children back to our classroom. I brought up the rear.

## DON'T TELL ME ALL CHILDREN ARE "SELFISH!"

• • • • • • • • • • • • • • • • • • • • • • •

And as I am walking behind the last little girl, Lavonya Perdue, she turned around to me and said, "Mr. Leedom, you didn't get any candy—take one of mine!" And the next child in line turned around and said, "Well, take one of mine!" and the next five children turned around and said, "Please take one of mine!" Can you believe seven children who had only just picked up five pieces as requested, would turn around and give one piece of their candy to their teacher?? I did take the students' pieces of candy because that action is part of the socialization process—children learn how in society we share; we give and take with each other. I still tear up when I recall the students' spontaneous behavior. Further, I want to declare, "I do not want you to tell me that all children are so selfish and self-centered!"

[Time Digression] As I reflect on my teaching career—spanning 40 plus years—I know that my natural bent toward kindness has fueled my feelings and actions. Drawing upon the synonyms for "kindness": benevolence, humanity, generosity, charity, sympathy, compassion, and tenderness can all be applied to my interactions as a teacher. When I taught kindergarten, I always had a box of money in the closet in case one of the students lost or forgot their lunch money: I would buy their lunch and ask for reimbursement from the parents later. I also was in charge of the Kindergarten Snack Program, so I always had food and beverage—for example graham crackers and milk available if a student came to school hungry. In a related circumstance, I protected my students from being forced by the vice principal "to eat everything on their tray before they went out to play." In the early days it was even worse: Federal regulations required that the cooks place sixth-grade portions of food on the kindergarten trays! I went "to battle-stations" and requested that the person in charge of food service for our district to come to our school to discuss the situation. (She came to our staff meeting and as she sat down at the table she said, "I know exactly what you want to talk about—but we are forced to do it; we tried providing smaller portions and the government fined us $30,000!" [When President Reagan became President, he got rid of these regulations.] Similarly, I "went to battle stations" to make it abundantly clear that "my students did not have to eat everything on their tray before they were allowed to go out and play!" (I am not inside the student's body; I do not know if the student feels sick or something; in other words I did not know how much of the food the student was comfortable eating.)

*MY VOCATION WAS TEACHING MONTESSORI
KINDERGARTEN BUT MY ADVOCATION WAS
SUPPORTING THE SUBMARINE ADMIRAL'S
STAFF IN NORFOLK VIRGINIA*

• • • • • • • • • • • • • • • • • • • • •

Way back in the **COLD WAR** with the Soviet Union, someone decided that IF the Soviets should shoot missiles at Washington D.C., maybe the President, the Cabinet, and Congress should leave Washington DC and hide under the mountain in West Virginia—known as Greenbriar. So, another someone decided that if the Soviets were going to shoot missiles at the Headquarters of the Atlantic Fleet Navy, maybe the Admirals and their staffs should leave Norfolk and hide under a mountain in Puerto Rico.

But someone should maintain the Norfolk offices, so, let's call in the Reserves! So, the Commander of the Submarine Force, U.S. Atlantic Fleet—known by the Acronym COMSUBLANT, promulgated a request for Reservists, particularly ***QUARTERMASTERS*** because their job is the safe navigation of ships and submarines around the oceans, should apply to be trained to take over the jobs in the Norfolk offices. That was in late 1972. The Commanding Officer of my Submarine Reserve Unit in Cleveland 4-92 came to me and said, "Leedom, this request "has your name on it; so, you should apply!" Okay. Sounds interesting. So, I did apply and was accepted. I reported to the Admiral's Staff in December 1972 for two weeks. I was the first Reservist in the country to apply, be accepted, and report for duty in Norfolk.

In those days, the Submarine Force had plenty of money, so every three months I would be given orders to fly from Cincinnati to Norfolk on Friday to "Stand Watches in the Submarine Operational Offices, learn and practice my job of helping plan submarine deployments. And then fly home on Sunday afternoons. In the early days, a car and driver would take me to and from the airport.

I was down to the office in Norfolk at least four times a year. I was single, SO I would re-activate myself back into the Navy in the summer time for six to nine weeks. [Anytime a sailor is on active duty for more than 30 days, that is considered Regular Active Duty.]

The result of spending so much time down in the Norfolk office was that I was able to qualify on my particular duty station. Our offices were classified as a Top-Secret Vault, so I had to be investigated and cleared to receive a Top-Secret Clearance. I had already been promoted to E7 Chief Quartermaster in April 1971. I worked diligently and became competent at carrying out my duties. Soon I started receiving excellent Performance Evaluations, so when I took the Navy-Wide Promotion Exams, I was promoted from an (E7) Chief Quartermaster, to an (E8) Senior Chief Quartermaster, and three years later, I was promoted to an (E9) Master Chief Quartermaster.

I spent eleven years as a member of the Staff, largely because I worked hard, I was competent, and if I didn't have enough work to do at my regular desk, I would go down the hall knocking on doors to see who needed help.

## WORKING FOR COMMANDER BILL GAINES IN THE SCHEDULING OFFICE

• • • • • • • • • • • • • • • • • • • •

In 1974 I knocked on the door of the Staff Schedular. He said "Come In." I said, "I have some extra time; do you need any help?" He immediately said, "Get in here! Yes, I certainly do need help. The Scheduling Office is a two-person office, and my Chief Quartermaster, Joe Gaskill, is away on Leave (vacation) for several weeks. So, I need you to fill in." I did. The scheduling office was responsible for generating a report every week detailing where every submarine in the Atlantic Fleet was. And we had over 70 submarines at that time. At the end of my several weeks of work, Commander Bill Gaines, as a thank you gift, gave me a copy of **SUBMARINE OPERATIONS OF WORLD WAR II.** It was a compendium of all of the United States submarine operations--- sinking enemy merchant ships, and sometimes enemy warships.

## THE SAGA OF THE USS NAUTILUS GOING UNDER THE NORTH POLE

• • • • • • • • • • • • • • • • • • • • • • •

I was extremely grateful. Digression: What I did not know at that time, was that Commander Bill Gaines had been a Second Class Sonarman on the *U.S.S. NAUTILUS (SSN 571)*—United States' very first Nuclear Submarine, as it went on its historic voyage under *the NORTH POLE.* **This occurred on August 3, 1958. Now this voyage did not happen on a whim! "Those stupid ignorant Soviets were not capable of much." But in October 1957 suddenly there was this object in the sky—a small object in the sky going beep, beep, beep—it was** *SPUTNIK BUILT AND LAUNCHD BY THE SOVIETS!! President Eisenhower was embarrassed and furious! He wanted to accomplish some feat to show the Soviets that United States was just as capable. So, he notified Captain Bill Anderson of the USS Nautilus (SSN571) to take his submarine and go under the North Pole!* **That was easier said than done. Captain Anderson tried twice and got lost under the Arctic Ice Cap because the Navy compasses were useless in helping him to find the North Pole. Finally, they took the navigating mechanism out of an Army Navajo Rocket, and now they were able to accomplish their mission! The Navigator was Lieutenant Shepherd "Shep" Jenks; and another person on board was Dr. Waldo Lyon of the Arctic Submarine**

Laboratory in San Diego. [I was able to meet Dr. Lyon years later when Captain Jack Sable of the COMSUBANT STAFF became the Commanding Officer of the Laboratory. Dr. Lyon had been the designer of the Under-Ice-Package built on the Sturgeon-class submarines. The Ice-Package consisted of a strong steel sail; a lever which dropped all masts and periscopes down 8 inches; and Sail Planes that could turn 90 degrees straight up such that this class of submarines could punch its way upward through up to six feet of ice. Dr. Lyon told me he told the Navy NOT to build the Los Angeles 688 class submarines without including the Ice Package, but the Navy went ahead without the package. Consequently, our USS Jacksonville (SSN699) (688 class) was trained to go up under the ice BUT we should not attempt to surface because we would severely damage the ship and would have to return immediately to our home base.

[Historical Digression.] Way back in the summer of 1972, I re-activated myself into the submarine Navy, specifically to Squadron Two, New London Connecticut for nine weeks. While the Squadron had requested my services, they really did not have much for me to do, so I went up to the Operations Office to see who was going to sea the following week. So, I was able to be a working quartermaster on the USS Nautilus (SSN571) while they were conducting Naval-Academy Mid-Shipmen Orientation. I also rode the USS Tullibee (SSN597), as well as the USS Lafayette (SSBN616). So, I regularly attend the USS Nautilus reunions.

## ATTENDING USS NAUTILUS (SSN571) REUNIONS

• • • • • • • • • • • • • • • • • • • • • •

In 2010, the reunion was held in Pigeon Forge, Tennessee. There was to be a Ship's Picnic in the Smokey Mountain National Park.

**We need to have our own car for transportation. An older woman overheard me making plans and she asked me to transport herself and her husband, which I gladly did. So, who was sitting beside me? Shep Jenks, the Navigator. He was just starting into some form of dementia. The next morning I observed them sitting in the Atrium of the hotel in order to greet old shipmates. I observed several shipmates walk up, say "HI, SHEP" shake his hand and walk away. I was upset that was no way to treat their former Navigator, so I went and sat beside them and adopted them; I took them anywhere they wanted to go. They invited me to come visit them in Martinez, California, but his dementia grew worse and he passed away. But what an honor to spend quality time with him. He made a point of saying "His Chief Quartermaster provided a lot of help when transiting under the ice."**

**Meanwhile,** Bill Gaines had stayed in the Navy and became an Officer. A few years later Commander Gaines was given command of the U.S.S. Gudgeon in San Diego. I contacted him and asked if I could bring my daughter and friends aboard for a tour? "Yes, Certainly."

Twenty plus years later, I found "Captain Gaines" in San Diego as the Commander of the *FLIP SHIP.*

I was extremely grateful. Digression: What I did not know at that time, was that Commander Bill Gaines had been Second Class Sonarman on the *U.S.S. NAUTILUS (SSN 571)*—United States' very first Nuclear Submarine, as it went on its historic voyage under *the NORTH POLE.* Bill Gaines had stayed in the Navy and became an Officer. A few years later Commander Gaines was given command of the U.S.S. Gudgeon in San Diego. I contacted him and asked if I could bring my daughter and friends aboard for a tour? "Yes, Certainly."

[Submarine Digression] In Score 2 First Half I used several pages to define the Diesel -Electric Submarine—which as largely a Surface ship with the ability to submerge occasionally. Now we are alluding to nuclear-powered submarine-which are majorly a different type of ship.

With the advent of nuclear Reactors in 1953, the United States Navy, with Admiral Hyman Rickover in command, began building submarines whose primary propulsion power came from the Reactors such as the famous USS Nautilus (SSN 571). How are they different from the Diesel-Electrics? First of all, the Navy invented an *OXYGEN GENERATOR* and associated equipment to scrub and cleanse the air of impurities such as Carbon Monoxide, and other undesirables. The equipment also reports the percentages of oxygen in the ship's atmosphere.

Second of all the steel hull is far thicker—to withstand greater operating depths. Third, the Navy experimented with different hull designs until they arrived at the "Tear Drop" design—rounded with no superstructure to interfere with underwater speed. Even the Sail and Bridge can be made streamlined and cause less water resistant. (In the Submarine Navy, we are concerned with *CAVITATION: Dictionary Page 331: 1. THE RAPID FORMATION AND COLLAPSE OF VAPOR POCKETS IN A FLOWING LIQUID IN REGIONS OF VERY LOW PRESSURE.* In other words this physical action causes submarines to make lots of noise—when one is trying to be stealthily quiet.)

Fourth, whereas the Diesel-Electrics were on the surface most of the time, nuclear powered submarines are rarely on the surface. They are on the surface to transit in and out of port. They are on the surface usually until they clear the shallow Continental Shelf. (This shelf is over 100 miles wide on the Atlantic Coast but is only 3-4 miles wide on the Pacific Coast.)

Despite having nuclear power—which also assists generating all the electrical power needed by the ship, a nuclear submarine has all the essential equipment that a diesel-electric sub has: a diesel engine connected to an electrical generator, sufficient fuel, a snorkel system for obtaining surface air into the ship, and multi-cell batteries.

This is emergency equipment in case the reactor breaks down at sea. They also have a Secondary Propulsion Motor to operate a separate and smaller the screw or propeller. Nuclear subs are much faster underwater, travelling in excess of 20 + knots. And they can submerge far deeper down to depths in the vicinity of 1000 feet!

While nuclear sub compartmentation does not allow them to suffer any major flooding, they are equipped with a powerful Emergency Blow System capable of providing positive buoyancy in a matter of a very few minutes "and making the sub "jump up out of the water as displayed in the movie *HUNT FOR RED OCTOBER.*

When I was serving as Chief of the Watch in the Control Room, that was my job to operate the switches of the Emergency Blow.

Modern nuclear submarines have the capacity to submerge and stay submerged for many weeks or months! Our submarine was submerged for 64 days during one operation.

+ + + + + +

*THE "ALL HANDS-ON DECK" GLORIOUS CHRISTMAS DINNER: MY STUDENTS TELL ME "NO" WHEN I SUGGESTED WE GO OUTSIDE AFTER DINNER*

• • • • • • • • • • • • • • • • • • • • •

**Returning to my Vocation** In November, 1982, two mothers

came to me and asked if they could do a cooking lesson with our students. Sure. So, they came the next week and the students made and baked Carrot Cake Cupcakes with Yogurt and Cream Cheese Icing. Delicious! It was the end of the school day; I marched my students down to the gym to get into their bus lines, then I went back upstairs. The two mothers were still there. I said, "OK, What?" They said now they wanted to do a complete Holiday Dinner before school ended in December. I said, "Certainly, here is a list of all the families." One was a caterer, so we did indeed have table cloths, china, silver, and actual candelabras (open flames were NOT prohibited in those days). The children helped to prepare a wonderful dinner. The parents told me, "Take the children outside to play and we will turn the classroom into a Restaurant. I did. They did. We had a delightful Holiday meal. The parents then said to me, "Take the children outside again, and we will clean up the room." I said to my students. "Get your coats; we are going outside." My students loudly said, "NO!" I said, "Why are you saying NO?" Students, "We want to wash the dishes!" I said, "Say what?" "We want to wash all the dishes!" I turned to the parents and said, "I'm sorry, but the students have spoken. They want to wash the dishes." So, we set up the three wash buckets; the students washed every single dish, and then they turned and said to me, "NOW we are ready to go outside!" How many kindergarten classes operate like that?? I loved my students.

### PATRIC (DURING HIS LAST YEAR) WRITES A TEN PAGE POEM "SWAN SONG" TO DEAL WITH HIS SAD FEELINGS

• • • • • • • • • • • • • • • • • • • • • •

I have taken time to share with you a number of my practices and strategies teaching kindergarten because it was the center of my life. It was what stirred my deepest passions. And I deeply cared that each student was able to develop whatever potential they had. And, over the seven years my kindergarten classroom was the most requested by parents. My last year teaching, I had 29 students: Eleven families had had me before and wanted their younger child to be in my room. Nine of the new families requested that their child be in my room. So, it was a very positive and warm year together. I wrote a ten-page poem titled *SWAN SONG* when I knew I was leaving.

## Swan Song

Words by Patric Leedom
Calligraphy by
Annamarie Borich

I will sing my Swan Song to you,
In celebration of your greatness;

I called to you to come and join me,
And you came and sat beside me;

I asked for your help in this mighty endeavor,
And you offered so willingly;

I struck a note upon my tuning fork,
And you vibrated sympathetically;

As the notes of the sitar and sarod
Now play a duet behind us,
You and I have danced this year.

\* \* \* \* \*

I will sing my Swan Song to you,
In celebration of our children;

It is something to be a child,
To be at the beginning of life's journey
When all seems so fresh and new;

How delicate and difficult it is sometimes
To bring a child into this world,
And you have brought your successes to me,
That I may make a contribution;

\* \* \* \* \*

Our children, their children, whose children?
Can we say they're ours?

They come down through our bodies,
But are they some extended organ?

Do their hearts beat when ours do,
Or do theirs have rhythms of their own?

Do their eyes see what ours see,
Even when facing the same direction,
Or do they have visions of their own?

Can they feel what we feel,
Or does their youngness stand in the way?

Can they really be like us?
No, they cannot, I'll have to say.

\* \* \* \* \*

And who are we, anyway?

Are we some self-created, isolated individual?

Or is each of us a composite of all
The moments of our days?

Of all the persons, pets, and places that have been intimate in our lives?

Of all the hurts and happineses that have
Saddened and gladdened us?

Of all the adventures, goals, and conversely, paths not taken?

Are not all of these and more,
Like pebbles dropped into the waters of our soul,
Whose ripples expand ever onward,
Influencing us forever?

Our children know not any of this,
Save a few pale words we say;
No, our children are not ours,
They belong to them.

\* \* \* \* \*

I will sing my Swan Song to you
In celebration of teaching

"Teaching" isn't teaching
If you think of it as one human being
Putting something inside the head of another.

If you have no eyes,
I can not give you color;

If you have no ears,
I can not give you sound;

If you have no tongue,
I cannot give you speech;
If you have locked away your mind,
I can not give you thoughts;

If you have locked away your heart,
I can not give you feelings;

If you have locked away your soul,
I can not give you life.

I can spread a feast before you,
But you must come and do the eating;

I can show you the symbols of our language,
But you must come and do the reading;

I can open my heart and extend my arms to you,
But you must come and do the loving.
No, I am not really a teacher.

I provide a place of learning,
But the magic of the learning act,
Comes from within the child,
And not from inside me.

\* \* \* \* \*

I will sing my Swan Song to you,
In gratitude for this life;

Patric Leedom

Now is the moment so precious to my soul,
Now is the moment for me
To make of it what I will;

Will I ignore its passing,
Or will I invite it in;

Will I whittle it into dust and shavings,
Or will I make it into a monument.

For all any one of us has, I believe
Is the eternal "NOW" moment.

The past—last moment, this morning. Yesterday
Is gone now, forever, never to return;

The future is not yet here,
And carries no guarantees for its coming;

Yes, I love my memories,
Some so polished with my touching;
And yes, my head buzzes with
The din of dreams, plans, and fantasies;

But how fragile this life really is,
In an instant, all can be for naught.

* * * * *

I will sing my Swan Song to you,
For yes, I am leaving,
But, do not feel rejected or deserted;

For in all the hours, days, and weeks,
We have been so fortunate to have together,
Have we not shared so much of
Ourselves with each other?

A heart once touched by a new love,
Can never feel the same;

Do you think I could come
And be so close to you,
And walk away unchanged?

\* \* \* \* \* \*

## WOULD YOU BELIEVE AN "ODD COUPLE" LIVING TOGETHER AMICABLY FOR THREE YEARS?

• • • • • • • • • • • • • • • • • • • • •

In the early years of my teaching in the public Montessori School, my salary was $12,000 gross which only allowed me a small amount for rent. So, I moved into a Studio Apartment—a bathroom, and one large space to include everything else.

I had a friend, Janice, who ran in the upper social circles. In 1977 she invited me to a lovely small dinner party. That evening I made the acquaintance of Albert and Ruth Steiner. Albert was the founder and owner of Kenner Toys—once the second or third largest toy manufacturer in the U.S.

Albert's first toy on the market was a gun that shot soap bubbles. It was a very creative business. (Later Kenner Toys was famous for producing **PLAY DOUGH, STAR WARS FIGURES**, AND MANY

OTHERS He was very concerned about promoting creative thinking and thinking "outside of the box" as a way of improving progress. He eventually funded the Chair position of such thinking at the University of Cincinnati.

Ruth came from a social worker background and had founded Camp Vega in Maine for wealthy Jewish girls. I became fascinated with Ruth and later asked if I could come to their home and visit with them. "Yes!"

Sadly, Albert dropped dead of a heart attack on Christmas Eve, 1977.

In the Autumn of 1978, I was over having dinner with Janice, and she informed me that Ruth Steiner has telephoned her and had invited the two us to her house for a larger dinner party. Janice also informed me that Ruth, now living alone, was looking for a woman to move in and be her companion. Janice suggested I could apply for the position. So, I telephoned Ruth and said I was delighted to accept her dinner invitation, and, if she would consider a man, I would like to apply for the position. Ruth responded, "I am so glad you are coming to the dinner party; but no, I am looking for a woman companion, and that was sweet of you to ask."

The dinner party took place a few weeks later on a Tuesday evening. I arrived. There were three large dinner tables of guests, a bartender and two cooks. And lo and behold, Ruth had placed me at her dinner table right next to her left side. Okay. The party lasted until 10:30 P.M. and the guests got up to leave. I said to myself, "Yes, that is the socially proper thing to do, so I stood up to leave. But immediately, Ruth said, "Please sit down and stay—I want to talk to you!" Well, okay. It turned out that Ruth did want to discuss the possibility of my becoming her companion.

We talked until it was midnight. I said, "Ruth, I am sorry, but I have to go home and get ready for school tomorrow." Ruth said, "What are you doing next Tuesday evening?" Well, we met every Tuesday for six weeks, including visiting her daughter Clara who was in the Home for Invalids—paralyzed totally by **MULTIPLE SCLEROSIS** except for her head. I would sometimes be responsible for Clara's caretaking, so we needed Clara's approval for me to move in. She gave it.

## *CLARA'S POEM*

• • • • • • • • • • • • • • • • • • • • • • •

Clara Was a brilliant writer of poetry. It is important to me to include here one of Clara's most poignant poems:

### A Disease

In the beginning you were shy:
The merest rustle of a sigh
Or the vibration of a passing shadow
Might whisper that you stood nearby.

But days went on and you grew bold.
You seized my hands in a firm hold,
The piano stuttered and the pencil dropped
From fingers that were numb and cold.

I clung to my old love and cried
And I dissembled and denied,
Concealing from the world and myself
That you had claimed me for your bride.

You walked with me in every street

And jogged my arm and tripped my feet;
There was a cane, a wheelchair, then a bed
And your dominion was complete.

Now in bed we lie entwined.
You are tyrannical but kind,
Gently you teach my body to obey
But you do NOT POSSESS MY MIND.

How curiously we are mated,
Cohabitating but separated:
From distant worlds I come to talk with you
In language that must be translated.

I, who detest dualism
Am here confronted with a schism:
Am partly yours, partly mine, and so am split
Like sunlight passing through a prism.

I had great respect and admiration for Clara. I learned to let her take how many gulps of air in order to finish a sentence. We had a great relationship.

In January 1979 I moved in with Ruth and began as her companion. Thus, began three of my best years in life! I paid no rent, nor any other house expenses. We had a maid—who cleaned my bedroom and bathroom, and a cook who served Ruth and me dinner every night except Sunday when Ruth—who was an excellent cook, served dinner.

And I was Ruth's companion. We enjoyed dinner together, we often sat in the living room discussing our lives. Right from the beginning she and I developed close rapport (or maybe we had already.) We were both born in May—10th and 13th! So, we operated on very similar views of life.

I did serve as a chauffeur for Ruth and her elderly friends. Sometimes Ruth bought me a ticket to plays and other events.

While I, myself, was never a member of the upper class, I lived around them and have received and acquired the social graces: not only had Matt Long been a solid member of the upper class, but mother married into a prominent "Old Money" family in the upper class. So, I was prepared for proper social behavior and conversation.

Albert and Ruth Steiner had gone in together with their friends, the Ed Seiberts [whom I knew from other connections.] and bought a beautiful three-story house overlooking the Ohio River. The Seiberts took the first floor, and the Steiners took the Second and Third Floors.

And there began three of the most important years of my life! Ruth Heller Steiner was one of the most brilliant persons I ever met. She was from a very scholarly family. Her father was one of the first Rabbis to graduate from Isaac M. Wise's new Reformed Judaism Seminary here in Cincinnati. Upon graduation he moved to New Orleans and became a leading Rabbi.

Ruth was born and raised there, and attended Sophie Newcomb College, the female equivalent to the male Tulane University. [By 1970 both colleges were combined into one.] While there, Ruth joined the Debate Team, and beat her Tulane opponent: Huey P. Long. Ruth's degree was in Social Work, so upon graduation, she moved to New York City, and eventually married the Director of Peter Stuyvesant Settlement House. Ruth gave birth to two daughters: Clara and Cecile. As her lawyer-Director husband developed heart problems, Ruth went to work, founding the Camp Vega, among other jobs.

Sometime after her first husband's death, Ruth re-connected with Albert Steiner in Cincinnati, through her Rabbi brother, Joseph Heller.

I had received my master's degree in Education with emphasis in Montessori in May 1976. Cincinnati Public Schools hired me to help start Sands Montessori School (Formerly Children's House West.) I was now in my fourth year of teaching all-day Montessori Kindergarten [one of five kindergarten classes.] I would get up early, way before Ruth; fix my breakfast and lunch and depart to school. I would arrive home between 4:00 and 5:00 P.M.; Ruth and I would have dinner, served by the cook, in the smaller dining room between the kitchen and living room. Always Ruth and I had pleasant dialogues about the day, and what might be planned for the immediate future.

Sometimes in the evening, I would go to my spacious bedroom in the front of the house, and do homework, and Ruth would do knitting in the living room listening to classical music, and her cat, Sugar, in her lap. Sometimes Ruth and I would just sit in the living room talking.

Ruth was very active socially. Once a week she would play bridge with world-class couples, who had played together for years. They offered to teach me the game of bridge BUT I had better get serious and learn quickly. I declined and stayed a "kibitzer." One Bridge-Playing evening, Libby Ackland became a second kibitzer. She was freshly retired as the "SOCIETY EDITOR of the Cincinnati Enquirer Newspaper. Cincinnati has adopted a few of the southern upper-class social institutions. One of those institutions was for girls; once they reach the age of 18, "They are put forward to the larger upper-class society circle of friends essentially announcing, "our daughter is now eligible for marriage.," That is called a Debutant Party. But how does one know what families are accepted and approved as upper-class families and therefore permitted to put on a Debutant Party. Who makes these decisions?

It turns out to be none other than the Society Editor for the Enquirer. To keep track of who is considered high society, the names are all listed in a "BLUE BOOK" So Libby and I were chatting about the Mitchell Family. Libby inquired if one of those Mitchells was "Perfect Pitch Mitch?" "Yes."

"Perfect Pitch Mitch" was my step-father's father! And step-father didn't appreciate his father enough. So, Libby told me to call Frank in the Enquirer Library and send me out both the photograph and newspaper story that Libby had written a few years ao. Frank did. I took them and created a plaque, which I then gave to step-father as a Christmas gift. Step-father was speechless for over ten minutes, and thanked me saying, "Patric, you could not have given me a finer gift!"

We often had guests for dinner; sometimes it was one or two couples, such as Art and Louise Spiegel, Ruth's attorney, who very soon became the Sixth District Circuit Judge. In cases of small groups, I became the butler and bar tender. [We always had 5 to 8 bottles of whatever guests usually drank...so we never ran out.] If it was a larger dinner party—a full table of ten or maybe two or three dinner tables, then Ruth hired a butler, a bar-tender, and extra maids. Sometimes Ruth gave a large party to promote some new artist and encouraged her friends to buy a painting. Sometimes it was a fund raiser for the Cincinnati Symphony.

Ruth had a regular annual travel schedule. She would travel to California to visit with her younger daughter Cecile and Jim B.; Ruth would travel to New Orleans—where she was born and raised—to visit with her sister-in-law, Mildred Heller; and Ruth would travel to the island of Antigua in the Caribbean for rest and relaxation which included swimming in the ocean. In those times it was my responsibility to make frequent visits with her daughter Clara—paralyzed from the neck down with Multiple Sclerosis in the Home for Invalids. It certainly was NEVER a chore to visit with Clara. She was very bright, humorous, and still dictating excellent poems. I learned a lot from Clara. We had many good discussions. I learned that with her Multiple Sclerosis, Clara needed to take three or four breaths just to speak a sentence. I learned Clara was angry when any guest, thinking they could help Clara "by finishing her sentences for her." I learned that Clara probably told me things she would not tell the ordinary guests. I learned that there were a number of Ruth's friends could NOT deal with Clara's condition, therefore the friends did not go to visit Clara. I learned that there were patients there with different afflictions—a brilliant former lawyer who had had a severe stroke and now could barely speak. There were others with deformed bodies, which brings to mind "Dixie." She was born with almost no legs, so she spent her days in an electric wheelchair. AND she was an Activist fighting for better services for the handicapped; she made telephone calls; she wrote letters.

[Time digression] One day a few years later when I was working on my doctorate at the University, I encountered Dixie motoring along on campus. It happened to be a drizzly day. I went over to Dixie, greeted her, and asked if I could help her. Yes. She was due to speak to a professor's class, but she wasn't sure how to find his building. So, I was able to direct her so she could quickly get out of the rain. Go Dixie! [End Digression]

Returning to Ruth's travels, when she was preparing for her first trip while I was her companion, I asked Ruth if I could give a dinner party while she was gone. Ruth said, "Certainly, my dear. This is your home. Let me show you where everything is." She took me over to one cupboard where all the 50 dinner plates were, another cupboard for the 50 sets of silverware, and another cupboard where the glassware was kept. And Ruth said, "Honey, if you break something, I will know you did not mean to do it, and besides, it is a "thing" and not a person." When Ruth walked away, Lois, the maid, came up to me and said, "Honey, please do not use any of the glassware. If you just look at it cross-eyed, it breaks. If the wash and rinse water is not in the exact temperature range, it will break!" "Ok, Lois, I promise never to use the glassware."

Over the next three years I probably gave eight or so dinner parties. I usually invited 24 people. Ruth had those little ceramic name place holders for each place setting, so I enjoyed figuring out where I desired each person to sit. I particularly placed persons who were "good conversation starters" at the heads of the tables. My cousin Chuck Woolford worked for a florist, so we always had flower spreads at each table. It was a Pot Luck Party. I provided the main course and everyone else brought the rest which I had coordinated. I hired two maids to help with the food and take care of the kitchen. What wonderful social experiences.

Sometimes Ruth's daughter Cecile and Jim would come for a visit. After two days Cecile said to me, "Patric, after dinner meet me in mother's bedroom. (Which was as large as some people's living room)" So we met. Cecile then spoke, "Patric, my mother is sloshing in money, and it makes her happy to spend some on other people. My mother tells me that you never let her spend money on you! And that makes her unhappy!" "Cecile, I did not move in here because of your mother's money." Cecile, "I know that! But I want my mother to be happy. Raise your right hand and swear that when my mother wants to spend some on you, you say "YES". "Okay, I will."

One-time Mildred Heller was flying up for a visit with us. I went to airport to receive her. In those days one could walk right up to the door where passengers were unloading. Lo and behold, the first passenger off the plane was Muhammed Ali and his entourage. The second passenger was Mildred. When we got down to the baggage claim, there was Muhammad Ali standing over by himself. I walked over to greet him. I did not want to discuss boxing, but I did want to discuss his "Saturday Morning Cartoons" that he made. They were very gentle cartoons with a moral in them on how we should be treating other people. I asked him how many cartoons were there? Ali, "Fifteen" I told him how much I admired them and hoped they would come back on television." Muhammed was very polite and gentle. And yes, I got to shake his large strong hands. After about 8 minutes or so, I believed I had imposed on him enough, so I thanked him and walked back to Mildred.

## *AN INVITATION TO MARDI GRAS*

● ● ● ● ● ● ● ● ● ● ● ● ● ● ● ● ● ● ● ● ● ●

A FEW DAYS LATER Mildred was talking about Mardi Gras in New Orleans and asked me if I have ever been? "No." "Oh, my dear, you must come down and see it. I will host you next February." So, I then had a wonderful time in New Orleans and was invited to a few parties. What people should know, is that the Madi Gras parades are 40 blocks long and come through the neighborhoods where it is not so crowded. The French Quarter is the worst place and almost every year someone gets killed or badly injured by the big heavy wagons.

A very impressive event was that Ruth was a member of a Literary Society, which met monthly, and different members would present papers they had prepared for the evening. I was often present. The President of the University of Cincinnati, Henry Winkler's wife Bea was a member. Sometimes they came to our house for dinner, and sometimes we went to their house.

One of my wildest adventures, was when I had just come home from school, Ruth asked me to take her car and drive over to the Belvedere Apartments and pick up her 99-year-old friend, Hannah Rau! 99 years old, huh? So, I drove over to the Belvedere and I could barely get out of my side of the car and open the passenger side door, when this little grey-haired lady came quickly down the walk, jumped in and said, "Hi Honey, my name is Hannah!" 99 years old, huh? [Sources informed me that Hannah lived to be 104 years old.]

Yes, she was! And a very sharp and delightful person. She was still a practicing Cloisonné artist, with a full studio in her apartment. She had Ruth and me over to dinner sometimes.

## *WE THREE ALL HAD BIRTHDAYS IN MAY: SO, WE HIRED A FRENCH CHEF FROM A FIVE STAR FRENCH RESTAURANT TO PROVIDE THE DINNERS*

• • • • • • • • • • • • • • • • • • • • • •

Well, the calendar is turning to 1980 and it became birthday time. All three of us, Ruth, Janice, and I had birthdays in May. I mentioned that one of my kindergarteners was the daughter of the Sous Chef at a local five-star restaurant. Ruth and Janice asked me to ask Marcel if we could hire him to prepare our joint birthday dinner. So, in January, our school had Parent-Teacher Conferences or in my classroom, I re-purposed them into a more positive event: "Parent Teacher Sharing Times." Marcel came in, we discussed the good progress his daughter was making. At the end I turned and asked him if we could hire him. He said he would glad to do it. So, in May he came out to the house early in the afternoon to prepare the food. At the five-star restaurant, days ahead he started marinating the "Coco-vine"—chicken in wine sauce, and he made the Salmon Patte. There were 27 of us—each of us was allowed to invite eight guests. So, Marcel brought 27 lobsters with him. He made "Home-made may-on-aise" in the kitchen and the rest of the food. For the birthday cake he made a cake with egg-white coating in which he wrote 'Happy Birthday.' This was my 40th birthday, and I have never had a grander time! We three paid for the food and wine--$427, but Marcel donated his services!!!

## *A TRIBUTE TO MY JEWISH SAINT AND BENEFACTOR*

• • • • • • • • • • • • • • • • • • • • •

I would like to honor Ruth Steiner with a tribute. Not only am I deeply grateful for my personal circumstances living with her, but I learned so much from her. Ruth certainly ranks high in my gallery of Role Models. She was brilliant in her thoughts and feelings. She was quite well educated. In her life's experiences as a Social Worker. (Ruth's aunt had been part of the Jane Hull Settlement House in Chicago.) Following Ruth's graduation from Sophie Newcomb College in New Orleans (Now part of Tulane University) Ruth moved to New York City and went to work for the Peter Styvant's Settlement House in Manhattan. She eventually married the director, a Mr. Cohen, and gave birth to two daughters.

The work of the settlement house in the 1930's into the 1940's was to rescue Jews from Europe and equip them to be successful in America. This included English language lessons. (Being Jewish, she and her husband attend a large Synagogue in Manhattan. Also attending was Anne Frank's father—the only surviving member of the "Diary of Anne Frank" family. Also attending was Joseph Hirschhorn—in the scrap metal business who later contributed the Joseph Hirschhorn Museum of Sculpture to the Smithsonian Institute.) I remember when the movie **HOLOCAUST** came out, I asked Ruth if she was going to see it? She responded, "Why should I? I lived through it!"

Through her Social Work of many years, she was very aware of the human condition; she was very compassionate, kind, and empathetic. I certainly benefitted from the way she interacted with me. I certainly already had these traits, but they grew stronger by interacting, and conversing with Ruth. While I was living with her, she was on the Board of one or two settlement houses. (When she died, they named one of them after her.)

For servants who had worked for her and her husband, Ruth paid small pensions to them, and especially paid the cost of swimming lessons for their children. I remember there was one elderly man, who now had cancer; she would pay him $100 in the spring for one hour of work in the spring, with his son, to go to the basement and bring up and place all the porch furniture. And then another $100 to come back in the Autumn and put it all away.

I asked her one time if she flew First Class when she travelled? Ruth responded, "Certainly not! The back end of the plane arrives at the same time as the front end! And the money I saved I would rather give it to some deserving person!" Ruth possessed mink coats. I asked Ruth if she always wore her minks when she attended social events. Ruth responded, "If most everyone attending was wearing a mink coat, then yes, I do. But if most of the guests were not, then I wear some of my perfectly good cloth coats!"

Ruth taught me and drove home the concept of ***NOBLIS OBLIGE:*** the moral obligation of those of high birth, of powerful social position etc. to act with honor, kindliness, generosity etc. A simpler definition might be: those with much abundance should share with those of low abundance.

So, Ruth and I often discussed how to interact in society. My self-confidence to interact with anyone in upper society or in positions of power soared. Long after I lived with her, to this day, I refer to her as "My Jewish Saint."

## *RUTH'S HEALTH AT 85 NEEDED A 24-HOUR-A-DAY FULL TIME COMPANION; SO PATRIC MOVES ON*

• • • • • • • • • • • • • • • • • • • • •

My companionship came to an end, when Ruth's health was declining, and she needed someone with her 24 hours a day. We stayed friends.

# CONTENTS

## Part Four: Dr. Patric Leedom's Autobiography
## NOVEMBER 19—OCTOBER 23, 2022

◇◇◇◇◇◇◇◇◇◇◇◇◇◇◇◇◇◇◇◇◇◇◇◇◇◇◇◇◇◇◇◇◇◇◇◇◇◇◇◇◇◇◇◇◇◇◇◇◇◇◇◇◇◇◇◇◇◇◇

# PART FOUR

## Dr. Patric Leedom's Autobiography

### NOVEMBER 19—OCTOBER 23, 2022

SCORE THREE FIRST HALF OF YEARS: Age 40 thru 50 Years

*RAFTING DOWN THE COLORADO RIVER FOR SEVEN DAYS!*

• • • • • • • • • • • • • • • • • • • • • • •

**1980 I** had turned 40 while living with Mrs. Ruth Steiner. In the summer of 1981, I had one of the thrills of my life: I purchased a ticket on a raft to travel down the Colorado River from Lee's Ferry—just below the Glen Canyon Dam—280 miles down to Lake Mead. Seven days and nights.

You might have guessed that I am attracted to all things "water." Over the years and travelling with my daughter around the United States for fifteen years, I had been to the Grand Canyon South Rim Overlook and Visitors' Center many times, eyeing the Colorado River way, way down there—is it a mile? And saying to myself "someday I am going to take a Raft Trip." Okay, now I am living with Mrs. Steiner rent free, so now I do have extra money. Goody! I contacted the Sanderson Brothers Rafting Company, paid $1,000 and bought myself a ticket. So, in July I pack all my things into my VW Square-back Car and off I go. I think I planned ahead and left a little early, which was good because when I was nearing Deming, New Mexico, the car engine got sick. I was able to limp into a car repair shop and leave it for a week to be repaired. I then took Greyhound buses the rest of the way to Flagstaff Arizona where I met Sanderson Brothers and all my fellow "River Rats." The companies always travel in two rafts for safety. Each raft can carry about 30 passengers, so there were 55+ people. We were staying at a Holiday Inn, where people could leave their cars for a week. We had orientation and received our "Wet Bags" and Ammunition Cans the night before; went to bed early, as Reveille was 5:00 A.M.

A bus drove us down to Lee's Ferry (which actually was a small vehicle ferry starting back in the 1800's). By Government Regulation all river tours embarked at Lee's Ferry; and the Government regulates how many rafts may be on the river at any one time—for a very practical reason: there are very few sand beaches where Rafters can stop for the night. The old-time rafts were constructed such that the passengers' Wet Bags and Ammo Cans of personal effects were secured in the middle of the boat, and passengers just made themselves comfortable leaning back on the bags.

Passengers were invited to help make the meals which was a wonderful way to get to know each other. There were portable tables brought from the rafts. Passengers went to bed and sleep shortly after the sun went down. The majority of the canyon has high obsidian walls which soak up the sun's heat all day long. So, at night, the temperature is in the 90's up to 100 degrees.

So, all one needs is a sleeping mat, some sheets, blanket, pillow, and you are comfortable. If you get too hot, just take the top sheet down to the river and drench it. Most passengers were up by 6:00 A.M. busy helping make breakfast. I think we launched back on the river between

7:00 and 7:30 A. M.

During the day, the scenery was gorgeous. And for Geological Aficionados there are 19 separate layers of sedimentary rock that the Colorado River has cut through. So called Rapids are rocks which have fallen off the cliffs into the river. On this 1981 trip the Government had let the level of the river go down low. There were two places where the passengers were off-loaded so the boat crews—two to a raft—could negotiate the difficult passages.

Interestingly when we were floating—no, wait, the rafts had outboard motors both to steer by and to provide forward motion. And I estimate (being a submarine Navigator) that the raft speed down the river was between five and six knots = River current plus boat speed. This reminds me that there is a "Code" on the river: if you see any raft in distress, everyone stops to help!

I could go on and on because I found this trip to be one of the most engrossing vacations of my life. But you might not be that curious about it.

The raft trip ended in Lake Mead. A high-powered craft was able to take aboard at least 60 persons, and they delivered us to a dock where a bus took us to the airport, and we were flown back to Flagstaff.

+ + + + + + + + + +

Once upon a time, I could not quiet my brain from insatiable wonder and curiosity. I had been associated with the U.S. Navy Submarine Force for 18 years. I had experienced two oceans, I had been full time crew on two World War II diesel electric submarines, and I had been (TDY) Temporary Active Duty on 16 other submarines. I was already experiencing nuclear submarines such as *the USS Nautilus (SSN 571)*

[United States' first nuclear submarine, which was the first ship to ever go underneath the North Pole (August 3, 1958.)] ***AND I ALSO RODE NUCLEAR SUBMARINE,*** the ***USS DACE (SSN 607),*** *the* ***USS TULLIBEE (SSN 597) and the USS LAFAYETTE (SSBN 616)*** .

*MY SUBMARINE EXPERIENCES LED ME TO*
*APPLY TO NASA FOR A STINT IN SPACE*

●●●●●●●●●●●●●●●●●●●●●●●●

So, my eyes turned heavenward, and I contemplated living and working in ***SPACE! I wrote to NASA and volunteered to be a school teacher and surrogate grandfather in their first space colony. I did not want to go up forever, but a nice two to three-year deployment seemed do-able. Here are excerpts from NASA' reply:***

***National Aeronautics and Space Administration Lyndon B. Johnson Space Center, Houston, Texas March 13, 1980***

Mr. William Patrick Leedom, East McMillan St. Cinti, Ohio

*Dear Mr. Leedom: Thank you for your recent letter and your interest in this Nation's manned space flight program. It may interest you to know that we receive hundreds of letters similar to yours from people all over the world asking about the status of the space settlement matter, or about space stations, or what subjects they should study, other qualifications, etc. in order to participate in space settlements.*

*A number of newspapers, magazines, technical journals...have in the past few years reported on various aspects of establishing space settlements... Most of the articles differed as to cost, the technology required, the time frame, and the size and functional capabilities of individual or clustered settlements....have long been the dream of space engineers and scientists.* **However, there is within NASA no recognizable need for a space settlement project now or in the near future and no plans at this time to establish a space station on the lunar surface. Therefore, space settlements are no longer being studied by NASA.**

Their reply to me was three pages long, with references to a number of NASA publications. "Again, we very much appreciate your interest in the National Aeronautics and Space Administration and your taking the time to write. Good luck in your future endeavors. Sincerely M. Scott, Office of Public Affairs." [And a thick packet of enclosures.]

Oh well it was a beautiful dream! And I did take action to fulfill that dream. Personal note: it was only three years later that I resigned from school teaching and took a two-year assignment as an Assistant Navigator of a nuclear Fast Attack Submarine—the USS BARACUDA (SSN659), which I helped to guide up into the Arctic Ocean for 64 submerged days of exploration.

1981. I was in my sixth year of teaching at Sands Montessori School. Mrs. Irene Linfert was my Teaching Assistant for the third year. We were the best team I ever had, and she ever had (she told me two years later.)

I have taken time to share with you a number of my practices and strategies teaching kindergarten because it was the center of my life. It was what stirred my deepest passions. And I deeply cared that each student was able to develop whatever potential they had. And, my kindergarten classroom was the most requested by parents. My last year teaching, I had 29 students: Eleven families had had me before and wanted their younger child to be in my room. Nine of the new families requested that their child be in my room. So, it was a very positive and warm year together.

I still enjoyed teaching kindergartners. I NEVER got tired of working with them. But I had told Ruth Steiner, that if I ever stopped living with her, I would leave teaching because the salary was not going to get much better.

While I lived with Mrs. Steiner, I paid no rent, no utilities, no food, no costs of any kind. It was all provided by her, and the maids who changed my bed and cleaned my bathroom. But back out on my own, my standard of living would certainly decline.

Back to teaching in Sands Montessori School. We had changed school principals. For the first year or two, everything seemed to be ok, but by the third year, trouble was brewing. Rumors began to creep around corners. I had always thought that Clare was a good principal, and I was one of the last to recognize that she was not. She had serious mental, emotional problems. She was a liar. She was afraid of most of us; so, she instituted certain teachers to be her "spies"—to telephone her at night and tell her "Who had been saying negative things about her." She had one set of rules for Black employees, and a different set for white employees. (She was white.) I do not think I want to go into detail about all the destructive behavior. BUT, I soon "saw the writing on the wall that I could not in honor and integrity coexist with the principal." So, it was a very positive and warm year together. I wrote a ten-page poem titled **SWAN SONG** when I knew I was leaving.

I had worked closely with the Parent Group Executive Board. When they knew I was leaving, first they invited me to come speak and share some of my observations about Sands Montessori School. Which I did—only Parents and I were at the meeting. Then they dedicated the last issue of the School Newsletter to me. **SANDS REPORTER, June 1983.** And in it they reported on our meeting.

## PARTING WORDS, THANK YOU'S, AND TEARS
• • • • • • • • • • • • • • • • • • • • • •

**DEAR PATRIC…THIS LAST ISSUE IS DEDICATED TO YOU, WITH OUR DEEPEST APPRECIATION AND MOST SINCERE AFFECTION TO A MAN WHO HAS SO NATURALLY GIVEN OF HIMSELF TO OUR CHILDREN AND TO THE SANDS SPIRIT. YOUR BEING HERE HAS DEFINITELY MADE SANDS A BETTER PLACE. THE NAVY'S GAIN IS TRULY OUR LOSS AND TO SAY YOU WILL BE MISSED IS A GROSS UNDERSTATEMENT.…**

"Last Thursday evening, Patric came to the Parent Group Executive Board meeting not only to socialize with friends but also to share with the group his perspectives and concerns relating to public school education in this city.…Patric has served on the Superintendent's Advisory Council.…He brought with him to the meeting his recently prepared position paper on the subject of retaining effective teachers.…entitled, "***WHO IS TEACHING OUR STUDENTS?***" As Patric progressed through his position paper, one particular thing struck me: his **sense of emotional commitment**.

"He spoke to two areas: 1) The Emotional Workplace; and 2) The Professional Workplace. He spoke of TRUST "being the most basic ingredient" in a relationship and how that relates to those involved in our schools.… He spoke of raising job satisfaction through ways of granting more responsibility (to teachers), showing recognition and appreciation on a more personal and specific basis.…His summarizing thought was a question that keeps crossing my mind and I'd like to share it with you:

"If we really want to get and keep good teachers, what actions are we willing to take to do it?"

Patric has written some "Parting Thoughts" to share with us… Lest We Forget. "I AM LEAVING Children's House/Sands after seven years with the warmest of memories and the greatest respect for what we—parents, students, staff—wanted to create and were successful in doing.

"My deep personal satisfaction from, and respect for my seven years here is that we have been engaged in a very positive, cooperative effort to produce a high-quality educational environment for our young individuals.

"My professional life at Sands has been congruent with my inner moral, ethical, and religious beliefs, many of which revolve around how do you treat other human beings, and how do you contribute to the well-being of others—to make our society a better place in which to live.

"I am grateful to have had the freedom to teach the grade level I most wanted, and the freedom to design both my physical classroom, and much of my academic curriculum my way. (These were the days before there were any state standards for what is to be taught in kindergarten.)

"Lest we forget. The freedom our Nation enjoys was won with a lot of sacrifice, blood, sweat, and tears. And several times since 1781 we had had to defend it. *"The price of freedom is eternal vigilance."*

"Our high-quality school program exists because of a lot of sacrifice, money, blood, sweat and tears, especially on the part of the staff and parents.…

"And it is in the nature of bureaucracy to tend toward mediocrity; when you put "HOT" and "COLD" together, you get "WARM."

(Within the Cincinnati Public Schools, Sands was rated the TOP of all Elementary Schools. And truly, parents slept on the sidewalk in

January just to gain a spot for their child in a limited number of seats in our school. One of my faculty doctoral advisors shared with me that he was one of those parents…)

+ + + + + + + + +

## *MY PARALLEL LIFE IN THE NAVY*

• • • • • • • • • • • • • • • • • • • • • •

Shifting over to my "parallel life" in the Navy, fortunately, not only was I a Master Chief Quartermaster, but I had been promoted to the **COMMAND MASTER CHIEF OF THE NAVAL AND MARINE CORPS RESERVE TRAINING CENTER** in Cleveland for the Third Weekend of the Month. My office was right outside the Commanding Officer's Office. We worked together as a team. One day in 1981, he called me into his office, and handed me textbooks for a brand-new Petty Officer Training Course—to help Reservists become qualified to be promoted. He said, "Master Chief, you are a teacher. Design a program so we can set up training for our young men." *I BELIEVE I CAN* "Yes sir. I can do that." I was being hosted for the weekend by my shipmate Doc Hemminger and his wife Judy and family—which I often did. (This was in the Cleveland area, and I lived 250 miles away in Cincinnati.) So, I took the textbooks back to their house and studied them and came up with a plan. The next morning, I went back into the CO's office to explain my plan.

I argued that the most efficient way to offer the training course, was, for him, on a designated weekend, to transfer all of the potential Petty Officer sailors to my care; and I would conduct the course all day on Saturday, and all day on Sunday. And while that would constitute less hours than the course recommended, I would cover all of the most important points, and we could guarantee completion—rather than offering the course for a few hours each of six different weekends and "have a nightmare trying to keep track of who had attended which of the chapters." The Commanding Officer immediately agreed that that was the best plan. I taught the course one weekend every three or four months for the next year, with successful completion by all of the sailors.

It was maybe a year later the Navy Reserve Center Commanding Officer called me into his office and shared with me, that in our entire Naval District, our Center was the First to implement the course with successful results. He said he was recognized for good leadership in the Naval District and he wanted to share the news with me. "You are very welcome, sir."

Meanwhile by 1983 I had had enough. Back in the Cincinnati Public Schools, the politics in the school building, and in the downtown district office, and in the Teachers' Union were deteriorating, so I was looking for a serious career change.

I knew it was time for me to look for "Greener Pastures." Remember that dream I had as a senior in high school wanting to "go around the world on a merchant ship?" Well, I started thinking that as a Master Chief Quartermaster who had navigated submarines around the world, that I could work my way up to being a navigator or Executive Officer of a merchant ship. So, I went to the United States Coast Guard— which issued merchant seamen's licenses- and I signed up and took the courses. [The Coast Guard was located in Cleveland, right behind the US Navy and Marine Corps Reserve Center.]

It took a few months, but I did it; I passed, and I was issued an "***ABLE-BODIED SEAMEN'S LICENSE*** enabling me to work on any American Merchant Marine Ship. So, then I started contacting American Shipping Companies. Sadly, I got the same replies, "We are sorry. You are ten years too late. We have just sold our fleet!" And some of the companies had actually not sold their fleets, but had "moved" their fleets to Panama, Liberia, or similar countries where there were no rules, no requirements for insurance, no wonderful pay for the sailors. Wow. That certainly is not for me.

## I TOOK A TWO-YEAR CONTRACT TO GO BACK ON ACTIVE SUBMARINE DUTY

• • • • • • • • • • • • • • • • • • • • • •

The Navy Recruiter, whose office was just across the hall, heard me talk about going back to sea. He came to me one day and said, "Master Chief, if you want to go back to sea, I will hook you up with a two-year contract—back in the submarine force." I said, "Let's do it!"

[Time Digression] All these years, from 1962 up through 1983 I had maintained a strong Navy Reserve Career in the Submarine Force. As a matter of fact, in December 1972 I was invited to join the Staff of the Commander, Submarine Force, U.S. Atlantic Fleet (COMSUBLANT), located in Norfolk Virginia. I was down to the office in Norfolk at least four times a year, and often in the summer, I went back into the Navy on Active Duty for six to nine weeks. My career path blossomed. In 1972 my Navy rating was (E7) Chief Quartermaster; in 1975 I was promoted to (E8) Senior Chief Quartermaster; and in 1978 I was promoted to (E9) Master Chief Quartermaster. So meanwhile, back on the Admiral's Staff in Norfolk, I had been substituting for the Command Master Chief of the Operations Center. He would call me up at home and ask me when I was coming down for the summer. Then he would put in a request for Leave (vacation.) One day in 1982 when I was down working in Norfolk, the Command Master Chief said to me, "Hey, I am retiring next year. Why don't you come back on Active Duty and come down and take my place?" Wow! Now that is an offer I can't refuse." Well, a few months later, he said to me, "Oh by the way, my wife is divorcing me, so I am not retiring!" OOOOpps, there went that opportunity, but I had already announced I was resigning my teaching position.

Back to the Drawing Board. The Navy Recruiter came to me and said I could choose any submarine base in the United States, including Hawaii. But my decision was pretty easy to make both my mother and stepfather were in ill health. They lived in western North Carolina—Bat Cave—about a six- or seven-hour drive from Norfolk. So, I chose Norfolk.

I had contacted the Submarine Personnel Detailer in Washington DC,--the person who assigns sailors to different commands (this includes ships.) I asked him if I could be assigned to a Fleet Ballistic Missile submarine because they had both a Blue and a Gold crew; they would go out to sea for 70 days on patrol, then come back and hand the ship over to the other crew. And the original crew would be in port for 60 days. I thought that would make for a decent life style; I might even be able to have a girlfriend (or wife. Was I crazy?) But the Detailer said, "Master Chief, we do not put any quartermaster on board an FBM above an (E5) Second Class Petty Officer, because all the ship does is go out to sea and "punch holes in the ocean!" [A Fleet Ballistic Missile Submarine is actually "an under-water missile platform that just happens to be a submarine."] They are given a "box"—a patrol area, and are expected to stay hidden, and be available to fire intercontinental ballistic missiles if the President of the United States orders them to." So, there is not much work for a quartermaster. "Master Chief, we need you on a Fast Attack Submarine, where we can use your knowledge and skills."

I was then assigned as an Assistant Navigator aboard the USS Barracuda (SSN 659). I reported aboard the USS Barracuda (SSN 659) on 3 August 1983 at age 43, just as the United States was "invading Grenada." When I first reported to the Barracuda, I remembered how social the crews were on my old diesel-electric subs; so, I thought, why don't I throw a party and bar-b-que at my beach residence for all of the chiefs on board. Twice I tried to schedule a weekend, and twice the ship got orders to get underway over that particular weekend. As I planned for a third time, the Chiefs came to me and said, "We appreciate what you are trying to do for us; however, the reality is, we spend so much time on board—even in port—away from our families, that once we get away (escape) from the ship, we do not even want to see each other. So, forget about a party."

After I had been aboard a few months, I totally understood what they were sharing with me. It was incredible how many hours the crew, and officers, were expected to be on board in port. For example, the normal working day is over at 4:30 P.M., but often crew members were kept another two to four hours before they were allowed to go home.….often arriving after the children were asleep in bed; and then, the crew members were expected to be back on board no later than 7:30 A.M. in the morning!!

+ + + + + + + + +

Remember several pages back, I chose to be homeported in Norfolk, Virginia, because both my mother and stepfather were in ill health. By Christmas time, 1983, my stepfather, Mark Mitchell, was in the Saint Joseph Hospital in Ashville, NC and never came home after that. He died a week after his son got married in January. I remember that Mother and I plotted that we would bring my daughter Julia, 19 years old, from California, to spend Christmas with our family in North Carolina. Julia flew into the Norfolk Airport during the week. On the weekend, when I was free, I drove her the seven plus hours to Bat Cave to spend time with her grandmother. Father Mark had some severe memory problems. We took Julia to the Hospital to visit her grandfather—with whom she had spent many hours helping to build miniature furniture with him and going for boat rides every day in Lake Lure. With Julia beside me, I said, "Mark, you remember my daughter, Julia?" And Mark looked at her blankly and said to me, "No, Patric, I don't!" Ouch. I was worried that Julia's feelings would be hurt, but if they were, she never talked about it. After bringing Julia to Bat Cave, I had to be back to work on my ship by Monday morning.

Julia was able to spend a whole week with grandmother and have a great time. Mother arranged for Julia to go horse-back riding with Mother's friend DeeDee who did have horses and loved to ride. I am just now thinking that Christmas of 1983 was the last time Julia and Grandma Joy ever saw each other. And that I didn't see Julia again until May 1985.

I was living in Virginia Beach, in the shadow of the 17-mile Chesapeake Bay Bridge. Virginia Beach is extremely flat land. If you desire a view of the Bay, you have to live right next to it. I was very fortunate. I walked in to a Real Estate Office right near the beach. I inquired about rentals near the water. The owner, Millie Shepherd, immediately said, well, I do have one available, but it is only available from Labor Day until Memorial Day. During the summer months. I rent the apartment for $400 week. But during the winter months, you may have it for $600 a month. We took a look at this second-floor apartment with a commanding view of the Bay, and I said, I will take it.

The apartment itself, was rather ordinary; two bedrooms, bathroom, kitchen with a dining area next to the viewing windows, a living room. The furniture was that special brand titled "This Side Up" furniture which was very sturdily made...like out of 2" by 4" boards. No problem. There was a nice deck overlooking the water. It was perfect for my needs. My submarine deployed during the summer months, so that was no problem. There was a very big storage facility for all my things, including my car, during the summer.

I looked around my new "neighborhood" on the beach, and I observed that many of the homes had a Hobby-Cat Sailboat setting at the back door. I wanted to be "in style." The Hobby-Cat Dealership was just six blocks south. So, I went and bought myself a 14 foot sail boat. The dealership just lifted the boat, placed a set of wheels under it, and just rolled it down the six blocks! It was an expensive "toy" but I, we did have fun on it. Actually, the boat was most enjoyable when there were three or more persons on board to stabilize it.

The Hobby Cat is known for its lightness and speed. The sails were very large in comparison to the "trampoline"—canvas sitting area. With only one person on board, the boat travels so fast that one is constantly tacking back and forth. And gusts of wind, if you are not alert, can tip you right over. I would say turn turtle, but the bay in that area was only six to eight feet deep. To "right" the turned-over boat, step one was to take a life jacket and attach it to the top of the mast (which is now under water.) The floatation of the jackets brings the mast back to the surface. Step two was to take the "righting rope" to the pontoon, fore and aft, then wrap the rope around yourself; put your feet on the up- turned pontoon, and begin to lean as far back as you can so your body is right angles, or perpendicular to the horizontal trampoline, and begin "bouncing your weight until the mast and sails, rises fully up and out of the water." And yes, the boat could be taken completely apart and placed in the storage facility, which was not that far away from the apartment.

+ + + + + +

### THE CAPTAIN AND I

• • • • • • • • • • • • • • • • • • • • •

[ Personal Digression] The first Capitan of the Barracuda and I developed a quiet mutual respect and friendship. It came to surface when I pestered the Captain for a Swim Call. It surfaced when we were high up in the Arctic Ocean where all the Meridians come together, and thus the Time Zones change quickly. The first day on scene, I kept saying, Excuse me, Captain, but we have just entered another Time Zone so I need to go through the ship and change all the clocks." He let me do those three times before he finally said, "Leedom, knock this shit off and just go to ZULU Time (Military Time, Universal Time.)" "Yes, sir!"

It surfaced one Thursday in Port When we were having our routine "Planning Board for Training. At one point the Captain looked across the table at me and said, "Leedom, I want you to order new curtains for the Periscope Stand." Would you believe I responded: "Captain, I would rather not order new curtains. I have just come back on Active Duty from teaching for seven years. And every year I needed to pay $1000-to $2,000 if I wanted my classroom to provide a very positive Learning Environment, AND *I needed a lot of supplies.!*" The Captain's eyes got really big, he glanced, then he began thinking. Finally, he said to me, "Leedom, my wife is a school teacher and I know what you are saying. Okay, do not order new curtains." "Thank you very much, sir."

### THE USS BARRACUDA DEPLOYS TO THE FAR NORTH

• • • • • • • • • • • • • • • • • • • • •

The Barracuda stayed in the Virginia Capes Operating Area mostly. We did make a trip down to the Caribbean for a week or two. In May 1984, we made all preparations for a major deployment to the Arctic

Ocean. I ordered all the charts we needed. The new Navy Regulations required that on major deployments that each sailor must has his own rack or bed. Our normal crew was 135 persons. We normally only had 90 beds on board. We were able to bring and place ten mattresses, mostly in the Torpedo Room; so that gave us a crew of 100. I was the "Schools Officer." That translated to: "Leedom, find schools and other places to put our 35 members somewhere off of the ship." That left the operating crew shorthanded of qualified watch standers, at least for the first few months.

We departed the Norfolk Naval Base in late March and sailed up north through the Greenland, Iceland, United Kingdom Gap, into the Arctic.

At that time, the Soviet Union was still in existence, and some U.S. military planners worried that World War III might be fought up in the Arctic. The Soviets knew a lot about navigating around the Arctic. But the US only had limited knowledge. So, our ship's mission was to learn about the Arctic Ocean and navigating under ice. Our superiors would send us periodic radio message as to where they wanted us to explore.

Once we were operating in the Arctic Ocean, **I received and plotted all the required legs of our orders. Later, I received an Admiral's CITATION.** Wherever I was, I had to stop everything and lay out the required track and check it for possible navigation hazards. We were submerged for 64 days.

As a "Thank You" Gift, the Submarine Force arranged for us to first pay a port visit to Edinburgh, Scotland, and then navigate down the English Channel to Southern England and the port of Portsmouth, England. Then we sailed home to Virginia. COMSUBLANT ordered us to stay out to sea for 24 hours to coordinate operations with another submarine.

## *ADMIRAL'S CITATION ON THIS WHOLE PAGE*

• • • • • • • • • • • • • • • • • • • • • • •

**Commander Submarine Force**
**United States Atlantic Fleet**

The Commander Submarine Force, U. S. Atlantic Fleet

takes pleasure in commending

MASTER CHIEF PETTY OFFICER

WILLIAM P. LEEDOM

UNITED STATES NAVAL RESERVE

for service as set forth in the following

CITATION

For professional achievement in the superior performance of his duties while serving as Assistant Navigator in USS BARRACUDA (SSN 659) from March to August 1984. During this period, BARRACUDA prepared for and conducted a highly successful independent operation of great importance to the defense and national security of the United States Government. This deployment was performed in an environment of great operational stress, requiring constant vigilance and keen operational competence. Master Chief Petty Officer LEEDOM consistently performed his demanding duties in an exemplary and highly professional manner. Displaying commendable leadership, superb skill and resourcefulness, he ensured the safe navigation of the ship in unfamiliar waters, thus greatly enhancing the ship's particularly high state of operational readiness. His sustained superior performance in an environment of operational complexity played a major role in the highly successful completion of BARRACUDA's mission. Master Chief Petty Officer LEEDOM's exceptional professional abilities, initiative and selfless devotion to duty reflect great credit upon himself and the United States Naval Service.

B. M. KAUDERER
Vice Admiral, U. S. Navy
Commander Submarine Force
U. S. Atlantic Fleet

## FINALLY, I GET MY SWIM CALL

• • • • • • • • • • • • • • • • • • • • • • •

**As we crossed the Atlantic Ocean and prepared to enter our home port in Norfolk, Virginia, we were requested to stay out in the VACAPES OPERATING AREA, TO DO A SOUND CHECK ON A FELLOW SUBMARINE JUST BEGINNING HER PATROL**

Since we had little to do, I went to the Captain,(again) and said, "Hey Captain, how about a Swim Call?" And the Captain said, "Oh god dammit, Master Chief, if you want a Swim Call, then YOU ARE IN CHARGE, and you organize it!" "Aye, aye, sir." And so, we had our swim call—maybe the first in many years. Half way through, I went down to the Captain's Cabin, and invited him to join us. He was lying on his bunk reading a book. He turned to me and said, "Master Chief, do you know what swims in the water, and has great big teeth?" I think that meant "NO!"

We spent the next six months operating in and out of our port in Norfolk.

## A TRAGIC ENCOUNTER

• • • • • • • • • • • • • • • • • • • • • •

One time when they sent us out to VACAPES Operation area, COMSUBLANT had screened our radio traffic so we had no knowledge of what was going on around the opening to Chesapeake Bay. The Squadron had sent us a radio message saying that as soon as we tied up in port the next day, they would give us a "Surprise Weapons Inspection." So, then the Captain radioed back and asked if we could come into port very early—like 5:30 A.M. Yes! So, the Captain was up until 2:30 A.M., preparing all the paperwork. At 4:45 A.M. we set the "Maneuvering Watch for Entering Port." The Officer of the Deck, started calling down to the Control Room, asking what was going on at the entrance to the channel. We had no information but there were a couple of ships anchored by Cape Henry Light, and lots of little white lights moving around on the water. The Executive Officer (XO) was on # 2 periscope trying to identify what the lights were. Generally, he called them fishing boats. Now we sometimes had problems with our Radar, and at this time, it was not working. As we got closer, the Officer on the Bridge called down "I have one white light way over on my starboard side, and I have another white light way over on my port side; what do I have? The Officer on the Periscope looked, and answered, "They are fishing boats. Okay. The Captain was NOT on the Bridge at this time. But as we continued to approach in the channel---oops—we discovered that those two lights were connected!!! It was some kind of craft, setting very low in the water, painted a dark grey. And it was laying right across the middle of the Channel!! The Officer of the Deck ordered "All Back Full!" And then he ordered: "All Back Emergency!" But we had too much momentum on the ship and so we kept coming; and we collided with it!! It rode right up on our sonar dome, and "opened it up like a Tuna Fish can!!"

Just as we collided, the ship stopped and started backing away. We discovered the craft was a "Self-Propelled Causeway 300 feet long, with a small tugboat built in on the stern." As we were backing away, our radar started working! However, the craft was only 18 inches above the water, and our Radar could NOT detect it. I was actually the Chief Witness to the Accident, because I was taking 2- or 3-minute fixes while we were navigating in the channel. And whenever I was not shooting bearings, I was trained on the craft. As soon as we were tied up in port, I took a legal pad of paper and started writing down twelve pages of everything I had seen.

All microphone communications during the Maneuvering Watch

were tape recorded. My boss, the Navigator, transcribed the entire conversations over the microphone. He handed the script to me with orders to make five copies and deliver them to the Squadron for the Board of Inquiry. "Well, wouldn't you believe that on this day the copier "misfired" that afternoon and made six copies. And "magically" one of those copies fell into my shirt." (Was that a Leprechaun at work?)

## THANK GOODNESS FOR RECORDED COMMUNICATION
• • • • • • • • • • • • • • • • • • • • •

In a day or two, I became aware there was a "Pissing Contest" between the Officer of Deck and the Captain. The Officer of the Deck insisted that "I had informed the Captain they were setting the Maneuvering Watch." And the Captain said, "I do not remember ever being informed!" So, I went home that night and reviewed my copy, and I discovered that the Captain had never been informed. So, the next morning I went up on the Submarine Tender ship, found the Judge Advocate General's' Office and asked to come in. My Captain was also sitting at the desk. I said to the lawyer, "Sir, if you will review the script of the microphone communications, YOU WILL SEE---THAT THE CAPTAIN WAS NEVER INFORMED!" The Navy Lawyer dug through a pile of papers on his desk, found the transcript, and said to me: "By God you are right!" So, my Captain was saved from a Courts-Martial, but he still lost his Command. [What if I hadn't made a "Pirated Copy?" and what if I hadn't bothered to share the news with lawyer?"] [In my humble opinion, the Captain did not deserve to lose his Command. He was a brilliant tactician, and he really cared about the crew.]

*So, when our collision happened and the Captain was in trouble, naturally I did everything to support him and show my respect and caring.*

As Assistant Navigator, it was my task to reconstruct the whole accident scenario, using data from several departments. Interestingly, I discovered that despite the Officer of the Deck ordering All Back Full, then All Back Emergency, the ship NEVER SLOWED DOWN, until just at the time we collided---The momentum of a very heavy submarine kept us moving forward.

## THE PRESIDENTIAL UNIT CITATION

Some months later, our ship was awarded **THE PRESIDENTIAL UNIT CITATION** for our accomplishments in the Arctic Ocean. THE PUC IS THE HIGHEST AWARD A SHIP CAN RECEIVE! (I was awarded an Admiral's Citation for my work.) When the P.U.C. pennant arrived, and I received it, I said the Executive Officer, "Captain Johnson was our Captain when we won this award. I would like to fly it the next time we go to sea, and then I would like to contact our Captain, go over to his house, and present it to him!" The XO concurred, and that is what I did—to the Captain's delight and appreciation.

## SHOCK OF THE CENTURY

[Digression] In Autumn of 1984—**SHOCK OF THE CENTURY!** Our submarine was headed out to sea for local operations. I went to our ship's mail distribution box. There was a letter for me. It had my name and address on the front of it. I turned the envelope over. It was from Mr. & Mrs. Stanley Worth of Carmel, California. Who? I opened the letter, my curiosity overcame my normal routine. I went straight to the letter writer's signature. And there was the Shock! It was from my former stepmother from the 1950's—**DARBY!** The one who mistreated me when I first moved in with my father. WOW! I had not seen nor heard from her for *29 years!* **You can understand why I was in shock.** So, I opened the letter and started reading. Synopsis: Darby had become an alcoholic and had joined Alcoholics Anonymous. She was following the 12th Step of making amends. She was apologizing for mistreating me! AND she was asking me to come back into her life!

How in the world did she find me??? Would you believe: Step One Darby and I are members of the same religious denomination. Step Two a minister who had served a church in Cincinnati and knew me, retired and moved back—to where? Monterey-Carmel—where Darby resided!! So, Darby approached him to help look for me. He found that I had lived in Cincinnati but had now reactivated in the Navy, and somehow, he obtained my Submarine address.

Well, when my submarine returned to port, and I was back in my apartment, I wrote her a long letter and included some photographs. Small shock—I didn't hear anything back!! I waited until the next Christmas and sent her a Christmas letter. Zippo! I got a letter right back: "Oh Thank God you wrote again! I had lost your address and was devastated." Darby and I began communicating, and deciding we would meet in person the following summer.

In March 1985, I made a special trip to Ashville, North Carolina to spend time with my mother, who was in St. Joseph Hospital recovering from several maladies and a broken hip. We visited for a couple days before I had to report back to my ship.

## USS BARRACUDA (SSN659) DEPARTS
## FOR THE INDIAN OCEAN

• • • • • • • • • • • • • • • • • • • • • • •

On April 1, 1985 at 2:00 P.M., the USS Barracuda (SSN 659) departed the Home Base, Squadron 8, Naval Operating Base, Norfolk, Virginia for the Indian Ocean. [We had been set to deploy to the Mediterranean, but the submarine that was supposed to be going on patrol in the Indian Ocean, "broke down." So, we were re-assigned. We headed south toward the tip of Africa. We steamed fairly close to the shore---between 20 and thirty miles out. BUT we had to be extremely careful because there are many stone pillars that rise up from the bottom of the ocean. To avoid them we had to sail underwater but near the surface. At most, our keel depth was 150 feet. After rounding the tip of Africa, we went up through the straits of Madagascar, and on into the Indian Ocean.

[Digression: over the years when my college students have made excuses that they did not HAVE TIME TO DO THEIR ASSIGNMENTS, I then tell them my story: We left port on April 1st, at 2:00 P.M. 27 days later, April 28th, at 4:00 P.M., I had my first ONE HOUR that was mine to do what I wanted. Before that I was working 16 to 18 hours a day!! So, it is hard to hear you say you did not have time!]

Our ship was assigned to work as an asset to a Task Group—an aircraft carrier—the USS Constellation (CV 64)—which is always surrounded with a host of support ships. We were assigned to a patrol GRID not far off of the coast of Somalia.

## *RED CROSS MESSAGE: COME HOME,*
## *YOUR MOTHER IS TERMINALLY ILL*

• • • • • • • • • • • • • • • • • • • • • •

It was on May 13, 1985 (my 45th BIRTHDAY—and the ship's bakers had made me a beautiful Birthday Cake! Thank You!) that I received the Red Cross Message: Come Home—your mother is terminally ill. A REPLACEMENT Captain and I arranged for me to take leave and go home. The Captain said I would be taken off the ship very early the next morning. He did not know yet whether I would be taken off by helicopter or small boat—but I should read up on both procedures.

## *THUS BEGINS MY WILD ADVENTURE AROUND THE*
## *WORLD TO BE WITH MY MOTHER—AND BACK*

• • • • • • • • • • • • • • • • • • • • • •

What I knew was that helicopter involvement with delivering personnel or retrieving personnel was very dangerous--too many things can go wrong, and the person is bashed into the side of the submarine. So, at midnight I was relieved from my "Chief of the Watch" duties and I went to bed.

At 5:00 A.M. the Surfacing Alarm Blew. Only a handful of men knew why. But after we surfaced everyone knew. While I was getting my things together, several young seamen came to the Chief's Quarters to see if there was anything they could do to help me! WOW! Thank you. And they did do errands.

Eventually I arrived in Crews Mess with my packed Sea bag and ready to depart. The Captain sent word that a Destroyer was 'Standing off on our Portside and was sending over a Whale Boat to pick me up. The plan was for the Crews Mess Hatch was to be opened for me to get on deck. So, at first one sailor tried to open the Hatch—without success. Then two guys with crowbars tried to open the hatch—without success. So, then the Captain changed the plan and I was to come up to the bridge and descend to the deck by a wooden and rope flexible "Jacob's Ladder." So, the Captain sent word for the Jacob's Ladder to be sent to the Bridge. There was a young seaman sitting next to me who said, "Master Chief, I don't believe that the Jacob's Ladder is on board. I think we left it at home in Norfolk in our garage." But the Captain did not yet have that information.

The captain got angry and rang the General Alarm for everyone to get up and "Find that God Damn Jacob's Ladder." Fortunately for me, the two, now three sailors with crowbars were able to open the hatch. So, I was able to arrive on deck with my full sea bag.

Sure enough, there was a Whale Boat waiting with one officer and three sailors on board. The ocean swells were in action: it was like trying to board a rogue elevator—first the floor is too high to climb up to; then it is too low to jump down to. Finally, I watched carefully until the boat was even with the sub, and I threw my sea bag over on to the boat. A few swells later when the floor once again was close to our height, I jumped over into the boat, and we were off. As the whale boat rounded the stern of our submarine and headed toward the Destroyer which was stopped and waiting on our Port side---about two hundred yards away, the swells and waves grew in height, and water splashed up and over the sides of our whale boat and on to us. Pretty soon we were all soaking wet from head to toe.

We arrived alongside the destroyer, which had its boat davits hanging down their starboard side waiting for us to connect. But once again, "the elevator" was out of control. One minute the whale boat was above the davit ropes, and then quickly below them. I was sitting toward the front of the boat; the davits had hooks on the ends of their ropes. Our boat had metal hinged "triangles with a large iron ring at the top. The concept was to get the Davit hook into that ring. All of a sudden, I observed the seaman in front of me thrust his arm and hand through the iron ring in an attempt to grab the swinging hook. I immediately screamed at the young sailor: **"Stop! Get your hand and arm out of that ring NOW!** (If he could have grasped the davit, the motion of the sea would have either pulled his arm off! Or else he would have suffered major damage. I turned to the young officer and said, "When is the last time your ship conducted a "Small Boat Transfer?" "We never have." OOOPPs!

Finally, we were hooked up and the ship pulled us up to the deck level and we got out—each soaking wet from head to toe. The ship's corpsman came running up to me and said, "I will take you down below and give you a complete physical exam!" I responded, "I'm FINE! It is my MOTHER who is ill!" The corpsman then asked me, "Didn't you fall over the side of the boat into the sea?" I responded, "Because I am all wet from head to toe? Look at the whole crew—we are all soaked head to toe."

Some of the ship's Chiefs escorted me down to the Chiefs' Quarters where I stripped off my wet clothes and put on dry clothes including a one-piece poopy suit." Someone in the Chiefs Quarters or maybe ship's service department, totally cleaned and dried my uniform. Eventually, I made my way back up to the ship's bridge. The Captain informed me that my helicopter would arrive over head in three hours. Okay. I ate a meal then waited. As it got close to the time, I wandered back up to the Bridge, and inquired: "What do you mean my helicopter will arrive 'overhead'"? The Captain answered: "Yes, it will hover over our front deck and lower a 'Horse Collar' device which will go under your arms. Now there is a big hook holding that collar; you will turn your whole head sideways as the helicopter is lifting you up into the helicopter." I said, **"Why do I have to turn my head?"** **"Because if**

**that big hook hits you, we want it to hit you on the side of the face rather than fully into your face!"** "Okay, I understand."

On time, the helicopter arrived overhead. They lowered the "Horse Collar." The Destroyer's sailors placed me into it; the helicopter crew hauled me up and pulled me inside. My first question was, **"Where are you taking me?" "We are taking you to an Aircraft Carrier,"** the USS Constellation (CV 64). Inside the helicopter, it was very hot and smelly and noisy. We flew with all of the doors wide-open. They gave to me headphones, both to be able to talk to the crew and to protect my ears from the noise.

We flew for well over an hour. I could not tell you how many miles we flew. I think we were going in a North Easterly direction. Finally, the Aircraft Carrier came in to view. But like some airports, the carrier did not have room on deck for us to land. So, we flew circles around the ship for maybe 20 minutes. Then we were brought down on deck. As I landed, a Navy Chief came to me and said, "Your plane will be leaving in about one hour." "Thank you." I looked around the flight deck, but I did not observe anything that resembled a passenger-type plane. I went below to the Chief's Quarters—which on an aircraft carrier—are huge.

### HOW WOULD YOU LIKE TO BE CATAPULTED OFF OF AN AIRCRAFT CARRIER?

● ● ● ● ● ● ● ● ● ● ● ● ● ● ● ● ● ● ● ● ●

I found an ice cream bar and made myself a Hot Fudge Sundae. Sure enough, as we approached the one hour, I was called back up to the Flight Deck. There was maybe a gathering of eight passengers, plus two Flight Deck sailors. Again, I looked around and did not see a passenger plane. The Carrier sailors started walking us across to the other side. As we approached the middle of the Flight Deck, an F-18 Tom Cat Fighter came directly toward us as he was preparing to take off. Our sailor escorts just stood still. The F 18 made a half turn to the right, and as he passed us, he looked out and smiled at us; then did a half turn to the left. As he did, his two big jet engines hit us with a full blast of his exhaust. I looked to our escorts. They took no notice. So, I assumed this was a routine event. I still did not see a passenger plane. Our escorts took us to the two "very large looking fighters." They were often called the "Whale" because they were originally designed to carry one large nuclear weapon. Their designation was A3D. **We were told somewhat in jest that A3D stood for "All Three Dead!" This was understandable because, the only way to enter the plane was through a hatch at the very bottom of the fuselage. So, if the plane crash landed on its belly, there was no way out! And you die!**

One of the escorts took four of us over to the first plane, and the other four went to the second plane. Inside there were only four passenger seats. I was in the back row. The aircrew man strapped us in: there was a "manifold" in the middle of our abdomen to which two straps coming up through our groin area attached, two more straps from over our shoulders, and two more from around our waist. **We were told we were going to be catapulted off the carrier. We would go from 0 mph to 100 mph in two seconds! So do not worry about breathing because you can't!**

The other plane was first to be placed on the catapult, so I could see the other plane flung into the air. Then it was our turn. There were two off duty pilots placed in front of me. As we were catapulted, the goggles on his helmet came flying back toward me but being on a bungy cord, they flew back (as in a cartoon.)

**Our flight from the Aircraft Carrier was in a South Easterly direction to Diego Garcia**—the American Base hosted by the "British

Indian Ocean Territory"---lasted at least six or seven hours. At one time in flight, the pilots of the two A3D's must have gotten bored because one plane flew with its right wing just three or four feet below the other plane's left wing. The pilots in front of me saw it and exclaimed, "What in the Hell are they doing?"

## MY FIRST EXPERIENCE WITH THE DIEGO GARCIA ATOLL
• • • • • • • • • • • • • • • • • • • • • •

Eventually as the sun was going down, we landed on Diego Garcia. I'm not sure I got anything to eat, but a taxi cab delivered me to an old deserted Quonset hut. I opened the door, turned on the light and saw sand all over the floor, and slime coming down from the front of the Air Conditioner. I was very tired. I plugged in the Air Conditioner... and it worked! So, I crawled into bed and went fast asleep.

The next morning, the taxi that came to pick me up, had not awakened me in time for breakfast. So, when I arrived at the "International Airport"—a very large Quonset hut—I looked around and saw that there was probably a snack bar on the opposite side of the Hut. In a short while the Filipino steward in charge, opened the metal rolling shutter. I got up and began walking toward the snack bar. I got half way across the floor and the electric generator quit, the lights went out, and the steward slammed the shutter closed. I went back to my seat. In maybe ten minutes, the generator started working, the lights came on, the steward raised the metal shutter. I got up and walked a little faster. I got to the middle of the room, the generator quit, the lights went out, and the Steward slammed the shutter closed. Damn.

In ten or so minutes, the generator started up, the lights went on, and the Stewart open the shutter. I practically ran to the Snack Bar. This time, the lights stayed on. I ordered a Bacon, Lettuce and

Tomato sandwich on toast and a cup of coffee. A man in green fatigues was standing next to me; he asked me what was going on with me. I explained that my mother was dying, and I was on a Humanitarian Evacuation (HUMEVAC). The man in green fatigues commented, "Well, we will have you off of the ground in about a half hour." And he walked away. I went back to my seat and ate my sandwich.

## THE LARGEST AIRPLANE I HAVE EVER SEEN; IT WAS AN AIRFORCE C5A WITH 32 WHEELS ON THE GROUND!

• • • • • • • • • • • • • • • • • • • • • •

In about 30 minutes our names were called, and they loaded us into a "School-Bus type bus" and drove us out onto the field. There set ***THE LARGEST AIRPLANE I HAVE EVER SEEN! IT WAS A C-5A WITH 32 WHEELS ON THE GROUND!*** I counted the wheels; I know there were 32. I was told the plane could carry two tanks at a time!! What? Wow!

We walked in line as we ascended the ladder into the belly of the plane. It was empty. I did not see any seats. So, I must have said out loud, "Oh, I see, we will stand all the way!" A young airman who was loading us, must have heard me, for he quickly said, "Oh no, Master Chief; do you see that ladder in the tail that leads up into the ceiling? Well, there are 75 seats up there." "Really?" So, I walked up the ladder and took a seat in the fourth row back. All of the seats faced rearward toward the tail. I have been told it is the safer way to sit in case the plane crashes. (My, that is comforting!) As we entered the seating area, we were each handed a box lunch. I was sitting eating, when that same guy in green fatigues came walking up the ladder escorting four Navy Captains and placing them in their seats. Then he quietly came over to me and whispered, "When you finish eating, I want you to go back down the ladder, walk to the front of the plane, and climb up that ladder."

I finished eating and followed his instructions. I arrived right up behind the pilots' Cockpit The man in green fatigues was Al Baker, the Flight Crew Chief. He introduced me to the young pilots (who could have passed for teenagers), explained their navigation equipment, **and Al asked if I would like a cup of coffee from the $6,000 coffee pot. Sure.** (Yes, it really was a $6000 coffee pot. The concept was, that if the plane crashed, they wanted the crew to have hot coffee to drink. (Really?) There were other such spending scandals happening in the military at that time.) Then Al Baker invited me to sit with him in the Comfortable Crew's Lounge with big over-stuffed chairs, and windows to look out of! Al said to me, **"Did you see those four Navy Captains I brought back to their seats? They wanted to sit up here; but I told them they had to be Admirals to sit up here. But Pat, you are a Master Chief, so you are welcome to enjoy the flight from up here!"** Okay! Wow! Thank You very much!

We sat beside each other and talked all the way from Diego Garcia to Clark Air Force Base in the Philippines. I do remember looking out the window as we were flying right over the top of the Malay Peninsula—Thailand, Singapore, and others. That was what seemed like an all-day trip because it was way past sunset when we landed at Clark. However, when one remembers that we were flying east while the sun was moving west it may not quite have been "all day long." It was very close to midnight when I sat down in the terminal; and I was told my flight would depart at 4:00 A.M., so just sitting for a few hours was the smart option.

## MY LAST CONVERSATION WITH MY MOTHER

• • • • • • • • • • • • • • • • • • • • •

Now there was a telephone booth in the corner of the waiting room; and I had a credit card. So, I walked over to see if I could telephone my mother. Yes, I could. I was able to reach Mother at St. Joseph's Hospital in Asheville NC. My mother had survived three different cancers: Cervix, Breast, and Throat. Mother had been a heavy smoker for years and years. So, it was no surprise when they had to operate on her throat, which left her with only a Whisper Voice. So, I did not want to try and engage her in a long conversation. I said something like, "Mom, I am coming home! I will be there soon to be with you!" And Mother responded, "Oh, that will be very nice." I did not know at that time, that that would be the last time I would ever be able to converse with my mother.

At Clark Air Force Base, I changed planes to I believe a C-141. It was a four-engine jet that could haul both passengers and cargo. There may have been thirty passengers at most. And there was a large jet engine on a wooden crate setting right in front of us. We were issued small yellow round sponges for our ears, because this was no luxury passenger plane; the noise was loud, and it was hard to get much sleep. The restroom was literally a form of Port-O-Potty We flew first to Guam, with an hour to shop at the store while the plane re-fueled; then on to Hickam Field in Hawaii, with an hour to shop while the plane refueled. And finally, to Travis Air Force Base.(Near Sacramento, California.) Then I was "on my own to travel across country."

[In the old days, in the 1970's, when a service person was HUMEVACed, THE Military Service provided door-to-door service. I know because I worked on the Admiral's Staff and participated in planning Humevacs.]

I telephoned Mother's Hospital Room from Travis; I got my sister Elizabeth Mitchell on the phone. I asked first, "How is Mother doing?" Liz: "Seems OK." Then I asked, "Do you mind if I take one more day, so I can travel down to Carlsbad, CA and spend a day with my daughter, Julia?" Liz responded, "One day would be OK, but I need to get back to Florida and take care of my family." That gave me the impression that Mother would stay alive some more. I flew down to Carlsbad; the family picked me up, and I enjoyed a wonderful 24 hours with Julia, and Jeannie, and Mel. Most comforting.

Then I caught a plane to Asheville, North Carolina. A family cousin, Charlie Johnson, a retired Presbyterian Minister, picked me up at the airport and drove me to St. Joseph Hospital. When I arrived at Mother's room, Liz was sitting there quietly, and Mother was in some form of coma. The nurse came in and shook Mother, saying, "Mrs. Mitchell, your son is here! Your son is here!" Mother opened one eye very briefly and said, "Yes, I know." And slipped back into the coma.

Cousin Rev. Charlie Johnson suggested that we all go back to his home and have dinner. It was a comfortable family meal with caring and support. After dinner, Charlie announced that he was going back to the hospital. An hour later, "Charlie called back to the house and said, "You had better get over here, now."

## MOTHER WAITED FOR ME TO ARRIVE HOME BEFORE SHE TOOK HER LAST BREATHS

• • • • • • • • • • • • • • • • • • • •

When we arrived, Mother had been moved from her regular room to the ICU and was now hooked up to all sorts of machines. The doctor asked us all to come with him into another room. Then he asked us, "Do you want us to do emergency Heroic measures to help keep her alive, such as put tubes into her lungs?" It was my decision to make; but we all voiced, "NO!" "She would not want that." The doctor then said, well, the end is near so let us go back to ICU. Liz took Mother's right hand, and I took her left hand; and we began saying, "Mom, we love you. You may go now, go in peace."

And within minutes the monitoring machines went FLAT LINE! Mother had taken her last breath. I could not let go. I just stood there crying and talking to her. It hurt me a lot. I held her hand until it was stone cold. Then we took our last look and drove home.

## THE COMFORTING ARMS OF FAMILY

• • • • • • • • • • • • • • • • • • • • • •

Liz asked me if I wanted her to stay with me. YES! Liz and I talked and cried all night long, telling stories and remembering some of the good times. We did not sleep a wink, but that was OK. I cannot think of a better way to be supported and comforted. It really helps to have a sister.

The next day, Liz and I moved down to Bat Cave cabin, and began sorting items for give away. There were mostly clothes that could be recycled to other people. Mark Mitchell III came down from Cincinnati, and Sally flew from Texas. I told my sisters and brother that mother had instructed me to be very generous and to tell my sisters and brother, that if there was anything, they wanted to remember Joy by, they were to take it. [When Father died in January 1984, he left the Contents of the House to Mother. So, now mother was willing to me "the contents of the house." So, it was mine to give away.] But only a few small items were claimed---a gold Broach from Spain, a Turquoise and silver Bracelet from New Mexico. I do not recall that Mark III wanted anything.

Mother had been cremated, so Liz and I drove over to the Funeral Home to claim this beautiful brass box with butterflies on it. In the lovely Episcopal Church, which the Mitchell family and Aunt Judith Colston had largely constructed using their money, we arranged for a Memorial Service for Mother.

[Time Digression]: After graduating college at Miami University, during the Depression, the first real job Mother could find was working in the Health and Welfare Department of Hamilton, Ohio. When Mother relocated to Albuquerque, and I was born, Mother went to work for the Health and Welfare Department. Years and years later, in August 1974, Father Mark and Mother Joy, decided to make the Bat Cave Cabin their year-round home. Once again, following her Health and Welfare knowledge and skill, Mom "adopted" all of the mountain country folk who lived right around the Mitchell Cabin on Route 9; if a mountain person received a letter from the "Govement" (Mountain Vernacular) Mother would put them into her car and drive right to that agency and become the spokesperson, so the Mountain person received everything they were entitled to. [Eventually the Buncombe County Department of Health and Welfare asked mother if she would go to work for them? Mother was honored and pleased but reminded them she was RETIRED.

Annabel Hudgins, aged in her mid-60's and only lately learned to read and write by babysitting her young niece in the first grade and observing her learning her letters,--Anabel was entitled to a new indoor bathroom! Which was installed! She utilized all of the other fixtures except the bathtub. Annabelle had never used a bathtub in her life, so was not going to do so now. She stored her canned food in the bathtub! I do want to comment, that when Mother sent me down to Annabelle's tar-paper shack to retrieve her grocery list, I often had to sit there while Annabel with great concentration produced some of the best cursive words you have ever seen! And Annabel Hudgins was downright proud of her new learned skill. [When Annabel's husband, Clan was alive, he purposely kept Annabel from learning to read and write.]

## "SAINT JOY OF THE MOUNTAINS"

• • • • • • • • • • • • • • • • • • • • • •

So, the Episcopal Nuns observed mother's welfare activities, so they gave her the name of "***SAINT JOY OF THE MOUNTAINS***". And that name stuck and had wide circulation in the Bat Cave--Chimney Rock neighborhoods.

We organized a Memorial Service for mother at the Episcopal Church of the Transfiguration (A church that both Sally C. Mitchell and her sister, Judith Braxton Colston had contributed the major amount of money to build the church.) Mother had been extremely popular and respected in the Bat Cave area. There was "Standing Room only!"

Again, because Mother had been cremated, the next day after the service, Liz and I performed a ceremony. Mother had not wanted to ever leave "her view of the mountains." And, since mother was very fond of her Scotch Whiskey Drinks, we unscrewed the bottom of the Cremains Container, spooned out some of the ashes, inserted small bottle of Scotch and screwed it back together. We had spooned the ashes into the wine holder : "A Day Without Wine is Like a Day Without Sun Shine." Liz and I walked around to strategic points overlooking the mountains spooning out some of the cremains, and we told mother that, "She was never going to leave her beautiful view."

Then Liz and I drove to Cincinnati and held a Memorial Service there at St John's UU Church for all the local friends and relatives. Next day, Liz and I buried mother between her mother and father in Greenwood Cemetery in Hamilton, Ohio where she had been born and raised. And we put a beautiful large white Lily on the Cremains.

It was time for me to report back to the Navy. I flew back to Travis Air Force Base. I boarded a Boeing 747 that was headed for Korea, so

I got off in Hawaii and boarded an Air Force Plane—back to Guam, back to the Philippines, back to Diego Garcia.

I was the last person off of the plane. The young sailor sent to greet us said to me, "You are off of the USS Barracuda, aren't you?" "Yes." "Well, yesterday, your submarine started into the channel past buoys One and Two; then President Reagan sent them a ***FLASH MESSAGE"*** ( THE HIGHEST PRIORITY) to get back up to the Iran-Iraq War. So, the submarine turned around in the channel and at flank speed went back to the war. You are stranded!" Oh, yes! Would you believe with all those plane changes, the airlines lost my luggage?

*STRANDED FOR EIGHT DAYS WITHOUT
LUGGAGE ON THE ATOLL OF DIEGO GARCIA.
IT WAS A BLESSING IN DISGUISE*

● ● ● ● ● ● ● ● ● ● ● ● ● ● ● ● ● ● ● ● ●

Hmmm, that is not all bad. I was given a nice room in the Chiefs' Barracks. My lost luggage included my check book. So, I took notebook paper and filled out all the necessary information, and I mailed these to my creditors! Well, I had heard that someone had done the same thing during WWII, only with a coconut shell, and it worked! In my case, two of the three creditors cashed "my notebook paper" and got their money. One did not.

Now, with no luggage, and therefore no change of clothing, I got permission from the "Mustang" Lieutenant Commander who was in charge of all Navy "Visitors" to the island...or Atoll, to wear a mixture of uniform and civilian clothes.

## *MY DAILY ROUTINE OF HEALING*

• • • • • • • • • • • • • • • • • • • • • • •

As I was a Master Chief, the Chief in Charge (who had previously spent three years being in charge of the seven chow halls in Antarctica; his Supply Base was in New Zealand—the closest land to Antarctica) of the base's chow hall at Diego Garcia and he gave me a pass to eat anytime I wanted to. Thank you. I started getting up at 4:30 A.M. and eating "First Breakfast" with the Radiomen who had to be on duty by 6:00 A.M. When I finished breakfast, I walked over to the Officer's Club—because there was a folding chair leaning up against the wall. I took the chair to the beach, such that I could face east. It was totally still night—dark when I sat down. I really needed an opportunity, a quiet opportunity, a nature-related opportunity to reflect upon my loss of my mother; to be open to all my feelings and thoughts. This was an outstanding time. After many minutes, the sky, one minute at a time, was absorbing the fore-runner rays of the SUN. Gradually, gradually I could begin to make out the objects on the beach. And some of those objects MOVED! I observed. And gradually I understood that the shells that were moving each had a Hermit Crab inside (except I do not believe the animal inside is a true crab.) And I understood that another species of crabs on the beach were "Ghost Crabs." You could only tell there was a crab nearby when it moved. Its body was almost transparent, and you thought you could see right through its body.

There were two more species of crabs only a few yards away. There were Coconut Palms within yards of the beach. Coconut Palms are a mixture of greens and browns in color. And once one looked very closely, there were crabs around the trees which "were painted to match!" Yes, their shells were a similar mixture of greens and browns. Behind the Coconut Palms there was dark reddish-brown soil; with the rains, there were shallow puddles. And in and around the puddles were large reddish-brown crabs!

I sat on that chair until the sun had fully risen several diameters high into the sky. Then, I got up, walked to my barracks, took a shower, got cleaned up for the day, and started walking down the road. For eight mornings I participated in my early morning ritual. This was an incredible, peaceful place, to reflect on Mother's passing. And for eight mornings I returned to my barracks room and cleaned up for the day. In the early days of my stay, I kept reporting in to Mustang Lieutenant Commander. One morning the Mustang LCDR said to me, "Master Chief, have you noticed we are on an island?" "Yes, sir." "In that case do not call us, we will call you!" "Okay."

## B.I.O.T BRITISH INDIAN OCEAN TERRITORY THE ATOLL OF DIEGO GARCIA. I MAKE THE AQUAITANCE OF THE BRITISH COMMODORE

• • • • • • • • • • • • • • • • • • • • • •

Diego Garcia was a "horse-shoe-shaped" atoll. It was 32 miles from point to point. The radio transmitting-receiving station was at the top of the loop—probably at least 10 miles from our Navy Installation. And I was walking toward the radio station. And every morning as I was walking, a bus with a Filipino bus driver, would stop and ask me to ride and talk with him, which I did.

## THE COMMODORE AND I ENGAGE IN DISCUSSIONS OF THE ATOLL'S HISTORY

• • • • • • • • • • • • • • • • • • • • •

[Time Digression.] Diego Garcia was "discovered" by the Portuguese in the mid 1500's. The name comes from the Navigator's brother. During the Napoleonic Wars, the French took possession of the Atoll. The atoll, when I was there, appeared to have 1,000,000 coconut palm trees (give or take a few thousand trees). Perhaps the French purposely planted many of them. Anyway, there had been a Copra processing plant on the far side or Western part of the Atoll. And perhaps the French were the ones who imported the Mauritians from Islands close to the coast of Africa. The Mauritians had a 300-year history of living on the Atoll.

I am guessing the British took over the Atoll when Napoleon was defeated. Anyway, for over a hundred years it has been "***The British Indian Ocean Territory,*** or B.I.O.T. (which geographically is 7 ½ degrees below the Equator and is the last parcel of land above water in the Chagas Archipelago. From north to south start with the subcontinent of India, then Sri Lanka (old name Ceylon), the Maldives' Islands,(2000 islands = 115 square miles), the Laccadive Islands and Coral Reefs, then a long strand of the Chagas Archipelago.

For many decades—maybe since 1898 when the Spanish lost the ***Spanish-American War*** and the United States took possession of several of the Spanish possession such as the Philippine Islands, the United States developed at least two major American Military Bases—one SUBIC BAY for the Navy, and Clark Airforce Base for the Airforce. The Philippines got its freedom from the United States in 1948; but allowed the Americans to stay. In the late 1960's, very early 1970's, the political winds changed, and the Philippines requested the United States to give back the bases. So, the United States went looking for another base location in the Indian Ocean. They talked to the British, and in 1972, the British allowed the Americans to build a base on Diego Garcia. The British then required both the French and the Mauritians to vacate the Atoll. Therefore, the Copra Plantation was abandoned; and the Mauritians—who have never lived on their ancestral island (Mauritius--a few hundred miles East of Madagascar, 750 square miles), were forced to emigrate. Diego Garcia is composed of volcanic stone—very hard. So, when a Mauritian died, they were covered with a few rocks. These graves were exhumed, and the bodies taken with the emigrants. [End Time Digression.]

Again, I had made the acquaintance of the British Commodore, who was in charge of the Atoll. He and his men enforced the traffic regulations on the island. For example, the top Speed Limit was **TWENTY-FIVE MILES PER HOUR!** AND not 26 OR HIGHER! I was often the Van driver, partially because I was now in charge off setting up the daily Beer-Baseball Game. Also, it was against regulations to harm any of the animal life on the Atoll; for example, there were cats, dogs, chickens, donkeys roaming around. The animals always had **THE RIGHT-OF-WAY!** The Commodore and I had pleasant discussions about the history of the island.

There were minimal recreation facilities available: There was a Bowling Alley, Several Ball Parks for Beer-Baseball Games, a swimming pool; I am not sure if there was a movie theatre, but I will guess yes.

However, once construction began on the American leased base, the British Government brought back to the Atoll, Mauritians who were skilled in the construction trade, to do most all, if not all, construction on the Atoll. I saw them at work, but I had no occasion to speak with them, so I really do not know their work agreements.

## I MAKE FRIENDS WITH THE FILIPINO WORKERS

• • • • • • • • • • • • • • • • • • • • •

At the same time, the British Government hired Filipino workers to come to the Atoll and provide all the "Service" work such as running the dining halls, do the truck and bus driving. (Especially for the Naval personnel who operated the Radio Station some 12 to 15 miles north of the regular base. I ate in the Officers' Dining Room frequently (the Chiefs' Club and dining room was under massive reconstruction.) I did get to know several of the dining room staff and the bus drivers. I learned that each person was on a twelve-month contract. And then they were permitted to go home to the Philippines for 30 days; if that person's work had been satisfactory, then that person was allowed to return for another 12 months. Several of the waiters explained to me that there were NO good paying jobs available in the Philippines in order to support their families, so the workers had little choice but to travel 1200 miles away, and not see their families. Some of the Philippine workers came to me and asked if there were any chores they might do for me such as mend clothing, shine shoes, or whatever, in order to earn some additional money.

Okay, that discussion was from the future... Now I am returning to May 1985, when I had just returned to Diego Garcia, with lost luggage. And I had received permission to wear a mixed Navy-Civilian outfit.

Also, within the early days, I heard about a Recreational Trip over to the Copra Plantation. So, I found that the "Medical Group" was planning such an outing. So, I joined with them and had a wonderful time snorkeling and picnicking. Very refreshing!

Came Sunday. There was one church on the Atoll. The Catholics held services at 9:00 A.M. and everyone else who wanted to, came to Church at 11:00 A.M. Then, those who wanted to, went to lunch together. I found out that the attenders came from a variety of different religions. The Head of the Red Cross, for example was a Unitarian. She was also heading up a melodrama play—"You must pay the rent" "I can't pay the rent." She was hoping I could stay around and play a role.

## DELTA FORCE IN THE LAGOON

• • • • • • • • • • • • • • • • • • • • • • •

These were the days when the United States needed a "Delta Force" stationed at Diego Garcia. This meant there were 10 plus ships anchored in the lagoon. These ships contained everything for conducting a war: Food, water, fuel, construction equipment, tanks, jeeps, and other necessary supplies and equipment. The ships, in effect were anchored and stationary in that they almost never got underway. So, some of the Officers off of these ships came to Church, had lunch with us afterward, and would invite me to come out and tour their ships, which I was glad to do.

## MY JOURNEY BACK TO THE USS BARRACUDA

• • • • • • • • • • • • • • • • • • • • • •

One morning I reported in to the Lieutenant Commander, I said, "I am a highly paid sailor, surely there must be some ship that can use my services." He responded, "Funny that you should ask—we were just going to call you! We are flying you over to the country of Oman [Which is adjacent to the country of YEMEN] , and from there back to your submarine." So, I said, "That is great! Now, our crew has been under water for 60 plus days. The men would sure appreciate receiving their personal mail." The LCDR agreed and called in the Mail Orderly and said "Go through all of the USS Barracuda mail bags and take out only the personal mail—none of the Official Mail. This developed into me taking custody of two huge mail sacks—at least three feet high!

## *OKAY, NOW WHERE? OMAN? USS CAMDEN (AOE2)*

• • • • • • • • • • • • • • • • • • • • • •

Within a few hours, I was flying to Oman—which is the eastern neighbor of YEMEN. As we landed, it looked like a Hollywood set with high sand dunes, and camels walking by on their own. Everything written was in Arabic including the soda pop cans! And it was hot—somewhere close to 100 degrees.

Two civilian men approached me and said, "You are off of the Barracuda?!" "Yes." "Good! We are on our way to the Barracuda to conduct a surprise inspection and we need an insider to partner with us." "Okay."

In a little while, a very large "Sea King" helicopter arrived and landed. There were many passengers as we were flying first to the USS Camden (AOE 2) which was a huge—big as a Battle Ship—Resupply Vessel.

We three men were given our own stateroom. Very nice. We were three days on board before it rendezvoused with the USS Barracuda. I spent much of my time up on the Bridge observing operations. We could refuel two ships at the same time! For example, there might be an Aircraft Carrier on our Port side, and a Destroyer on our Starboard side. ***TALK ABOUT SOME EXCEDINGLY DIFFICULT SHIP HANDLNG*** by all three ships! They could refuel 24 hours a day. At night time they would attach those chemical plastic lights—that come in colors-attached to the lines and hoses, so everyone could see where each was.

During the day, there was some comic relief: First, whenever we were actually refueling a ship, the Captain commanded that the music ***BABY ELEPHANT WALK BE PLAYED OVER ALL OF THE SHIP'S LOUD SPEAKERS.*** And second, when we were refueling smaller ships in the daytime, an officer--"Fast Eddie" would have himself high-lined over to the other ship and with a spray bottle and squeegee and wipers, he would proceed to wash the front windows of that ship! (I actually was able to have dinner with him back on Diego Garcia. He was a "Jolly Good Fellow!")

When I observed the Quartermaster Navigation gang, I felt like crying: They had twice as many quartermasters to do half as much work as we did; for example, the Chief Quartermaster ONLY STOOD Junior Officer of the Deck. The First-Class Quartermasters only shot stars and sunlines; the Second-class quartermasters did the actual navigating with charts, Loran, etc. The Third-Class Quartermasters ONLY TOOK NOTES IN THE Quartermaster's Notebook—speed and course changes, and other items needed for court documentation; the other Third-Class Quartermaster only worked in the "Chart Room correcting charts and publications." I really was upset. For the first time in my Navy Life, I wish I had left submarines and gone to surface ships. On our sub, *we were always behind.* In those days, submarine quartermasters "Non-Volunteered" meaning they no longer wished to serve on submarines; some QMs' were able to go to Officer Candidate School, some QMs simply got out of the Service. Beyond my first months on board—when I had Second Class-- David S. to assist me, I virtually had no one QM that I could count on for competent help. The result was, I had to do all of my work, but then do a large portion of their work; I literally was working 16 hours a day.

## *SO, WHAT DO SUBMARINERS EAT?*

• • • • • • • • • • • • • • • • • • • • •

One afternoon at meal time, I sat with the Chief in charge of the meals on the USS CAMDEN (AOE-2). He asked me, "What do you submariners eat?" I replied "Well, it is either canned or frozen." He then asked, "Don't you guys have any fresh vegetables or fruits?" "No, because we have been gone from our port for 60 days, and we do not have a garden on board." The Chief then said, "Master Chief, I am going to 'hook you up' with thirteen cases of fresh fruits and vegetables!" Wow! Thank you.

## RENDEZVOUSING WITH THE USS BARRACUDA; BACK TO DIEGO GARCIA

• • • • • • • • • • • • • • • • • • • • • • •

The next day, we rendezvoused with the Barracuda. And just to get me, the two three foot tall sacks of mail, the thirteen crates of fresh fruits and vegetables, it took two "Zodiac Boat" (rubber inflatable boat) trips to accommodate my things, and the two "Mysterious inspectors." [It took until a ship's reunion some years later before the crew learned that I had orchestrated those gifts.]

We continued our Task Force Assignments. We were operating as part of an Aircraft Carrier Task Force. After a month or so, we completed our assignment, and were "Released" to head into port at Diego Garcia.

## I CAN'T GET AN ACCURATE FIX!

• • • • • • • • • • • • • • • • • • • • • •

As we were entering the short channel, my Navigator started hollering. "What is wrong, sir?" "I can't get a god damn pin point fix!" "Well, I am shooting the prominent landmarks for a bearing." "It is not you, Master Chief; it is this chart! Nothing seems to be where the chart shows. Master Chief, you know how to take a sextant and hold it sideways and measure angles?" "Yes, I do." "Tomorrow, you take the sextant and the ship's truck, drive around the Atoll and ***find where*** *these objects actually are!" "Yes, sir!"*

So, the next day, I did take the sextant, some note paper, the ship's loaned truck, and I did drive around shooting distance angles. I made the assumption that the Water Tower was where the chart showed it, because THE TOWER HAD BEEN THERE 30 YEARS!

So, I climbed up on ladders, I climbed up on the roofs of buildings, and I shot angles. I came back to the ship, got out a new copy of the chart, laid down my new bearings, and yes—most of the newly built tanks, towers, and piers were not exactly where the chart indicated. In a day or two we had the opportunity to go out to sea on some exercise, and then return to port: Pin Point, pin point, pin point. My new chart worked like a charm. So, then I took out another copy of the harbor chart, added the locations of tanks, towers, and piers, and took it down to *the Harbor Master. I said, "Would you like to know where these landmarks used for navigation, actually are?" "Yes." The Commodore later thanked me for my work.*

Days before our arrival in Diego Garcia, I had been telling the Captain, what a great place the Copra Plantation was for recreation. So, when we arrived in port, I went to the office that schedules such trips. However, the Chief in Charge said, "NO! No one is going over to the Copra Plantation. The Commodore is angry because no one obeys his rules—building fires, leaving trash on the ground, and FEEDING THE DONKEY BEER!~ So he has locked the gates. No one goes over!"

*WRONG ANSWER!*

• • • • • • • • • • • • • • • • • • • • •

Well, I turned around and headed straight for the Commodore's Office. "Knock, knock!" "Come in, Master Chief." "Sir, I have been telling our crew what a wonderful experience it is to have recreation at the Copra Plantation." "No. It is locked shut! No one obeys my rules!" Then I spoke up and said, "Sir, what if I take personal responsibility; we will take three enormous trash bags, police the area, clean it up; we will not build any fires, and we will not feed the donkey beer (which was an alcoholic animal with his abdomen almost dragging the ground—a real beer belly.) The Commodore walked over to the window, rubbed his chin, and said, "I know your crew has been underwater for 60 days; I would like to do something nice for them. **"Master Chief, if you will take personal responsibility, I will open the gates." "Thank you, sir."** I went back to the boat and told the Captain what the requirements were. And we did go over to the Copra Plantation and had a wonderful time; and followed all of the Commodore's/ my instructions.

Since I had spent eight days by myself on the Atoll, the Captain assumed I knew my way around the recreation facilities, so he put me in charge of organizing daily Beer-Ball Games. Which I did.

[Time Digression]: once I returned to the USS Barracuda, and we pulled into port at Diego Garcia, all of us chiefs went over to the Chief's Club to have a drink. Now this was under primitive circumstances: The Bar, literally, was a broad board laying across two barrels! There was a bar tender behind with access to the alcohol, ice, and glasses. So, after a few drinks, we decided it was time to eat dinner and we headed a few hundred yards over to the Officers' Club dining room. I was walking toward the back of the group. **The Maître's Dee** started to walk us back to a back room for dining. Then he spotted me and said, "Oh, it is you, Master Chief!" and he promptly turned the group around and we headed toward the best table in the house—right next to the big picture window! [End Digression]

## MY TWO-YEAR CONTRACT WAS EXPIRING

● ● ● ● ● ● ● ● ● ● ● ● ● ● ● ● ● ● ● ● ● ●

My two-year contract with the Navy was coming to an end. So, I was departing from the USS Barracuda here in Diego Garcia. After the ship departed, the P3 Orion's (Anti-submarine warfare planes specially outfitted for identifying and attacking submarines under water, were going to engage in some warfare exercises with the Barracuda.) The First-Class Engineman who was also departing and I got permission to fly with the Orion crew, and we did. It was a very long day. The exercise called for dropping lines of sonobuoys on each side of Barracuda's track and listening to see if we could detect him. I had ear phones on so I could hear all of the conversations. Yes, we could detect and hear the submarine passing by. It sounded like a Freight Train passing by. I requested that the Plane captain notify the sub that they were very noisy.

We flew into the night. And all of a sudden, the aircraft windshield lit up with **"Saint Elmo's Fire"**—electrical charges that scampered all of the windshield. I have not seen it before nor since. But it was exciting to watch.

As we landed back on Diego Garcia, the first order of business was to "Go through the ***BIRD BATH"* What?** Would you believe it was a total wash down of the entire plane! When planes fly low over the ocean, they pick up salt and other chemicals all over the hull. But the showers wash them clean.

## THE COMMODORE GIVES ME A GREAT SEND-OFF

● ● ● ● ● ● ● ● ● ● ● ● ● ● ● ● ● ● ● ● ● ●

The next evening, I was standing in line, waiting my turn to be loaded onto a bus and taken to my plane. The line was not moving yet. The front doors opened and who walks in, but the Commodore and a guest. He spotted me in line and came quickly over to shake my hand and tell me he was glad I had come to visit Diego Garcia, and he was sorry to see me leaving. "Thank you very much sir; it was my honor." I meant that; the Commodore was the highlight of my visits to Diego Garcia.

We boarded the plane—some kind of four engine combination of passengers and cargo charter flight. I say it that way, because a few months later, one of this company's planes crashed and burned. (Was it this one?)

This must have been a Tuesday, Thursday, or Saturday flight because it was heading west to Egypt, Italy, Ireland, and the United States. If it had been Monday, Wednesday, or Friday Flight, it would have headed east to the Philippines etc. and then the U.S.

My flight brought me to Norfolk, Virginia. And in less than week, I was released to go back to Cincinnati.

## *OKAY? SO, WHO AM I NOW?*

• • • • • • • • • • • • • • • • • • • •

Okay, who am I now? And what am I going to do with myself. I had done a job interview back to my old school-Sands Montessori School, but as I later found out, the person who interviewed me was not the person doing the hiring. So, no job. I decided that if I had a First Grade through Eighth Grade Teaching Certificate, I would have an easier time finding job. I went to the University of Cincinnati, Department of Teacher Education and asked what I would need to do to obtain the 1st thru 8th certificate. Dr. Al Ciani advised me to take these three courses, and then I could add them to my certificate. I went and registered for those three courses, and then I went to the Veterans Administration Office on campus and requested that they pay for my three courses. They said No. I said yes. They said no. I said why won't you pay—you used to? They said, yes, in the past we did, but the rules have changed, and one must be in a "Degree Granting Program in order for us to pay." Oh! So, I went back to Dr. Ciani and told him I need to be enrolled in a Degree Program. Dr. Ciani replied, you will have to speak to Dr. Linda Amspaugh, the Assistant Chair of our Department. She is not here today, but you can call her on Monday. Thank you.

## MY "FAIRY GOD-MOTHER" COMES TO MY RESCUE: PATRIC OPTS FOR GETTING ANOTHER GRADUATE DEGREE

• • • • • • • • • • • • • • • • • • • • • •

Monday morning. Ring, ring. Hello Linda, it is Patric Leedom here! I need to be enrolled in a degree granting program. "Oh my gosh, Patric, not ten minutes ago the Chair, David Naylor, instructed me to find a graduate student to work in our Department. Pat, could I interest you in being that person?" "Yes, I would be glad to do it." "Okay. We will sign your admission papers and you can fill them in later!" "Thank you, Linda."

[I had known Linda Amspaugh for 20 years, as a member of our church]

Initially, I signed up to go into the **MASTERS IN READING DEGREE.** And in the Fall, I signed up for all reading courses. [Linda A. and I are still friends in 2022.]

Now "A funny thing happened on my way to a graduate degree." I was 45 years old and about the average age of the faculty. So, the

Department of Curriculum and Instruction started giving me faculty-like assignments. My very first quarter, I was made Chair of a Faculty Committee to organize a Conference for 500 area teachers to come to a Program on Language and Literature. And I did it. I even went to the custodians and asked if they could please shine the brass railings in the stairwell. They did it. Faculty started remarking that they had no idea those bars were brass. I wrote the Custodians a Letter of Commendation.

## PATRIC COMMENCES A DOCTORATE

• • • • • • • • • • • • • • • • • • • • • •

**Later on, that Quarter, Linda Amspaugh suggested that I stay and do a Doctorate.** I said I would really have to think about that one. I had started one at Northwestern University in Evanston, Illinois, but it was the wrong time for me. But I went around our Department consulting with faculty members, and I consulted with several graduate students in our department. Finally, I decided that a doctorate was "do-able." So, I signed up.

Doctoral Degree. I enrolled at the University of Cincinnati Department of Curriculum and Instruction in September 1985. I was living on Bishop Street adjacent to campus in one of the large apartment complexes with 20 units. It was easy to walk to campus and walk back home. The walls were paper thin, and the floors were "cardboard" thin. So occasionally we had to communicate with neighbors to quiet it down.

I was very fortunate with the Military GI Bill for schooling. I had been released from Active duty in June 1967, so that gave me a ten year "Window" to obtain advanced degrees. I had started my master's degree in Montessori at Xavier University in the fall of 1972. I graduated with my Masters in May 1976. The "Window " closed on my GI Bill although I still had around three years of support on the books.

It was 1985 when I began the Doctorate, and magically the GI Bill "Window" opened once again; however, for some strange reason, my 36 months on the books turned into 49 months!! I do not recall the actual monthly payment but somewhere around $500 a month. So, I was able to scrape by. And as I earlier described, I took a part time job consulting with the U.S. Shoe Company for four years. And **I also took on another part-time job Playing "Vanna White" on the stage for the Fernald Nuclear Processing Plant**. National Lead Corporation had administered the Plant on behalf of the Department of Defense. But in 1987, the government decided there were problems—for one instance the training of Project Engineers was way behind. So D.O.D. hired Westinghouse to take over the Administration and to expeditiously bring the training up to date. I was hired by Barnwell Engineering Company to present the new required forms, and to explain to the audience of Project Engineers how to fill out each line. This was a year-long process. I was invited to join Barnwell Engineering Co. full time as they serviced all the other uranium plants in the United States, But I declined—my heart was in education of teachers.

It was officially a Doctorate in Curriculum and Instruction, but Dr. Howard Johnston was just starting up a strand of Corporate Training and Development and asked me if I was interested. Yes. So, I took courses in that field as well as teacher education.

+ + + + + +

I had taken my daughter, Julia, on a car trip around the United States every summer for fifteen years. On one summer, I would drive to Solana Beach, Julia's home, pick her up and drive all around the U. S. "The West Coast Circuit" –seven times. Up U.S. 395 to Reno, then across Nevada to Idaho (Craters of the Moon),to Wyoming (Yellowstone National Park—always based in the Old Faithful area. We were there in August 1974 when President Richard Nixon resigned;

there was only one TV in that local, and we all squeezed to view it). On to Nebraska (Recreation of Buffalo Bill's Wild West Show and Congress of World Riders.) Julia and I worked our way south to New Mexico, to Arizona (Grand Canyon.) and home to California. On opposite summers Julia would fly to Cincinnati, and we would do the "East Coast Circuit"—we had done it eight times. From Cincinnati we would drive to Florida, Orlando, to my sister Elizabeth and family (and usually went to Disney World.) And from Orlando we drove to Fort Augustine (Originally built by the French, but when the Spanish Galleons full of gold started sailing by, the Spanish could not tolerate having enemy in Fort Augustine so the Spanish massacred them and took over.) the oldest recorded settlement in the United States. From there we drove to my mother's in Bat Cave, North Carolina for a week. From there to Washington D.C. to the Smithsonian for three days. [In 1976 for the Bicentennial we made a special stop in Philadelphia to see the Relics of the American Revolution. It was at that point Julia said to me, "Gee, Dad, this is a wonderful trip, BUT I have never heard of any of these persons for the Revolution." Me: "Kid, haven't you ever studied American History?" "Yes, Dad." "Well, what did you study?" "The Twentieth Century!" It was on another trip on the East Coast when Julia's friend Beth, a year older than Julia, joined us and was just learning to drive. So, every day I supervised Beth driving the car. Anyway, for years I, we had been stopping at my sister's in Florida, and for a visit, and for years my sister begged me to take her much younger daughter, Christina along. And for years I declined.

## PATRIC IS HIRED TO TAKE TWO TEENAGE GIRLS FOR A 27 DAY ADVENTURE AROUND THE WESTERN UNITED STATES

• • • • • • • • • • • • • • • • • • • • • • •

Well, the day came when Julia-the active teenager--no longer wanted to travel with me. That is the summer my sister Elizabeth said, "Now will you take my daughter around the United States and I will pay you?" And I agreed. I had just met a family in Cincinnati who had a thirteen-year-old daughter, Sara. When they heard I was driving Christina around the United States, they said, "Well, take our daughter Sara too! And we will pay you." "Okay!"

Okay, so for 27 days, I drove two teenage girls around the United States!! That is not totally true. Christina had just obtained her driver's license and my sister wanted me to instruct Christina a lot during our trip. [I actually was or still am a Professional Driver with a Chauffer's License; I had already driven across the United States multiple time— more than 30 times.]

We drove from Ohio to Indiana, Illinois, Wisconsin, Minnesota, South Dakota (Visiting both Mt. Rushmore and Crazy Horse), Wyoming (Visiting Yellowstone National Park), Nevada, California, Arizona (Visiting the Grand Canyon), New Mexico, Texas, --where we visited my stepsister Sally, on her horse ranch—leaving Christina with her aunt—and I drove Sara on to Arkansas Tennessee, Kentucky, to Ohio. As I drove up to Sara's house, her mother said to me, "Boy, I'll bet you are glad this trip is over!" "I said NO, not really. I had to come back to go to school."

In 27 days, we only had ONE argument: we had just checked in to the Old Faithful Inn in Yellowstone. The girls said they wanted to visit the Gift Shops. I said okay BUT we have dinner reservations downstairs at 6:00 P.M. Meet me by the big stone fireplace clock at 6:00. Well, I am standing down there at the clock at 6:00 P.M. and no girls…finally at 6:15 they arrived. We had an instant discussion that in the future, I could not afford to let them go by themselves IF they could not watch the time. That was it. Absolutely no problems after that.

OH YES—many minutes ago there was a reason I took the girls on a trip around the country. When we left San Francisco—and my daughter Julia had flown up from Solana Beach and joined us—we drove down to Monterey to one of their famous museums.

## DARBY AND I RECONNECT AS STEP-MOTHER AND STEP-SON

• • • • • • • • • • • • • • • • • • • • • •

Darby and I had arranged that I, we, meet her at the museum where she was a docent. Imagine—meeting someone again after 29 years!! We hugged and visited for 45 minutes or so. Darby invited me to her home in Carmel Valley for Christmas, and I agreed. Then the girls and I continued our summer trip, but at Christmas I bonded back with Darby, and with her mother also a Julia, who looked across the table and said, "Pat, you are my only grandson!"

[Historical Digression] As of this total re-bonding between Darby and I, we became very close, with biannual visits, alternating summers, and alternating Christmases for the next 35 years. We really loved and cared for each other, and the relationship provided a wonderful beautiful strand to my life.

In January 2017, Darby telephoned me in Cincinnati and requested that I fly out to California and be with her as she passed away at age 93. I will be forever grateful that I did.

+ + + + + + + + +

## *JUST ONE MORE NAVY ACTDUTRA EXPERIENCE*

• • • • • • • • • • • • • • • • • • • • • •

It was now the summer of 1986. I was three months away from retirement from the United States Navy Submarine Force. I called the Reserve Detailer in Washington D.C. and requested to do one more two-week Active Duty for Training. They said they would look around. A few weeks later they called me with orders to the Reserve Minesweeper Squadron, at the Naval Base in Charleston, South Carolina. Hooray! When I arrived at the Reserve Minesweeper Squadron, they really didn't have much work for me to do. So, I telephoned the Commodore's Office of the whole squadron, announced who I was, and said I would be glad to go to sea on any minesweeper that might need my services.

On Friday, they called me with orders to conduct a Navigational Operational Inspection on one of the minesweepers already at sea. I would be joining a Lieutenant Commander at 6:00 A.M. Saturday morning and a small boat would pick the two of us up at the pier. We boarded the minesweeper, returned back out to sea, and began conducting exercises. I was stationed in the Combat Information Center (CIC). My focus was Reduced Visibility Navigation.

As the day concluded, my LCDR companion and I were in the ship's Wardroom beginning to assemble our notes. The Captain of the ship walked in. I spoke up and said, "Captain, you have three major problems with the Reduced Visibility Navigation operations. Here is Problem 1, Problem 2, and Problem 3. Now, here is Solution 1, Solution 2, and Solution 3." The Captain thanked me very much; my partner and I returned to port Saturday night.

On Monday morning, the Commodore himself telephoned me and said, "I understand that you know a lot about Reduced Visibility Navigation. I would like you to go aboard all of my minesweepers and conduct training on Reduced Visibility Navigation." "Aye, aye, Sir. Please give me a day to generate a Lesson Plan and I will be glad to assist you."

The next day I went over to the Submarine Base and borrowed one of their Navigation Operational Procedures. Discussion. Navigation is not a real high priority in the Surface Fleet, so their NAVOPORD is only ten pages long. The Submarine NAVOPORD is One hundred and ten pages long! Definition: Reduced Visibility Navigation is anytime a ship is unable to see more than a thousand yards or so ahead. This could be fog, dust, snow storm or other such situations. I wrote up a Lesson Plan detailing various methods a ship can avoid danger in Reduced Visibility. I did go aboard the Squadron's Minesweepers—perhaps six, including one in the shipyard, and conducted about an hour's worth of training on each ship. The final day the Commodore called me into his office and provided me with a verbal BZ Well Done and a nice Performance Evaluation.

I am very proud that even during my last days at sea of a 24-year career, I was able to be of great service to the U.S. Navy! Now it is 34 years later; I am retired as an E9 Master Chief Quartermaster, with a decent monthly pension and a great medical plan; I even receive some extra benefits as I am a Viet Nam War Veteran. But in my heart, I know I have earned it.

+ + + + + + + +

## MY SCHOOL LIFE AS A DOCTORAL STUDENT

• • • • • • • • • • • • • • • • • • • • • •

Now, as the University of Cincinnati, Department of Curriculum and Instruction was paying my enrollment fees, and providing a stipend,

I needed to do things for the Department. The first was to teach a Junior Second Semester course on ***INSTRUCTIONAL PLANNING.*** This involved taking the knowledge and skills one learned in earlier courses, and now forming them into Lesson Plans, and presenting them in class. I loved it. Taught it every quarter. The second task was to go out into the field and supervise our students who were either in Pre-Student Teaching placements, or students who were doing their full-blown Student Teaching.

This too, I thoroughly enjoyed, partly because I had a lot of knowledge and skills, and I was working on behalf of the students' best interests. For example, I would watch a student teacher teach her/his full lesson, and then the two of us would go off into a private space. "Okay, tell me what I did wrong!" Patric, "I have a better way to start. You tell me three things that you thought went well?" "Aren't you going to tell me what I did wrong?" "Well, we might get to that, but tell me your good news." Students could come up with two, and I would have to tell them the third. They were not focused that way. Now, if there was a problem area, I would say to the student, "If you could teach this very same lesson over again to these same students, would you do anything differently?" This would give the student a chance to identify a possible problem area. "And what might you do differently?" This gave the responsibility to the student to come up with solutions. And a number of times, the student had not done anything "wrong."

Sometimes it was the "Clinical" teacher-supervisor that was creating problem situations-such as allowing the students to talk among themselves while the student-teacher was teaching the whole class. In these instances, I would call for a three-way conference, and together we could think up some solutions.

+ + + + + + +

## *MY SISTER ERIN GETS MARRIED*

● ● ● ● ● ● ● ● ● ● ● ● ● ● ● ● ● ● ● ● ●

[Digression] The time now is the summer of 1987, and my sister Erin was getting married in San Francisco. I took Julia with me. I had had a few glasses of champagne at the reception (but not inebriated.) I turned to Julia, "Honey, do you have your driver's license?" "Yes, Dad." "Would you be OK driving us to Frank and Andy's across the Bay, where we are staying?" "Yes, Dad." "Okay, here are the keys. I observed her driving very carefully as we drove to my former housemates. The next day I asked Julia again to do the driving to our destination. My goodness she was so smooth and professional behind the wheel!! Finally, I said, "Julia, *WHERE DID YOU LEARN TO DRIVE LIKE THAT?"*

"I learned from you, Dad." Me, "I never taught YOU to drive." Julia, "Yes Dad. Remember when you were instructing Beth on how to be a careful and safe driver?" "Yes." "Well, I was leaning on the front seats listening to everything you told Beth!" Me, "Wow!"[My daughter must have caught the confidence of "*I BELIEVE I CAN.*" Come to think over my daughter's life, yes, she does exhibit the attitude/disposition 'I Believe I Can.' [End Digression]

+ + + + + + +

I believe it was at the beginning of my third year— 1987--I was asked both by the Associate Dean of Graduate Studies, and the Chair of the C & I Department to manage the College Of Education's Lecture Series. [There were two Education faculty members who became co-chairs of this committee, but they really did not like each other. So, we never had a committee meeting with all three of us. I would meet separately with one faculty member, and then later a separate meeting with the other.]

We brought in three famous Educators/Researchers to lecture each quarter. My bosses would hand me name and telephone number. It was then my job to do everything else. I telephoned the desired Speaker and asked if they would come to UC. If the answer was yes, and most of the time it was yes, it was my job to type up a contract, provide airline tickets; make hotel reservations, create a publicity flyer to be distributed around the College and city.

[I will digress: when I needed help with folding stapling, labelling, sorting the Circulars—between 200 – 300—I went across the street and engaged the students in the high school Special Education Class. They were "glad to have something meaningful to do." And they were excellent at their tasks because they had done it several times before. Now, in these early times before Standards were created for each subject area and for every grade level and category—so there were no requirements for what Special Education students were supposed to do.]

Resuming as the manager of the Lecture Series I would reserve the auditorium; go to the airport and greet our guest and take them to the hotel. Then I had to organize the Reception: arrange for the food and beverage to be served. Occasionally one of my bosses would take the guest to dinner, and I was usually included. Often, then it was my job to take our guest back to the airport.

Over a two-year period, six academic quarters, I brought to campus three lecturers each quarter for a grand total of eighteen presentations. I remember many of the lecturers, but two really caught my attention: Dr. Ruth Randall, Commissioner of Education for the State of Minnesota. It was she who initiated Nation-wide 1) Open enrollment—parents could choose to send their children to another school district if it was performing academically better. 2) taking college courses during a student's senior year in high school, which would double count. The second lecturer was a Latino Professor studying the successes of

Latino school children in the mid agricultural valley of California. I forget what her original research questions were, because when she started observing in the classroom, she discovered that some students were doing quite well, while others were doing poorly. And they were all from the same neighborhoods! What accounted for these major differences? After weeks of researching, she discovered that the school had two kindergarten teachers. Teacher A took the responsibility of educating the parents on how to communicate and negotiate with the school administrators. Teacher B did NOT take that responsibility. What a difference one teacher can make!

But as I needed to focus more on my doctoral program and other Corporate Training jobs, I relinquished the Lecture series. Interestingly, the graduate student who took over for me was also named Pat. Sometimes the faculty got confused between the two of us. I finally said to the faculty; "I am the tall one, and he is the short one." Do you think it mattered that Patrick Anyalewechi was from Nigeria, and I was Caucasian from the U.S.?

*I NOW HAVE THE ASSIGNMENT OF ADVISING
EVERYONE WHO ALREADY HAS A DEGREE, BUT
NOW WANTS TO BECOME A TEACHER.*

• • • • • • • • • • • • • • • • • • • • • •

I believe it was the beginning of Fall 1989 when our Department Chair, Piyush Swami, requested that I become an Academic Advisor for all the persons who did have a bachelor's degree, but it was not in Education. "Now Patric, if you would be willing to do this job, then we will take you out of the "Graduate Student Office" —8 to 10 Graduate Teaching Assistants occupied one large room—and give you your own office, secretarial help, a computer." "OK, I will do it." I was taken out and given my own office-sort of—Dr. Janet Bohren and I became

Office mates. (And we are still friends today in 2020!")

I believe I met with according to carefully kept records: **twelve hundred persons.**

I would analyze their transcript, use as much of it to fill the Education Program, and usually I informed them that it would take two more years of Education-related courses. I would tell the secretaries what days and hours I was available to meet with interested parties. So, when I would come in, the secretary would hand me my list of appointments. Two months into the Quarter—November 1989 I picked up my list and was about to go out the door to my office. But I stopped. There was a name I recognized. I turned around and went back to Lilly. I put the list down, pointed to that name and I said, "Did this person say anything when you made the appointment?" **"Why yes, Patric, she said 'Oh, this is going to be interesting!'"** Lily: **"Patric, why did she say that?" "Well, Lily, she is my second ex-wife--SHELLEY!"** Please do not put anyone else in the slot behind her; I would like so time to speak with her."

Shelley did come in. We had not seen each other for 18 years! But we were civil and cordial. And I think that was the beginning of rekindling our friendship. (She had re-married about three years after our divorce and had given birth to three daughters.) I told Shelley the same thing I generally told everyone: I can take two years' worth of your courses, but there are two years of very specific teacher-education courses you will need. In Shelley's case, she decided that was too much. She and her husband, Ian, had a job offer down in North Carolina at a Church Conference Center, and so they chose to move there.

## AS A "REWARD" I AM NOW REQUESTED BY THE DEAN TO CREATE AN ACADEMIC ADVISING CENTER FOR THE ENTIRE SCHOOL OF EDUCATION

• • • • • • • • • • • • • • • • • • • • •

At the end of that year, the Dean of the College asked me to launch an Academic Advising Center for the entire **COLLEGE OF EDUCATION—7 DEPARTMENTS!**, and they hired four persons to work for me as advisors. And I did it. At first, we were on the Fifth Floor in a vacant office. [Years later, the Advising Center was given a huge spacious area on the Third Floor.]

+ + + + + + + +

As I was constructing a philosophical framework for my doctoral dissertation, I telephoned Dr. Sheldon Stryker at Indiana University, in Bloomington, Indiana, and he invited me to come over and visit with him for the day, which I did. I was very honored to meet with him and discuss his theory. His renown theory—**STRUCTURED SYMBOLIC INTERACTIONISM** – Had two main themes. The first theme was: we form a sense of ourselves, etc.—others being parents, guardians, extended family, clerks in stores as we experience the way others treat us, speak to us, interact with us. The second theme was: to what social groups do we aspire to become a part of: how do they dress? How do they talk? How do they walk? and other physical gestures etc. ? I understand his theory does appear in beginning psychology textbooks.

## TO AUGMENT MY SMALL STIPEND FROM THE UNIVERSITY, I TAKE ON TWO CONSULTING JOBS: U.S. SHOE AND FERNALD NUCLEAR PLANT

● ● ● ● ● ● ● ● ● ● ● ● ● ● ● ● ● ● ● ● ● ● ●

My stipend from the Department was still not enough to pay all my bills. So, since I was taking Corporate Training and Development courses, I decided to seek employment with corporations. One such Corporation was U. S. Shoe.

Digression: my early five years' work in construction aided me in carrying out my many assignments with the U.S. Shoe Corporation, e.g., to help them convert their factory workers from a "Long-Linked Process" where a worker stands all day operating one and only one machine in the making of shoes—to a Japanese-style quality team approach—where workers needed to know not only their own job, but those jobs to the left and right of them. We label it the Japanese model but in truth, it was C. Edwards Demming, an American, who went over and taught the Japanese how.

+ + + + + + +

A second **CONSULTING** story with a different moral. Going back thirty some years, I had a wonderful older friend, named Byron Dann. ("By" for short.) He was old enough to be my grandfather. We became very close friends. After his retirement, he purchased a fair-sized Gemini Catamaran sailboat, which he kept housed in the Florida Keys. Once or twice a year, he and I would journey to Florida and go out sailing for five or more days in the National Marine Sanctuary. We would moor at one of the organized Dive sights; and that way we were the first to start snorkeling in the morning, and the last in the evening. By was very bright. He had become a chemical engineer, and later a mechanical engineer. He worked for Proctor and Gamble. Whenever

P & G was erecting a manufacturing plant for food products, By was always in charge. By retired when he was 65. But almost immediately P & G hired him back when there were production problems to be solved. I loved to hear his stories. I became aware that By was in his eighties and P & G was still hiring him. I remember when we were in his convertible heading south and I finally had the courage to say, "By, I don't mean to insult you, but how come they keep hiring you to problem solve?" By answered, "The younger engineers do not know how to do it." I then said, "Well, how do you do it?"

By began. "When they contact me for a consulting job, I remind them of my requirements: I can go anywhere in the plant I want to; I can talk to anyone I want to; I can take off and go away for a few days; and I can facilitate the final problem-solving meeting."

When they agree, and I travel to the plant, I meet first with the management to hear and understand what they think their problems are. Then I go down on the factory production floor and select workers to talk to. I go up to one *and I say, "Hi! I am your Fairy God Father and if I could solve one* problem for you, what would it be?" I spend days collecting the workers' needs. Then I disappear for a few days; I might go to the Zoo, or a nice public park, etc. and my mind is processing all of the information. One day, Eureka! I think I have it. So, I go back and call a final management meeting and begin laying out what I think would be the solutions." [NOW HERE COMES THE IMPORTANT LESSON:] "Often as I am discussing my plan, someone at the table speaks up and says something like "Oh, and we could do this process another way…" And By responds, "Good Idea! Let's Add that to our solution!"

In other words, By does not have what may be labeled "Ego-Ownership" of the solution. By is approaching his consulting "as a team member—working together to solve problems," he is highly effective.

I believe he was around 86 when he finally stopped consulting.

+ + + + + +

So, when my mind starts saying "I BELIEVE I can" a lot of what I am thinking is, "Well, I am not sure I know exactly how to do that, but if I team with others and ask around, I probably can learn how. Or in rare cases I will need to do some exploration myself and devise a way to do it."

In my years of teaching teacher education candidates, I started telling them, "You know when you have a doctorate and are hired, they start giving you all kinds of tasks and responsibilities you have NEVER done before. But if you have a doctorate, they figure *YOU KNOW HOW TO ASK QUESTIONS!*"

My mind is nagging me to tell another story from my teaching experiences. Over twenty-five years ago, I was introduced to the latest iteration in psychology of how human beings learn. The umbrella term is "*CONSTRUCTIVISM.*" While there are more versions of the definition, here is what I have taught: When there is new information presented to the student *No learning takes place unless the learner (student) seeks connections and associations with the learner's PRIOR KNOWLEDGE; thus, it is the learner who CONSTRUCTS THE MEANING OF THE NEW INFORMATION coming in.* So, in my classes when I ask a question, and someone answers which does not match up with what I had in mind, I respond, "Steven is using Constructivism. He is relating the words of my question to what he already knows. Now, would someone else like to add to the answer to my question?" I continue until the student responses come close to what I had in mind. I discuss my question to the class and the responses near the direction I was going, and then I go back and acknowledge the earlier responses and validate the students for exercising Constructivism. This way, I confirm that our class atmosphere is a SAFE PLACE. I, we, welcome all students to use their minds and offer responses.

+ + + + + +

# CONTENTS

## Part Five: Dr. Patric Leedom's Autobiography
### NOVEMBER 23—OCTOBER 26, 2022

# PART FIVE

## Dr. Patric Leedom's Autobiography

### NOVEMBER 23—OCTOBER 26, 2022

SCORE THREE SECOND HALF OF YEARS: Age 50 thru 60 Years

*TRAINING CONSULTANT CONTINUES FOR U.S. SHOE*

• • • • • • • • • • • • • • • • • • • • •

Actually, I want to provide or "set the stage." Primarily, I was now a "Doctoral Candidate" having passed all the course work and passing the oral exam." I was living just off campus on Bishop Street so I could walk back and forth to the campus. This was handy because I was often working and writing in the office seven days a week. While the University paid my tuition and provided a Stipend, it was not enough to survive on. So, I had to have outside employment. In 1987 I was employed by the U. S. Shoe Corporation as a Training Consultant.

As a training consultant for the U. S. Shoe Corporation, I was working to install their new form of manufacturing titled the QRM Program—Quick Quality Response Manufacturing; I, we, were working to change the factories' work forces' style of manufacturing from **"Long-Linked" where a worker stood at a machine all day** *long, all week long, all month long…* to a Quality Team Model where a worker might now perform several of the operations. I wrote **The Workers' Participation Manual;** I wrote **The Trainers' Instruction Manual;** I oversaw the "architecture of the training" the design of the manuals, the conditions of the Training Classrooms. I monitored the performance of the new Japanese-type Quality Teams.

In addition to providing services to the manufacturing Modules, the Corporation asked me to create a Course on becoming an electrician for the maintenance staff'. I developed an Electricians' Training Course for the Maintenance Department—(U. S. Shoe Co. liked to hire and promote from within) I simply went to the Navy and adapted their Electricians' Training Program; I did create weekly quizzes.

And I was asked to provide additional training for the Leather Sorters Staff. I brought a speaker in from Massachusetts, Egon Nifle-a master tanner.

I also learned a new "*favorite word: IMPUTRESCIBLE (Random House Webster Unabridged Dictionary 1998, Page 963. Imputrescible adj. not liable to decomposition or purification; incorruptible: a tanning process to make skins imputrescible [1650-60] To augment the training I went to the last full-service tannery in the United States and made a video-tape* <u>DOOR-TO DOOR</u>*

*VIDEO-TAPING 43 STEPS OF CONVERTING BLOODY COWHIDES INTO SHOE LEATHER*

• • • • • • • • • • • • • • • • • • • • • •

Then I was asked by the Leather Sorters Department to create training for the sorters so the company could be justified in raising their hourly wage by 25 cents. It was all up to me. I decided to focus on the

"BIG PICTURE" of how animal hides and skins could be converted to shoe leather. I brought in Mr. Egon Kniffle from Massachusetts—he was a master tanner—to explain the tanning process. The Leather Tanners Council of America was located right on UC's campus, so I worked closely with Mr. Frank Rutland. One day I got the idea that if we could show the workers a video of the entire process Start-to-Finish in a tannery, they would be more committed to their jobs. I asked Frank for such a video. Days later, he reported there was no such video. So, I talked Vice President Jim Duff into purchasing a video camera and tripod for me, and paying my expenses to go to Lynn, Massachusetts, to the last "full-service tannery" in the United States. He did, and I did. A Mr. ROB Jordan, who had previously been employed by U. S. Shoe Co., was now employed by the CARR Leather Tannery, and Rob was my host, guide, and narrator through the 43 steps of converting bloody-cow-hides into shoe leather. This is my tape : DOOR TO DOOR. [WHICH I STILL HAVE MY COPY.]

## PATRIC WORKS TO ADJUST THE WORKERS' PAY AND THE DAILY QUOTAS

• • • • • • • • • • • • • • • • • • • • •

Returning to U. S. Shoe. Over four years I had gotten to know many of the workers on a social basis, and they felt free to tell me anything. Early on when U. S. Shoe set up the Last-through-Pack-Modules, there was a "Three-Tiered Pay System." The workers with the lowest pay told me they were not inspired to work hard because of their low wages. So, I went to Corporate to John and Walter who created the pay system, and told them it was not working--"You're killing the Team Spirit"; so, they re-arranged things and made it a flat pay rate for all-except the "Toe Laster" because that person had a very critical job to correctly affix the uppers to the lowers. Secondly, months later, workers discussed their pay system with me to wit they had a quota of "pairs" to manufacture each day. If they produced a lower percentage, then their hourly wage was reduced by that percentage! I took on the challenge of using a stopwatch to time the various functions. After a week or two, I was able to go to corporate and announce that the quotas were too high—it was killing the workers' pay. So, corporate lowered the quotas!

### PATRIC BECOMES THE COMMUNICATION CONDUIT BETWEEN THE FACTORIES AND THE CORPORATE MANAGEMENT

• • • • • • • • • • • • • • • • • • • • • •

Short story. I would walk out on the Mods and a worker would call me over and whisper in my ear problems, problems, problems. I would say, "Why don't you tell the Foreman?" Oh, No, the Foreman does not want to hear that, they would be 'hateful' to me." About once a week the Foreman would call me over and tell me problem, problem, problem, and I would say, "Why don't you tell the Factory Manager?" "Oh, No, the Manager doesn't want to hear it, he would be hateful to me." Ever so many weeks, the Factory Manager would call me into his office. Shut the door, and tells me about problem, problem, problem. I would say, "Lawrence, why don't you tell Corporate?" " Oh, no, they do not want to hear it."

So, Lawrence, why are you telling me?" "Because Corporate listens to YOU."

A few weeks later I would be walking down the halls of Corporate, and a Vice-President would stick his head out of his office door and say, "Patric, may I see you in my office?" "Yes, Joe, what can I do for you?" "So Patric, what is going on out in the factories?" "So, Joe, why are you asking me?" "Come on Patric, the Managers only tell me what they think I want to hear, not what is really going on. So, I don't know what is going on. But I know that you know what is going on and you know I don't know, so tell me, Patric, what is going on in the factories?" "Ok, Joe, but I will not mention any names."

In January 1991, my four-year Training Consultant Contract came to an end. U.S. Shoe Corporation owned several subsidiaries including Lens Crafters. For whatever reason, U.S. Shoe Co. took the CEO of Lens Crafters and made him CEO of the Shoe Manufacturing Division. When I arrived at the Flemingsburg Shoe Show Case Factory—80 to 90 miles East of Cincinnati—I was told that the new CEO would flying in by helicopter at 10:00 A.M. OK, so I went about my research duties. At 10:00 A.M. the helicopter lands and soon the new CEO and entourage began touring the factory. I was very well-known to the Shoe Division because I had worked for them on various projects—the main being converting the manufacturing from Long-Linked—where a worker stood all day at the same machine-to now being organized into the C. Edwards Demming Japanese Quality Team Modules where workers were linked to each other in the "Last-through-Pack Modules. I also created an Electricians Course for the Maintenance Department, and created information training for the Leather-Sorters Department including travelling to Lynn Massachusetts to the last full-service Tannery in the U.S. and videotaping the 43 steps in converting bloody cow-hides into shoe leather, and I had written a 16-page report focusing on some of the manufacturing difficulties.

So, as soon as the entourage reached the Mod where I was working, the new CEO came right over to me to make my acquaintance. Shook hands and said, "Hello." And they moved on their tour. About 12 minutes later, I felt a tap on my shoulder, and it was the CEO by himself, asking me to step over to a quiet corner; he wanted to discuss me how I saw things in the factory. I am sure he consulted many others, but within 30 days, U. S. Shoe Co. sold the manufacturing Division to Nine West Corp. which used offshore factories.

## *U.S. SHOE LOSES TO OFF-SHORE MANUFACTURING*

• • • • • • • • • • • • • • • • • • • • • •

[This was a major catastrophe for some workers. They had come to work at the factory as a teenager---maybe not graduating high school or completing the Elementary grades. Standing at a shoe making machine was the only thing they knew. When the factories closed, these workers panicked! A few committed suicide!]

Getting back to my great disappointment-- I was in the middle of trying to install a GED (General Education Degree) here in the factory for the workers. Over the last two years I had conversations with some workers about the level of their Formal Education in school. Very few had completed high school, and a significant number had not completed 6th grade or even 4th grade. One worker reported to me, "I know I learned to read in the elementary grades, but I have not read anything in 20 years!" So, I surveyed these workers: "Would you like to have GED [General Education Degree here in the factory?" "Yes!" So, I went to the State of Kentucky and asked if they could help us install a GED Program in the factory?" "Yes, we will! We will supply the teachers, all the textbooks etc. and we need a Formal Letter Of Invitation from the Factory Manager. You just give us a classroom and the workers." "That's a deal!" So I went to Charlie, the Factory Manager, and explained I needed a formal letter from him to the State inviting them into the factory." "Oh yes, I will do that." But week after week, I checked with him and he had not done it…then the factory was sold! Well, at least I made a solid effort to get the job done.

+ + + + + +

Even though I recently turned 80, I want to include in this Score an essay I wrote 30 years ago when I was turning 50.

### EXCERPTS OF SEVEN REFLECTIONS ON TURNING 50 YEARS OLD

● ● ● ● ● ● ● ● ● ● ● ● ● ● ● ● ● ● ● ● ●

Parts of me remain very childlike and probably always will. Notice I did not say "**childish.**" Three years ago, I wrote and delivered a sermon in my church entitled ***CELEBRATE THE CHILD WITHIN US!*** In it I quoted from the author of ***I'M OK—YOU'RE OK,*** Dr. Thomas Harris. He wrote, *"In the child resides creativity, curiosity, the desire to explore and know, the urges to touch and feel and experience…"* Dr. Harris suggested that is the **Natural Child** within us that is "***part of the phenomenon of intimacy.***" This is the type of childlike that I choose to remain…..

**REFLECTION NUMBER THREE What is the wellspring of my need to reflect?…[P.4] Most of us live within three inter-related spheres of reality. 1. The reality of the existent parts of world and universe around us which may be unknown to humans. 2. The socially constructed reality of human knowledge, and 3. And our own personal sense of who we are and what we are about; our sense of "SELF"—our own inner reality—which in part has been influenced by the first two realities. My wellspring flows from my inner reality.**

**For me it has always been important to acknowledge and embrace whatever age I am…..For a healthy life we need to let go of the past and recapture the energy and attention that is drained from us when we cling to the agony and ecstasy of what once was…**

Up to the age of fifty, I have had several careers. To name just a few of those contributing careers, I have been a construction worker, a labor foreman, a union member, an office manager, a purchasing and expediting agent, a restaurant manager, a teacher, a school administrator, a building manager, a speech instructor, a Navy sailor, A Command Master Chief, A Command Career Counselor, A University Supervisor of teachers, and a teacher of teachers,

Back to my Reflections on turning 50. "Now I can call upon a rich supply of mental (emotional?) tools to assist diverse sets of people with a variety of problems and needs….I am feeling very alive and affirmed….

Many theorists, such as Dr. Sheldon Stryker with whom I consulted, particularly from the fields of psychology and sociology, argue that we " *"construct our SELVES"* **BASED IN LARGE PART ON OUR PERCEPTIONS OF OUR SOCIAL ENVIRONMENT. In different words, we develop a sense of who we are from the feedback we receive when we interact with others in our everyday lives.**

**REFLECTION NUMBER SIX Do I harbor any secret wishes to be younger? Not really. To be younger would mean to give up some of the rich tapestry of events, influences, and memories which I have worked so hard to include in my life.**

Worse, to be younger means travelling backwards along the path of one of the most important journeys of life: figuring out (or constructing) what "life is all about, AND figuring (or constructing) meaningful roles and identities for myself in relation to my perceptions of life.

## IS PATRIC IN DANGER OF BECOMING
## LIKE THE VELVETEEN RABBIT?

• • • • • • • • • • • • • • • • • • • • • •

A corresponding goal of mine has been to become authentic and real like the Velveteen Rabbit. (By Margery Williams with Illustrations by William Nicholson.

In case you have forgotten, the story begins:

There was once a velveteen rabbit, and in the beginning, he was really splendid. He was fat and bunchy as a rabbit should be; his coat was spotted brown and white, he had real thread whiskers, and his ears were lined with pink sateen."

The velveteen rabbit lived in a child's Nursery along with many other toys, but most particularly with his friend, the **SKIN HORSE.**

*"What is **REAL?" asked** the Rabbit one day,…Does it mean having things that buzz inside you and a stick-out handle?"*

*"Real isn't how you are made," said the Skin Horse. "It's a thing that happens to you. When a child loves you for a long, long time, not just to play with, but **REALLY** loves you, then you become **REAL."***

**"Does it hurt?" asked the Rabbit.**

**"Sometimes," said the Skin Horse…"When you are REAL YOU** DON'T MIND BEING HURT."*

*"Does it happen all at once, like being wound up?" he asked, "or bit by bit?"*

*"It doesn't happen all at once," said the Skin Horse.* **"YOU BECOME.** *It takes a long time. That's why it doesn't happen to people who break easily, or have sharp edges, or who have to be carefully kept. Generally, by the time you are REAL,* **most of your hair has been loved off, and your eyes drop out and you get loose in the joints and very shabby. But these things don't matter at all, because once you are real, you CAN'T BE UGLY, EXCEPT TO PEOPLE WHO DON'T UNDERSTAND."**

*Patric: "Boy, am I feeling beautiful and Real! Much of my hair has been loved off, my eyes need crutches (glasses), and I do feel an occasional ache in my joints. And I know I have been and am really loved by children of all ages for a long, long time… [And this was written a few years before I earned my doctorate in Education and began teaching teacher-candidates in college. Now I have binders full of loving thank you notes! And this is still happening into my late 70's and early 80's."*

On May 13, 1990 I turned 50 years old. My friends Paul and Beverly Dudey threw me a big Birthday Party to which 50 persons were invited. It was wonderful and the last time I had a huge birthday party. Some one gave me a gift—a Tee Shirt "THIS IS WHAT 50 LOOKS LIKE!" I was into the last phases of my doctorate.

+ + + + + +

## PATRIC EARNS HIS DOCTORATE

• • • • • • • • • • • • • • • • • • • • • • •

In May 1992 I defended my dissertation—311 pages-an Ethnography (Also known as Qualitative study—as opposed to a Quantitative (numbers) study.

I graduated with my doctorate in Curriculum and Instruction in May 1992.

That same week the Chairperson of the Curriculum and Instruction invited me into his office and said, "You are not leaving our Department until I see you sign a Teaching Contract!" Wow! I have never heard of such a thing! They kept me in my office—I was sharing an office with the faculty member in charge of Educational Technology, Dr. Janet Bohren. We were a complementary team. Everyone in the Department said to me, "You deserve to stay with us after all the work you have done on behalf of the Department and the College of Education— e.g.in addition to normal responsibilities such as teaching courses and supervising field students/student teachers I also became a major academic advisor for persons needing the Bachelor Degree transcripts to see what it would take to receive a degree in teaching (including my former wife, Shelley) and supporting our faculty advising since I knew the programs better than they did.

The Department kept me in my office for a year. I HAD USE OF ALL THE Department Equipment and Services. I read the Chronicle of Higher Education (which carried advertisements of teaching jobs all across the United States and some foreign countries. I responded to 180 advertisements. I applied for three categories of positions: Professor of Elementary School Teaching, Faculty in charge of all Field Placements including Student Teaching, and Assistant Director of the Student Academic Advising Center. I received 18 interviews which is high percentage. I went on 8 in person interviews, and ten telephone interviews, including Barrow Alaska, and Fort Kent Maine—the last settlement on U.S. Route 1 before you enter Canada—very remote.

+ + + + + + +

## IN 1992 HURRICANE ANDREW ARRIVES IN FLORIDA AND WREAKS HAVOC; PATRIC VOLUNTEERS TO GO DOWN AND HELP WITH REPAIRS

• • • • • • • • • • • • • • • • • • • • • •

In August 1992, Hurricane Andrew (Category 5) came across Florida just south of the edge of Miami to on down to the north end of the Keys. I had just graduated with my doctorate, and so I did have flexible time. I decided I needed to drive to Florida the week after and help our church district's Disaster Team. Members of the church in Cincinnati contributed money, and a big box of construction tools to me.

My Florida Involvement. Since December of 1987, I had been attending a church camp called S.W.I.M. in Homestead. We used Camp Owassa Bauer, a Dade County Park, used as children's camp in the summers was nestled in the agricultural farm area.

Homestead is where the Florida State Turnpike has its Southern Terminal. From then on South is U.S. Route 1. Homestead is perhaps some 20 miles south of Miami, and maybe 10 miles to the entrance to the Everglades National Park. Cutler Ridge is the community between the two. I have taken pains to provide a geographic location, because in August 1992, this is exactly where Hurricane Andrew came ashore and caused massive destruction. Picture a 40-mile swath with its Northern boundary the southern neighborhoods of South Miami—Kendall-down to Homestead. Nestled below was "Florida City." Which was the low-rent district for minorities, and it was very poorly constructed. For example, most of the roofs of the houses were only held in place by a scant few nails. As a result, most of the homes had their roofs lifted off by the hurricane and deposited upside down in the front yard.

So, I drove to Miami and was hosted by my church friends Bob Jacober and Janice McArthur. The leaders of our Disaster Team, Ed

Cossum and his wife Mary, were staying there too. Bob was a painter by trade, and he loaned and extension ladder which I secured to the roof of my station wagon. Every morning we all got up and drove down to Florida City to the Missionary Baptist Church—they were directing us to the residents who needed help. The area of destruction was now under control of the U.S. Army and National Guard. We had to obtain special passes in order to enter the area and have permission to work. It was a "war zone" with most every home and building damaged, all of the palm trees had "snapped off" around the 15-foot height, and "live electric cables were still laying across several roads. Most all businesses were closed. There was one Shell Gas Station that was open on Route 1—to both provide gas AND they used electric frying pans to provide limited breakfasts.

For my second trip down in September I received an invitation to come for a job interview at St. Thomas Aquinas College in Miami. I arranged to come down a week early and do more disaster relief. My hostess was Florence Cohan in Miami and my partner—who shared the same couch-bed, was Allan Levin from Washington DC. This trip we focused upon the Centro- Campesino—Mexican Labor Camp which needed a lot of help, and Florida City Residents.

One day when Allan and I had finished nailing tarpaper down upon a hot roof, and we were just driving away from the house, we spotted a group of local young men lying down under a large shade tree drinking something from brown paper bags, Allan and I said to each other: "Let us get this straight—you and I have flown or driven 1500 miles to come down here and provide labor services, AND the local young men are just lying around under a shade tree???

On another day, we were working at Centro Campesino which National Guard had taken over as their encampment. And providing cooked meals for everyone involved. I was talking with a young female soldier who was working hard to scrub clean some of the large baking pans. A young local boy came up, saw the soldier working hard and commented, "Hey man, why are you working so hard? Just let 'someone else' do it!"

## LIFE-LONG-LESSONS-LEARNED

• • • • • • • • • • • • • • • • • • • • •

Another life-long lesson I learned after speaking with both middle-class victims and poor working-class victims: The middle-class victims—who lived in a nice apartment complex in Cutler Ridge—where the roof had been ripped open and the rain waters had damaged antique furniture and paintings on the walls, were telling me they were so upset by the material losses, that they were making appointments with their psycho-therapists to deal with the stress. The poor working-class victims just told me in a matter-of-fact way, "Well, we have lost everything before; we will just start over."

I remembered this lesson five years later when the Ohio River Valley suffered "a hundred-year flood" and many homes suffered water damage. My house was built up high on a bluff, but the Ohio River rose over 65 feet above flood stage. Our village of Buena Vista was flooded to the extent that no one could enter or leave our village due to both roads were flooded with three feet of water over them!!!!

+ + + + + +

## THE TALL STACKS FESTIVALS

• • • • • • • • • • • • • • • • • • • • •

In October 1988, Cincinnati celebrated its BICENTENIAL.

There were many events held all over the city. But a very special week-long event was a Tall Stacks Festival on the Waterfront. Steamboats and Paddle Wheel boats came from far and wide: Minnesota, Iowa, Illinois, Missouri, Louisiana, Pennsylvania, West Virginia, Kentucky (which included boats from Ohio BUT Kentucky owns the Ohio River, because Kentucky became a state in 1792; whereas Ohio did not become a state until 1803.) And the large overnight Queens came: The Delta Queen (with a twin in Sacramento—the Delta King—both built in Scotland in 1926.)

The Mississippi Queen built in New Orleans in about 1970, and the American Queen (with full luxury) built somewhere in the 1980's.[One Christmas I received a beautiful gift of a photograph of all three Queens during a Tall Stacks Festival from my step-brother, Mark Mitchell]

The term "**TALL STACKS**" refers to the large smoke stacks on the original 1800's steam boats, with the stacks purposely built high enough to keep the grit and ashes from falling on the passenger decks. Nowadays most of the small touring boats run on diesels—even with a paddle wheel turning in the water behind them. I would describe them as Day Charters who only take passengers out for a lunch or dinner cruise of a couple of hours. That includes the Belle of Louisville which is an authentic Steamboat.

So, during Tall Stacks all the smaller boats did take people out for a lunch/dinner cruise. The three Queens did not take passengers out for the one-day meals. They either discharged passengers debarking in Cincinnati or embarking for a several days cruise down the river.

## PATRIC IS PROMOTED TO SUPERVISOR

• • • • • • • • • • • • • • • • • • • • • •

I missed attending the 1988 Tall Stacks, however, it was such a popular feature of the Bicentennial, that investors decided to repeat the festival every four (sometimes three) years. But in 1992, I came aboard at 5:00 A.M. the first day as a "volunteer" but I teamed up with a supervisor and helped figure out solutions to logistical type problems. At the end of that first day, my supervisor told the bosses to make me a supervisor. And I worked as a supervisor for the five remaining Tall Stacks Festivals. I had my own golf cart for three of them—allowing me to rove around solving problems. ( I believe it was 1992 when NBC's Today Show came to do their broadcast. I became Willard Scott's assistant e.g., holding his coffee when he was ON AIR. By 2003 I was shifted to loading boats for cruises down by the docks. They gave me Dock 1 & 2 which were down the cobblestones where I had no radio contact with them, and passengers had a terrible time with cobblestones.

In 2006 [the very last Tall Stacks Festival in Cincinnati—they cost too much and a few times the investors lost money.] I was shifted to Docks 11 and 12 with boats moored right there in front of us. I thought, "Oh boy, is this going to be easy compared to 2003. Well…in a little while the wife and husband management team, John and Teala McQuilkin, came by in their golf cart. They informed me that not only did I have Docks 11 & 12, but I was the boat loader for the Majestic Floating Theater, and I was responsible for the concrete handicapped ramp, and the whole East Entrance to the Festival!! It was way up on top where I couldn't see it. They said to me, "In case you think you have the most demanding station—you do! You are the only person we trusted to do it." Gee thanks, I think. I was supposed to have 14 volunteers working for me, but I never had quite that many.

I was on station each morning at 5:00 AM. The last two mornings, the Coordinator of the Volunteers disappeared. So, I was selected to be the new Coordinator and distribute all the volunteers to their appropriate dock. I made sure I had at least the minimum number of volunteers to cover all the critical points in my stations (And some of those volunteers quietly begged me to be on my station for better management.)

During the second night there was a huge rain storm all boats untied and survived loose under power on the river. The next day they each were moored at a different dock! So, we supervisors had to create a new map. And there was tremendous radio traffic to get the passengers to the correct dock.

With all the rain for days, the river kept rising, so at the end of the festival, the American Queen was trapped! With her tall non-bendable stacks, she could not fit under any of the bridges. She was trapped for several days. I don't know if she damaged her paddle wheel, but she donated one to Cincinnati and that's why today, if you travel along the waterfront, you will see this huge paddle wheel mounted as an attraction.

# LETTER FROM PATRIC TO JOHN MCQUILKIN

• • • • • • • • • • • • • • • • • • • • • • •

---

**Patric Leedom**

| | |
|---|---|
| From: | Patric Leedom |
| Sent: | Tuesday, October 10, 2006 1:40 PM |
| To: | 'John McQuilkin' |
| Cc: | Patric Leedom |
| Subject: | Tall Stacks |

Hello John and Teala.

What a pleasure to be part of your team again this year. There wasn't a good opportunity to thank you on Sunday so I thought I would do it now.

Despite all of the uncertainties and minute to minute changes, I thought Boat Loading on the Docks went well. While the number of volunteers was thin at times (and I only know the morning shift) we made due.

On Sunday morning, when I noticed Dock 10 had a big crowd to board, I walked over and told Carl Fischer that he was welcome to "borrow" a few of the Dock 11 volunteers. A little while later he did, and after the boarding, they came back.

One thing I found to be very helpful was my going aboard the boats, (mostly the Harriet Bishop) and in a team way, coordinated everything with the Captain. He complimented our crew for doing an excellent job. One comment he made, was that on Friday, when no boats were departing, he had hired a band for entertainment and was prepared to show the guests a good time, but then we--all Tall Stacks people--discouraged going aboard that morning. He said he lost $4000 that day.

On my shift, the exit stairs and ramp seemed to go well. It does take at least two volunteers at the top, which I had all except for the last day. I am aware that different supervisors have different concepts of who may come down the stairs and ramps. For example, I gave permission for families with strollers to use the ramp, and for people who were nervous about walking the small stairs--usually elderly--to use the exit stairs instead.

On exiting from the boats, I remember one radio conversation about letting people climb the gate stairs rather than walk all the way to the east exit stairs. I heard Teala say that if things were not that busy, that that would be alright. I wanted to second this idea. I did have some "over 50 year-olds" pause in front of me and say "just how far do we have to go before we can get up?!" Certainly if anyone asked for a cart I called one.

Speaking of which, I thought the Transportation Office did a very supportive job. Every time I called for a cart, it was there within 5 minutes. Kudos.

Here is a partial list of the volunteers who came the first day to Docks 11 and 12, and returned every day afterwards: Jack Feldkamp + Joan Langen; Mary Ellen Ihle; Carole Dever; Barb Lindower; Erik Ehrle; Mitzi Reynolds; Kathy and Pat Flischel; Barb Shaffer, Dave Devel. For the 10:45 Shift Rilla Foster; Mary and Kelly Woodruff; Tom and Lorraine lientz; Regeanna and Al Morgan.

I would like to note that many of the 10:45 Shift came down shortly after 10:00 and started; and several of the 6:30 Shift stayed late if we were in the middle of embarking or disembarking a large number. On Sunday, a number of the off-going volunteers came over to me to thank me and say they had a good time and would be willing to come back next Tall stacks. I am not aware of any volunteer who was unhappy with his or her assignment. I am not aware of any volunteer violating any rules, or being less than a welcoming ambassador. Speaking for Docks 11 and 12, I think the operations went very well.

I hope to work with you again in a few years. Sincerely, Patric Leedom

1

+ + + + + + + +

## BACK TO DOCTORAL JOB INTERVIEWS

• • • • • • • • • • • • • • • • • • • • •

Back to job interviews. It is now the summer of 1993. I had applied to Shawnee State University in Portsmouth, Ohio. When they telephoned for an in-person interview, they said I would be applying for the Math and Science Methods position, and that I had to do a demonstration lesson with students. I agreed. When I got off of the phone, I re-examined their Chronicle Ad; it said NOTHING ABOUT A MATH AND SCIENCE POSITION! Whoa! I turned to our Math and Science Departments for help. Bob Drake, in the Math Department, gave me some terrific understanding of current philosophies, and current textbooks. So, I created an interactive lesson plan. [Note: all through high school I was very strong in math and science, so I was very comfortable.]

So, I drove out to Shawnee State for two-day interview. My interactive lesson was a "hit." Toward the end of the final day, the Dean of Education looked across the interview table and said to me, "You are not a specialist in anything. But, you have done this and this and that and that...why you can teach any course we offer!" "Yes, I can!"

## SHAWNEE STATE UNIVERSITY PROVIDES A CAREER

• • • • • • • • • • • • • • • • • • • • •

Three days later, when I was visiting my sister Liz in Florida, the phone call came that I was hired! Hooray! And I stayed at Shawnee State University for 24 years, teaching a variety of different courses. [I stayed because I was very comfortable—I was in home territory because my Leedom family had been one of the three families that settled the Manchester area and Adams County. I still have a first cousin living there.]

My contract commenced in September 1993. I sometimes tell people that I was 53 years old when I finally decided what I wanted to do "when I grew up." In terms of living quarters, I decided I wanted to live along the Ohio River west of Portsmouth and closer to Cincinnati (where all my support groups were. It turned out that the Dean of Engineering, Dave Winters, was needing to sell his house—19.4 miles west of campus. I went out to see him and within an hour, Dave said, "Move in today!" I did. Within a year Dave moved home near Toledo, but I stayed in the house for 23 years. For my needs, the house was perfect. Dimensions were for the large rectangle 32 feet by 64 feet. The small rectangle on the river side was 12 feet by 20 feet—with all windows and doors. This was my "Florida Room, and the place where I did most of my grading of papers.

In 1993, Shawnee State Center for Teacher Education was just one program: Elementary First through eighth Grades. Gradually we were able to establish a Secondary Program.

+ + + + + +

## DESCRIPTIONS OF MY TOWN OF BUENA VISTA, AND MY PROPERTY ON "SILT STONE"

• • • • • • • • • • • • • • • • • • • • • •

Buena Vista, Scioto County (just a few hundred yards from the Adams County line.) In 1993 I purchased a home 20 miles west of Portsmouth, right on a bluff overlooking the Ohio River. I even had a U.S. Coast Guard Navigation Aid on my property. During the day, it displayed a large 4' x 4' Green Reflective Board that tow boats could use as a target to guide them down one leg of the "V" that the river formed. At night, there was a flashing Green light.(Across the river was the RED markers and light. In the U.S. when you come from sea, it is always "RED, RIGHT, RETURNING." Coming up river from the gulf is coming from sea.

My property had an interesting history. Way back in 1812, the pioneers discovered large quantities of "SILT STONE" or "FREE STONE." It is similar to Sand Stone, which has to be cut with the grain. But Free Stone can be cut in any direction. The settlers began mining the stone and hauling it down to the river to a convenient cove for loading barges—on my next-door neighbor's property. My property became the "Cutting Yard" where they formed window sills, door jams, and other coverings such as the faces of the Suspension Bridge in Cincinnati. Over the years the workers began using the tailings or left overs to build a wall along the river's edge, and slowly filling dirt behind the wall. So, a hundred years later or so, my property became a built up "Bluff."

When I moved in, people said, "Aren't you afraid of being flooded?" I replied, " I don't think so; do you realize how high the river would have risen—30 some feet above the normal depth—millions of gallons before it could reach my property."

### THE "100 YEAR'S FLOOD THAT I SAID WOULDN'T HAPPEN-HAPPENED

Well, in life, sometimes you have "to eat your words." On the last weekend of February 1997 there was a very unusual freak rain storm that dumped at least 13 inches of rain for days up and down the river like to Falmouth and Cincinnati. That Sunday I was in Cincinnati attending the evening installation of a minister. I didn't leave town until evening. As I drove across the Maysville Bridge to Ohio, there was a group of highway workers with a large sign saying ROAD CLOSED.

While they were discussing various routes I could not go, a caravan of cars and trucks came driving up Route 52 heading west. When they stopped next to us, they said I could drive home if I was willing to drive in water and mud and go around fallen trees. So, I did. Thank goodness because by the next morning, I would have never made it. The next morning, I got ready to go to school and turned my car east to head down Rout 52. A local man standing on the side of the road said, "Where you going?" I said to school. He said, "Don't you see the three feet of water across the road?" And as I looked, I could see where the road dipped the water was over the fence. Oops, no school today!

The water was flooding our small village. Fortunately, on Sunday, Roger Stephens went to our little grocery store, asked what they needed from town—milk, bread etc. Then he took his 18-wheeler semi steel hauler and drove the 20 miles into town. Got the groceries and drove back before the water got too high.

I remembered this Hurricane Andrew lesson four years later when the Ohio River Valley suffered "a hundred-year flood" and many homes suffered water damage. My house was built up high on a bluff, but the Ohio River rose over 65 feet above flood stage. Our village of Buena Vista was flooded to the extent that the following day, no one could drive in or out of town because the water was three feet high on our only road US 52. On both sides of the village.

Somewhat fortunately part of our town—adjacent to U. S. 52--was built up on a knoll such that where the fire station, store, and church were out of the water, and residents could get meals at the fire station and sleep in the church pews. We were able to drive our tractors and cars up to the Fire House Parking Lot to be safe. I loaded clothes and school books in mine. Many of the homes did suffer some inches of water in the house. Because my house was built up on a mound of dirt with an extra layer of cinder block, I only took water to within ½ inch of the floor joists.

As I prepared my house—by building wooden platforms both in the garages and some in the house—I own a large king-sized waterbed and I built a sizable platform 4 feet above the bed upon which I placed quite a bit of my possessions. I placed my 60 photograph albums up on top of the refrigerator.

As I was working, the Assistant Fire Chief came to my home and said, "Patric, from the news on the Emergency Scanner, the water is predicted to rise so high, your house will either suffer major flooding OR it will break loose and float down the river!" (In my mind I was thinking: Why, thanks, Charlie, for that wonderful news!") But, remembering Hurricane Andrew, I said to myself, "Well, I have done all I knew to prepare. And if it all washes away, I do have insurance, and as the residents of Florida City said, "Well, we will just have to start over. I will survive."

Buena Vista Village was totally isolated for four or five days because the water was three feet high on both side of Route 52. I actually was able to sleep in my bed—under a few thousand pounds of furniture I had place on a platform right above my bed. And it was terrible—my outdoor hot tub was in great shape so I could climb in and enjoy the flood water just two feet below me. (Awwww poor me.)

However, I had two housemates-Medical Doctors from Romania. Maria had some gorgeous antique furniture and expensive paintings. She panicked, and almost had a "melt down." I finally shared Mark Twains' remark: "I never knew a man with a million dollars; but I knew a lot of million dollars 'that owned men!" Maria did not appreciate my humor.

## *I WAS ASKED TO WRITE THE NEWSPAPER ARTICLE ON OUR COMMUNITY'S CELEBRATION*

• • • • • • • • • • • • • • • • • • • • • • •

Months later in November 1997, our Fire House Community decided to throw an Appreciation Dinner for the local Heroes who helped so much. I went to the Portsmouth Times Newspaper and asked the Editor if he could send a reporter to cover the Event. We talked for an hour or so. He said # 1, I do not have a reporter available. # 2, you are a professor and son of a major newspaper writer, why don't you write the article? OK, so I did. We were given two 12" columns including pictures.

## *GENEROSITY AND CHARITY*

• • • • • • • • • • • • • • • • • • • • • • •

At the college level there have been times when I have bought clothes for a student so she could look professional when she became a student-teacher; and there were times when I bought all the books for a student to ensure their ability to succeed in required courses. In generosity, I began publishing books of the students' essays and final papers at my own expense, so future students would have exemplars of excellence to guide their work.

In sympathy, I can think of three times when a student-teacher's mother suddenly dropped dead, and I arranged for the student to take a few weeks off to grieve, before continuing their teaching. On one of those occasions, when the student lost the person who was their "emotional rock and supporter" I hugged the student and said, "Your mother (grandmother) is gone, BUT I am here! And you ARE going to graduate in June, and I will walk every step of the way with you!" And she did; and we did; and now she is an outstanding teacher such that other teachers want their children to be taught by her! And, here in 2022, we are back in touch 18 years later! Shawna wrote recently _**"I probably wouldn't be a teacher if it wasn't for you!"**_

There also have been numerous occasions when a student has had a crisis at home, and I have arranged for them to turn in their work at a later time when they were up to it.

There have been occasions where a student was not performing up to expectations for one reason or another—in one case there had been a "date-rape" the semester before which caused the student serious emotional traumas. In each case I created "Contracts" delineating the required academic performances that must be accomplished in order to graduate. I left it up to the student to then write out HOW that student was choosing to redirect their behavior. We both signed and dated the contract. And in every case, the student fulfilled the contract.

Another example of compassion was if a student turned in an assignment that was not close to the exemplar that had been shared, I simply wrote on the paper: "I am stopping grading this paper because it does not match the exemplar you were shown. Would you like me to show you the exemplar again, and you can try again to complete the assignment?" After that, it was up to the student to choose.

After years of teaching and being painfully aware that many college students are lacking in self-confidence, self-esteem, and a positive belief in themselves, I, being influenced by the Montessori Philosophy of being positive, I utilized this strategy in my college classrooms.

When I was teaching a freshmen college course "Introduction to the Teaching Profession" I distributed the instructions for the final examination to my students the fifth week of the semester; and for about 20 minutes allowed them to view an exemplar of excellence: they had ten weeks to work on the Final Exam. And none of the questions had only one right answer! For example: #1 Why do human beings go to the trouble of creating schools? What are the purposes? #2 What do you think the community's roles and responsibilities should be? #3 What do you think the teacher's roles and responsibilities should be?...the parents?...the students?... #6 You may create the educational environment of your dreams; what curriculum would you put in it, and why would you choose that particular curriculum? To this day I am still proud of how many students chose to wrestle with these questions and create their own responses. I have a notebook full of outstanding examples. I was motivated by my deep concern that U.S. schools are not teaching higher order thinking skills. Not only did I want to "stretch Students' minds" with this assignment, but I wanted them to deeply process the knowledge and skills, such that they would have them when they got their own classroom.

+ + + + + +

## I ACCEPT A POSITION OF PRAXIS III ASSESSOR FOR THE OHIO BOARD OF EDUCATION
• • • • • • • • • • • • • • • • • • • • • • •

In 1998 I took the training to become a PRAXIS III Assessor of First Year Teachers. The new teacher began in the fall, and sometime in February or March I would contact the teacher and coordinate when would be a good day for me to come and observe. The Praxis consisted of an Interview Instrument of four categories and 19 elements. In my pre-observation conversations, I always discussed if they had a particular student with serious behavioral problems, please let me know ahead of time, or have the student sent to someone else's classroom. Either way, it would not count against them. I also always discussed that if they were in the middle of lesson, and they realized the lesson was not appropriate on that day, that it was fine with me if they wanted to stop and change to a more appropriate lesson –that is a mark of Professionalism. On the phone I tried to develop and atmosphere of trust and respect. In my ten years as an assessor of over 40 teachers, I only had four or five who did a "set up" such as have a thick stack of dittoed assignments and were told DO NOT LEAVE YOUR SEAT OR TALK! (yes, this did happen.) In 2008 the Praxis III system was replaced by the Resident Educator four-year program in which I did not participate.

The most challenging PRAXIS III assessment I have ever done was at the little country school in the very back woods. I arrived when a snow storm was just building up steam. The Candidate fortunately was very understanding. Every half hour or so, the principal would get on the loud speaker and announce a changed game plan for handling lunch. But the snow kept pouring down. There was a third plan, but within minutes the principal was announcing the school was closing for the day. The Candidate and I had become a tight team "just roll with it." I could already assess that she was a very good teacher with excellent classroom management. I was supposed to interview her for the fourth and last Part. Instead, I handed her all the pages, " you fill it out on your own and mail it to me." She did. Everything was fine. A good teacher/professor always needs to stay flexible.

## SUCCESS FOR ALL READING PROGRAM

• • • • • • • • • • • • • • • • • • • • •

I travelled all over the southern part of Ohio for ten years. What struck me was the different curriculum organizations. The biggest difference was Many Elementary Schools on the western Side of Ohio adopted *THE SUCCESS FOR ALL READING PROGRAM.*

Most typical elementary teachers arrive in the Autumn with a new class of students reading on a variety of levels. Most teachers do not have the luxury of a Teacher Assistant or second adult in the classroom. So how does the solo teacher organize her or his reading program? Certainly, it can not be individually (unless it is a Special Education Classroom.) Should it be all in one group? And I have seen that done several times particularly at the Kindergarten, or First Grade Level. Ok, so now the teacher divides the class into three groups: I am assuming, from my own experiences, that the top level are students who grasp the meaning of the lesson with one lesson and are ready to move on the next day. The Middle Group may be able to absorb two or three lessons per week and may need reinforcement the following week. The lower group are students who for whatever reason, have not quite mastered the concept of reading or the "Word Attack Skills" and also for whatever reason have poor retention from day to day. I would guess there still are some students still left on their own such as the highly gifted or the mentally challenged,

BUT, there is a university research program on teaching students to read known as **SUCCESS FOR ALL.** It is a rather simple program. Each school has a Success For All Reading Teacher-Facilitator-Coordinator. During the first week of school, that teacher and her/his assistants test the reading levels of all students. Then depending on the students' scores, they are placed in groups with students who are scoring about the same level. When I or you walk into a classroom where students are reading. And many Success For All Schools Programs require reading to be going on going on all over the school at the same time every day (and includes the secretaries and custodians!) So, When I walk in, I may see kindergarteners, first, and second graders all reading together—because that is their comfortable level. In another classroom I may see Second, Third, and Fourth Graders all sitting beside each other because that is their proficiency level. Voila. Every student in the school receives appropriate reading instruction and practice.

After nine weeks, the Success-For-All teacher-facilitator and her / his assistants test all of the students again. Adjustments are made: Some students show the skills to do better in a higher group, some stay in the same group, some are changed to a group more suited to them.

Despite my urging and promotions, we did not have Success For All in our Southern Ohio local school districts. Several "Scores" back in this autobiography I described my methods of teaching reading such that out of five kindergarten classes, my class always had the best annual overall reading scores. Essentially, I kept a Matrix Grid with the 40 Modern Curriculum Press Phonics books listed across the top, and the 29 students down the "Y" Axis so anyone coming to help with reading could instantly tell what book a specific student was ready to master. I usually had one, two, sometimes three parents come in and help with reading; I also designated two or three of my highest reading kindergartners to instruct the developing students.

And the students themselves developed some "accidental motivation." On their own, they would start counting the number of books mastered by different classmates. If that student perceived he or she was behind a friend, they then begged to read a book.

## OHIO DEPARTMENT OF EDUCATION REORGANIZES THE CLUSTERS OF GRADE LEVELS

• • • • • • • • • • • • • • • • • • • • •

Change is a given. In 1999, the Ohio Department of Education reorganized the grade clusters away from Elementary and Secondary Programs, to "Early Childhood Programs Pre-school through the Third Grade." To "Middle Childhood—Fourth through Ninth Grade Programs." The reason for such a wide-spread is that each district decides which grades will be considered 'Middle School e.g., Fourth through

Sixth, or maybe Seventh Grade through Ninth. And Adolescent through Young Adult (AYA) Tenth Grade and Up.

I took advantage of this new distribution and overhauling of our programs. The Number One Complaint from New First Year Teachers is that they "did not receive enough education and training in CLASSROOM MANAGEMENT. So, I "snipped off two credit hours from another course or two and created 'Guidance and Classroom Management." The concept I used was "How does a teacher take all of their students and create an Educational Environment such that each and every student wants to be in attendance every day because "good things are happening" [Definitely NO Boring Lessons—the teacher needs to find a way to make it come alive.] Each and Every student feels welcome and respected. Each and every student feels safe not only from classmates but also from the teacher (some have a tendency to embarrass students in front of other students.) And each and every student perceives a positive connection between the teacher and the student. In order to expose my teacher candidates to much of the current research literature on Classroo Management, I required the students to buy four different textbooks, and I loaned them two more. [Obviously, one cannot learn everything in one Semester, BUT I was assisting the students in developing a Professional Library to consult. I required students to submit two-page memos during the semester, and the Capstone was to write a five page + paper on "My Emerging Pedagogical Philosophy." And it was up to each student to think deeply and critically to state where their emerging philosophy was at that moment in time, knowing they would keep growing.]

What I hope becomes obvious to the reader is that I am inspiring students to use the Higher Order Thinking Skills.

# CONTENTS

## Part Six: Dr. Patric Leedom's Autobiography
## NOVEMBER 22, 2022

‹‹‹‹‹‹‹‹‹‹‹‹‹‹‹‹‹‹‹‹‹‹‹‹‹‹‹‹‹‹‹‹‹‹‹‹‹‹‹‹‹‹‹‹‹‹‹‹‹‹‹‹‹

# PART SIX

## Dr. Patric Leedom's Autobiography

### NOVEMBER 22, 2022

SCORE FOUR FIRST HALF OF YEARS; Age 60 thru 70 Years

### BEHOLD: A NEW MILLENIUM

•••••••••••••••••••••••

In December 1999, I was in San Clemente, California (Just 15 miles south of Laguna Beach where we both went to high school) with Christine (soon to be my wife) to celebrate New Year's Eve and the changing of the Millenniums from the thousand years of the teens, to the 2000's and the scare of the Y2K and the fears about computer date problems with shifting millennium. We were at our favorite Sea Food Restaurant on the Dock in San Clemente! And we watched the last sunset fade into the watery horizon. It was indeed a beautiful experience.

I turned 60 on May 13, 2000 but it was overshadowed by an impending wedding. It was my first attempt at marriage after a 29 years' wait. I married one of my former classmates from Laguna Beach High School. In the late 50's we had a couple of courses together—Christine was a Junior and I was a Senior, but we never dated. We re-met at a

"Four Class Reunion 1958, 1959, 1960, 1961 in 1989. We enjoyed dancing together. We began writing and occasionally visiting—but we both decided to look for someone closer to our homes i.e., California and Ohio. Ten years later, not having found mates, we became serious resulting in our marriage July 29, 2000 in Long Beach, California.

## BINGO! ALASKA COMPLETED THE LAST STATE OF MY TOURING THE UNITED STATES

• • • • • • • • • • • • • • • • • • • • • •

For our honeymoon, I arranged for us to take a passenger ship cruise up to Alaska. I Think We Can Do This. At the "Captain's Cocktail Dinner the second night, I went up to him quietly and said, "I have driven submarines around the world; do you suppose I could come to the Bridge and observed how this ship navigates?" He responded, "Write my secretary a letter." I did and a few days later I was invited up to the bridge. There were about 12 passengers on the tour. The Captain whispered to me, "When these people leave, you stay!" I stayed for about two hours. The ship's crew was more interested in how I navigated submarines!" I learned that this cruise ship had "Bow and Stern Side thrusters." We were deep into Glacier Bay observing the Glaciers "Calving": On the front wall of the glacier, every few minutes a huge chunk of ice would fall away into the Bay. After 20 minutes of passenger observation the Captain turned on both the bow and stern thrusters and the Cruise Ship turned 180 degrees on its pivot-point! So, I got to observe it all! [After "9/11" a friend of mine took a similar cruise; but when he asked to observe the Bridge—there was no way!]

On land in Alaska, we liked the Museums in a few towns/cities and the overnight and the outdoor train car ride FOR A TWO NIGHT OVERNIGHT tour of Denali National Park.

At the end of our Honeymoon trip Christine and I decided that she should stay in San Clemente where she had a job, her family members, and friends. And that I should return to Ohio where I lived and had a faculty position at Shawnee State University. (There was really NOTHING in Ohio for Christine.) But on every break from school, I flew out to San Clemente. We lasted this way for almost two years, but we discovered there were some fundamental differences in personality, so we divorced.

## CONGRESS HASTILY INTRODUCES THE UNFINISHED NO CHILD LEFT BEHIND LAW
• • • • • • • • • • • • • • • • • • • • • •

In 2001, the No Child Left Behind Law was enacted by the U. S. Congress and required compliance of all States who hoped to receive Department of Education funding. A few years later I heard a discussion on radio of some of the faculty who had been writing the "No Child Left Behind Act." One faculty member stated that they had not finished writing the Requirements when the World Trade Center was attacked and destroyed. Congress persons were wanting to show the public that the Congress persons were "doing something" in all the chaos. So, they came in and grabbed up the "No Child Left Behind Legislation" even though it was not finished.

Continuing from the earlier discussion about **No Child Left Behind** –it was installed from the Federal Department of Education and had 13 categories that must be met by every school district or they were punished. This to a massive amount of memorization so students would obtain decent scores on the High Stakes Testing. An unplanned result was that schools rarely taught Bloom's Taxonomy Higher Order Thinking Skills such as Analysis, Synthesis, Critical Thinking, Creative Thinking, and Complex Evaluation.( So millions of graduates from

Public Schools were launched into adult life with limited abilities to think deeply.) An unintended consequence was, "IF IT IS NOT ON THE TEST, WE DO NOT TEACH IT." So often there went out of the curriculum Social Studies such as History, Geography, Civics, and citizen responsibilities in support our Democratic form of Government.

I have taught College Freshmen for 23 years, and in EVERY Freshman class the students often confess and comment that they only memorized for the test, and "No One told them to REMEMBER ANYTHING!"

+ + + + + + + +

## MAJOR STRUCTURAL SHIFT IN THE OHIO DEPARTMENT OF EDUCATION OF GRADE CLUSTERING

• • • • • • • • • • • • • • • • • • • • • •

Change is a given. In 1999, the Ohio Department of Education reorganized the grade clusters away from Elementary and Secondary Programs, to "Early Childhood Programs Pre-school through the Third Grade."

To Middle Childhood—Fourth through Ninth Grade Programs" [the reason for such a wide-spread is that each district decides which grade will be considered 'Middle School e.g., Fourth through Sixth, or maybe Seventh Grade through Ninth.] And Adolescent through Young Adult (AYA) Tenth Grade and Up, and the Ohio Department shifted from antiquated Certificates (which could provide PERMANENT CERTIFICATES) to a new LICENSURE SYSTEM which did require a periodic renewal.

I shifted to instructing Early Childhood but did keep teaching Freshmen—"Introduction to the Teaching Profession" for all Education

Students in the Department. Then I TAUGHT SENIORS: Math and Science Methods for the Early Learner. My other courses were all Seniors. At that time period in U.S. Education Teaching Programs the number one complaint from Graduates was that they were given few to no courses in Classroom Management.

This might be a time to paint the picture of my life as a professor at Shawnee State University. This was the longest location—home and school—where I had stayed in my life! I was there from September 1993 until June 2016! It was the most "routinized." In the early years I did teach courses to Freshmen, Sophomores, Juniors, and Seniors.

Being a Professor of Education is a rather challenging career. **"YOU ARE NEVER AHEAD OF THE GAME!" T**HE RULES KEEP CHANGING.

*IN 1989, NCTM PUBLISHES A RADICAL NEW COMPREHENSIVE SET OF STANDARDS FOR GRADES K-12; OTHER EDUCATIONAL DISCIPLINES FOLLOW THIS LEAD*

• • • • • • • • • • • • • • • • • • • • •

The Curriculum Standards Movement for the fifty states came into existence when NCTM published its first set in in 1989 when the National Council of Teachers of Mathematics published its Set of Standards for Mathematics for grades One through Twelve. Ohio immediately adopted them. Then one by one the other disciplines decided they should have Standards also. And several years after that, many of those standards were revised. These became the requirements for both Ohio classroom teachers and professors of Teacher Education.

Down through the 23 years, I served on Departmental Committees such as Chair of a Faculty Search Committee, University wide committees such governance—usually Faculty Senate, Shawnee Education Association department representative to the Union (NEA). And Chaired the University-wide Facilities Committee for 18 years.

### BIRTH OF AN ALL-ENCOMPASSING DESIGN OF EDUCATIONAL LEARNING ENVIRONMENTS THAT LED TO EASIER CLASSROOM MANAGEMENT
• • • • • • • • • • • • • • • • • • • • • •

I took advantage of this new distribution of grade levels and its overhauling of our programs. The Number One Complaint from New Teachers nation-wide is that they "did not receive enough education and training in CLASSROOM MANAGEMENT. So, I "snipped off two credit hours from two other courses. [*NOTE: Our Department was limited to the total number of credit hours for our degrees.]* The concept I used was "How does a teacher take their students and create an Educational Environment such that each and every student wants to be in attendance every day because "good things are happening" [Definitely NO Boring Lessons—teachers need to find a way to make it come alive.] Each and Every student feels welcome and respected. Each and every student feels safe not only from classmates but also from the teacher (some have a tendency to embarrass students in front of other students.) And each and every student perceives a positive connection between the teacher and the student. In order to expose my teacher candidates to much of the current research literature, I required the students to buy four different textbooks, and I loaned them two more. Obviously, one cannot learn everything in one Semester, BUT I was assisting the students in developing a Professional Library to consult. I required students to submit two-page memos during the semester, and the Capstone was to write a five page or more paper on "My Emerging Pedagogical Philosophy." It was up to each student to think deeply and critically to state where their emerging philosophy was at that moment in time, knowing they would keep growing.

The selected four main textbooks were: HANDBOOK OF CLASSROOM MANAGEMENT: RESEARCH, PRACTICE AND Contemporary Issues edited by Carolyn Evertson and Carol S. Weinstein.

BEYOND DISCIPLINE From Compliance to Community by Alfie Kohn.

THE TACT OF TEACHING: The Meaning of Pedagogical Thoughtfulness by Max van Manen.

And ELEMENTARY CLASSROM MANAGEMENT: Lessons from Research and Practice by Carol Weinstein from the above Handbook, and Molly E. Romano, and Andrew J. Mignano, from the above ***Handbook of Classroom Management.***

Students wrote two-page Memo every two weeks on their readings, and they selected themselves to meet in small discussion groups on topics of their reading choices. Later in the Semester when they were sent out into the schools for Field Work, they then shifted to writing two-page memos on their Field experiences memos. The final for the course was to write at least five pages on "MY FINAL EMERGING PEDEGOGICAL PHILOSOPHY."

After the first few semesters of teaching the course, I realized the students were doing amazing final papers, so I started "publishing" them using our University Print Shop. I made plenty of copies so not only the current students could purchase one, but I had extra copies for future classes to understand clearly the kind of written work for which the course was striving. It was an outstanding educational experience.

+ + + + + +

Every student who was hoping to graduate from Shawnee State University was required to take a "Capstone" Senior Seminar Course to do research on a particular topic and produce a well-written Academic Research Paper. OK. Now the course instructions do say the Instructor controls the topics. And some instructors required all students to write on the one topic the instructor chose—such as Conspiracy Theory. We Education Professors were not happy about that. So, first my colleague Dan Dan Huang took a plunge and started teaching Senior Seminar, and a semester later, I took the plunge. I only taught once a week on Monday nights. I did have control of the topics, but I encouraged each student to choose something in their discipline and to check for possible Research Literature to see if it is sufficient on the topic, and then come to me and we would discuss and eventually approve the topic. I joyfully taught the course for seven years. Admittedly I mostly had Education students in the course, but any student from any discipline at SSU was eligible to enroll in my course.

*FOR YEARS IN MY SENIOR AND FRESHMAN COURSES, I HAVE UTILIZED TWO PAMHPLETS FROM THE FOUNDATION FOR CRITICAL THINKING*

• • • • • • • • • • • • • • • • • • • • • •

So, after I had taught Senior Seminar Research course a few times, I added two small pamphlets: ***The Thinker's Guide to ANALYTIC THINKING: How to take Thinking Apart and What to Look For When You Do*** and a second one ***The Thinker's Guide to FALLACIES: The Art of Mental Trickery and Manipulation.*** Both booklets were from the ***FOUNDATION FOR CRITICAL THINKING.***

A semester or two later, my seniors were telling me, "Boy, if I had had these booklets in my freshman year, it would have made a major difference in my learning!" So, I talked to myself and said, "Gee,

Patric, you do teach a freshman course, so include the booklets in that course!" And I did.

In all of the courses I taught, I looked for ways to stretch students' thinking. Early in the Freshman course—***Introduction to the Teaching Profession*** --I organized the course such that I gave out the instructions for the Final Examination the fifth week of the course. And I put an exemplar from previous Introduction to Teaching classes into their hands for 20 minutes-so the students could get a concrete example of a well-written Final. There were ten essay questions such as: Why do humans go the trouble of creating school? What do you think the Community' roles and responsibilities should be? The Teacher's, the Parents, and the students? AND there were not specific answers to those questions. Students had to wrestle with the concepts and figure out their own philosophies.

+ + + + + +

As a "Generalist Professor"[Meaning I was not identified with a specific disciple such as math, English, science, or philosophy] I was teaching a multitude of courses, I joined and participated in four Professional Organizations: National Council of Teachers of Mathematics (NCTM); National Science Teachers Association (NSTA), Association for Supervision and Curriculum Development (ASCD) and the American Education Research Association (AERA). I was always on the prowl to be sure my textbooks were the latest in research.

# CONTENTS

## Part Seven: Dr. Patric Leedom's Autobiography
## NOVEMBER 23—October 26, 2022

# PART SEVEN

## Dr. Patric Leedom's Autobiography

### NOVEMBER 23—OCTOBER 26, 2022

SCORE FOUR SECOND HALF OF YEARS; Age 70 thru 80 Years

*I WISH TO LEARN WHAT LIFE HAS TO TEACH*

• • • • • • • • • • • • • • • • • • • • • •

*"I wish to learn what LIFE has to teach, and not, when I come to die, discover that I have not lived."*

*From Henry David Thoreau*

*Comment: Very early in my life I discovered that my insatiable curiosity was coupled with confidence and a belief that I could figure out solutions to many of life's challenges.*

## MY TRIP WAS INTERRUPTED BY DIVERTICULITIS

• • • • • • • • • • • • • • • • • • • • • •

All of my life I have generally enjoyed excellent health. In 2009, imagine the nerve of some doctor who told me that I have **diverticulitis!** "No, I couldn't possibly have that!" Well, in the summer I was making one of my Western Swings to visit friends and relatives. When I arrived at my brother Casey's in Palo Alto, I started feeling poorly. I thought maybe it was his cooking because he used lots of spices. On the fourth day, I was travelling to my sister Erin's in Suisun/Vallejo. But as I got closer, I started doubling over in pain. I telephoned Erin. She said you are close; drive to my house, jump out of your car and into mine and I will take you to a very good hospital in Vallejo. The diverticulitis I said I didn't have, I did have, and it had broken open and I had a severe case of Peritonitis. They did surgery and removed 8 centimeters of my Sigmoid Colon and left me with a Colostomy Bag. I was in the hospital 6 days, then in a Convalescent Facility for five days, and then Casey nursed me for several days in his Palo Alto Apartment.

When it came time to drive back across country, my longtime friend Howard Landau took time off from work to help me drive the car back to Cincinnati.

[I want to recognize Howard as one of the many unsung heroes of the Viet Nam War. When Howard joined the Navy, they sent him to the Monterey School of Languages. He was taught two dialects of the Viet Namese Language, and one of the Mountain Tribe language-- Montagnard. In Viet Nam, Howard was given a very special assignment: his uniform had absolutely no markings on it, so most persons could not identify him. He would fly in helicopters with Generals and Admirals. When they would land to discuss things with a village chief, Howard would just stand off to the side and listen. When the Generals or Admirals reboarded the helicopter, Howard would tell them what he heard the village chiefs discussing. On a very special occasion, his Vice Admiral boss came to him and said, "Howard, I am not going to order you to do this; but we have a very special need and you are probably the only person to do it: walk across the demilitarized zone and negotiate with the North Viet Namese soldiers for the release of some captured Americans." Howard did it and won the release of the American soldiers." Howard is now deep into Alzheimer's, but I thought the public should know his contribution to our country.]

## WHAT IS GOING ON? OH NO—NOT A STROKE!

• • • • • • • • • • • • • • • • • • • • • •

Early in February 10, 2010, I went around my University Department hallways saying, "Wow. I feel very strange like I have never felt before." I said it three times throughout the day. I went home that night and went to bed. At 2:00 A.M. I got up to use the bathroom, and I did a slow slump to the floor. I made it to the bathroom and back into bed and then I noticed my left arm and hand were not quite responding in their usual way nor my left leg and foot. Then I said, "OK body, wuz happenin?" I figured I did need medical help, but it was so early so I waited until 5:00 A.M. to call my doctor in Cincinnati. He said, "How soon can you get here?" I said "Three hours." He said, "Okay, we will be waiting for you." So, I packed my bags and headed to Cincinnati, 100 miles away. I did stop at McDonald's to get a sandwich, but I noticed I had great difficulty walking. As I got near University Hospital, I telephoned and said, "I can get to the garage, but I can't walk. Could you send a wheel chair for me?" "The young lady on the other end said, "Just a moment….Okay drive your car to the entrance of the Emergency Room and then we will bring out a Wheel chair." I said, "But what about my car?" She said, "Honey, don't worry about your car!"

The nurses and doctors began immediately working on me, poking me with needles. Nobody had yet said **STROKE** , but I figured it must be something like that. About that time a young Admission Clerk came flying around the curtains and said, "We are going to admit you; you just need to sign these forms." I thought to myself, "Do I tell her I have had a stroke? Do I tell her it is on my left side? Do I tell her I am left-handed?" Fortunately, I had taught beginning writing for 7 years in Kindergarten, so I just said, "Ok, hand me the forms. And like a Kindergartener, I slowly printed my name.

It wasn't until around 4:00 P.M. that they wheeled me into my room, and one of the doctors brought a computer with her and for the first time said **"You have had a stroke! And here is a picture of your brain with the blockage!"** When I called my office at Shawnee sometime later, they were not only surprised but a little upset with me 1) for not asking for help immediately at 2:00 A.M. but 2) Driving by myself 100 miles to a Cincinnati Hospital!

It took me six months or so to recover—with a lot of physical therapy; but it was not what I consider a Major Stroke—most people cannot tell I have had one. I tell people "That the Delivering Stork got confused and landed on the wrong house!" What I know is that I can not multi-task as well as I once did. When too many things come at me, I need to back off and regroup.

+ + + + + +

## MY CANADIAN BIRTHDAY

• • • • • • • • • • • • • • • • • • • • • •

I turned 70, on May 13, 2010. I didn't want to celebrate alone so I took a fancy birthday cake and drove up to Waterloo/Kitchener,

Canada and be with the Marvin Warkentin family. It was a wonderful caring family-type birthday Marv and I met on the handball courts at San Francisco State University in 1962. We have been very close friends since then. In 1969 when I was relocating to Evanston, Illinois to attend Northwestern University, Marv and I took a nine-day cross-country trip where we philosophized most days and into the evening in our sleeping bags.

## NEW SCHOOL MONTISSORI'S 40TH ANNIVERSARY

• • • • • • • • • • • • • • • • • • • • • • •

Autumn 2010 was also the scene of a very special celebration: earlier in this book I spoke of being a founding staff member of the New School Montessori, founded in September 1970. While I moved on to the Cincinnati Public Schools in September 1976, I never broke my ties to the New School. Not only was I very proud of the excellent education being provided, BUT my Step-father's family—the Mitchell's-- had built the Castle-like home in 1891-used by the New School and I was introduced to the family home by Great Aunt Monica Mitchell-Hoppe-Fenton-Lawson who had sold the home to the Catholic Archdioceses in 1927. I am the building Historian.

So, 2010 was the scene of the 40th Anniversary of the School. I was on the planning Committee; many of the former teachers, parents, and students came back for the three-day celebration! It was grand! What I will comment in 2020, is that there will be no more grand Celebrations—so many people passed away or can't travel or don't have the interest. There was a 50th Celebration in the Planning but the Coronavirus cancelled all that.

+ + + + + +

## *CINCINNATI'S UNITED STATES SUBMARINE VETERANS INC. HOSTS THE NATIONAL CONVENTION*

• • • • • • • • • • • • • • • • • • • • • •

Looking back at October 2010, Our Submarine Veterans' Base was the Host for the National United States Submarine Veterans Convention. Our Cincinnati Area group formed a Planning Committee and I was on it, and we worked it for two years. We contracted with a large sprawling Motel in Kentucky off I 75 and Butter Milk Pike. While we wanted to plan really exciting programs and tours off-campus, our BIGGEST CONCERN was **NOT TO LOSE MONEY AND GO DEEP IN THE HOLE!** So, we costed out every activity and tour, and cost of hotel rooms and meeting rooms. We were actually so good at this we came out with a profit of $26,000.00!! We paid back the National Organization their Seed Money and a little more. But they wanted a lot more. We still have a nice nest egg to keep our base going.

I was selected to be the Master of Ceremonies! Probably because I gave speeches all the time at the University and other Organizations. Typical of me, I had the sound system turned on when only one or two people were there to tell me if I was loud enough and I enunciated each word crisply and carefully. One of my unusual pleasures was to have Mr. Donald Brandt PLEASE STAND UP! Donald had been a fighter pilot in WWII and was shot down by the Japanese right next to Guam Island. A submarine, I believe the USS Stingray, was dispatched to retrieve him. Don was already in a one-man raft and the Japanese were firing at him. When the submarine came in on the surface, the Japanese fired on the ship. So, the Stingray made a hasty exit out for a mile then submerged and came back in with the periscopes raised. It took three circling passes for Don to get the idea to grab on to one of the scopes. When he did, the submarine drug him out perhaps a mile, surfaced, and took him aboard.

Another pleasure for me was that we had invited the Commander, Submarine Group Two in New London Connecticut. The Rear Admiral and his Lieutenant Aide came a few days earlier, so I had a chance to become acquainted. It was also my task to instruct him how to use our microphone to be heard clearly. He later sent me a Thank You Note and said call him if he could do anything for me.

The following summer I went to New London and was his guest for the day. I got to do the two things I asked for: 1) Meet with the Commander of the Submarine School to discuss the quality of young sailors, and 2) experience the Navy's brand new "Star Wars" System of Navigation. The Executive Officer took me down to the Training Room and put one of those "Virtual Reality Helmets" on my head, then they started up the system. "OH MY GOD" Fantastic! The Officer-of-the-Deck on a Ship's Bridge now has the ability to see all of the floating contacts with their courses, speeds, and CPA---Closest Point of Approach--all calculated. In effect, the Officer-of-the-Deck is totally unhooked from the Navigation Team down in control. [Over the many years, there have been far too many ship collisions and groundings—hundreds every year!] I was very pleased to enjoy the system.

+ + + + + +


## I ACCEPT A POSITION WITH THE
## OHIO BOARD OF REGENTS

• • • • • • • • • • • • • • • • • • • • • • •

Shifting back to my role as a college professor, in 2010 I volunteered to work with the Ohio Board of Regents in a program titled Curriculum Equivalency Management System (CEMS) The concept here was if a student took a certain basic course in one State University and transferred to another, and if the Board of Regents had declared that

that course was equivalent State-Wide, then the receiving University could not make the student take the same course over again. It was a great concept. Essentially, the Board of Regents required that at all State Colleges' and Universities' syllabuses for the identified basic courses must be EQUIVALENT. I became a member of the Educational Basic Courses evaluation panel. The system required all state institutions to email their syllabi to the Ohio Board of Regents. There was a panel for each discipline composed of faculty from various Colleges and Universities from across the state. I was accepted as a Panelist from Shawnee State for all of the Identified Basic Courses. (In terms of the Education Department: ***INTRO TO THE TEACHING PROFESSION, EDUCATIONAL PSYCHOLOGY; EDUCATIONAL TECHNOLOGY, AND INTERVENTION SPECIALIST.***

After two years, I became the Lead Panelist—meaning that the syllabus was emailed to me first. If I thought there was merit to the syllabus, I submitted it to the rest of the Education Panelists—usually 8 to 10 persons. But if I thought the syllabus did not meet the (my) requirements, then I rejected it back to the sending institution. My requirement was fairly simple: does your syllabus clearly demonstrate that each and every student has mastered the required Regents' Standards content? If that is not easily identifiable, I rejected it.

I developed the reputation of rejecting the most syllabuses of any of the lead panelists. In my mind I was strongly supporting the high standards—and better education for the students and the State of Ohio. I gave my phone number to the Board of Regents and told them I welcomed phone calls from the rejected institutions. And usually, one conversation with me cleared up the problem, and usually, when the corrected syllabus arrived, our panel would approve it. However, my letter of rejection contained my/our requirements so sometimes a phone call was not necessary.

When I was first informed that I had that reputation for rejecting the most CEM syllabuses, I did not know if that was a criticism of me, or a Kudo. Turns out it was a Kudo, and I was asked to do a presentation on my methods for all of the other Ohio Board of Regents CEMS Panel Leads.

I retired from being Panel Lead the same time I retired from Shawnee State in 2016. Even though I was 76 years old, I was not ready to retire; but the State Teachers Retirement System changed its rules, and I was allowed only one more year under the old rules, before I would be forced into the new rules which were not as financially friendly.

＋ ＋ ＋ ＋ ＋ ＋ ＋ ＋

## *JIM PETRO'S LETTER REGENTS*

• • • • • • • • • • • • • • • • • • • • • •

University System of Ohio
**Board of Regents**

John R. Kasich, Governor
Jim Petro, Chancellor

June 15, 2011

William "Patric" Leedom
Shawnee State University
940 Second Street
Portsmouth, OH 45662

Dear Patric:

Thank you for your service this past year in supporting the accessibility and quality of higher education in Ohio.

As a faculty reviewer for the Education Career-Technical Assurance Guide (CTAG) Review Panel, your contributions as a member of this team were a credit to your profession, your institution, and your state.

Credit transfer pathways are the cornerstone of a strong system of public education with partnerships among secondary and adult schools, colleges, and universities. Without your service and that of your colleagues to help build these linkages, the wide network of high-quality transfer options offered today to Ohio students could not exist.

On behalf of the Ohio Board of Regents and all the students of the University System of Ohio, I would like to thank you for dedicating your time and offering your talents and expertise to this important work.

Sincerely,

Jim Petro
Chancellor
Ohio Board of Regents

Cc: President Rita Rice Morris, Shawnee State University

30 East Broad Street | 36th Floor | Columbus, Ohio 43215-3414 | phone 614.466.6000 | fax 614.466.5866
www.uso.edu

## *A STUDENT OF MINE CREATES A QUILT OF MEMORIES IN MY HONOR*

• • • • • • • • • • • • • • • • • • • • • •

On a side note, back in May 2011, a freshman student of mine, April McCleese,-(Seen on the Front Cover standing with me)-in appreciation for my teaching, presented me with a king-sized quilt with 57 photographs, many of them submarine related, and when I found out what she was doing, I added 21 "Badges" of both submarines I served on ---USS Capitaine, Rock, Jacksonville, Sterlet, Ronquil, Caiman, and Nautilus plus events like Shellback, Golden Shellback, Northern Run, (Arctic Ocean Run) Blue Nose, Tonkin Gulf Yacht Club from Viet Nam. The Rear Admiral and his staff—stationed at the submarine base in Groton, Connecticut--enjoyed seeing the quilt. And I have taken the Quilt twice to the Submarine Force Museum adjacent to the Base, and the curator twice [as of 2022: Make it three times] has said "When you are through with the quilt, send it to us and we will hang it!"

## BACK TO QUARTERMASTERING
## ON SEVERAL SUBMARINES

• • • • • • • • • • • • • • • • • • • • •

[Time Digression] Returning to Autumn, 1970. I have mentioned elsewhere that I served in the Navy Submarine Force Reserves for 24 years and had ridden 24 different submarines. Well, at the Groton Connecticut Submarine Base, Summer 1972, I was attached to Squadron Two for Nine weeks. The office didn't always have enough for me to do, so I kept putting myself to sea on Submarines.

First a small story, then a Big story. One day, the FBM USS Lafayette (SSBN616) (Fleet Ballistic Submarine) pulled into port. I said to our Operations Office, "Put me on that submarine." He said, "We can't." I said ,"Why?" He said, "Because we don't control it." I said "How can I ride it?" He said, "Only if they ask for you." " Give me the telephone number." Okay, so I went down to the USS Lafayette and knocked on the side of the Sail. They said, "come in." So, I dropped down to the Control Room and the Chief Quartermaster said, "May I help you?" "I said yes. I see that your ship is going to sea for Midshipman Orientation and I wondered if you could use an extra hand." The Chief Quartermaster dragged me into the Executive Officer/Navigator's Stateroom. The Chief Quartermaster said, "Sir, we have a live one here." The XO said, "Give me that telephone number. "Yes, we want him!" The Chief Quartermaster then said to me, "Tell me your name again." "Leedom." "You know, I have an Aunt and Uncle in Cincinnati." I said, "Yes, Uncle Bob and Aunt Mildred!" Surprise. Dale Liggett was related to Aunt Mildred and I was related to Uncle Bob. Small world!

Now for the Big Story. Another of the Squadron Two subs was the famous USS Nautilus (SSN 571). And it was going to sea for Mid Shipmen Orientation, so I requested to serve aboard and did. [So now I am a bona fide crew member.] Some of you elder readers will remember that the USS Nautilus was the first ship to go under the North Pole, August 3, 1958! What you do not know is the Back Story. You do remember the Soviets launched in October 1957 **SPUTNIK** as the first Satellite to orbit the earth. That really upset the United States because for years we bragged that the Soviets were too stupid to do anything like that! But, oh my god, they did it! President Eisenhower was very upset and said to the Nautilus' Captain Bill Anderson, "Well, take the USS Nautilus and go under the North Pole; we want to show the Soviets that we are just as technologically capable!" It took three tries—that is another story—but with the help of the navigation component out of an Army Navajo missile, the Nautilus submarine did it!

As the years went by, I started attending USS Nautilus Reunions. And in September 2010, I went to the Reunion in Pigeon Forge, Tennessee. On the first night, we were supposed to go to have a Ship's Picnic in the Smokey Mountains Park. I said to the Convention Convener, "How are we getting to the Picnic Grounds?" He told me, "You have to have your own car." "I said, no problem." A little grey-haired lady came over to me and asked, "Would you please take me and my husband to the picnic?" "Yes, ma'am!" I got my car, she got into the back seat, and her husband got into my passenger seat. We are driving to the picnic. Who is sitting beside me? The **NAVIGATOR WHO GUIDED THE NAUTILUS UNDER THE NORTH POLE !! Shep Jenks!!** He was very friendly and talkative and made sure to tell me that his Chief Quartermaster helped him to navigate under the pole. You could tell he was just on edge of some kind of dementia. The next morning, they were sitting in the hotel lobby. I watched as several different shipmates of his walked up to him shook his hand, said "Hi, Shep." And then they walked on. After several occurrences, I decided that was the wrong way to treat him. So, I went and sat beside him. I stayed with them and took them wherever they wanted to go. They invited me to visit them in Martinez, Calif. But his dementia got bad so I was never able to make the visit, and he died a few months later.

A related story. I was invited to join the Submarine Admiral's Staff (COMSUBLANT) in December 1972. They kept me for 11 years largely because I always kept busy. In the summer of 1974, I didn't have enough work at the front desk, so I went down the hallway knocking on doors. The last door I knocked on the voice said, "Come in." I said sir, I have some extra time, do you need any help?" He said, "Get in here, and that is your desk right over there." He was the Admiral's Schedular and he was tasked with generating a weekly report on where all submarines in our command were located and their readiness e.g., New Construction, Having an Overhaul in a Ship Yard, Deployed on missions, etc. I worked with him until the regular chief came back from leave. Commander Bill Gaines was so appreciative, he gave a large volume of **SUBMARINE OPERATIONS OF WORLD WAR II AND A NICE Thank You note.** Over the years I got together with him, when he was the Commanding Officer of the USS Gudgeon (SS 567) in San Diego—he welcomed me to tour the sub with my daughter and step siblings. And then again just a few years ago when he was the Officer-in-Charge of the famous Scripps Oceanographic Institute Flip Ship (barge) that could be towed out into the ocean and, similar to a submarine, with valves and pipes, could invert the ship 90% down into the water for scientific research.

I did not know that he had been a Second-Class Sonar Petty Officer as the Nautilus went under the North Pole!! Finally in 2018 at a USS Nautilus Reunion in Groton, Connecticut, I was able to catch up and have several warm conversations with Bill Gaines. [End Digression] ] *I attended the USS Nautilus (SSN571) Reunion this past July 2022. The last night was a Banquet; and following the end if the Banquet, all Nautilus Crew Members were asked to Line Up. And when they did, each person was handed a small black box, and inside the box was a version of a $500 wrist watch; this watch had been specifically designed for the Nautilus Crew Members. On the front side there was an image of the Nautilus and underneath was* *written Nuclear Submarine SSN 571. On the reverse side was: an engraving of the Nautilus under the ice. Below the sub was written "World's First Nuclear submarine. Around the circular is written: IN HONOR OF VETERANS OF THE United States Submarine Service. My version was manufactured by the VOSTOK European Co. It is a diving watch capable of descending to 300 meters. Wow! I am so honored to have it.*

At the age of 75 in 2015 I was on a good and happy roll. I loved my career, I loved my courses, and I loved my students [Many of my Senior Students had also been my Freshman Students; and they helped set the ambience for those who were new to me.

+ + + + + + + + +

## STUDENTS REFLECTIONS ON THE QUALITY OF LIFE IN OUR CLASSROOMS

• • • • • • • • • • • • • • • • • • • • • •

As I am nearing the end of my full-time teaching career, I am going to pause, and share with you some of the feedback I have received from students over the years. Only a few professions provide feedback on how well one meets their goals. I am humble and very fortunate that a number of students chose to give me feedback on what I had hoped to accomplish.

*The next few pages contain letters and comments from my students over a twenty-year period*

# PROLOGUE

As a teenager, I was extremely active in my church denomination youth district. I worked closely with a number of ministers, who would take me to lunch and suggest that I enroll in seminary so I could become a minister too. I was pleased with the discussions, but I knew too much about the political hassles and divisions within the congregations, and I knew I did not have the required personality. So, I never went to seminary. However, ever since then I have thought of myself as a minister, and my students—be they Kindergarteners or College--students—I have thought of my classes as my congregations and I was there to care for them, to support them, to lift them up for a stronger belief in themselves. And that has been true my entire career of teaching.

## 1. Dr. Leedom [A SHY STUDENT] Wednesday, MAY I, 2019

I wanted to thank you for a wonderful semester and for being **the most caring, understanding professor that I have had yet. You have been an incredible model for the teacher that I would like to become.** You truly made me, and many others, feel comfortable in the classroom and allowed me to get out of my **comfort zone** while **speaking out in class.** This course has not only made me **feel more confident heading into the field of teaching,** but **confident in my writing ability, forming my own thoughts, and truly *Listening* to others.** I hope that you get the chance to teach this class again, for it would be a huge disservice to future students if you do not. *Lauren Fitzgerald*

## COMMUNITY/FAMILY CLASSROOM

2. Rachael M. October 20, 2015.

As I was doing the readings, chapter seven in "***BEYOND DISCIPLINE***" really stood out to me, I had never experienced a ***"Community Classroom"*** until I was in Dr. Leedom's Intro to the Teaching Profession." In that class, we had our classroom set up ***"Family Style."*** I met my two college best friends in that course Thanks to the way the classroom was run as a family and as a community. This type of environment is very respectful and supportive of the teachers, the student, and the classmates. To quote Alfie Kohn: "To say that a classroom is a Community is like saying that "***CARE***" and ***"TRUST"*** are emphasized above restrictions and threats, unity and pride replace winning and losing, and where each person is asked, helped, inspired to live up to such ideals and values as ***KINDNESS, FAIRNESS, AND RESPONSIBILITY.*** A CLASSROOM COMMUNITY SEEKS TO MEET EACH OTHER'S NEED TO FEEL COMPETENT, CONNECTED TO OTHERS, AND AUTONOMOUS. Students are not only exposed to basic human values, they also have many opportunities to think about, discuss, and act on those values, while gaining experiences that promote ***EMPATHY AND UNDERSTANDING*** of others....." [End quote]

Rachael continues: "…When I was part of this type classroom, I felt comfortable with my peers, I gained friendship as I have previously mentioned, I made connections with my peers and professor, and I was always treated fairly and kindly…"

3. *Stephani D. to Patric: April 2020* **To Appreciate my own Self-Worth**

*Well yet again, let me say thank you for your constant support.*

*That semester [When Stephani was in my Into to Teaching Course 2015] ended up being the beginning of an important chapter for me in terms of **finding and beginning to appreciate my own sense of self-worth. A lot of it I think may be due to the REFLECTIVE** nature of your class. In a lot of professors' classes, **you can identify their personal philosophies on education and the slight push toward [STUDENTS] BELIEVING THE SAME. HOWEVER, THROUGH YOUR CLASS, IT WAS PURELY THE OBSERVATION [we made] AND THEN MORE SO HOW THIS RESONATED WITH US PERSONALLY. This reflective nature caused me to have to look at some things outside of the classroom as well....**Thank you for your kind words and reassurance on my journey. I am glad to be back in touch!*

*4. Brooke T. December 8, 2014*

*Hello Dr. Leedom, I wanted to tell you what I'm about to tell you in class today, but I am, what I refer to as a "cryer" and I didn't want to cry in front of everyone. My grandmother was a school teacher and she was very passionate about what she did. She would allow students to go home with her so she could help with any struggles that they were having in class. She would make sure that their home lives were not affecting their school work negatively...She passed away in hospice in 1997 but even while she was in hospice, she made sure everyone else was okay and doing fine.*

*I wanted you to know that from you and your class, **I felt that same feeling. The feeling of true care and love for your students. I cannot tell you how grateful I am for you and the and the amount of care you give us students.** It really was a blessing to have you as a professor...The comfort that I felt knowing that I am learning from someone who has the same heart for teaching as my \*grandmother is indescribable!...*

## CARING

5. Dear Dr. Leedom June 6, 2006

As you know this has been a difficult year for me. Not only did I have to complete my methods courses and student teaching but more importantly **I lost my Mom.** *I can never convey how grateful I am to you for your support through this time. In January, I didn't think I could ever finish this quest I had begun.* **You told me, "Shawna, you WILL graduate in June and I'll be right there with you!"** *From that moment on I never doubted that I would graduate this year. Well, here I am! Please know I will never forget what you did or what you said to me, in a time when it felt as though my whole world was collapsing around me.... Shawna Q.*

## MAKING A DIFFERENCE

### 6. Dear Dr. Leedom May 2016

**Thank you for getting me through student teaching 20+ years ago—not the greatest school experience. But you helped me learn a lot from it & it continues to shape who I am as a teacher.**

**Thank you for teaching me that I can say "NO" & that it's okay to do so.**

**Thank you for teaching that I am not responsible for how others interpret their reality or feel about it. That is a burden I don't need to carry.**

**God Bless You, Patric. See you soon.**

*Remember that each day Is a new beginning And that what you do makes a difference.*

*You've been "making a difference" for many years...my classroom is partly your classroom, my students have been & will continue to be partly your students. The guidance you've given me continues to be passed on, like a ripple in a pond. Thank you.*

*With Love, Lora R.*

## EXPECTATIONS

7. January 10, 2013 What I remember most from EDUC 1115 [Introduction to the Teaching Profession] though, is how much Dr. Leedom expected from us. He set high goals and expected us to submit in-depth observations, genuinely considered reflections and well thought-out, well written papers. I noticed immediately that although it was my first semester at Shawnee, he had higher expectations for our class than any other professors did. However, I was able to surprise myself by rising to the challenge, truly investing my time and thought into my assignments, and doing far better than I thought I would. The class was made memorable to me because Dr. Leedom was one of the first teachers I had ever had at the time who set high, measurable goals and actually expected his students to be able to reach them. He believed we could, so we believed we could....However, as I always say to people who ask me if they should take a class with Dr. Leedom, "He is one of the toughest teachers you may ever have, but if you put in the effort, you'll learn so much more." Kristen L.

## GRATITUDE

**8.** Dr. Leedom April 29, 2013

I cannot say thank you enough for the amount of time and effort that you have invested in my education. **What you do for your students is rare and special. I have NEVER ENCOUNTERED ANOTHER TEACHER THAT DOES WHAT YOU DO; YOU CLEARLY LIVE FOR YOUR STUDENTS.**

When I entered the education program, I was apprehensive and worried that I would not receive the kind of education that I desired. I wanted an authentic, hands-on, and meaningful education that I could utilize in the kind of classroom that I wanted. I am proud to say that I received exactly what I wanted, and I have **you** to thank for that! The amount of creativity, passion, and brilliance behind each of your courses is remarkable. **I have been SO impacted by you and your coursework....**

"I remember talking to Grace (Her older sister whom I had taught a few years prior) about my feelings on education, **and she would say "just wait until you have Dr. Leedom."** I understand why she said that now. You have helped me become more knowledgeable, **CONFIDENT,** and open-minded teacher. I have incorporated Science and Social Studies into my classroom at Northwest every single day, **and you are the one that let me believe it was possible!"**

"I am excited to embark on this new chapter of my life! I will always remember and use things you have taught me and helped me understand. You should feel proud in knowing that you do **change lives, and you have helped the world in many ways."** Sincerely, Olivia M.

# INSPIRATION

*9. Professor Leedom December 12, 2015*

*I knew from the first day of our class that I was going to enjoy it. Never did I expect for one class to impact my whole outlook on life itself like this class for me. Now I want to be the best teacher I can because **YOU inspired** me to be more positive and have **confidence** that I can make a difference in someone's life....But not only did you impact my education positively, I believe you also helped me become a more passionate person and more motivated to do better for myself and my daughter....I have so much more **confidence** in myself because I had the freedom to share and express my thoughts without judgment from you or my peers. I love the atmosphere you created in our classroom. I know you have thanked me for sharing and you have no idea how appreciative I was to hear that. It's not often that my thoughts or opinions feel **validated or like** anyone is interested in what I have to say. Therefore sharing (speaking up in class) is something I rarely do....I just want to thank you so much for your positivity and understanding that we needed the atmosphere you provided and let us help form the **family** that we are today. You allowed us to explore and share and it developed into a wonderful experience that I don't believe any of us will forget. Kristen E. ( An older student in her mid-30's)*

10. **A LETTER TO MY STUDENTS.** An unusual event happened one year. My Senior Methods class waited until the end of the following semester to produce a notebook of each student's thank you letters. I was deeply touched, so I wrote back to them.

Dear **"Your 2006 Spring EDEC (Early Childhood—K-3) Graduates."**

I can not rest until I tell you how much your thoughts and words mean to me. I was deeply touched, to the point of tears;...

One does not, should not, go into teaching expecting that students will appreciate and thank you for all that you attempt to do and give. Sometimes a few students at the end of the quarter will take the time to say "Thank You." But when a whole class organizes to say thank you a quarter later, that is very special.

And we did not have a smooth and easy time of our classes together. There were 22 of you when the Cap is 15. Far too many for an instructor to give much individual attention. But you understood and did not complain. And the textbooks! Or rather, the non-books! I HAVE NEVER HAD SUCH A QUARTER WHEN SO MANY REQUIRED TEXTBOOKS WERE UNAVAILABLE!

Some of you wrote, "Thanks for being a great professor." I am not always sure how to interpret that. If one is a **CONSTRUCTIVIST,** and I am one, then we know it is the student who constructs the meaning of what they are hearing, or reading...Maybe what I do is to try to gain your full alert attention and to challenge you to see some new visions, new understandings, new possibilities.

And the requirements for being a professor do not include creating "a Popularity Contest." Nor making students "happy," and learning "fun" all of the time. During class time there is a very dynamic tension between what the instructor believes is important and wants to get across and taking the students and their LEARNING Styles and needs into account.

A few of you commented how much it meant to you that when you had some difficult times, that I stood beside you, supported you, and provided assurance you were going to make it and graduate. I do NOT say and do things I do NOT mean. I really believed in you....

Thank all of you. Love Patric Leedom

## PATRIC'S COMMENTARY IN REGARDS TO THE STUDENTS' REFLECTIONS

• • • • • • • • • • • • • • • • • • • • • •

As I have been typing these comments and evaluations, and reflecting, I realize that within the framework that I have suggested:—40 plus years in the classroom have been my longest continuing efforts to accomplishing my educational goals! Every year is different; every year often brings a new population of students, and sometimes the State Standards Requirements change. It certainly has required my attendance at educational Professional Conventions to keep abreast of some of the latest new ideas, and keeping up on strategic research that helped me to grow. Often, I came home from a Convention with new research and/or new textbooks to utilize in my courses. I was open-minded, I was willing to explore new viewpoints, and sometimes make some major changes to my knowledge bases and skills. Teaching and learning hopefully is a very active, evolving process.

I have already written that while I chose not to go to seminary, I did always consider my students to be my congregations—giving me the responsibility to lift up my students, and to be more successful in the Academic as well as social world.

Having said that, I was always very careful to stay far away from Religion and Politics in the classroom! While my religious values guided my interactions with the students, no students ever knew what my religion was, nor my political views—they have no place in a General Education Classroom.

I share that I was only married for two years during my 40+ years--and decided to stay single after that. So, I really was "married" or heavily committed to my profession as a teacher or professor. It really was my "CALLING." I put in hundreds of extra hours per week, setting up my lesson plans, supplies, and equipment. Over the last 20 plus years I did spend many weekend days in the office. For every single academic assignment, I required of my students I provided a "Handout" of exemplars for each assignment. Truly for my Introduction to the Teaching Profession, I had 25 different Hand-outs! And that requires hours and hours each semester to organize all that.

## HOW I INTERPRETED MY RESPONSIBILITIES

• • • • • • • • • • • • • • • • • • • • • • •

And, as I have written elsewhere—and Rachael M. alluded to it, I arranged to provide a "Community" or "family-like" positive learning atmosphere. Every year in my Introduction to the Teaching Profession classes, students were able to make some very close friends. And quite a number of shy students commented that this was the only course where they felt safe, secure, respected such that they actually "Spoke Up in Class!"

Over the years I developed close and trusting relationships with Principals as well as teachers. It was maybe six years ago that I was handling a huge personnel abuse situation in one school. I went to the city public school and said to the Principal, "I need three elementary placements by tomorrow and don't ask any questions" within one minute or less, the Principal said "You have got them!" The same day I went out to one of the country schools, and said to that Principal, "I need two elementary positions for my student teachers by tomorrow, and don't ask any questions." Again, the Principal said, "You have got them!" Now THAT is TRUST!

I interpreted my role as a University Supervisor to frequently be on the scene to make sure my Pre-Student Teachers, or my Student Teachers were performing professionally, and if they needed redirection, I was the one to do it! But the reverse was true too. If I found a Clinical teacher abusing or stifling my Student Teacher, I was the one "in a flash" to remove that Student Teacher to a healthier situation in another school district.

Interesting story. I walked into one rural Elementary School and I wound up conversing with the Second Grade Team who were on a break. Two of the Team Members were students whom I had rescued from unhealthy situations. They said to me, "If ever you need us to help you with such a situation, you can count on us!"

I departed and journeyed to a second rural Elementary school. There I found one of my Student Teachers in the empty cafeteria seriously crying her eyes out. As I got her to calm down enough to talk to me, she told me how horrible she had been treated including chewing her "rear end" out in the Hallway in front of other teachers and students!! Oh my god! It only took me two minutes to say, "Jennifer, GO HOME. You are never coming back to this school again! I will telephone you tonight."

Wouldn't you believe I made a Beeline back to the first school, and back to the Second Grade Team. It only took them one minute or less to say, "Please bring her over in the morning and we will welcome her with open arms!" That night I telephoned Jennifer and told her to meet me in front of that school first thing in the morning!" Believe me, that team made sure Jennifer was going to have an OUTSTANDING rest of the semester!

Second story. I was still working on my doctorate at the University. It was the end of a semester. I went to one of my Student Teacher's

Classroom. The classroom Clinical teacher had filled out an Evaluation on my Student Teacher. It was awful. I had known there were frictions between the two. The Clinical teacher was young in her twenties, and my Student Teacher was in her 40's. I did not say anything to either teacher. But I took the Evaluation back to the University to my boss and told her how upset I was. My Boss carefully said to me, " Tear It Up !, and you write a new one for your Student Teacher, and on the bottom, write what you have done that the Clinical teacher did not do a professional job in your estimation." Thank you, Nancy! I went back quietly to my Student Teacher and explained the situation.

I am so glad I learned that tool; some clinical teachers should never have a Student Teacher under them. And later at Shawnee State, I did tear up evaluations three more times in 20+ years. We faculty created a Confidential List of Clinical Teachers NEVER to use again.

**Interestingly, my same orientation that I had for my college students also was evident in my caring for the sailors for whom I was responsible: While this is not the place to go more into my Navy Submarine life; (however, especially after I was elevated to E7 Chief, E8 Senior Chief, and E9 Master Chief,) I tried to watch over the men assigned to me, or if I was Duty Chief, then it was all the men in the Duty Section.** One time when I attended the Planning Board for Training, I spoke up to the Captain and said, "Captain, we need a rule on board that if a lower rated man has spent all day engaged in very heavy work—like rebuilding an engine, he must be allowed four hours of sleep before we ask him to go topside as a security watch. You know how often they fall asleep, come before you at Captain's Mast, and are reduced in rate." The Captain responded, "Master Chief, I know what you are saying; however, we have too much work to be done on this ship. Master Chief, when you are Duty Chief, you can run the watch anyway you want!" So, after that I put out the word and enforced it—four hours sleep before "going up on the roof."

+ + + + + +

## *THE STATE TEACHER RETIREMENT SYSTEM'S FINANCIAL CONSIDERATIONS BROUGHT MY TEACHING CAREER TO A CLOSE*

• • • • • • • • • • • • • • • • • • • • • •

I was prepared to teach for several more years. There was no compulsory retirement age. But the reality interfered. State-wide in Ohio there was a growing financial problem in the near future. In Ohio there are five publicly funded Retirement Systems including the State Teachers' Retirement System. All five systems took a hard look at the money coming in, and the money being paid out. All five agreed that without changes, their retirements systems would all run out of money in about 20 or so years. So, each system designed its own new rules.

In STRS the new rules were: a teacher needed to be 60 years old in order to retire, and a person must have worked 30 years in order to retire. Under previous rules the formula for computing one's Final Average Salary was to take one's three highest earning years, add together and divide by three. Under the new rules, the Final Average Salary was taking one's five highest earning years and dividing by five. [Some persons had been "gaming the system" by taking on extra assignments to boost those three highest years].

STRS wrote me a letter and said, "You may work one more year under the old rules. But if you stay after that, we will put you under the new rules and you will lose money."

## I RELOCATED BACK TO CINCINNATI AND INTO A RETIREMENT COMMUNITY

• • • • • • • • • • • • • • • • • • • • • •

"Say no more, say no more!" And I formally retired on June 1, 2016. Much earlier in my Retirement thinking, I thought I would first relocate to Cincinnati. Take an apartment or condo overlooking the Ohio River for a few years, then move to a Retirement Community. But as the last year drew near, I decided to skip the middle step and just go straight into a Retirement Community. I searched and interviewed about five different Retirement Communities. Finally, I selected the Twin Towers Retirement Community because 1) It was the most affordable, 2) It was conveniently located to services I wanted—such as my church—5 miles away, my hospitals 7 miles away, and the downtown area, 10 miles away, and 3) It was a very familiar neighborhood because I had gone to the Ohio Military Institute for three years and the Ohio State Historical Marker that our OMI Historical Association had erected in 2007-was located just 1000 yards away from the campus of Twin Towers!

When I was still teaching at Shawnee State, I attended several Marketing Luncheons at Twin Towers and got to be friends with the Marketing Agent. I looked around and told her what quarters I was interested in. At the January 2016 meeting, she quietly announced to me that she had just what I wanted—an end patio apartment with a screened-in porch. She showed it to me, and I put a down payment on it.

So now I am living in a very desirable "Man Cave" apartment with no immediate neighbors. I see woods and trees out of my back windows, I see woods and trees out of my side windows, and occasionally wildlife—deer, wild turkeys, birds, squirrels and one day a Coyote! So, my relocation to Cincinnati was quite satisfactory.

## ONE LAST ENCORE

● ● ● ● ● ● ● ● ● ● ● ● ● ● ● ● ● ● ● ● ● ●

I was hired back to teach part-time at Shawnee for a year. And then in 2018 the University of Cincinnati hired me in the School of Education to teach **TEACHING AND LEARNING IN A DIVERSE CLASSROOM.**

"Our Texts" were a large variety of journal articles and textbook chapters comprehensively covering the spectrum of the kinds of students who are enrolled in teachers' classrooms. I was told I could make changes in the curriculum content. Half way through the course, I realized there was no "CAPSTONE" to pull together all of the rich theories and concepts, I wanted an instructional activity which would assist the students in remembering important knowledge and skills three, four, five years from now when the Teacher Candidates were in charge of their own classrooms. Therefore, I established an *"EMERGING MULTICULTURAL TEACHING PHILOSOPHY* essay paper. I instructed students to select four or five of the critical insights and focus on them and go deep in your paper elaborating how you would introduce the subject; how would you monitor the progress of the change in students, and how would you make corrections.

NOW THERE WERE 31 STUDENTS ENROLLED IN THE COURSE. But only 13 of them turned in outstanding papers. Out of those thirteen essays I now have a book in publication: *A Companion Reader for any Teacher, Professor, Administrator who wants to make their Courses more Multiculturally Relevant.*

# CONTENTS

## Part Eight: Dr. Patric Leedom's Autobiography
## NOVEMBER 23—October 26, 2022

# PART EIGHT

## Dr. Patric Leedom's Autobiography

### NOVEMBER 23—OCTOBER 26, 2022

FIFTH SCORE OF YEARS; Age 80 and Beyond Years

*VIEW FROM AGE 82*

• • • • • • • • • • • • • • • • • • • • • •

I want to publicly acknowledge that I have been successful in life due to many, many others who took the interest and time to contribute to my journey.

Some looked out for me with food, clothing, shelter, medical insurance, and tips on how I could be safe in life.

Some others worked to educate me and helped me to climb the mountain of knowledge. Some others challenged me to develop a critical thinking mind—to learn many ways of viewing and participating in life's journey, and to be able to understand with an open mind, other person's points of view. Some others have "opened the doors of promotion" for me—that I could grow and prosper in my careers. I am very humble and grateful for all of these gifts. And I hope that I, in turn, have worked to provide these gifts to help others be successful in their lives' journeys.

This past weekend, my Companion, Barbara, came home with an intriguing book:

*LEADING FROM WITHIN: POETRY THAT SUSTAINS THE COURAGE TO LEAD*

● ● ● ● ● ● ● ● ● ● ● ● ● ● ● ● ● ● ● ● ●

*Jossy-Bass 2007 ISBN 978-0-7879-8869-2*

### FORWARD

### By Madeleine K. Albright

Madeline Albright provides a description of ***LEADERSHIP*** THAT STRONGLY RESONATED WITH MY STYLE OF LEADERSHIP.

"One of the most moving stories to come out of September 11, 2001, involved a passenger on United Flight 93, which went down in Shanksville, Pennsylvania. The passenger, Tom Burnett, called his wife from the hijacked plane, realizing by then that two other planes had crashed into the World Trade Center.

"I know we're going to die," he said. "But some of us are going to do something about it." And because they did, many other lives were saved. Since that awful morning, the memory of their heroism has inspired us. It should also instruct us.

The reason is that when you think about it, "I know we are going to die," is a wholly unremarkable statement. Each of us could on any day say the same. It is Burnett's next words that were both matter-of-fact and electrifying. "some of us are going to do something about it."

These words convey the fundamental challenge put to us by life. We are all mortal. What divides us is the use we make of the time and opportunities we have....

It is possible, of course, that we are all so busy using time-saving devices that we don't have time to do anything meaningful. Or we may have the right intentions, but instead of acting, we decide to wait—until we are out of school, until we can afford a down payment on a home, until we can finance college for our own children, or until we can free up the time in retirement. We keep waiting until we run out of "untils." Then it is too late. Our plane has crashed and we haven't done anything about it. We have lived our lives, but we have ***not led.***

"As the poems and commentaries in this volume attest, leadership is a concept with as many facets as life itself. The book's thesis, though, is that true leadership comes not from the sound of a commanding voice but from the ***nudging of an inner voice—from our own realization that the time has come to go beyond dreaming to doing.***

The question of course is, What to do? The answer must be determined by each of us in accordance with our own circumstances and values, but the past has given us clues.

Leadership is found most often in simple acts of self-expression, when conscience overcomes reticence and we make our presence known by challenging a falsehood that has been advertised as truth, calling injustice by its name, stopping to help another, or on one memorable occasion, daring to take a seat at the front of the bus. [MLK JR. CIVIL RIGHTS MOVEMENT.]

We think of great leaders as famous, and some of them are, inspiring others to follow: Gandhi kept on his desk a bronze casting of Abraham's hand; Martin Luther King Jr. carried in his heart Gandhi's doctrine of creative non-violence; generations of community activists have found their calling in response to the summons of Martin Luther King Jr.

There are, however, many more models created by people whose names will never be etched in marble or memorialized in a book. Leadership can be found in the reliable presence of a parent, the outstretched hand of a friend, ***the extra effort of a teacher,*** and the determination by any of us not only to ask the best of ourselves but also to encourage other to live lives rich in accomplishment and love...."

## *PATRIC'S HISTORY OF LEADERSHIP*

• • • • • • • • • • • • • • • • • • • • •

I would like to provide a synopsis of my growth into leadership:

- When I enrolled in Ohio Military Institute at age 11, I was shocked into discovering I could become a strong student. As I became ranked as First in Class, I was the Academic Leader and the Military Leader. This led to further leadership positions in the school structure.
- As I moved in with my Dad in California, he introduced me to the LRY Church Youth. I was so turned on I began growing in leadership Councils. First I became Vice-President of the District; and then at 17 years old I became Chair of the Summer Camp Planning Council. During that time period, I took the initiative to organize a meeting of the LRYers in Arizona, New Mexico, and El Paso, Texas. From this conference a new Desert Federation was launched.

- Also during this high school period, several ministers took me to lunch to interest me into going to a seminary and becoming a minister. I chose not to go to seminary, BUT ever since I have always regarded my students as my Congregation—to reach out to them, to inspire them to become excellent teachers. And for me to be available to the students to help them when they encountered difficulties.
  - o As I stabilized my college life in San Francisco State College, I became the President of the College YMCA. And I served for two years on the Associated Students Judicial Court.
  - o I joined the Submarine Naval Reserves in 1962. I took advantage of every opportunity to grow in promotion. By my transfer to my second full-time-assigned submarine as a new Second-Class- Quartermaster, I became the "Leading White Hat" which meant I was in charge of the lower rated quartermasters. In 1972 as I had attained E7 Chief Quartermaster, I was invited to serve on the Admiral's Staff which controlled all of the submarines in the Atlantic Ocean. I kept busy and was then promoted first to E8 Senior Chief Quartermaster, then E9 Master Chief Quartermaster. I began serving as the backup Command Master Chief for the office.
- On my way to earning my doctorate, I also became the Academic Advisor for our Department. Then the Dean of the College requested me to create an Academic Advising Center for the entire School of Education.
- As I reflect upon these leadership roles what was my driving force?
- In the beginning at Ohio Military Institute I was learning that good things happen to you when you followed the rules and took your responsibilities seriously.
- In the high school LRY group, it was my strongly believing

in that the organization helped teenagers to live a better life.

- In being a professor, it was largely my inner voice that saw the value of helping students to become inspired, to believe their careers as teachers would lift up the minds and emotions of their students.
- There is another element I have not mentioned: many of the leadership positions I have held,--I did not go looking for—other persons requested me.
- One might say-Success builds upon Success. It becomes a kind of habit of being willing to accept positions of responsibility.
- As I am 82, while I am reducing the number of responsibilities, I still do provide services. I feel quite satisfied and proud of my life's accomplishments.
- Back in May 12, 2020, I wrote some reflections about entering the age of 80:

## REFLECTIONS ON TURNING 80 YEARS OLD

• • • • • • • • • • • • • • • • • • • • • •

### By Patric Leedom May 13, 2020

**REFLECTION ONE** Hooray! I have arrived at this age with my mind, emotions, spirit, body, and heart in decent functioning order.

**REFLECTION TWO** I have not yet ended my career in Teaching Education. I didn't retire from Shawnee State University until I was 76 in 2016. I taught part-time until I was 78, including a course at the University of Cincinnati: *Teaching and Learning in a Diverse Classroom;* and out of that-as I wrote earlier, I have a book in publication: ***A COMPANION READER FOR MULTICULTURAL AND DIVERSE EDUCATION COURSES.***

**REFLECTION THREE** In terms of financial planning, I was conservative starting when I was 36 and began a career with Cincinnati Public Schools under the State Teachers' Retirement System. Later, I added to it when I taught at Shawnee State University for 23 years. The STRS recognizes Military Service so I ended up with 35 ½ years--yielding a comfortable pension.

I also stayed in the Navy Submarine Reserves for 24 years—I ended as an E9 Master Chief Quartermaster, also yielding a very supportive pension. And due to my many other jobs, I also receive Social Security; so, I am financially comfortable.

**REFLECTION FOUR** When I headed toward retirement from SSU, I decided to move directly into a Retirement Community in Cincinnati. Coincidentally, I live in a Patio Independent Living apartment within Twin Towers Retirement Community—which is 1000 yards from where I went to the Ohio Military Institute for the 6th, 7th, and 8th grades.

**REFLECTION FIVE** I became a "Rough Carpenter" when I was 19 years old and working building houses in Los Angeles—next to Hollywood. So, I have been using those skills all my life. In my "Man Cave" I have built an 8' x 8' false wall peg-board Masonite where I display paintings, photographs and I constructed some nice shelves in between the two sheets, and added some overhead-lighting. In my kitchen, the right half has become "my office" and I again hung a 4' x 8' peg board with a large shelf at the table level for displaying art work, photographs, a model submarine and "pooka's" for storing papers and books that I use frequently.

**REFLECTION SIX** Despite my displaying "shyness" up through high school, I have become active in several life-long organizations—my church, my church-affiliated week-long camps, United State Submarine

Veterans Inc., American Legion where I have been a judge for 21+ years in the High School Oratorical Contests, and recently a Commissioner in the Buckeye Boys State, and staying in touch with long, long time friends, so I am very well socially connected and never suffer loneliness or depression—especially during these Coronavirus times.

**REFLECTION SEVEN** Starting as a young child, I developed (or maybe inherited) a strong curiosity about things or places coupled with a strong need to go adventuring and exploring. I developed a strong disposition for "I Believe I Can!" I have travelled a lot including two trips around the world by submarine and airplane and visiting all 50 United States. I have risen to leadership positions in many organizations starting first at the age of 11 in the Ohio Military Institutes' 6th, 7th, and 8th grades. Then later at 16 when I was very active in the Church Youth Group Federation.

Parallel with the above traits I also developed (or inherited) a very strong sense of Responsibility. And coupled with that a strong sense of perseverance e.g., it took me five colleges and universities, 6 ½ years to obtain my bachelor's degree. And it took seven years to obtain my doctorate in Curriculum and Instruction.

**REFLECTION EIGHT** As I sit here at age 80 looking back over my life and achievements, I am largely quite satisfied and proud. That does not mean I would like to live it all over the same way. There were a number of negative experiences, but I weathered my way through them.

**REFLECTION NINE** Back when I was 16 years old, and active in a church youth federation, I came to a philosophical point of declaring "I always want to be and experience the age I am." I do not want to be a day older, nor do I want to be a day younger! And that philosophy has served me very well right up until today! I am largely content and comfortable with my life, and I willingly accept the aging process.

**REFLECTION TEN** I turned 80 on May 13, 2020 in the middle of a Corona Virus Pandemic and Social Isolation. While at least 140 other countries are struggling with the Virus, United States has the most cases; currently around 2,400,000; and the most deaths currently around 125,000 as of August 2020. Now in JANUARY 2021, THE CASES ARE 5,000,000, and the deaths are 420,000! [By July, 2022, I have heard more than 1,000,000 Americans have died of Covid!]

## *THE COVID VIRUS COMES TO THE UNITED STATES*

• • • • • • • • • • • • • • • • • • • • • •

This event is the most is the most difficult and crippling of our society since the "Great Depression of the 1930's!"

Because of massive quarantining at home our economy ground down to a near stop—at least for awhile. Some states are beginning to "Open Up—go back to work—go back to buying in stores and restaurants. We have been most fortunate that medical laboratories have been able to quickly produce vaccines. However, the virus appears able to morph into other variants, so I think we will need to continue to be cautious and prudent when we participate in public gatherings.

+ + + + + +

## *A SIGNIFICANT LADY ENTERS MY LIFE*

• • • • • • • • • • • • • • • • • • • • • •

Recently, my life has experienced a "Game Changer": For the first time in 20 years, I encountered a woman with whom I believed I could establish a significant relationship! Barbara is a member of our church, and a participant in a Wednesday evening spiritual growth group. I asked her if she wanted to have dinner with me before the next group evening. She said yes. And we have been growing more and more together.

I experience Barbara as a person who is:

- Sensitive, kind, and giving
- Thoughtful and generous
- Warm, affectionate, and caring
- Someone I feel safe with, and can fully relax when I am with her
- Someone with whom we can openly share our needs and wants
- Someone who is accepting of what I have to offer

I feel a profoundly tender, passionate, affection, and desire for her.

I feel a warm personal attachment to her. I look forward to growing old together.

## BARBARA'S THOUGHTFUL ANALYSIS

• • • • • • • • • • • • • • • • • • • • •

My significant companion, Barbara, has penned a very thoughtful analysis of our relationship:

"Patric asked me if I would consider sharing some of my thoughts and feelings re our relationship. I have always been an introvert and prefer to remain in the background, and so I was hesitant. Still, I recognized the amazing and unexpected new dimensions our lives have taken on since we have come together, to borrow a phrase from Patric, our relationship has been a "**GAME CHANGER**" for both of us. And yes, I feel it has been significant enough to be included in his autobiography, and so I agreed to contribute.

I am 71 years old at this writing, and Patric is 82 years old. We are older, but I hope we are wiser too. Call us crazy if you will, but we actually entertain the possibility that together the best years of our lives may still be ahead of us. Our ages are irrelevant.

It has come as a revelation (to me at least) to realize that "old" people in love can love each other with the same intensity (and yes, physical desire) as lovers in their 20's. I guess I never thought about it before, but why wouldn't they....love is love is love is love!

Patric and I have talked at length about the how and why of our tremendous attraction and chemistry that brought us together. One thing we have come realize is that our relationship probably never would have "worked" if we had come together at any other time in our lives. It was a perfect confluence of circumstances, I suppose. So what if we didn't fall in love until we were in our 70's and 80's. ***CARPE DIEM*** is my advice to all the geriatric folks reading this.

I do recall that before I would allow any deeper feelings for Patric to grow, I needed an answer to a very important question: ***Do you have room in your life for a girlfriend?***

Yes! He is 82, and you may laugh at this, but anyone who has read this far in Patric's autobiography already knows that he has had, and continues to lead, a very active life, and is involved in a myriad number of activities. I was not about to allow myself to become emotionally involved with him without some assurance that he was also ready for a long-term relationship. I held my breath until Patric assured me that he could definitely make room in his life for me.

Some of the thoughts I am sharing here may raise a few eyebrows; but, ask yourself this question: does the need to love, and to be loved, ever lessen?

Consider for example the condition in neglected babies and children called "Failure to Thrive." This condition is also diagnosed in the geriatric population. There are physical reasons for the decline in these individuals for sure, but there are also psychological and emotional components, including depression.

Babies deprived of touching and cuddling are particularly prone to this syndrome, as are senior citizens who find themselves missing the comfort and interaction with other people. I ask you to consider again (before you raise your eyebrows) does the need to love, and be loved ever lessen?

Yes, Patric and I will continue this perhaps less than conventional love/partnership that has grown between us, supporting one another and sharing emotional and physical love we have for each other for as long as we are given. Let it be.

Thank you, Barbara! I certainly see this relationship continuing far into the future. I tell Barbara, "My life has become more WONDERFUL since we have connected."

## EPILOGUE: WRITING AND PUBLISHING BOOKS

● ● ● ● ● ● ● ● ● ● ● ● ● ● ● ● ● ● ● ● ●

I am ending this book at the age of 82, but that does not mean I don't envision many more years and challenges that "I Believe I Can" accomplish. But do not picture me sitting home alone for hours twiddling my thumbs! I have plenty of important projects to do. For example: writing and publishing books! Who knew?

My first book is based on the love letters my second wife and I wrote when we were engaged—Shelley living in Cincinnati, and I living in Los Angeles in 1970 before our wedding. That became **_METAMORPHOSIS OF A YOUNG MAIDEN_**. It caught the eyes of six literary scouts so now I am working with marketing firm. [This book has caught on fire: Two different book publishers and promotors have taken charge; The second agent is World-Wide connected, and is sending my books to Frankfort , Germany for the European Book Festival, and so on.

At age 78 I taught a university course **_Teaching and Learning in a Diverse Classroom_** and out of our essay final exam, I published **_A COMPANION READER FOR MULTICULTURAL AND DIVERSE EDUCATION COURSES._**

My third book—which you are currently reading, and will be published in the Winter of 2022 is an "abridged autobiography."

**_"I wish to live my life deliberately… I wish to learn what LIFE has to teach, and not, when I come to die, discover that I have not lived." From Henry David Thoreau._**

I wish to thank all my readers for sharing this journey with me! I now present some final offerings. Sincerely, Patric Leedom

*RALPH WALDO EMERSON ON SUCCESS*

● ● ● ● ● ● ● ● ● ● ● ● ● ● ● ● ● ● ● ● ● ●

To laugh often and much;
To win the respect of intelligent
People and affection of children;

To earn the appreciation of honest
Critics and endure the betrayal
Of false friends; to appreciate
Beauty; to find the best in others;
To leave the world a bit better,
Whether by a healthy child, a
Garden patch or a redeemed social
Condition; to know even one life
Has breathed easier because
You have lived.
This is to have succeeded.

Ever since I started writing this autobiography, I have always thought an appropriate ending would be the words of Paul Anka's song 'My Way.'

[In my attempts to provide an official reference for credit, I was only able to acquire:

"The song was, however, originally composed as (a French song) "Comme d'Habitude" ("As Usual"), written by Jacques Revaux and Giles Thibault along with Egyptian-born French singer Claude Francois. Canadian singer Paul Anka added the English words, turning it into the classic we now know."]

Here are a few of the words:

*MY WAY*

● ● ● ● ● ● ● ● ● ● ● ● ● ● ● ● ● ● ● ● ● ●

AND NOW THE END IS NEAR
AND SO, I SAY I... STATED MY CASE
OF WHICH I AM CERTAIN

I'VE TRAVELLED EACH AND EVERY HIGHWAY
AND MORE AND MUCH MORE THAN THIS
I DID IT MY WAY
REGRET I HAVE HAD A FEW
BUT THEN AGAIN, TOO FEW TO MENTION
I DID WHAT I HAD TO DO AND SAW IT THROUGH
ON THE BY WAY
I PLANNED EACH CHARTED COURSE
AND MORE THAN THIS I DID IT MY WAY
YES, THERE WERE TIMES WHEN I BIT OFF MORE THAN I
COULD CHEW I GUESS YOU KNEW
I LOVED, I LAUGHED, AND I CRIED
I'VE HAD MY FEARS AND MY SHARE OF GLORIES
I DID IT MY WAY.

www.ingramcontent.com/pod-product-compliance
Lightning Source LLC
Chambersburg PA
CBHW051128120626
46547CB00012B/716